NATURE'S
Altars

NATURE'S
Altars

Mountains, Gender, and American Environmentalism

Susan R. Schrepfer

UNIVERSITY PRESS OF KANSAS

Published by the University Press of Kansas (Lawrence, Kansas
66049), which was organized by the Kansas Board of Regents and is
operated and funded by Emporia State University, Fort Hays State
University, Kansas State University, Pittsburg State University, the
University of Kansas, and Wichita State University

Library of Congress Cataloging-in-Publication Data

Schrepfer, Susan R.
   Nature's altars : mountains, gender, and American
environmentalism / Susan R. Schrepfer.
       p.   cm.
   Includes bibliographical references and index.
   ISBN 0-7006-1369-2 (cloth : alk. paper)
   1. Nature conservation—United States—History.
2. Environmentalism—United States—History. 3. Mountains—
United States—Psychological aspects. I. Title.
   QH76.S365 2005
   333.72′0973—dc22

                                            2004025533

British Library Cataloguing-in-Publication Data is available.

Printed in the United States of America

10 9 8 7 6 5 4 3 2 1

The paper used in this publication meets the minimum
requirements of the American National Standard for Permanence
of Paper for Printed Library Materials Z39.48-1984.

This volume is dedicated to my family

(Edward Ortiz; my father, Robert Schrepfer;

and my daughter, Amy, especially)

and with great appreciation to Judith A. Steen

CONTENTS

ACKNOWLEDGMENTS

I owe a professional debt to the Sierra Club, whose History Committee sponsored many of the oral histories used in this work, as well as to the National Endowment for the Humanities, which funded a three-year project, directed by myself and Ann Lage and administered by Willa Baum of the Bancroft Oral History Office, to interview past and present Sierra Club leaders and to gather archival materials on the history of the wilderness conservation movement. I want to acknowledge as well the assistance of many librarians, particularly those at the University of Washington in Seattle; Yosemite National Park; the New York Public Library; the University of the Pacific in Stockton, California; Bancroft Library in Berkeley; the Appalachian Mountain Club; the American Alpine Club; the Denver Public Library; the Sierra Club; the Mountaineers; and Mazamas, particularly Jeff Thomas. Above all, I want to thank the interlibrary loan and reference librarians in Rutgers University's Alexander Library. I am grateful to the readers of the manuscript, whose comments were extensive, helpful, and often too kind: Vera Norwood, Katherine Morrissey, and Jennifer Price. That this book has been published is due in large part to my editor, Nancy Scott Jackson, whose superb editorial eye improved the text substantially. She never seemed to lose faith that, through the difficulties life sent my way, I would indeed finish this book.

Maxine Lurie of Seton Hall University read the manuscript and gave me good advice. Among the faculty of Rutgers University who helped me were Jonathan Lurie, who encouraged me to work with the University Press of Kansas; Jack Cargill, who applied his linguistic skills to the first chapter; and Philip Pauly, who brought to the entire manuscript his knowledge of the history of American science and his sense of humor. The women in the Department of History at Rutgers have been unfailingly supportive, particularly Phyllis Mack, who read the chapters on women and discussed feminine perspectives at length, greatly to my benefit. Bonnie Smith and Ziva Galili encouraged me. Lora Dee Garrison loved the premise of the book and read the manuscript throughout. I want to thank as well a number of young scholars who assisted me: Abigail Lewis, Justin Lorts, Kelly Enright, Jason Rimmer, and Peter Mickulas. Fellow historians and outdoor enthusiasts Ann Lage and Richard C. Davis brought to my early drafts their extensive knowledge of the Sierra Club and the western mountains.

The pleasures of researching this project included climbing in the Rockies, the Cascades, and the Sierra, and diving into dusty archives from Boston to Yosemite with my partner, Edward G. Ortiz. I appreciate his support and patience. My mother, Rita Schrepfer, who died during the years I worked on this book; my father, Robert; my brother, Steven; and my sister-in-law, Diane—they all gave me shelter and solace during my travels and my travails. To my classicist daughter, Amy Schrepfer-Tarter, for trips to the library, for walks in the woods, and for listening kindly to strange stories of men and women in the mountains, I say: *gratis tibi ago.* Above all, I am intensely grateful to Judith Steen for her clear thinking, her editorial skills, and for her years of encouragement. Among my most satisfying memories are of sitting at her dining room table in Santa Cruz discussing passage after passage, chapter after chapter, and drinking espresso, while her husband, Joe Michalak, made lunch in the kitchen and the kittens dashed quietly through the room, as if afraid they might be edited out, as had so many of those wordy passages. The mistakes in the book are, of course, all mine.

Christmas Hill, a small rise in California's rolling coastal range, looked out over the town of Gilroy and the fields, orchards, and ranches of the Santa Clara Valley. Once known for its produce as the "valley of plenty," much of the Santa Clara is today Silicon Valley, and Christmas Hill hosts a garlic festival that draws thousands of visitors each year. In the late 1950s, however, the hill was an obscure knoll enticingly situated off a narrow road that led across the wash of Uvas Creek and out of town. Even then, an old barbed wire fence divided the hill into two ecological zones. On the creek side grew a mature stand of gnarled live oak; the dappled sunlight that filtered through its canopy fed a richness of shrubs and wildflowers. The other side of the hill was a semiarid grassland, the product of cattle grazing the region since the Spanish had established, two centuries earlier and ten miles southeast, a mission at San Juan Bautista.

Never again would I know a place in the way that I, as a child, knew that hill and its lessons in natural history. I would later climb Mt. Whitney in the Sierra Nevada and appreciate North America's other high ranges, but Christmas Hill was my mountain and, however compromised, my wild place. Along with its valley, the hill was swept up in the population increase, industrial development, and suburbanization that would, ironically, make the commercial growing of garlic a thing of the past in Gilroy. Ultimately, this book grew out of my interest in such changes, an interest that in the 1970s impelled me, as it did others, to study the new field of environmental history.

In the manner of hills, research projects have histories of their own. An early focus on San Francisco's Sierra Club led me to explore the origins of the wilderness movement in the United States. That in turn led me back to the mountains and an awareness of the unique role they played in the evolution of the idea of wilderness and its flowering as an ecological perspective, particularly because of their power to draw human attention to their soaring heights and because, ironically, of their biological fragility. Aldo Leopold, forester and wildlife ecologist, called the taking up of an ecological perspective "learning to think like a mountain." I found the history I write of less in boardrooms than at the heights. Memoirs, climbing narratives, old maps, and early photographs introduced me to the Sierra's past and to those who had once tramped the range: from Sierra Club President Aurelia Harwood to Lieutenant Nathaniel Fish McClure, from author Mary Austin to herder Frank Dusy and his dog Dinky, from rock climbers Marjory Farquhar and David Brower to photographer Ansel Adams. I directed my attention to other North American ranges and climbing groups, and to a cultural context that spanned the Atlantic Ocean and dated back to the early nineteenth century.

Looking to the mountains made me aware of the participation of women in the histories of outdoor sport and the wilderness movement. Their presence on almost every summit and in every conservation organization made it imperative that I highlight their influence. In the final analysis, however, what emerged is less a history of men and women than of masculine and feminine viewpoints. Initially I had thought it possible to present them together—masculine and feminine, male and female—but this approach compromised the richness of each. Instead, a history of mountaineering and conservation emerged in which gendered perspectives twist and turn, converge and diverge.

INTRODUCTION

Yosemite

December 10th, 1872

Dear McChesney:

I am glad to know that you miss no opportunity in seeking Nature's altars. May she be good to you and feed your soul while you labor amid those Oakland wastes of civilization. I love [the] ocean as I do the mountains—indeed the mountains are an ocean with harder waves than yours.

Farewell, write again. I am lonely.

—John Muir, *The Life and Letters of John Muir*
(ed. William Frederic Badè)

A long line of climbers made its way up the glacial slopes of Oregon's Mt. Hood. The men wore bowlers, white shirts, vests, and trousers with suspenders; the women, long, dark skirts, full-sleeved white blouses, and netted hats. Men and women alike sported goggles and turned faces swathed in greasepaint toward the sun-dazzled snow. Holding onto a single rope anchored to the glacier, they inched forward, dark silhouettes against the ice. Of the three hundred who began the ascent in separate parties on that summer day in 1894, only 193 reached the 11,239-foot summit. They called themselves "Mazamas," a Native American word for mountain goat. Although arresting in itself, the 1894 trek is significant because it became relatively common. Over the next two years, 600 people made this ascent with the Mazamas. Hundreds more soon scaled other peaks in the Cascades as well as in the Sierra, the Rockies, and New England ranges.[1] Wives, lawyers, teachers, engineers, clerks, and other workers across North America trekked up slopes, mapped steep terrains, and studied natural history. The heights fired the imaginations of Americans, sparking efforts to save such rugged regions and shaping perceptions of what wilderness was and what it should be.

Mountains were North America's last, and its first, wilderness. Last, because new settlers slipped around or hurried through the high ranges, leaving them islands of seemingly unknown lands, places of exotic peoples ripe for the rapacious curiosity of nineteenth-century travelers, who in their mind's eye constructed the meeting of mountain and valley as the coincidence of two stages

Figure 1. Cloud Cap Inn party as it reached the summit of Mt. Hood, July 19, 1894. Twenty-two climbers were in this group, which was led by H. D. (Doug) Langille. Participants in the July climb established an alpine club, which they named the Mazamas. Courtesy of the Mazamas, Portland, Oregon.

of history. And first, because it was the mountains that the United States initially and officially established as wildernesses.

The physical features of any and all landscapes are construed through the cultural assumptions of the viewer. Yet the earth's heights have been among the most emotionally laden of topographies, and although wilderness is often defined as barely imprinted by human beings, it is a political creation that is richly embroidered with human aspirations. The word *mountain* denotes a geographical place, but *wilderness* is a concept and today a status assigned by law. This book is a story of how mountains were made wilderness. National legislation removed native and pastoral peoples and designated the heights as sites of recreational use, scientific study, and aesthetic inspiration.[2]

The love of mountains generated a wealth of written and visual materials in the nineteenth and twentieth centuries. As one mountaineer pointed out in 1879, alpine exploration concerns itself with the adventures of the mind as well as of the body.[3] The result has been a richness of letters, sketches, diaries, maps, journals, photographs, and chronicles, many published in specialized journals or popular magazines. This work draws on these diverse records. The Sierra Club, with its history of vigorous conservation activism, of high-quality publications, and of outstanding climbing, anchors the chapters that follow, but individuals and groups from places as diverse as Seattle and Boston, New York and London, broaden the story.

The sport of climbing developed in the mid-nineteenth century throughout Western Europe, the British Empire, and North America. It shared much with the other sports, such as bicycling, that Victorians embraced, as well as with their passionate interest in landscapes, travel, and natural history. Alpine sport was, however, the most Victorian of enthusiasms, with its imperial imperative in which were embedded assumptions about race, class, civilization, national identity, and gender.[4] These assumptions were what gave climbing its characteristic quality and at the same time made it unique.

But what is a mountain or, for that matter, a mountain climber? Most of us conjure up images of individuals roped to rock faces or icy walls that soar into the clouds—a Matterhorn, perhaps, or a Mt. McKinley. The gentle 1995 comedy *The Englishman Who Went Up a Hill But Came Down a Mountain* reminds us, however, that height is a subjective measure, even when mathematically calculated. The movie, directed by Christopher Monger and purportedly based on a true story, tells of two English cartographers who visit the Welsh village of Ffynnon Garw and measure its nearby peak, only to find it ten feet short of fitting the category of "mountain." The villagers respond to the official threat to downgrade their peak to a hill by piling it ten feet higher with rocks and then forcing the cartographers to measure it yet again.[5] The line between a mountain and a hill is, in short, a subjective judgment. The present study takes such subjectivity to heart, setting no topographic criteria.

Nor does the work adhere to strict requirements on who qualifies as a mountaineer. The rock climber hanging suspended by pitons and nylon ropes from a vertical face is largely a mid-twentieth-century phenomenon, whereas the sport of alpinism in North America and Western Europe dates back at least two hundred years. Whether people scrambled or roped up an incline is less important than the attraction of the heights. Hearty walkers tramped the ranges of North America, only to gaze up at the summits. This volume looks at those people, but it also encompasses those who scrambled halfway up, at alpinists who reached the icy summits, and rock climbers who scaled vertical surfaces.

The "who" and the "what" of mountaineering are explored here, but it is the "why" that engages this study. By telling us why people risked their lives and comfort in certain landscapes and how they perceived them and why they wanted to save those landscapes, this history reveals the ways in which religion, social class, ethnicity, and nationality shaped the American experience of the natural world. This same history simultaneously throws into relief the influence of gender. Gender—the idea that society and history shape our sexual identities—has analytical power when used as a lens through which to view a specific group at a specific time and place.[6] In this instance, it explains a great deal about many of the Americans who were in professional or service sectors of the economy and who joined their efforts to enjoy and to save specific terrains.

America's conservation movement and the popularity of outdoor sport grew in part out of the ways in which men thought of themselves. Nineteenth- and twentieth-century men looked to terrains that they visualized as both threatening and metaphorically feminine in order to cultivate the "primordial" impulses they variously wished to refine, thwart, or sublimate. They sought arenas in which to exercise control over the external world and their own bodies. In wild areas, they exercised strong emotions—anger, fear, hate, and love—in the ambivalent agenda of escaping from, yet succeeding in, everyday life. Courting hardship and risking death, they experienced sublime moments of spiritual transcendence over material bonds. Measuring themselves against the peaks, they honed physical, emotional, and spiritual identities, and they inscribed those identities on the landscapes and codified them primarily in the policies of the federal government. Scholars have identified the conventions of the romantic sublime as central to modern interest in wild nature, but they have paid less attention to the masculine and imperial connotations of those conventions, with their promise of personal transformation and empowerment in places that romantics visualized as desolate, womanly, and frightening.[7]

From the European Alps to the Cascade Range of the Pacific Northwest, men reenacted the struggle for civilization. Their fantasies reflected the conviction of nineteenth-century theorists that human societies had evolved— in the manner of biological species—from the primitive to the modern by the action of broad social entities surviving in a hostile but malleable physical environment. Men reasoned rhetorically: where better to demonstrate civilized behaviors than in rugged places seemingly untouched by urban, industrial life?[8] Later, American and European climbers alike would follow this logic to the Himalayas and to Kilimanjaro, but their initial forays brought them into contact with their own supposedly unscaled heights and primitive peoples, be they Native Americans, guides, or herders, or merely local residents.

North America's peaks became symbols of the "pathway" of civilization, signposts in what literary critics today term the "master narrative" of conquest. The continent's ranges, because of their north-south axis, were particularly daunting for those moving east to west. Nevertheless, it was primarily in lore that the heights became for English-speakers final crucibles, sites of legendary respite from the sweep of civilization, and last occasions for territorial mastery: Natty Bumppo hunting in the Adirondacks, Daniel Boone in the Alleghenies, Zebulon Pike claiming his peak in the Rockies, Jedediah Smith crossing the Sierra Nevada, and Kit Carson scouting western passes. These men inspired subsequent generations. In such rugged places, Aldo Leopold argued, American men justified the "Blood of the Conqueror" by reenacting the triumphs of their forefathers.[9]

Historians have implicated a "crisis" of masculinity experienced by turn-of-the-twentieth-century American men who reacted to the feminization of family and workplace. To counter women's new power, such historians argue, men and boys took to the outdoors, often in the exclusive company of their own sex, in organizations such as the Boy Scouts.[10] Although the history that follows makes clear the roles played by masculine expectations in framing interest in the creation and conservation of wilderness, it adds complexity to the association. The history of the wilderness experience shows men's commitments to outdoor sport extending across two continents and two centuries even as it reveals an ebb and flow in their understandings of manliness, as well as differences among contemporaries.

Surveyor Clarence King and naturalist John Muir, both arriving in the Sierra Nevada in the 1860s, delighted in the terrors of the abyss; but King's climbing narratives expressed aggressive imperial tropes of the sublime, whereas Muir advanced a vision, no less frightening, of domestic sublimity. Nor can sexual exclusivity explain the striking parallels in the experiences of men and women, and of boys and girls, or in the actions of men who chose to spend their leisure in the company of the opposite sex.[11] The history that I present here suggests less that middle-class American men felt intimidated by modernity than that they felt so secure that they reached out to create walled gardens in the wild that could protect what they and their female companions visualized as the even more threatened virtues of femininity.

The traditional emphasis on men's motives in conservation and in sport slights the role of women and the influence of feminine perspectives. Both were central to enjoying and protecting the natural world. Examining the actions and perceptions of women in tandem with those of men reveals the analytical power, but also the limitations, of socially defined identities. Faced with the ambiguities of industrial life and of unsettled cultural norms, middle- and upper-class Americans of both sexes looked to the natural world as a source of scientific, historical, and emotional authenticity. Botanical studies shaped feminine visions of wild nature, whereas geology, in particular, underscored masculine perceptions. Both sexes were affected by the symbolism of socially created roles and by the assumption that middle-class men and women should occupy separate spheres: women the domestic and men the public. That symbolism served less to keep women out of the mountains, however, than to invite them in. At the same time, it shaped their perceptions of these rugged regions and of themselves.[12]

Not encouraged by society to express the powerful emotions that men often cultivated, nineteenth- and twentieth-century American women reshaped the masculine conventions of sublimity.[13] They did so by using their own historically constructed, metaphoric ties to nature, the study of botany, and powerful Victorian visions of domesticity and motherhood. The feminine versions of the sublime that they formulated emphasized the warmth, life, intimacy, freedom, and comfort provided by the natural world. They achieved spiritual transcendence in the wild by right of a life force that they felt pulsing through themselves, the plants, the animals, and even the rocks. Their language established their claim to explore wild lands and to have a voice in the public disposition of such places. Although masculine conventions determined which landscapes the United States designated as wilderness—the vast, rugged, and desolate—the feminine, domestic, and naturalist sublimes pioneered ecological perspectives, influencing land policies. In the first three decades of the twentieth century, the activism inspired by these visions reinforced, even as it contested, the imperial tropes of the masculine sublime.

In the mid-twentieth century, however, the feminine presence lost visibility, subsumed into the national desire for a traditional social topography. This cry brought a new urgency to the politics of conservation. Cold war anxieties fed a bomb-shelter mentality that made high, rugged terrains seem safe, reassuringly American, and conducive to family life. A vision of masculinity prevailed that encompassed the multiple roles of father, husband, and soldier. Psychological theories of human development and popular understandings of history portrayed wilderness as essential to the survival of the world. Fascination with presumably primitive places and peoples grew as some Americans questioned the assumption that modernity guaranteed a happy future. By the late 1950s, wilderness advocates had transformed their cause into a modern social movement and broadened their agenda into a critique of western civilization.

A lobby led by the Wilderness Society and the Sierra Club won congressional enactment of the Wilderness Act in 1964. Echoing conventions of the masculine sublime, the act protected the highest regions of the Cascade Range, the Rocky Mountains, the Sierra Nevada, and the southwestern United States. By designating places of seeming desolation that invited struggle and required the muscles of man or beast, the act expressed views articulated by the Wilderness Society's Robert Marshall, U.S. Supreme Court Justice William O. Douglas, and Sierra Club executive secretary David Brower. However, the act also defined wilderness in terms of a more feminine perspective, as a community of life, a vision that owed much to naturalists from John Muir to Lucy Braun and Rosalie Edge.

As a consequence of the multiple and fluid meanings that North Americans have imparted to their mountains, public support for wilderness as a land management policy has grown astonishingly. Only a handful of influential Americans lobbied for the establishment of parks in the Yosemite region of the Sierra Nevada in the nineteenth century. By the close of the century more than a dozen organizations had endorsed the designation of the Sierra and Sequoia Forest Reserves. By the 1920s a broad spectrum of public-interest groups, from youth clubs to native plant societies, cheered when the U.S. Forest Service classified the highest and most rugged portions of its national forests as either wilderness, wild, primitive, or limited-use areas. In 1964 Congress passed, with an overwhelmingly positive vote, the Wilderness Act, protecting more than 9 million acres, many of them in the Sierra and most in America's mountains. When in 2001 the Forest Service dedicated an additional 11.5 million acres in the Sierra Nevada to protect old-growth timber, the spotted owl, and other species, the news (if not welcomed by all) appeared in newspapers across the nation.[14]

Even as the protection of such lands elicits increasing public support, however, scholars challenge the logic and the history of wilderness. Pondering the improbability of a place in which humans are but visitors (as the 1964 Wilderness Act reads), critics suggest that the wilderness areas now maintained by the United States represent a national fantasy turned into implausible policy. Historical studies, including this one, provide evidence of mountain people deprived of homes and of use rights by the establishment of public parks and wilderness reserves.[15] In assuming an ideal ecological balance that is unaffected by humans, twenty-first-century land-use managers often struggle to distinguish, for example, between those fires that are deliberately or accidentally ignited, which they try to extinguish, and the seemingly more natural lightning fires, which are often left to burn.

Although critics charge with some justification that the idea of wilderness is in meaning elusive and in rhetoric self-justifying, the American public increasingly prizes landscapes that symbolize, even when they do not concretize, the limits beyond which the modern industrial and urban order must not reach. Twenty-first-century Americans do well to protect such spaces, honoring, even as they challenge, those elements of our nineteenth-century legacy that these sites epitomize: the Victorians' keen sense of history, their strong appreciation of the natural world, and their clear, if surprisingly fluid, visions of masculinity and femininity. Perhaps it does not matter that our efforts to save wild places represent a policy embedded in myth; the value of wilderness, like that of history, lies as much in the reality of the past as in the uses we make of that past. Protecting wilderness not only saves biological communities and evidence of earlier inhabitants but also preserves centuries of a multilayered, cultural history, of meanings imposed upon meanings, realities laid upon fantasies, and fantasies set against the force of very special places.

Part I
(En)gendering the Wilderness, 1860s–1914

Traveling through the High Sierra in the summer of 1864, the men of the California Geological Survey encountered what they described as "a wilderness of mountains, barren and desolate," with needle-sharp pinnacles, precipices of "naked and shattered granite," cold, and filled with deathly silences.[1] Scanning the rugged horizon, they identified what they thought was the highest point in the range. They debated seeking its summit, one concluding it would be madness; another said that it would be as difficult as getting onto a cloud. The young Yale-educated topographer, Clarence King, decided on the attempt. Despite freezing temperatures, pain, and danger, he reached the top, only to see a higher bluff to the south. Seven years later he returned to conquer that bluff, which he now knew to be the highest peak in the United States. He again described a landscape that offered no "air of virgin hospitality." Nature, deviating from her nurturing mode, frightened and intrigued him. He clawed his way up through fog, any slip being "a death fall." Narrowly escaping a plunge into the abyss, he reclaimed his nerve to reach the top. There he noted a pile of rocks that had "solidly built into it an Indian arrow-shaft pointing due west." He conceded the "hunter's pride" of his predecessor, confident in his own superiority over the "half development" of such people and his right to name the peak for the chief of the California survey, geologist Josiah D. Whitney. King returned East to publish his narrative, *Mountaineering in the Sierra Nevada*, announcing what he believed to be the first ascent of Mt. Whitney.[2]

Meanwhile, an Italian team and two Englishmen, Edward Whymper and John Tyndall, were waging a three-way battle to reach the

Figure 2. Left to right: J. T. Gardiner, Clarence King, and packer Richard Cotter on the 1864 California State Geological Survey of the Sierra Nevada. Courtesy of University of California, Bancroft Library.

highest point of the deeply serrated Matterhorn, one of the most formidable peaks of the European Alps. As he climbed, Whymper marked how far he had come from the cities and tourist baths, places of degenerate men and women—silly, indolent, chattering creatures who called death "droll." At the heights, death was faced of necessity and, if not defeated, then heroic. The summits were the domains of the "true man," known by the cairns he erected. Whymper agreed with Tyndall that civilized men too often succumbed to effete and "fatty degeneration." When asked, "Why climb?" Whymper pointed to "the development of manliness, and the evolution, under combat with difficulties, of those noble qualities of human nature—courage, patience, endurance, and fortitude." [3]

In 1865, on his seventh attempt, Whymper won the "first ascent" of the 14,780-foot tip of the Matterhorn. He, too, described mastering fear, a treacherous terrain, and superstitious local peoples who thought the summits were inhabited by "the spirit of the damned." He claimed that he was forced to drag along mercenary and often terrified guides as he laid siege to the peak with implements of "Alpine warfare"—ice pick and rope. Mocking locals who, he said, believed devils would harm those who dared to trespass on the summits,

Figure 3. "The Summit of the Moming Pass in 1864," on the
Matterhorn. Engraving by Edward Whymper from Scrambles
Amongst the Alps *(1871).*

he hurled rocks down on the Italian team scaling the southern slopes. Building his cairn and planting a banner at the top, he declared that "the world was at our feet and the Matterhorn was conquered." But on the descent, three of his fellow climbers and one guide fell three thousand feet to their deaths. Shortly thereafter, Whymper reported that there appeared an unearthly apparition in the clouds, an arch with two crosses. He illustrated his 1871 narrative *Scrambles Amongst the Alps* with engravings of the crosses and a body falling through space etched against grotesque escarpments. Lighting bolts outlined jagged spires. The Matterhorn itself appeared in the guise of an enraged dragon, a man astride its jaw, his ice pick raised as if ready to attack.[4]

Whymper's *Scrambles* and King's *Mountaineering*, both published in 1871, established the alpine narrative as a literary genre that blended the forms of the natural history essay and the travelogue. Both men described mountain inhabitants and topographies as well as their own physical and emotional reactions. They reflected on precipitous places and precarious moments, anticipating readers much like themselves—middle and upper class; educated and interested in natural history, athleticism, the aesthetics of place, and moral imperatives embedded in nature. The genre became prescribed in form and prescriptive in message.

The stylized character of these narratives, the close circle of author and audience, and the choreographic qualities of the sport itself all provide ideal lenses through which to view patterns in nineteenth- and twentieth-century American middle-class culture. The very discipline of form, however, also highlights variations, shifts over time, and differences in social identities. Equally popular with men and women, climbing and its literature elicited distinctly masculine and feminine responses, making gender a central theme in the story that follows.

While *Mountaineering* and *Scrambles* became classics, shelved and read in public and college libraries throughout the English-speaking world, both adventures had actually ended badly: Whymper's with deaths, King's with embarrassment. The American surveyor had climbed the wrong peak, not Mt. Whitney. When the California Academy of Sciences revealed his error in August 1873, King raced west to organize another expedition. But he reached Whitney's 14,498-foot summit, only to find there the names of two other parties. Two local men from nearby Lone Pine had claimed King's "first" and named Mt. Whitney "Fishermen's Peak" in defiance of the California Survey. According to King, their effrontery reflected the "low prejudice" of most Californians against the niceties of science and sport.[5]

King and his supporters considered the name "Whitney" suitably "suggestive of pre-eminent rank among men as well as mountains"—a matter of presumed class status, manly accomplishment, and scientific credibility. The designation anticipated the recreational and scientific uses they envisioned for the peak, uses seemingly commensurate with its namesake's stature. King, who later headed the U.S. Geological Survey, felt that the local residents of the San Joaquin Valley slighted his mentor when they lobbied the California legislature for "Fishermen's Peak," even pursuing their case in the courts.[6] As the survival of the name "Mt. Whitney" testifies, however, the peak's future belonged to those who, seeking intangible rewards, climb it by the thousands each year rather than to those who lived and worked in the hot, dry towns fringing the range.[7]

For Victorians like Whymper and King, the competitive sport of mountaineering, the aesthetic conventions of landscape appreciation, and the process of topographic naming were all fraught with social meaning. It was not simply that one would never name a mountain such as Mt. Whitney for a woman. Immortalizing a man by identifying him with a peak and mortalizing a peak with a man's name were filled with assumptions as to who was an "appropriate" man. The parameters of proper manhood excluded the Native American and the presumably foreign herders one met in the Sierra—all of whom, King believed, were disqualified by their race, moral deficiencies, and debased lives. The peaks of the Sierra should honor men, he argued, but not *these* men.

Although Susan Fenimore Cooper and John Muir challenged King's ideas of naming places and described unique experiences of mountains, most American men emulated King as they set out to give "the gift of names to the unknown peaks, . . . the gloomy canyons, and sequestered lakes."[8] In their view, these recesses lay ripe for the taking. Even as they challenged the rights of local users, they fantasized about virgin peaks and replicated the acts of possession employed by Europeans from Columbus to Vancouver. They visualized their sport and their lives as products of an imperial civilization built on acts of discovery made by individual men. Their claims to affinities with explorers were flights of fancy but not entirely specious, given that they mapped terrains, renamed the topography, and otherwise took intellectual and physical possession of place.

The ability to narrate is the power to create identities for place, self, and others.[9] For Americans, the idea of the unknown has been intertwined with the reality of mountains. These were among the last areas settled by English speakers, but the coincidence of fact and perception explains only in part the equating of mountains and wilderness. Seeing America's heights as empty was a matter of artifice, language, and gesture. Creating wilderness was a conscious act of a discrete, if singularly self-defining, group deeply influenced by the nineteenth-century natural sciences, the popularity of geography, the relatively new sport of alpinism, and trends in western aesthetic culture.

The title of Part I, "(En)gendering the Wilderness," refers to the ways in which the construction of identities coincided with the exercise of power in the Sierra Nevada. It also refers to the processes whereby Americans brought masculine and feminine perspectives to such mountains.

Place Naming in the High Sierra

Belying the language of visitors like Clarence King, Native Americans and other peoples had long lived in North America's mountains and named them. The combined weight of Victorian commerce, nation building, and science demanded formal mapping by public survey-ors, but informal maps had long existed—in men's minds or drawn in dirt or on rocks or on the backs of greasy fry pans. The topogra-phy of the Sierra Nevada functioned as a palimpsest, that medieval parchment on which text was superimposed upon text, each layer seeming to erase earlier images. As with the palimpsest, patterns of the past are discerned by bringing older documents to the fore. Suc-cessive trails and shifting nomenclatures not only record a history of occupants but also identify the purposes that mapping has served and the visions that name-givers held of themselves and of the range. For each group of people, mapping and naming represented not only a way of locating themselves in the mountains but an effort to de-scribe such places, others, and themselves. The power to narrate was the power to create identities and ultimately to determine the fate of the Sierra and comparable ranges.

The Sierra Nevada stretches the length of California, some four hundred miles, from Carson Pass, near Lake Tahoe, south to Walker Pass. On maps the range appears to be a continuation of the more northern, glacier-clad, and volcanic Cascade Range, but it is not. The Sierra originated as detached earthquakes and lifted a portion of the earth's crust, forming an eastern margin, so that the crest is off-center and rises abruptly out of plateaus to the east. From that perspective, the range presents a jagged summit wall; passes are high and few. The peaks of the main crest average ten thousand feet above sea level, with many over thirteen thousand feet in elevation and a few over fourteen thousand feet. The approach from the west is more gradual, interrupted by foothills and deep canyons chiseled by glaciers and cascading waters. In summer the eastern slopes are warm and dry, and the western flanks form a rain shadow that traps the summer moisture off the Pacific and the winter snowpacks that feed the rivers. The range's length curves north-south with the coastline but is far enough inland to have gone unrecorded by Europeans until the eighteenth century. State-authorized mapping of the interior of the range awaited the arrival of American surveyors in the mid-nineteenth century.[1]

European explorers had long assumed the right to rename topographies uninhabited or inhabited by what they termed "uncivilized" peoples. The Spanish called the range "Nevada," for "snowy," and "Sierra," for "range of mountains," from the Latin *serra*, or saw.[2] By using the language of their pastoral faith and their shepherd savior, they laid claim to the rivers that watered their livestock. Spanish names like "El Rio de Nuestra Señora de la Merced" (Our Lady of Mercy River) celebrated a collective, religious, often feminine presence. The suggestion that place naming is a strategy of colonial expropriation is borne out by the history of the Sierra. When the Spanish lost control of the range, many of their place-names disappeared or, as happened with major rivers such as the Merced, were shortened and Anglicized.[3] The English speakers who followed John C. Frémont into the range glorified, as he had, the manly and implicitly racialized act of individual discovery.[4]

Settlers began moving into the Sierra in the 1850s and 1860s, finding their way on old byways, whitish lines etched in the granite, that were, a resident recalled, "like bear trails never on high ground. Worn for centuries, never departed from." Most of these newcomers sought gold, timber, arable land, and pastures for their cattle and sheep.[5] Herders, cattlemen, miners, loggers, and homesteaders quickly gave their own names to the creeks, bridges, trails, mills, corrals, camps, and mines they claimed. "Horsethief Canyon" celebrated local history, but most new arrivals honored the valuable meadows with their own surnames: Fox, Fuller, Gabbot, Gomez, Halstead, Hoffman, Haskell, Ladeux, Leidig, and McGann. Of such owner/user names, Henry David Thoreau complained: "*Flint's Pond!* Such is the poverty of our nomenclature. What right had the unclear and stupid farmer, whose farm abutted on this sky water, whose shores he has ruthlessly laid bare, to give his name to it?"[6] Indigenous people had used names to convey information; and the Spanish, to honor

Christianity. The new settlers used their surnames to celebrate ownership and use rights, while the surveyors and climbers who followed favored surnames that reflected their roles as explorers and scientists.

Legitimizing, facilitating, and visualizing political control, official maps serve as "graphic tools of colonization."[7] Maps had long been military tools, describing routes and locating inhabitants, defensible sites, and essential resources. Inhabited by potentially hostile indigenous peoples and ethnically diverse settlers, most of the Sierra lay beyond the intimate control of English-speaking Americans, prompting the California legislature to commission Josiah Whitney in 1861 to carry out a geological survey. Whitney chose as assistants Yale graduates Clarence King, William Brewer, and J. T. Gardiner (also known as Gardner), and German topographer Charles F. Hoffmann. The state's legislators were interested in commercial and military advantages, but the surveyors—geologists, biologists, chemists, and topographers—bragged that they had no pecuniary interests. Feeling akin to English and German explorers in the Arctic and the Congo, they visualized the Sierra as one of the "yet unknown portions of the earth."[8]

They turned their attention first to Yosemite Valley, only ten miles in diameter and etched some three thousand feet into the range's northwestern flank. In 1851 the so-called Mariposa Battalion, commissioned by California's governor, had dispersed the valley's Ahwahneechee residents and their leader, Tenaya. Tourists followed so quickly on the heels of the militia that the line between the two must have seemed indistinguishable to the vanquished. By the time the California Survey had arrived in 1863, the valley already commanded national attention. Influential audiences had read descriptions of Yosemite by Boston clergyman Thomas Starr King or had seen sketches by Thomas Ayres, paintings by Albert Bierstadt, and photographs by Carleton Watkins.[9]

Determined that the ideal future uses of the area would be recreational, scientific, and aesthetic, the surveyors joined the lobby to make the valley a park, bringing the process of mapping together with a conservation ethic. In 1864 President Lincoln transferred the fifteen-mile-long "'Cleft' or 'Gorge' in the Granite Peak of the Sierra Nevada" to the State of California to be held "inalienable for all time" for "public use, resort, and recreation." The act mandated the valley be kept as itself "for all time," suggesting its right to a natural integrity that, if violated, might justify its recession to the federal government (as happened in 1905–1906). Ironically, the law claiming an "inalienable" right of public usage obliterated all Native American claims.[10]

When the surveyors arrived, Mono peoples still controlled the plateaus to the east and, along with other native groups, used the Sierra for refuge and subsistence. Hundreds, including Tenaya's people, had filtered back into Yosemite Valley. Acknowledging that these people had "a name for every meadow, cliff, and waterfall in and about the Valley," Whitney recorded the names with the help of an Italian translator; yet the survey did not locate, on its 1865 map of the region, a single place-name used by the Native Americans.[11]

Whitney called Yosemite's people "degraded . . . beings, who must die out before the progress of the white man's civilization." King initially liked what he saw as heroic "Indian paterfamilias" and "proud-stepping 'braves'" who traveled "unhampered and free" ahead of "submissive squaws." He identified with an old man's sorrow at the loss of a spouse but was appalled when the man took a new wife seemingly without ceremony or mourning. King theorized that the development of these people had been arrested by the natural upheavals that had produced the range; or perhaps the "burden of shadowy myth-born fears had robbed their daily life of all dignity." He wanted these "living savages" studied as evidence of human progress, but he also wanted their "moral topography" erased from the land. In the eyes of the Yale-educated surveyors, as of the Mariposa Battalion and the valley's new hotelier, James Mason Hutchings, Tenaya had been a man of "latent power" before his defeat, but he was now merely a "dirty old man" with the bodily vermin of his race; ignorant and willful; unworthy of his surroundings and deserving to be honored with no more than a small, shallow, lake in the valley.[12]

Hutchings and other white settlers had for several years bestowed English-language names, such as Mirror Lake and Bridal Veil Falls, on the sites of the Yosemite Valley. The men of the survey were not impressed by the "sentimentality" of the names chosen by what they called the "emotional" Hutchings and other newcomers, but they made the new designations official—even as they recorded legends that explained the meaning of such Native American place-names as Tissaack. Seeing the beautiful, fair-haired maiden Tissaack sitting on the southern rim of Yosemite one morning, the god who had long protected the valley's people became infatuated with her and neglected them. Soon there was no corn; "the green leaves became brown." Kneeling on a dome, the maiden asked the Great Spirit to bring back the flowers, grasses, and acorns. With an awful sound, the rock split, killing her but sending "a sweet murmuring river through the Valley." Although English speakers, who liked stories about maidens, recorded the legend (making its authenticity suspect), the name "Tissaack" beautifully evokes the flow of the Merced River, the valley's topography, its seasons, and its drought cycles. When the survey recorded the cliff's new Anglicized name, "Half Dome," Tissaack lost its feminine and indigenous identities.[13]

Moving into the range south of Yosemite, the surveyors encountered places they called "entirely unknown," where "no human foot has ever trod"—even as they followed old footpaths. They were not the first Euro-Americans in California's mountains, as they learned on Mt. Shasta, a dormant volcano north of the Sierra. Knowing that Frémont had attempted to reach Mt. Shasta's 14,161-foot summit, but failed, the surveyors had labeled it "unconquered" and embarked on its ascent; once at the top, however, they found what Brewer called a "California conglomerate": tin cans, broken bottles, hymn books, newspapers, and playing cards, probably left by prospectors. Moving into the Sierra, the surveyors found the prospectors' food and directions useful. The Native Americans, however, proved elusive and disquieting, their signal fires telegraphing the intruders' movements. Everywhere the surveyors saw signs of Native Americans, including meeting a group of mounted warriors.[14] Neither their presence nor that of the prospector, however, dampened the surveyors' enthusiasm for celebrating themselves (with peaks called Mts. "Brewer," "Clarence King," "Gardiner," and "Cotter"). They chose "Silliman" for Brewer's chemistry professor at Yale, "Abbott" for a surveyor, and "Goddard" for an engineer. Few of the peaks they named escaped this commemoration of manly, Anglo-American individualism and of modernity's academic and technological underpinning.[15] When they left the range, however, they had named only a few of the peaks.

Government surveys of the range remained minimal for the rest of the century, leaving mapping to the climber. The line between exploration and sport had always been thin. King's first "grand assault" of a peak on the main divide of the Sierra, although accomplished when he was still with the California Survey, was made less for purposes of measuring than for fun. Asking packer Richard Cotter whether "he would like to penetrate the Terra Incognita with me at the risk of our necks," King had been thrilled by Cotter's reply: "Why not?"—the reply confirming King's sense that there was in Cotter's "manhood no room for fear or shirk." At the top, King rang his hammer on the rock, claimed for the peak a new voice, and "reverently named the grand peak MOUNT TYNDALL," for John Tyndall, the geologist and author who had claimed the "first ascent" of the Weisshorn.[16] The English critic John Ruskin had denounced such imperious relations with the heights as attacks on "sacred places," and he satirized the likes of Tyndall for looking on the Alps "as soaped poles in a bear-garden, which you set yourselves to climb, and slide down again, with 'shrieks of delight.' When you are past shrieking . . . you fill the quietude of their valleys with gunpowder blasts, and rush home, red with cutaneous eruption of conceit."[17] Ignoring Ruskin's critique, most American men who climbed sought competitive sport and a chance to act the explorer. One recalled standing on a peak he had just named Mt. Winchell: "Formal salutations were addressed to the witnessing mountains, and double charges of gunpowder fired over the cañon and forest, arousing crashing reverberations that leaped from cliff to distant cliff. . . . 'Every mountain now had found a tongue.'"[18]

The trickle of tourists grew into a stream in 1869 when the first transcontinental railroad was completed. Sightseers arrived in Yosemite Valley carrying *Hutchings' Tourist's Guide to Yo Semite Valley* and Whitney's *Yosemite Guide-Book.*[19] Though intrigued by legends dubiously recorded as "Indian" in the guidebooks, visitors rarely sympathized with the actual human beings eking out an existence selling baskets, begging, acting as guides and packers, posing for photographs, or fishing and gathering berries for hotel guests.[20] Only the historical "Indian" was celebrated. The U.S. Geological Survey's 1905 map of Yosemite Valley recorded few names that were even remotely indigenous.[21] Native American names that had appeared on early English-language maps for other parts of the Sierra disappeared as well.[22] Given the opportunity, newcomers to the Sierra, as to the Cascade Range to the north, seldom resisted the urge to rename.[23]

It was a rare (and often female) visitor who objected to this reencoding. Helen Hunt [Jackson], who later critiqued the treatment of Native Americans in her *A Century of Dishonor,* visited Yosemite in 1872. Like almost all visitors, she found no noble savage, but she did chastise whites for abandoning the original designations of place. Constance Frederica Gordon-Cumming, a British missionary touring in 1878, found jarring the contrast between the scenery and what she saw as filthy stragglers. Yet she felt "a thousand pities that wherever the Anglo-Saxon race settles, it uproots the picturesque and generally descriptive native names of mountains and streams, and in their stead bestows some new name, which at best is commonplace, and too often vulgar." Early-twentieth-century travel writer Mary Roberts Rinehart also challenged reflexive renaming, calling it an effort to eliminate Native American history.[24]

Fewer still were critics like Susan Fenimore Cooper. The daughter of the American novelist and an author remembered for her own, less heroic, nature writings, Cooper called it "a miserable dearth of words and ideas" to baptize a "stern and savage" peak "by the name borne by some honorable gentleman just turning the corner, in honest broadcloth, close buttoned to the chin."[25]

Figure 4. "Indian Village in Yosemite Valley." Photograph by Charles E. Townsend, 1898. Native Americans had lost control of the valley in the 1850s. The Mariposa Battalion, largely responsible for the dispossession, saw the event as a process of conquest and rebaptism, replacing the valley's name Ahwahnee with what they mistakenly believed to be that of the vanquished, "Yosemity." As this photograph shows, Native Americans filtered back into the valley and maintained a presence for decades. Courtesy of University of California, Bancroft Library.

Concluding their 1871 suffrage campaign in the West with a trip into Yosemite, Elizabeth Cady Stanton and Susan B. Anthony protested the use of men's surnames for the trees—for example, the "General Grant Big Tree." Seeing only men immortalized on the Calaveras Sequoias, which Stanton called "the daughters of the Earth," the two visitors wrote—on cards they attached to the trunks—the names of a dozen leading women.[26]

The practice of using men's surnames persisted. A nine-thousand-foot peak near the South Fork of the Kaweah River (now in Sequoia National Park) was known to native people as the site where the Eagle God and the Wolf God had created the Wutchumna people, and they named the peak accordingly. In 1872 a General Land Office official renamed it Homer's Nose for guide John Homer. Later in that same decade, a lawyer, an ex-Confederate officer, and a minister from nearby Tulare County honored their Princeton professor of ge-

Figure 5. Two Native Americans on horseback with women alpinists in the background to the right, Cascade Range, ca. 1900. Courtesy of Manuscripts, Special Collections, University Archives, University of Washington.

ology and astronomy, Charles Young.[27] Despite such gestures, many sites remained unnamed. John Muir would leave them so.

Muir's life is legendary among conservationists and environmentalists. He himself cultivated the almost mythic tale of his escape into the Sierra in 1868 from a boyhood of rural drudgery and the demands of a wagon shop.[28] He did not name as he traveled the Sierra, eventually denouncing the practice as a gesture of possession, which to him was the antithesis of wilderness. Telling a friend of having once "met two very rare and beautiful species of orchids in the wilds of British Columbia," he added: "Hush! we won't mention their names, for so rare were they, so delicate, so fragile, and so altogether lovely, that even to pronounce their names might frighten them away." Muir used names only to illustrate by geological analogy, calling, for example, all steep-sided Sierra valleys carved by water and by ice "yosemites."[29] According to another Sierra climber, Muir remained "a very poor sort of explorer. He could aptly describe every place he had seen, but you could seldom tell where it was, for he seldom oriented himself. . . . The terrain was high and wild, and much of it blank on the so-called maps," yet he "bestowed no place names and made no diagrams."[30] Muir said merely, "I care little about names." With no small irony, given the fact that many others would so honor him, he boasted of not having left his name "on any mountain, rock, or tree in any wilderness."[31]

His brag was integral to his vision of wilderness as lying outside of human history, a somewhat disingenuous vision. He knew that others had lived and still lived in the Sierra. Visiting the South Fork of the Kings River in 1873, he tried to imagine the lives of the Monos.[32] He preferred the indigenous name for Hetch Hetchy Valley to the proposed "Smith Valley," and he recorded other original names.[33] But the living survivors he occasionally encountered had no place in his Kings Canyon. His uninhabited paradise was an ideal, but not entirely a fiction. He had entered the canyon when its population was at an historic low. The Native Americans who had not died or fled from there had hid; the canyon's Spanish past was evident only in its name honoring the three kings of the nativity; the prospectors who had come there had left, empty-handed. Muir seized the moment to define wilderness not as a place of Native Americans, Spaniards, miners, hunters, or pastoralists but one of idyllic, timeless innocence, a place to be preserved against the force of commerce.[34]

When campaigning for congressional support of Yosemite National Park in the 1880s, Muir constructed a similar vision of a Garden of Eden whose fate hung in the balance, focusing on Tuolumne Meadows. The meadows had been homesteaded, mined, trampled by some fifteen thousand sheep, and grazed by Angora goats for almost a generation, but Muir told the story of a virgin land threatened.[35] Seeing sacred places about to be defiled, Congress established Yosemite, Sequoia, and General Grant National Parks in 1890. Pressed by eastern supporters to organize citizens to ensure that the federal government managed these areas with care, Muir allied himself with men planning an alpine club for California.

Alpine clubs dated to the 1850s and had quickly spread throughout the British Empire, western Europe, and North America.[36] British clubs, the Appalachian Mountain Club, and the Oregon Alpine Club of Portland had already wed the sport to conservation.[37] American mountaineers were among the most active conservationists, advocating, for example, that Washington State's Olympic Mountains be established as a national park and lobbying for Alaska's Mt. McKinley National Park.[38] Aware of these precedents, William Armes, a professor of English at the University of California in Berkeley, proposed a Sierra Club. In September 1892, two hundred fifty men gathered for a meeting of what its president, John Muir, called "Our Alpine Club." Most were professors of history, art, English literature, German, and the natural sciences, testifying to the influence of western culture's aesthetic traditions and sciences on American conservation.[39] The new club, like similar groups, quickly attracted a cross section of well-educated professionals: lawyers, physicians, teachers, and engineers.[40]

Shortly after it was established in 1892, the Sierra Club staked its claim to the Sierra with a two-part map of the highest reaches of the range. J. N. LeConte, a University of California professor of engineering, had surveyed the area and drawn up the map. It showed uninscribed lands stretching along the main summit of the Sierra from Mt. King to Bishop Creek, and embracing Mt. Gordon above Tehipite Canyon. From the Kings River Canyons and Mt. Whitney in the south to Yosemite Valley in the north, a plethora of peaks appeared to invite "first ascents." The map visually represented an emptiness on which might be written a new history. The men of the club set out to claim this "terra incognita."[41]

Although it might well be said that the mountains of California had captured the heart of the Sierra Club, its soul came to reside in San Francisco's Academy of Sciences, housing the "Mother Maps" on which it recorded its members' peak-by-peak conquests of the Sierra.[42] In their club room, the men hung a portrait of the president of the Alpine Club of London—Edward Whymper of Middlesex—alpenstock in hand. Whymper himself returned the honor; when his portrait was damaged in the 1906 earthquake, he replaced it and left the club a bequest in his will.[43] Displaying Whymper rather than a painting of Daniel Boone or even of Clarence King, the Californians celebrated mountaineering's transatlantic origins. Publishing a bulletin, contacting correspondents in Europe, and making pilgrimages to the graves of Whymper's companions, the new group emulated, much as did others in America, the Alpine Club of London.[44]

Because most climbing and conservation groups were headquartered in urban areas, historians have argued that appreciation of wilderness was born in the city. Although most of the Sierra Club's early members lived in or near major cities, one-fifth had their homes in California's Owens and San Joaquin Valleys—in rural areas or small towns, such as Chico, Fresno, Reno, Merced, and Bakersfield.[45] Membership correlated only partially and not necessarily causally with urban living. The men who established the Sierra Club, like the founders of these other groups, are best characterized by their high levels of formal education, their white-collar status, and the ways in which they described themselves.

They visualized themselves as part of an international "brotherhood"—a "mountain-seeking fraternity."[46] They linked their efforts to the Royal Geographical Society of London and similar groups, and they located themselves within a transatlantic history of geographical expansion.[47] As President Charles Fay of the Appalachian Mountain Club (AMC) explained, the first European explorations over the seas had led to the discovery of new lands, but "long after the sea had lost its terrors the mountains were still left to their solitary grandeur."[48] Emulating Captain George Vancouver, who baptized peaks in the Cascade Range for the English lords of the admiralty—Baker, Hood, and Rainier—American climbers sought peaks that were "not only unexhausted, but even unnamed and unseen."[49]

They lobbied the federal government to protect these "unknown lands." Determined to preserve the forests and other features of the Sierra Nevada, the men of the new Sierra Club lobbied for federal forestry, campaigned against efforts to reduce the size of Yosemite National Park, and invited nationally prominent conservationists to join them. *From the hills cometh our strength,*" Secretary of the Interior John Noble said, accepting his invitation, "and I am glad that that stronghold is being preserved by the efforts of the SIERRA CLUB."[50] The members approached Josiah Whitney, Clarence King, General A. W. Greeley of Arctic fame, John Wesley Powell of the Colorado River, Tyndall, and Whymper (but not Ruskin), conflating the modern ideas of conservation and exploration.

The men of the club called their organization a vote against individualism "run mad" and bragged of having no material motives.[51] Other western climbers similarly distinguished themselves from those who went into "the wild for profit—to mine, log, or chase, or killing." Their sport represented an "intellectual conquest," something "quite modern" and characteristic of "civilized nations."[52] Like American intellectuals in general, climbers argued that only educated cosmopolitans possessed the scientific, aesthetic, and spiritual sensibilities to appreciate natural landscapes.[53] They described those who actually lived in the mountains as incapable of appreciating their own landscapes, so that conservation required that federal scrutiny be intensified.[54] The assumption that the physical world shaped human culture served climbers well as they pressed authorities to preempt the rights of those who used the mountains for hunting and gathering, mining, or grazing livestock.[55]

The early 1890s were a turning point for the Sierra only in part because of the Sierra Club and Yosemite National Park. The 1891 Forest Reserve Act, passage of which owed much to the lobbying of professional foresters and preservationists such as Muir, authorized that public domain lands be reserved from private sale or claim. President Harrison set aside fifteen million acres in the western mountains. The Sierra Club called this inadequate and petitioned Congress to place *all* federal timberlands under permanent military control.[56] President Cleveland added twelve million acres, four million of them in the Sierra and Sequoia Forest Reserves, which together incorporated two hundred miles of the Sierra's western divide from Yosemite to Kings Canyon.[57]

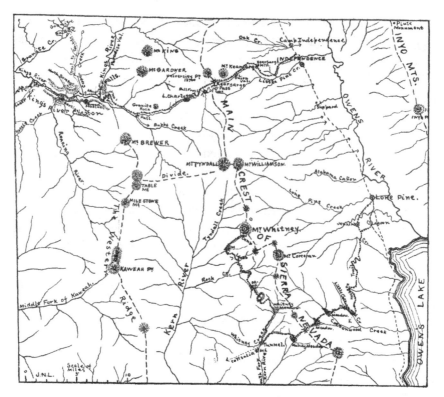

Figure 6. Map of the High Sierra surrounding Mt. Whitney. Section of 1894 map by J. N. LeConte entitled "A Portion of the Sierra Nevada Adjacent to the Kings River," reproduced in Sierra Club Bulletin, *May 1895. LeConte's original maps are held in the University of California, Bancroft Library, Map Room.*

The uses people were at that time making of the new reserves, as was true of Yosemite National Park, remain visible today on maps and in narratives from the late nineteenth century.[58] The sheepherder was at home "in every part of the High Sierra" and would, one climber conceded, draw you a diagram on "the sooty bottom of the 'fry pan,'" if you asked directions.[59] Extant maps show a wealth of human artifacts and trails. Byways laced the upper Kings River and its North Fork; bridges and established fords led into the presumably most remote regions. Meadows and peaks in abundance bore designations, most of which would later disappear.[60] Climbers denigrated the herder's place names and offered new ones. On six peaks in the upper Middle Fork of the San Joaquin River they honored men in the evolutionary sciences, beginning with Charles Darwin.[61] The Sierra Club quickly staked its claim to the peaks of

Figure 7. "Trespassing in Yosemite National Park."
Sheepherders and their dogs in Tuolumne Meadows, with their
flocks in the distance. Photograph by Charles E. Townsend,
1898. Courtesy of University of California, Bancroft Library.

Kings Canyon, of Tehipite Canyon, and of the southern portion of the main divide. In an area some twenty miles wide and one hundred fifty miles long, its members honored each other, their heroes, and influential friends, including Gifford Pinchot of the federal Division of Forestry.[62]

Along with Pinchot and the U.S. Cavalry, which patrolled the reserves, the men of the club shared the goal of removing the sheepherder, a process for which they found the language of patriotism helpful. William Dudley of the Sierra Club complained that "the herder is a foreigner, a non-citizen, a parasite, who intends eventually to move back to France, or Portugal, or Ireland, whence he came, and carry with him all his gains pilfered through sheep-raising on land not his own." The cavalry, arriving in May and departing in the fall,

Figure 8. "After the Ascent of Mt. Davis (12,308') in the Sierra Nevada, August 27 & 28, 1891." Shown, among others, are Lt. Milton F. Davis of the 4th U.S. Cavalry and Dr. E. W. Beers, a Methodist minister. Photograph taken in Yosemite Valley by George Fiske. Courtesy of University of California, Bancroft Library.

chased out cattlemen and herders who trespassed into the parks and reserves, pursuing the latter with vitriol because they were unpropertied "foreigners."[63]

The sheep were so numerous that they represented a significant intrusion of market forces into the range, threatening its soil and its vegetation.[64] Sheep also trampled the wildflowers and ate the fodder that hikers required for their pack animals. In 1895 four climbers who traveled from Fresno to Mt. Whitney with twelve donkeys bearing camp chairs, food, and a large stove were annoyed to find that the resident sheep had left scant feed for their animals. "Throughout the whole trip," the four were "much disappointed to find the otherwise delightful water near the sources of the streams, so unpleasantly flavored by having passed through meadows where the sheep had grazed." Hikers soon took to carrying lemons to disguise the urine flavor of the waters.[65]

For years the herders defended their use rights in the courts and the state legislature. Only after more than a decade of military and legal action were these trespassers—nomadic, alien, and destructive—driven out of the Sierra's public forests and parks.[66] Each summer, hikers would follow indigenous and grazing trails, but it became increasingly difficult to identify the origins of these byways.[67] Herders' place-names were forgotten or removed, and few traces remained of their Spanish, Chinese, French, or Basque languages. Their surnames left a somewhat larger heritage. Those on today's maps reflect nineteenth-century social hierarchies: McGree Creek honors a homesteader; and Mt. McGee, a geologist. Jack Main's Lake, named after a herder, was renamed for the daughter of a superintendent of Yosemite National Park, and Sheep Mountain became "Mt. Langley," for an astronomer. The new names honored scientists and recreationists rather than those who worked the land.[68]

Perhaps the most explicit gesture of reencoding the range involved Frank Dusy, who pastured large flocks in the North and Middle Forks of the Kings River for twenty-five years. He explored the rivers with his dog Dinky, built a home, and in 1879 took the first photographs of Tehipite Canyon.[69] Hiking in the Palisades in the 1870s, Lilbourne Winchell of Fresno County named a fourteen-thousand-foot spire for Dusy, placing the name on official maps.[70] In 1903, J. N. LeConte told Winchell that the Sierra Club was "struck by the unfitness of the name" and renamed it "North Palisades."[71]

The U.S. Board on Geographic Names in Washington, D.C., had come to recognize climbing clubs as the official "name-givers" of the Sierra, the Cascades, the Rockies, and New England's mountains. Revealing the fine line between military subjugation and establishment of domestic order, the board had initially represented the Departments of State, Treasury, War, Navy, and the U.S. Coast and Geodetic Survey. Even after 1906—when all its members were drawn from the U.S. Geological Survey—the board continued to consider the alpine clubs as authoritative, urging them to contribute to the nation's "Mother Maps."[72] The board's new chairman that year advised the Sierra Club to retain Native American names, those from the Spanish Mission period (if euphonious), and those from the Gold Rush, even if "rude and uncouth." His guidelines seemed to signal a new sensitivity to historical names, but regional clubs continued to favor English surnames and the board continued to accept them.[73] One climber quoted the lines of a poem: "I like a mount that bears a name, . . . the name of a friend of intimate fame."[74]

In 1901, inspired by successful group climbs organized by the Mazamas, the AMC, and others, the Sierra Club decided to sponsor annual summer High Trips. Club secretary William Colby hoped that by leading John Muir's disciples into the mountains, he would build a politically active constituency—warriors for the wilderness. Colby promised prospective participants that experiences of cold weather, hunger, and discomfort would be minimized.[75] As another club leader explained, "[O]ne cannot enjoy either grand scenery or good temper with a disgruntled stomach or a chilled body. Mountain trips should be for pleasure and recuperation, not discipline and stoicism."

*Figure 9. Portrait of Frank Dusy, Thanksgiving Day, 1873, at
age thirty-five, captioned "A Stockman Ahead of His Time."
Dusy, an adventurous climber and one of the first to
photograph Tehipite Canyon, pastured his flocks along the
North and Middle Forks of the Kings River for many years.
Courtesy of University of California, Bancroft Library.*

Climbers were advised to "take plenty," from feather quilts to butter, lemons
to chocolate.[76]

On its first trip, the following year, the club invited women, a decision that
brought substantial subscriptions. Each summer thereafter, its High Trip drew
over a hundred men and women. A stagecoach bounced hikers in from the
San Joaquin Valley through the Sierra foothills to Muir's beloved Tuolumne
Meadows, which the club had since purchased. Participants then spent four

(EN)GENDERING THE WILDERNESS

Figure 10. Sierra Club High Trip in Yosemite National Park, with Chinese cook in the center of camp, ca. 1904. Courtesy of University of California, Bancroft Library.

weeks in the Sierra, walking an average of ten to fifteen miles a day from one base camp to another. Each stop afforded opportunities to scale the peaks; evenings brought campfires, group sings, natural history talks, and impromptu skits. Dunnage and food arrived at each base camp well ahead of the hikers; the supplies were transported by packhorses and some seventy mules led through the night by Mono peoples—shadows of those who had once controlled the Owens Valley and hunted in the Sierra.[77]

Historians have described the Sierra Club as uniquely American and distinctly Californian.[78] But the appreciation of the natural world represented by the Sierra Club could be found emerging throughout North America, the British Empire, and Europe.[79] Modern conservation, whether referring to wise use or to wilderness protection, was not born in North America's Far West. Rather, western civilization made that West its conservation project. What was new was the opportunity to implement appreciation on public lands. Westerners copied European topographic nomenclature ("peak" and "mount"), shared European aesthetic standards, and patterned outdoor clubs after those of the eastern United States and Europe. Most founders of western clubs had been born in the eastern United States, and had brought to the mountains of the Pacific a fascination with natural history and sport that was rooted in a transatlantic culture, even as they claimed a new right of place. Their enthusiasm was a product of place and of time. Over the next twenty years, similar organizations multiplied across North America.[80]

The Sierra Nevada was, as well, largely mapped during these years. By World War I, the range had new topographic designations acceptable to a cosmopolitan audience and certified in a distant capital. Of the Sierra's 358 peaks higher than nine thousand feet above sea level, 205 had acquired Euro-American surnames that celebrated engineers, topographers, climbers, federal officials, scientists, philosophers of science, and a few recognized artists and photographers. Of the eleven peaks higher than fourteen thousand feet, all but one honored geologists, topographers, or astronomers. The urge of English speakers to favor men's surnames, and these particular surnames, had its wellspring in more than self-congratulation, the difficulty of pronouncing Native American names, or limited knowledge of the land.

These designations conveyed political and cultural authority, erased the history of the range itself, and decontextualized its topography. Rather than identifying a site embedded in time and place, these designations celebrated taking possession as a manly act. The new nomenclature reflected the social identities and aspirations of its givers, who had chosen the names of men of such seemingly transcendent importance as to make the appropriation of the land appear inevitable and final. Few surnames met this criterion better than those of nineteenth-century natural scientists, experts in systems of knowledge that were European-centered yet purported to embody universal truth. To their givers, such designations had the added virtue of portraying a territorial expansion that was free of commercial and political self-interest while justifying the processes by which earlier owners and users, from Native American peoples to Basque herders, were dispossessed.

The new maps of the Sierra's topography can be read as gendered texts. Western culture's traditional use of female metaphors to describe the natural world assumed a new dominance in the nineteenth century. To Victorian Americans, sexual identity sent clear signals of meaning, and they used its attendant assumptions to make new lands welcoming. California's *Sunset* magazine, for example, encouraged readers to visit the Sierra, noting, "Nature almost virgin and of surpassing beauty awaits the coming of her chosen ones."[81] Writers metaphorically feminized nature, even occasionally describing mountains as maternal, succoring the flora and fauna at their bosoms, and being buffeted by the masculine elements of rain, storms, wind, and sun. The

Sierra's streams welled "out of the earth, ice-cold from its mother . . . , kissed by that passionate lover, the sun."[82]

When English-speaking newcomers reached the Sierra, Rockies, and Cascades, however, the nature they found there did not accord with these metaphors. Of the High Sierra, King exclaimed, "I have never seen Nature when she seemed so little 'Mother Nature' as in this place of rocks and snow, echoes and emptiness." Ascending the peak called Grand Teton, a man declared that "our haughty lady" proved "a snarling wolf."[83] Perhaps, then, it is not surprising that the Sierra's peaks, in particular, became fanciful embodiments of individual men, replete with substantive presences and analogous body parts of faces, brows, flanks, shoulders, backs, ribs, and feet.

In general, North America's alpine topographies were rarely given female names. Nature was assumed to be feminine, but control over it was masculine. Although occasionally cited as an exception, Mt. St. Helens in the Cascade Range is not. Its name, chosen by Captain George Vancouver, honors the British ambassador to Spain, the Baron St. Helens. Exceptions did include analogies of peaks and breasts. Twin Teats, Nellie's Nipple, and Squaw Nipple Peak sexualized the topography.[84] The taller the peak, the less likely it was to be given a female name (only four of the Sierra's eighty-two peaks higher than twelve thousand feet and named on federal maps before 1950 honor women). For the most part, men were the name givers. Had women had a greater say, more peaks might honor women. The highest Sierra peak commemorating a woman—13,037-foot Mt. Genevra—was named by a woman. As it was, naming transformed the mountains of North America into metaphor and image, making the land a written text. The heights lent natural authority to debates regarding social class, the ideal ethnic identity, and the proper spheres of men and women.

The aversion to female ascendancy grew in the early twentieth century, and a number of women's names disappeared. The demise of some is shrouded in mystery; others were removed by fiat.[85] In the Sierra, the Board on Geographic Names renamed Jenny Lind Cañon—chosen by miners for the Swedish singer—"Big Arroyo."[86] Settlers had called a 13,016-foot peak in Inyo County "Mt. Alice." Although "Mt. Alice" appeared on early U.S. Geological Survey maps, the board, with Sierra Club concurrence, redesignated it "Temple Crag."[87] In 1877 seven men and four women from nearby Porterville named a peak near Mt. Guyot for Anna Mills, a local teacher and a climber of "plucky perseverance." A century would pass before the name gained board approval.[88]

In 1906 the chief of the U.S. Board on Geographic Names advised the Sierra

Club to avoid petty or obscure names, citing as examples those recognizing women. No geographic feature could be named for a woman, he wrote, unless she was a saint, and only a landowner had the right to honor an aunt or sister. With partial accuracy, he complained: "Our mountain regions are filled with Maud peaks, Mary lakes, etc., *ad nauseam.*" To him, there was "no more fitting monument to the great men of the past . . . than noble mountains bearing their names." When a great man dies, he urged, look for a peak to name for him.[89] There is nothing worse, the AMC's president agreed, than "a poorly named mountain." When the town of Lincoln, Massachusetts, named a nearby peak "Elizabeth Thompson Mountain," the AMC vetoed it for "its intrinsic inappropriateness."[90]

The few sites honoring women were bodies of water. Billed as the lovers of commanding peaks, waterfalls soothed granite walls, stroked cliffs, and added beauty, tenderness, and sound.[91] The name "Bridal Veil Falls" captured an Englishwoman's notion of obvious femininity as "the bride of the Sierra."[92] A rich biological symbolism associated water with fertility and nurturance. "Bridal Veil" imparted a moral lesson, as did "Virgin's Tears," a trickle on the other side of Yosemite Valley. Berkeley Professor Joseph LeConte explained that El Capitan preferred to look at the bride rather than at the "seamed, and channeled, and wrinkled" face of the virgin. LeConte pronounced fitting the marriage of Bridal Veil's beauty and El Capitan's strength, and he admired the commanding names English speakers had given to other cliffs. He thrilled to the "bald, awful head" of Half Dome glittering in the sunlight with Mirror Lake nestled at its feet, "fast asleep, her polished, black surface not yet ruffled by the rising wind."[93] All was right in a world where men soared above the limits of the material and where women lie embedded in the earth. Social order rested in the oppositional forces of strength and beauty, production and reproduction.

Elements of power were thought masculine; waters, feminine.[94] The few Sierra features named for women before 1940 were lakes, although some feminine names were later applied to adjacent creeks, canyons, or peaks. In the 1860s the men of the California survey named Eleanor Lake for Whitney's daughter; Lake Nina for Hoffmann's sister-in-law; May Lake at the foot of Mt. Hoffmann for his fiancée; and Lake Frances for a friend.[95] For the next century, men would name lakes for wives, daughters, and friends (rarely for mothers). Charlotte Lake was named in the 1870s; Florence and Jennie Lakes, in the 1890s; Helen and Elizabeth Lakes, in the 1900s; Cora, Dorothy, Edyth, and Wilma Lakes, in the 1910s; Lakes Bernice and Doris, in the 1920s; Lakes Betty and Bright Dot, in the 1930s; Lakes Anne and Beryle, in the 1940s; and Lake Midge, in the 1950s. Acknowledging friends, wives, and daughters by the

Figure 11. "Dryads." Five women dressed in tunics and scarves dancing around Fairy Lake, Mt. Rainier. Photograph by Asahel Curtis, ca. 1931. Courtesy of Manuscripts, Special Collections, University Archives, University of Washington.

use of first names followed a convention that owed much to the tradition that women changed their surnames at marriage. But the practice also assumed that femininity was more generic, abstract, and natural than masculinity, so that, for instance, one honored all Helens as much as a specific Helen.[96]

Although it does not take a stretch of the imagination to link Victorian prescriptions for womanhood with such portrayals, the message was not simple. When Meriweather Lewis named a branch of the Missouri River "Maria's River," for a cousin, he considered that its muddy, boiling waters were inappropriate to the purity of a lady, but that its roses and "the wild and simple yet sweet and cheerful melody" of its birds warranted "Maria."[97] Potentially inferior and reactive, water was also a powerful material force. In summer, especially, lakes were the life of western ranges. Trees, flowers, insects, and animals clustered at their edges. Equating womanhood with such fecundity was logical and, in a world that prized motherhood as women's sole occupation, potentially empowering. Yet men overwhelmingly described lakes in passive terms, minimizing their reproductive force. Mountains symbolized power; placidly sequestered "limpid waters" epitomized purity and evoked the urge to protect. Animate yet quiet, such waters "nestled in the chilled embrace of the rock floor," slept in the moonlight, smiling up into the sky at dawn, drowsy at dusk.[98] Like life-giving waters, wives and daughters were to be submissive and self-effacing.

Few landscapes were more popular than still lakes.[99] Manuals of the day detailed the exacting requirements necessary to capture photographically such scenes: clear early light, dawn breaking, and calm waters. Tourists posed on the rim of Mirror Lake so that their images were reflected in the water beneath those of the cliffs.[100] Mirror Lake was the only topographic site mentioned in passage of the bill making Yosemite Valley a public park. By the 1870s, this wide and shallow lake, reflecting the profile of Mt. Watkins that honored its photographer, was among the best known of Yosemite's attractions.[101] This fascination with this exact imaging reflected more than enthusiasm for a new technology.

Clear, still, liquid bodies looking up at the stern cliffs offered the perfect Victorian tableau. Mirror Lake appeared "exquisitely cradled in the very midst of stern granite giants, which stand all around as sentinels, guarding its placid sleep." A Sierra peak, one man wrote, is most "perfectly reflected in the bosom of the water."[102] Women seemed to like the analogy, emphasizing the color, beauty, and life of these waters lying in rock hollows.[103] "The sun shone down," a climber commented, "on a wild waste of barren peaks and ridges with tiny lakes nestling at their bases." For some there was an element of mystery in the lake.[104] J. N. LeConte, in a rare act, honored his wife Marion (Helen Marion Gompertz LeConte) with a 12,719-foot peak and its lake, which he described as "fringed with tiny meadows on one side, and guarded on the other by fine cliffs of white granite, which could be traced far down beneath the clear waters till lost in their blue depths."[105]

In her slender classic *Land of Little Rain*, Mary Austin described the Sierra near her Owens Valley home. Her fascination with lakes, as with nature in general, lay less in their beauty or reflectivity, however, than in their mysterious, even evil, qualities: "The lake is the eye of the mountain, jade green, placid, unwinking, also unfathomable. Whatever goes on under the high and stony brow is guessed at." Lakes often sit, she cautioned, in such "deep cairns of broken boulders" that one could neither get close to them nor get "away unhurt." She recalled one on the Kearsarge trail as "still and wickedly green in its sharp-lipped cup." Other visitors also found lakes unknowable, even frightening.[106]

Most, however, described lakes simply as sheltered and tranquil places possessing little power beyond that of nurturing their surroundings.[107] Muir loved glacial lakes that "nestle in rocky nooks and hollows about all the high peaks and in the larger cañons, reflecting their stern, rugged beauty and giving charm and animation to the bleakest and most forbidding landscapes." Of Lake Tenaya in winter, he wrote, "the ice was so clear and unruffled, that the mountains and the groves that looked upon it were reflected almost as perfectly as I ever beheld them in the calm evening mirrors of summer."[108] Climbers described the reflective surface of Pamelia Lake in the Cascades and the quiet waters of Lake Louise that "doubled and intensified" the impression of the cliffs. Wrote a hiker, "Rae Lake is one of the most beautiful . . . of our Sierra mountain lakes. It is encircled by a wonderful array of towering peaks which it mirrors on its island-dotted surface." One man visualized a lake as akin to his wife (named for her by friends) and named the lake's island after their infant daughter.[109]

Such metaphors reinforced the advice on good conduct offered to middle- and upper-class ladies. *Overland Monthly* told those graduating from high school in 1873: "The noblest aim of every true woman is not the happiness which serves herself, but the joy that she may irradiate to others. And, however obscure and quiet may be her sphere, the world will feel her ennobling influence . . . that she distills about her from day to day."[110] Like alpine lakes, women were to be secluded, nurturing, and selfless. Construed as pure, passive, and transparent more often than mysterious or life-giving, lakes were mirrors in which men could see themselves.

Although it is possible in retrospect to see that the aesthetics of naming concretized social expectations, what men and women sought in the natural world, was, ironically, evidence of the intrinsic correctness of their expectations. According to one man, nature made clear the laws of God, which included "the laughter of children, the unmeasured sacrifice of motherhood, and the ceaseless yearning of all men for a wider outlook and nobler existence."[111] Well into the twentieth century, soldiers, officials, tourists, and climbers imparted a consistent vision of the conquest of nature and of the society that had achieved that conquest. The mountains came to emulate in vertical space the social values of hierarchy and authority. From a diversity of motives, then, the Sierra's topography became a monument to English-speaking colonialism.

Masculine Sublimes

In the summer of 1913, fifteen-year-old William O. Douglas and nineteen-year-old Doug Corpron camped overnight in the northern Cascades. At dawn they watched the sun rise behind an oval-shaped rock rising two thousand feet above Tieton Basin. As the light touched "her crest," the rock known as Kloochman became for the boys a "symbol of adversity and challenge." They resolved to climb the rock, the name of which was, appropriately, they said, an Indian word for "woman." At first the ascent was easy, but after the first six hundred feet they were forced to inch up, bodies pressed against "gnarled and chewed teats pointing to the sky." Reaching a cul-de-sac, they found that they could not proceed. Retreat was possible only if Corpron, suspended by his fingers six hundred feet above the valley, let go and dropped six inches to a foothold. The maneuver would require his companion to grasp the rock with one hand and take the full weight of his friend's body with the other. Corpron had, in an earlier moment of fear, told Douglas that should he fall, Douglas was to tell his mother that he had loved her and his father that "I was brave and died unafraid." Corpron released his hold. Straining against the weight, Douglas imagined himself standing "sick and ashamed" before his friend's parents, "testifying to my own inadequacy." His arms held. The boys descended—only to try again.

On the second assault it was Douglas who found himself dangling by his fingers: "I did not see how I could possibly hold. I would slip, I thought, slip to sure death. I could not look down. . . . But in my mind's eye I saw in sharp outline the jagged rocks that seemed to pull me toward them. Fright grew in me. The idea of hanging, helpless

200 feet above the abyss brought panic. I was like one in a nightmare who struggles to shout—who is then seized with a fear that promises to destroy him." He accused himself: "You are a weakling. Weaklings die in the woods." Then he recalled a "domestic scene"—his mother sitting in their living room telling him his father's last words: "If I die it will be glory. If I live, it will be grace." Douglas asked God "to give him guts, to give me power." In this moment, he "first communed with God." Surrendering to deity and father, he found identity, strength, reason, and control. He did not fall; Corpron reached him and the two made the summit. On her gnarled teats, Douglas was reborn. The experience was at once revelation and rite of passage.[1]

The episode was a young man's bravado described by Douglas forty years later, in 1950. By then a justice on the U.S. Supreme Court, he believed that his brush with death had made him a conservationist and empowered him as a man. Already a strong advocate for wilderness in the Pacific Northwest, Douglas went on to serve on the Sierra Club's board of directors and to deliver an opinion for the court arguing for the rights of nature in a case involving the High Sierra.

Across centuries and continents, men described such transcendent moments, often writing chronicles that bore structural parallels to memoirs and novels of war and to the westerns of American fiction. Men's alpine narratives, like these other genres, are set against spare, natural landscapes. The three literary forms share a halting rhythm. They open with anticipatory scenes that lead into false advances followed by retreats, new offensives, spells of monotony, crises of endurance and pain, and "thence to the end or closure, which consists of transformation, reaffirmation, recognition, victory, apotheosis, or defeat."[2] All three genres were recipes for manhood. Each was "haunted by death."[3] The structural similarities were not coincidental. Men often wrote of climbing as a contest; their language was frequently warlike, if loving, and the effect of the mountain was cathartic. Multiple and shifting social expectations of appropriate behaviors and feelings drew men onto the peaks and into movements to save wild and scenic places.

By definition, landscapes represent both external objects and perceptions of objects. Simon Schama argues that "a whole world of associations and sentiments" encloses and gives meaning to any and all scenery, even that which we know to be wild. The men who climbed in the United States during the nineteenth and the early twentieth centuries brought cultural associations that had grown out of the European understanding of America and the American understanding of Europe. Alpinists on both sides of the Atlantic Ocean followed Edmund Burke's lead in praising landscapes for their sublimity. Romantics prized whatever was foreign, exotic, desolate, and mysterious, if not grotesque, landscapes that were chaotic, raw, barren, irregular, and frightening.[4] By right of its Latin origins, the word *sublime* conveys the idea of elevation, a sense of awe, and connotations of masculinity. *Sublime* defined mountains and men's experience of them both by its etymology and by the associations given to it in the nineteenth century.[5] Seeking truth in emotion and reason together, romantics visualized the material world in surprisingly postmodern terms as a construction of the human mind and an extension of the social self. Nature was a window through which they saw themselves, others, and the divine.

Mountaineering also offered the opportunity to merge the romantic aesthetic with the social topographies of gender. Men's language was built on western culture's traditional portrayals of the human body, particularly the female body, as analogous to the natural world. Metaphoric forms and literary conventions inherited from European history contoured the American experience. The peaks were forbidding, but they were also feminine; they enticed men, who responded with emotions ranging from love to lust to anger. Mountaineering reflected a masculine sense of the proper relationships between the sexes. Victorian men approached wilderness fearfully but with the desire to dominate, and the protectiveness, curiosity, and emotional intensity that their cultures urged them to feel toward their wives.

Despite the ostensible spontaneity in these writings, men's descriptions of sublime moments had, by the late nineteenth century, become conventional and the sport of alpinism a set of rituals. That men kept seeking fresh heights to master and to write about attests to the determination of climbers to locate themselves within history, but it also suggests that they continued to find these forms relevant to their lives. Alpinism was replete with martyrlike suffering, elation, and catharsis. The formation of ideal and material identities converged, as they did when William O. Douglas conflated mother with nature, and self with father and God. Men courted, copied, and choreographed the convergence of spirituality and athleticism. The ritualized experience of struggle satisfied religious impulses and suited an agenda of physical maturation.

Consciously or not, William O. Douglas had mimicked the poet Samuel Coleridge's descriptions of rock climbing in the Lake District of England in 1802, a pastime Coleridge himself referred to as a "sort of Gambling" and to which he admitted being addicted. After a day of scrambling up crags and skirting precipices, he began his descent, only to find himself stranded on the narrow ledge of a "smooth perpendicular Rock," unable to go up or down. To fall meant death. "My limbs," he reported, "were all in a tremble." Lying there on his back with the "sight of the Crags above me on each side, & the impetuous Clouds just over them," he fell into

> a state of almost prophetic Trance & Delight—& blessed God aloud, for the powers of Reason & the Will, which remaining no Danger can overpower us! / O God, I exclaimed aloud—how calm, how blessed am I now / I know not how to proceed, how to return / but I am calm & fearless & confident / if this Reality were a Dream, if I were asleep, what agonies had I suffered! what screams!—When the Reason & the Will are away, what remain to us but Darkness & Dimness & a bewildering Shame, and Pain that is utterly lord over us, or fantastic / Pleasure that draws the Soul along swimming through the air.

His rational thought conquering dread, his pleasure overtaking pain, he rose, only to find below him stones piled so that he could move along them. A rent in the rock permitted him to slip down between the semienclosing walls. Escaping "bewildering Shame," he reached a shelter where he sat listening to a thunderstorm and uttered a cry that echoed across the Atlantic: "O how I wished for Health & Strength that I might wander about for a Month together, in the stormiest month of the year, among these Places, so lonely & savage & full of sounds!"[6]

Coleridge, who with other poets and essayists cultivated romantic thought, often described the love of nature as hierarchical. Appreciations of the beautiful (natural objects that could be enjoyed for their inherent form, such as flowers) and of the picturesque (having elements of a picture, often associated with gardens) were simpler, they argued. More complex and higher was appreciation of the sublime ("that which seemed infinite in size or power, and thus could not be comprehended or fully understood by men because it transcended human judgment").[7] Poets and essayists often gendered this hierarchy. Ralph Waldo Emerson suggested that only because of its "high and divine beauty" could nature "be loved without effeminacy." Coleridge distinguished between a man who described a great cataract as sublime and a woman who responded, "Yes! and it is not only sublime, but beautiful and absolutely pretty." In the poet's eye, the woman had failed to transcend nature's physicality to find higher meaning. Because this woman noted only beauty, a scholar explained, she had obviously resisted "the direct experience of Nature," preferring to convert it into "an image."[8] But this example more accurately invites us to argue that the masculine sublime represented a strong distancing of self from the immediacy of one's presence in the physical world, a distancing that uncommon landscapes merely exaggerate.

Figure 12. Members of the Mountaineers, 1907, in Washington's Olympic Mountains. Courtesy of Manuscripts, Special Collections, University Archives, University of Washington.

The Alps were the archetypal romantic landscape, but North America's alpine clubs embraced their own heights as well. The Appalachian Mountain Club's president, Charles Fay, found New England's darkly forested and stormy heights sublime. "Wild, black tempest-clouds" suddenly parted, he wrote of a scene in the White Mountains, to reveal a "weird, rocky peak in unspeakable grandeur, standing out against a lurid background of rain-clouds illuminated with ghastly, yellow light."[9] Men tramping the Cascade Range reveled in the abruptness of volcanic peaks, blinding snows, dangerous ice sheets, and crevassed glaciers.[10] In the Sierra, glaciers had cut deep, narrow valleys out of the range's upthrust granite and abandoned chaotic moraines, dangers to gladden the heart of a romantic.

For all that they drew on natural histories and real places, however, these conventions celebrated more than reality. Arriving in the summer, when they might have described the Sierra as a "gentle wilderness," as later conservationists would, most nineteenth-century visitors avoided the range's harsh winters. Nevertheless, they commonly portrayed it as "sublime and awful," a "bewildering confusion of peaks" whose vegetation suggested a "nether world."[11] Despite the often sunny beauty of Kings Canyon, early hikers wrote of a "deep, dread, silent, stupendous amphitheater; . . . crowded with adamant mountains, pinnacled crests, thunder-scarred cliffs, green lines of forest, snows in eternal sleep, horrid gorges, yawning gulfs; . . . nude, primeval granite— cold, soulless and silent as death."[12]

Such descriptions of desolation were stylish and roundly applauded in North America and Europe. The tropes of manly exploration had been well established by the early nineteenth century and were not unique to the American West. Henry David Thoreau narrated for a popular magazine a sublime moment on Maine's Ktaadn (the modern spelling is Katahdin) in 1846. Historians have portrayed Thoreau as recoiling from a place so unlike Walden Pond, but his experience of Ktaadn is more correctly understood as sublime horror. Reaching the five-thousand-foot summit, he was disoriented by its savagery. He trembled with joy, his sense of awe exaggerated by the earth's departure from its role as nurturing mother. "Here was no man's garden," he wrote. "It was not lawn, nor pasture, nor mead, nor woodland, nor lea, nor arable, nor waste-land. It was the fresh and natural surface of the planet Earth. . . . Man was not to be associated with it. It was Matter, vast, terrific,—not his Mother Earth that we have heard of." His distancing was palpable, exquisitely intellectual: to come into contact with the "*solid* earth!," "the *actual* world!" he exclaimed! "*Contact! Contact! Who* are we? *where* are we?"[13]

Growing out of the spiritual impulses of eighteenth- and nineteenth-century poets and essayists, including Thoreau and Coleridge, sublimity came to reflect "the vastness, the power, the terror of Deity." It was the terrestrial vision of God, what one analyst has called "the aesthetics of the Infinite." The idea of sublimity addressed those mysteries—such as the inevitability of death, the existence of God, and the possibility of divine salvation—that could not be grasped by reason but rather required intuition. Nevertheless, the idea also built upon advances in the natural sciences that revealed the creative force of vast time and space, so that sublimity reconciled spirituality and science.[14] Mountains became altars for the often secularly educated climbers, many of whom found institutionalized religions increasingly inadequate. As Christian churches and clergies weakened their hold on America's intellectual life, experiences of sublime landscapes provided sustenance for some. Rugged landscapes allowed men to glimpse God, as Coleridge had, or, as Douglas did, to shout at him. "Wilderness glows with divine light," Muir wrote, "throbbing and pulsing with the heartbeats of God."[15]

In wilderness, Muir and men like him felt their souls gained authority. Experiencing and describing powerful landscapes served them socially as well as spiritually. Claims to empirical understanding and physical mastery recon-

Figure 13. "Overlooking Cowlitz Glacier," Mt. Rainier, 1897. Courtesy of the Mazamas, Portland, Oregon.

ciled the potentially effeminate love of nature and the seemingly frivolous joy in leisure with society's demand that men work hard. Simple praise of beauty was acceptable from women, whom Victorians idealized as the aesthetic arbiters of everyday life, those who arranged the flowers and shopped for apparel. Women's very bodies served aesthetic ends. Less so did the bodies of middle- and upper-class men. Clad in black, Victorian men's appropriate sphere was less the consumption of time or goods than the production of ideas and commodities; such men readily embraced a message of power.

Wild landscapes became meaningful within the context of middle-class norms that prescribed for men (but not for women) the cultivation of anger and fear presumably well suited to a competitive commercial order.[16] Men spoke of being perversely drawn to the heights. They imagined peaks defying them and conjured up an anger that impelled them upward.[17] One was, Fay shuddered, "almost powerless to resist the strange fascination of the terrible." Yet the reflexive response to vertigo was empowering. "The ascent of a mountain . . . is remarkably fitted to development of this sense of power." One might be nearly dizzy with fear, but out of this "temporary sense of oppression springs a reverent sense of power."[18] Out of this "sudden madness and paralysis of the soul" sprang the experience of the masculine sublime.[19] Crossing the Alpine ravine of Mont Terrible on a narrow bridge with little more than a rope line for the parapet, a climber found himself overcome with demonic self-doubt and unable to move. Only at the critical moment did he find, in Christianity, salvation from the hell of the mountain.[20]

Muir experienced the sublime moment while scaling an avalanche gully on Mt. Ritter. Brought to a halt, arms outstretched, he was unable to move up or down the mountain: "I *must* fall," he thought: "There would be a moment of bewilderment, and then a lifeless rumble" down the precipice. "Nerve-shaken," his mind seemed to fill with "a stifling smoke. . . . This terrible eclipse lasted only a moment, when life blazed forth again with preternatural clearness. I seemed suddenly to become possessed of a new sense. The other self . . . came forward and assumed control." His muscles stopped trembling; his legs and arms moved with precision. Had he been "borne aloft upon wings," he recalled, "my deliverance could not have been more complete."[21] Muir invited this reflexive emotional transport in 1874 by lashing himself to a tall conifer in Yosemite Valley to experience the winds of a high country thunderstorm.[22]

Explicitly or implicitly, such moments represented a physical purging, a martyrlike faith that elation would follow self-abasement. Muir had grown up in a home he remembered as dominated by a devoutly Christian father who made the boy work so hard that his health was damaged. As an adult, despite a less-than-robust body, Muir became a strong mountaineer who disavowed physical comfort, eating little and walking far—habits of abstinence that facilitate revelation. He deliberately disassociated himself from his body, moving at times beyond asceticism to self-flagellation. Ascending a rock above Tenaya Falls one summer in 1873, he stumbled, made several involuntary somersaults, and was knocked unconscious. He awoke only feet from a potentially fatal drop, unclear as to what had happened. He felt "angry and worthless" and chastised his feet: "That is what you get by intercourse with stupid town stairs, and dead pavement." He resolved on the most vigorous exercise, forcing his "humbled body over the highest practicable precipices, in the most in-

Figure 14. Members of the Mountaineers on Mt. Baker, April 13, 1913. Courtesy of Manuscripts, Special Collections, University Archives, University of Washington.

tricate and nerve-trying places I could find." That night he slept on a naked boulder, denying comfort for his "ill-behaved bones" by not seeking "plush boughs" and by not using "spicy cedar-plumes for pillow." In the morning, he found his body under control, his "nervous trembling" gone. The process of purging was made complete in the almost confessional tone of the description he wrote for the *Overland Monthly* of this moment of weakness.[23]

Some historians have deemphasized the influence of gendered assumptions on shaping the wilderness experience. John Sears argues that public parks and forests "both preserved a part of the wild . . . about which men had fantasized—and domesticated it. Free of Indians and the hardships of settlement, the parks offered the delights of recreational camping to those with the leisure to 'rough it' for pleasure. . . . [T]ourist attractions . . . were . . . free of being identified as either male or female space."[24] William Cronon similarly suggests that wildernesses, once publicly protected, became "tamed" and therefore ungendered, and he labels Muir's experiences of such spaces as that of a "domesticated sublime," the wild made tame, contrasting this sublimity with the experiences of someone like Clarence King.[25] Nevertheless, Muir's sporting prowess was as legendary as his portrayals of the crushing and concentrated energies that had created the canyons of the Sierra. He experienced the sublime moment and its attendant self-abasement. His wilderness was no tamer than that of his near contemporary, King. Both looked into the abyss.

The phrase "domestic sublime" might define Muir's love of nature, an emotion similar to that which nineteenth-century society encouraged men to feel toward wives and children. Coleridge had spoken of something similar when admiring the Lodore and Borrowdale mountains through rain and drizzle: "It was a dream such as lovers have,—a wild and transfiguring, yet enchantingly lovely dream, of an object lying by the side of the sleeper."[26] Like Coleridge, American men confessed strong affections for nature, even love, albeit a love that did not preclude dread, sexuality, or the urge to disarm. For centuries men had visualized nature as feminine and harbored dreams of subjugating it.[27] Their sexual imagery had sustained "the heroic stature of male colonizers who conquered and penetrated dangerous, unknown continents."[28] Muir's reevaluation of the metaphor complemented his pleasure in women's company. He climbed with them, sponsored the first women to join the Sierra Club, and was a solicitous husband and father.

For Muir, the feminine was delicate and reactive; the masculine, powerful and assertive; yet both described natural features. He used the indigenous names—Wapama Falls and Tueeulála Falls—for the waterfalls of Hetch Hetchy Valley because he found them appropriately gendered. "LáLa descends so softly that you scarcely feel sure she will alight at all," he wrote; but Wapama, with such "weight and energy . . . that you half expect him to penetrate the ground like a hard shot." And again: "LáLa dwells confidently with the winds; . . . but Wapama lives back in a jagged gorge, unreached by the winds, which, if they could go to him, would find him inflexibly bent on following his own rocky way."[29]

Muir, however, had been nurtured by a culture made skeptical of heroic masculinity by the Civil War. As well, his domestic sublime corresponded with Victorian society's positive reappraisal of womanhood. By the 1860s, middle-class Americans had come to prize motherhood and to value a man's sentimental and sexual love for his wife, seeing it as the glue that bound together the family and, by doing so, bound society. Such appraisals allowed men to articulate a more caring posture in relation to both women and nature. The metaphor of the female earth could now elicit a sensual and protective, if no less adversarial, response.

Muir's description of a winter walk in Yosemite blended sensuality and spirituality. As he looked up from the valley floor, Half Dome appeared as a madonna, her crown encased in azure blue; "purple drapery flowed in soft and graceful folds" around her. He rejected Half Dome's new name in favor of that describing the Indian maiden Tissaack. He had gazed on her a thousand times, he wrote, and "heard her voice of winds, or snowy, tuneful waters." As he lingered timidly about her skirts, she revealed her soul to him. Eventually the urge to trace the path of Yosemite Valley's glaciers compelled him to forsake Tissaack for a side canyon and the work of measuring, but at the end of the day, his task done, he ran back, the elated lover. He looked at Yosemite's peaks, lit by the love of "their god and father," the sun, and found "their faces shone with responsive love!"[30] His Sierra may have reflected the soul of God, but their face was decidedly feminine.

He was not alone in his ardor for nature. William Brewer had written to his wife of his longing to see the Rocky Mountains and of his first view of them in 1869: "Need I say that I gazed with delight or that I wished, as I have a hundred times the last two days, that you might see them with me." He called them forbidding but looked at them "often and fondly."[31] Claiming to be Yosemite Valley's first tourist, J. M. Hutchings lovingly praised the Sierra. Standing before a one-thousand-foot waterfall in the valley, he and artist Thomas Ayres watched "the changing drapery of its watery folds." To Hutchings's query, "Is it not as graceful, and as beautiful, as the veil of a bride?" Ayres had replied: "I propose that we now baptize it, and call it, 'The Bridal Veil Fall,' as one that is both characteristic and euphonious." The name captured for Hutchings the thrill of watching "gracefully undulating and wavy sheets of spray" that fell in "ethereal folds" as if, "in very modesty, to veil its unspeakable beauty from our too eagerly admiring sight."[32] Other men shared such flights of fancy.

Joseph Nisbet LeConte, professor of geology and a founder of the Sierra Club, did not take his wife along when he climbed in the 1870s because, like many of his day and class, he believed that the more civilized a society, the more manly its men and the more womanly (and separate) its women. A sentimentalist who found the distinction between men and women to be the chemistry of attraction, he was given to expressions of affection for his wife's "dear heart," and he believed that "the manly heart rejoices in woman." He also loved Yosemite, where the undulating motion of Bridal Veil lulled him, he confided, into delicious reverie, the scenery "mingling with his dream." Swimming at the bride's feet, he attempted to peek, with "sacrilegious rudeness," under her veil but "got pelted beyond endurance with water-drops, by the little fairies which guard her beauty."[33] Although Bridal Veil's name reflected the frontier vision of a "virgin" continent chastely awaiting its pioneer groom, it also signaled the emergence of a new role for man in relation to nature—that of lover and protector.

Figure 15. Joseph Nisbet LeConte and four women in Yosemite National Park, 1890s. Courtesy of University of California, Bancroft Library.

The earth's metaphoric femininity had symbolically assisted English speakers' mastery of a frontier, but it now allowed some men to frame affection for the natural world as an extension of a socially acceptable sentiment. Charles Fay campaigned, as did Muir, to protect nature from exploitation, to keep her femininity safe within parks and reserves. In 1887 the Appalachian Mountain Club (AMC) announced its intention of "protecting Nature and enabling man to enjoy her beauties and her grandeur." Men fantasized about rescuing nature from the consequences of her own bounty. In a period when women were encouraged to stay in their homes, protected by men for men, the idea of placing a boundary on nature flowed logically out of the metaphor of the female body. Fay told of approaching his "first mountain" with an innocent longing that ended in a "tryst!"[34] Much like the cloistered wife in the "walled garden" of the idealized Victorian home, wilderness was to remain pure and comely, excluded from the realm of the commercial and industrial, beloved of those privileged and strong enough to know her well.

In the years after the Civil War, the reality of the Victorian home as a "haven in a heartless world" came under siege. The hierarchical and deferential values that rested on the premises of women's submission and men's dominance were being compromised by the individualistic and commercial values of the outside world. All the more reason for nature to afford respite and the opportunity to reassert masculine dominance.[35] Assuming the household's function, wilderness offered men sanctuary from the outside world and the consolation that would prepare them to reenter that world. Muir himself moved frequently between the wilderness and his orchard ranch. Much as the idealized home was assumed to be immune from the greed and ambition endemic in middle-class men's business and professional lives, wilderness offered freedom from the pressures of work and opportunities for rejuvenation. Most men who climbed sought thrills, commemoration, and dominion—emotions not antithetical to the home—but Muir looked for a genuine alternative to competitive culture even as he worked to care for his ranch, his wife, and his daughters, to establish himself as a writer, and to protect the Sierra against commercial exploitation.[36]

Although the achievements of King and Whymper had been those of conquest, those of Muir and LeConte were of immersion. King's response to Mother Nature had been that of alienation; Whymper's, of hostility; Muir's and LeConte's of affinity. The experience of Whymper and King was heroic and egotistical; Muir's, self-effacing. Muir's Sierra was a "Garden of Eden," warm, intimate, and nurturing, symbolically sanctified by the presence of the serpent. Geology was the favored science of romantics because it seemed to describe powerful natural forces, such as the cataclysmic earthquake that Whitney hypothesized had created Yosemite Valley. Muir more accurately identified another, no less powerful cause—glacial ice eroding the granite of the range over centuries—but he described those glaciers as "tender snowflowers noiselessly falling through unnumbered centuries."[37] He found beauty in the monumental geological past as well as in the smallest creatures. "Nowhere will you see the majestic operations of nature more clearly revealed beside the frailest, most gentle and peaceful things." His wilderness abounded with "lessons on life."[38]

He wrote of how he listened to the tales told by new plants he met and asked the boulders where they were going. "Brooding over some vast mountain landscape, or among the spiritual countenances of mountain flowers," he wrote, "our bodies disappear, our mortal coils come off . . . and we blend into the rest of Nature." Departing from masculine conventions, he found no hint "of lawless forces" among mighty cliffs and domes, "no word of chaos, or of desolation" but rather common processes of creation. Although some men described the Sierra's Tuolumne Canyon as barren, he called it "a botanical garden." "Few persons have," he said, "anything like an adequate conception of the abundance, strength, and tender loveliness of the plants that inhabit these so-called frightful gorges."[39] His love of wildflowers, in particular, defied middle-class expectations of what a man should be.

The natural sciences were heavily gendered in the nineteenth and early twentieth centuries, with women favoring botany over biology or geology. Conversely, when men studied botany, they flirted with being considered effete. Many men therefore emphasized elements of athleticism, exploration, empirical vigor, and aesthetic meaning in describing their collecting of botanical specimens. Male botanists often deflected suggestions of effeminacy by studying North America's conifers. They visualized, for those who read their studies, what became known as "climax forests"—of firs, spruces, cedars, larch, and pines—calling the ancient giant of these stands a superior form of life that had striven through history "to escape enemies, overcome crowding neighbors, and bring forth its diversified fruit." Looking to the Sierra's *Sequoiadendron gigantea*, one of the oldest and largest trees, and then believed to have once dominated western landscapes, American naturalists declared that the tree epitomized the fittest in the competitive struggle for existence.[40] Muir loved conifers but was unrestrained in his enthusiasm for flowers.

By the time he helped found the Sierra Club in 1892, Muir was not only locally prominent but had a small national following. His blurring of the boundaries of gender, his sense of the sacred, his iconoclastic denial of material culture, and his penchant for wandering in the wild had all been particularly appropriate to American culture from the mid-1860s through the 1880s. In the last decade of the century, however, the strictures of manliness tightened. As historian Mary Blanchard says: "The reassertion of the sense of the individual man as a fixed social unit, not a self-created person, affected larger intellectual circles." Masculinity came to depend "on social cohesion," as a growing class of professional men formed business, civic, and social associations.[41] In contrast to the unassuming figures of John Muir and Joseph LeConte—with their long beards, slight builds, and gentle demeanors—definitions of the manly physique emphasized muscular strength. Men still sought inspiration in the mountains, but they often spoke in a language of savage sexuality.

In the summer of 1894, three college fraternity brothers who had become, respectively, a judge, a doctor, and an artist traveled north from San Francisco to climb California's Mt. Shasta. Judge John Glascock narrated their adventure, beginning with their determination to escape "the busy turmoil of life . . . to gather strength, elasticity, and moral equipoise from her [nature's] sacred touch." He described how, as they advanced onto the mountain, "the varnish of civilization rubbed off." "Bah! talk of our boasted nineteenth century civilization; it is but the thinnest of veneers. Scratch it, and you disclose the savage." They "killed, cooked, and ate," and they concluded, "Evolution still holds. You are a savage at heart." They climbed hills and explored hidden canyons. The judge confided: "She [nature] led us step by step to the summits of her beauty, seduced us into the secret places of her hiding, and day by day revealed the arcana of her being." When Mt. Shasta finally rose before them, however, they saw not simply a "mass of stone and earth; it is a living personality, following, confronting, and peeping over your shoulder, peering into your affairs, and laying your very soul bare to its awful scrutiny." The dormant volcano loomed "impenetrable, vast, and the higher you go the more it grows, dominating you from its supreme height, questioning you from the summits of immeasurable age—stern, immutable, monolithic." Try to run and the peak "laughs at your impotent efforts to escape." An old man they met on the trail informed them that Mt. Shasta was alive and that it followed him like the eye of his mother. In the end, the fraternity brothers reached the summit and stood astride the top, their fear having been mastered. Their wives had accompanied them to the base of Shasta, but the presence of women had not diminished the men's triumph, which they saw as savagery winning out over civilization and effeminacy.[42]

No less an American than Theodore Roosevelt argued that the survival of manly virtues and, by extension, of civilization required the periodic exercise of savagery.[43] The idea that modernity might threaten masculinity dated back to the early 1800s, but the equation resonated more strongly with Americans as the century (and presumably the frontier) drew to a close and the United States became increasingly urban and industrial.[44] Glascock's experience on Mt. Shasta, however, represented only a temporary stripping away of the men's identity, a "round trip," as historian David Pugh calls it, "into the primitive and back again."[45] The trip proved that the three climbers were rational, scientific men, in control of their nerve and will, of their environments, and even of their own savage urges. They enjoyed engaging in and reading about a sport that pitted men against nature and each other. Theories of social evolution made struggle the vehicle of social and economic progress, positioning men's competitive edge as the driving force. The rituals initiated by Coleridge, Whymper, King, and others were reenacted because they symbolized assumptions of superiority: racial, class-based, and, perhaps above all, gendered.

Just beneath this crust of confidence, however, apprehensions simmered. Pugh finds the level of insecurity to have been so high that he defines nineteenth-century American masculinity as a "psychosexual state of being."[46] He locates the origins of male anxieties within the unique confines of American history and culture, rather than within the broader transatlantic context evident in alpine sport and romantic rhetoric. Nonetheless, his argument does suggest that mountaineering attracted men because it afforded them the opportunity to release those tensions that defined their identity. Their narratives permitted them to verbalize insecurities and to brag of savage urges, even as they chronicled the processes of channeling these feelings into elevated moral, intellectual, and social purposes.

Social analyst Peter Gay argues that nineteenth-century men feared that their world was out of control. Both sides of the Atlantic experienced dramatic changes in the configurations of social classes, in levels of mechanization, in physical environments, and in gendered expectations. These changes caused men, Gay suggests, high levels of apprehension with commensurate rates of aggression. The search for such diversions as competitive sport represented a deliberate "cultivation of hatred."[47] Repetitious use of the word *attack* in men's narratives defined the act of grasping or gripping that is essential on steep grades, but it also connoted aggression and violence, as do other words common to men's alpine sport, such as *assault, mastery,* and *conquest.* Men fantasized peaks as being malevolent feminine enemies.[48] The sport invited men to struggle against a powerful metaphor of the opposite sex at a time when women's independence was growing. The emotional reflex generated was similar to that which Annette Kolodny detected among nineteenth-century American-frontier farmers, who used a language of mastery to compensate for the vulnerability created by their dependence on a new and difficult land.[49]

Masculinity was often articulated through a language of place. This was particularly clear in literary representations, such as those of mountains in climbing narratives or those of the West in popular novels. Although it is possible to impart metaphysical and psychological meanings to a mountain and to the West, readers saw these locations as "absolutely real," making what transpired there appear authentic. Such places transformed two elements of men's lives: work and risk. The effort and struggle of daily life could be transferred into a situation in which both suddenly appeared to have a point, usually survival. The desire to be physically relocated, in fact or in fantasy, signaled a need for purification, for freedom from everyday life. Barren landscapes transformed labor and danger into what Jane Tompkins calls "the saturated moment." This moment concretized the classic opposition between what men saw as the world of illusions—culture, society, and class—and the real world of overriding purpose, suffering, and even death.[50]

This world of place was, however, also feminine. Douglas's story of Kloochman and Glascock's narrative of Mt. Shasta located the identity of the mature male as opposing a powerful maternal presence. Those experiencing the sublime moment were often young men for whom it symbolized both the break from a parental past and an anticipation of sexual maturity. As often as nature beckoned to men as if it were a mother, it represented the no less frightening figure of a lover, her voice often sweet, and at other times demanding, but always seductive. Narratives opened with frenzied anticipation of the thrill of intimacy. Peaks were virginal, promising the erotic ecstasy possible only in the "inexpressible gladness of their conquest." Men were irresistibly drawn to places that threatened to unman them.[51] They described peaks as personal protagonists.[52] One climber recalled the excitement of seeing "looming in the distance, entirely isolated, the rugged, spiny, and unscaled summit of Mt. Humphreys, . . . its whole aspect one of defiance."[53] Men's rhetoric betrayed an ambivalence toward the feminine: fear and anger mixed with desire. Historians have suggested that men resented the extension of feminine prerogatives in the nineteenth century, yet alpine narratives also reveal that men increasingly found it socially acceptable, indeed natural, to love womanly figures, whether in the form of Douglas's nurturing mother, the wives camped with the fraternity brothers below Mt. Shasta, or Mt. Shasta itself.

The stakes in the encounter were high. One either triumphed or suffered shameful defeat, perhaps even death. Indeed, the imminence of death still bracketed the moment. Unlike other sports, climbing was defined by harsh topographies, and the specter of mortality was reinforced by the imperative of split-second decision making. Philip Stanley Abbot was a twenty-nine-year-old Harvard graduate, Boston lawyer, and member of the AMC when he experienced in the last thousand feet of difficult snow work on the Weisshorn the "saturated moment," or what he called the "*summum bonum*" or "fullness of life":

the memory of that next hour is one of the keenest and most unmixed pleasures I have carried away—letting oneself go where the way was clear, trusting to heels alone, but keeping the ice-ax ready for the least slip,—twisting to and fro to dodge the crevasses—planning and carrying out at that same instance,—creeping across the snow-bridges like snails, and going down the plain slopes almost by leaps,—alive to the finger-tips,—is a sensation one can't communicate by words, but you need not try to convince me that it isn't primary.

This primal moment of life, stripped to bare essentials, was played out against a landscape that Abbot called "not sleeping, but dead."[54]

Men encoded their own mortality onto places they called "still as death," weird and cold, "nude, . . . soulless, and silent as death."[55] Even naturalists described such landscapes as barren and lifeless.[56] Men sought to reclaim the authenticity of struggle, to escape from the complexities of ordinary life and the banalities of mundane spaces. Their unease was concentrated and released in one moment of terror. Men conceived life in places of death.[57]

In 1896 Abbot and a small group of friends set out on what they called a "conclusive struggle" with Canada's Mt. Lefroy, the highest point of the continental divide. An earlier failure, they explained in their narrative, had whet their desire. They again skirted icefalls, avalanches, and ferocious cliffs. Negotiating a glacial death trap, they reached the divide at 9,850 feet, finding "the snowy hills of God . . . absolute, stupendous, sublimely grave." They felt an exquisite thrill approaching the peak: "Nothing can surpass the supreme exultation of such a moment . . . ; the great silence, the virgin peak almost won. . . . Perchance the coming conquest, perchance the quickening heartbeat, enhanced the beauty of this second view." Suddenly, silently, Abbot fell. His companions descended, finding his body surrounded by "an infinite sky." They named the cleft into which he had fallen "Abbot Pass."[58] The Sierra Club eulogized his paternal lineage that dated from Cotton Mather, Nathan Hale, and those who died at Gettysburg. The AMC asserted that climbing involved the control of fear, making the sport appropriate for such "a leader of the republic."[59] Abbot's grasp of moral imperatives had demonstrated his superiority. Inherent in his death and in the memorials that followed were assumptions about class and ethnicity, blood and lineage, femininity and masculinity.

Empowered by grief, Abbot's companions returned, sevenfold, for a third assault. Gazing up at Lefroy's "ghostly white shape, . . . with unsatisfied desire," they began. This time they reached the top, to sit astride it in triumph. "For a radius of a hundred miles the world was ours," they wrote, "a wilderness of uncultivated valleys, of peaks and glaciers." After their descent, the struggle having been won, they saw their erstwhile protagonist "as never before," this great symbol of the natural world transformed under their feet.[60] Lefroy became a saga, Abbot Pass a shrine, and Abbot himself the quintessential hero that young men might emulate.[61] By courting death in relation to a metaphorically feminine earth, men perhaps sought to prove that they had been created by their own hand, not by the accident of having been born of women.[62]

Men continued to speak of peaks as at once maternal and seductive. Climbers remained obsessed with "first ascents," accomplishment and memory, beginnings and endings. Even later, questioning the obsession, they perpetuated the metaphor: "The fetish of the 'first ascent' has as little value in mountaineering as in personal relations," a man commented. "If it were applicable, we should lose all interest in widows, divorcees, married women, and the majority of spinsters. The attraction of a mountain as of a woman is inherent."[63] This metaphor reinforced the illusion of how separate men were from that which they sought to master. They rarely spoke of rugged places as home. Even Muir wrote of Mt. Rainier: "The view we enjoyed from the summit could hardly be surpassed in sublimity and grandeur; but one feels far from home so high in the sky."[64] When King called the wild a "true home," he meant that which was the opposite of civilization.[65]

Four years before his death, Abbot had commented that man was present on the highest peaks "on sufferance merely, and not in man's usual role as the master of creation."[66] A physician and climber confided: "Nature well knows the hiding of her strength. She stands without discomposure . . . , serenely confident of her ground. You will recall, that the opening definition made the Solitude identical with Nature, leaving out only man. And now, what is left after you have subtracted man from Nature, is much." Men were "but children in relation to wilderness." Its ways of knowing were intuitive, theirs were rational and empirical.[67] The doctor echoed Coleridge's praise of nature's "silent preference for intuitive nonverbal understanding."[68] Men intruded on "her majestic repose."[69] Such imagery assumed that humanity and the natural world were separate spheres, but emphasized the alienation of men.

The idea that one might love wilderness seemed to represent a reversal of the colonial drive for mastery and a rejection of the commercial world in which climbers lived and prospered. However, mountaineering was a sport of artifice. Participants sought and described desolate places. As well, repetitive conquests reinforced the assumption that even these places had in fact bowed to men's mastery. Each successful onslaught on a peak underscored the correctness of the society that had achieved it. Mountains made only salutary stabs at men's vanity. The language of masculinity made nature seem less fecund, portraying landscapes so barren as to dispel any lingering doubt that one should look to nature rather than to culture for progress. Horizons of rock and ice seemed to deny the reproductive force of nature, reinforcing the impression of men's technological and cultural ascendancy over the material world.

Turn-of-the-century American men relished romantic landscapes. The Alps were all the more "dark and forbidding"; the Rockies and the Sierra, still savage.[70] Lincoln Hutchinson opened his 1902 narrative of Red-and-White Peak: "I have sometimes been asked what charm there can be in the higher levels of the Sierra, when the forests are gone and nothing remains that is not dead and forbidding." He responded: "Such a scene!—wild, desolate, cold, forbidding, fascinating! White granite for miles, black shadows; . . . jagged fantastic peaks and pinnacles with alpine intensity of light and shadow. . . . And withal the intense quiet and loneliness of the place, a seeming new world on a new planet where man and words are as nothing. The thrill of it all. . . ." He recalled how he and his friends had come face to face with the peak they "had come to conquer. . . . Directly before us on the opposite side . . . rising two thousand feet above our heads and looking down defiantly upon us." He detailed the struggle, foothold by handhold, and the thrill of imagining himself the first. He built a rock cairn and placed inside it a Sierra Club canister with his name and those of his companions. They decided against renaming the peak but mapped its topography and photographed the scene.[71]

Such formulas marked the masculine sublime as a colonial fantasy. In the 1890s the idea of empire fired imaginations. American climbers emulated explorers of known social stature, correct ethnicity, and cosmopolitan perspective—the navigator Vancouver, the alpinist Whymper, or the topographer King—"[f]or true appreciation is discovery."[72] Praising their European ancestors for solving the "problems of the unknown" in the Alps and the Caucasus, Americans cast themselves within the "seemingly inevitable repetition of history" by which each of the world's mountain ranges was being conquered.[73] Of his "final and supreme effort to master the coveted" North Peak of Mt. Rainier in 1892, a man recalled how halfway up he and his friends had found themselves on glacial ice in the dark. Proceeding was dangerous but preferable to "ignominious retreat." Was such risk worthwhile? the man asked, his feet frozen in the attempt. His answer was yes, as it had been for "zealous navigators." However, "when victory at last crowned our final effort," he found that the coveted was no longer "a virgin and unexplored peak—for just about two weeks before our mastery of it, Dr. W. Riley of Olympia and two companions reached its summit."[74]

Mountaineering was reinforced with the rituals of taking and of telling the tale. It flourished in the context of a cultivated memory. Americans claimed peaks they visualized as female yet powerful, barren, forbidding, and disorderly; "sheer unloveliness" fascinated them, their adjectives making the peaks distant from urban and even pastoral landscapes.[75] "Very far from the world," men reenacted mastery.[76] Of California's Matterhorn, one wrote: "We had come for glory; our attack should be directed against the peak which was the highest and apparently the most difficult of ascents." The night before, he had dreamed of the "terrors inseparably coupled with the dread name of the Matterhorn." He was acutely disappointed when the ascent proved easy.[77]

Climbers visualized local people, whether in the Americas, Asia, or Europe, as finding in their own heights "only ghosts and witches."[78] Appreciation of sublimity was seen as defining a modernity rooted in the natural sciences and western aesthetics—a conjecture that historians have echoed.[79] It was often the guide and the porter with whom alpinists compared themselves. They were often oblivious to the irony inherent in the near invisibility of those who tended them. They admired the skills and endurance of Swiss and German guides in the Canadian Selkirks and Rockies, but they found even them wanting in scientific and aesthetic sensibilities. At their annual meetings, AMC members listened to chronicles of the ascents of Mexican peaks in which indigenous guides and bearers were dismissed as taciturn and lazy, dirty if picturesque, little more than part of the scenery. Climbers thought guides and bearers were oblivious to the meaning of manly sport and deemed them little more than boys.[80]

The imperial overtones of the wilderness experience conflated the drive to establish federal authority over portions of the United States with the exercise of national power overseas. Nathaniel Fish McClure's military career and his adventures illustrate this convergence of imperialisms. In 1894 Lieutenant McClure led the Fourth U.S. Cavalry up the Sierra's Tuolumne River, taking herders prisoner and scattering their flocks. Pursuing what he described as "an enemy" with its own maps, trails, and place-names, he recorded those names and determinedly added to the land surnames drawn from his regiment. The Sierra Club hung his maps in its club room.[81] Five years later, stationed in Puerto Rico, McClure described for the club his mastery of El Yunque.[82] Now a captain, he and his first sergeant penetrated a "virgin forest" filled with "gloomy forebodings" to reach the summit, where he lit what he said was the first campfire to illuminate the peak. He claimed that its flames had amazed his guides, who, left to themselves, would simply have lain on their blankets to sleep in the damp and gloom. He described his guides as cowardly and uninterested in his efforts to determine the exact altitude of this, the island's highest peak. He had lit Puerto Rico's darkness, measured its heights, and surveyed its breadth.

Four years later, McClure was stationed in Manila. The Sierra Club sent him record boxes from San Francisco to deposit on the summits of the Philippines.[83] Setting his sights on Mt. Pinatubo, which he assumed was the highest point on the islands, he again encountered a "dark and gloomy" landscape and "native Negritos unwilling to reach the top whether out of fear or superstitious dread," and who were uninterested in his survey. The appropriation of the Philippines by the United States seemed legitimized by the failure of residents to recognize the value of their own land, much as the appropriation of the High Sierra had been justified by the "superstitious" natures of herders and Native Americans. El Yunque, McClure proudly told the club, had become "the last mighty sentinel on the eastern front of our glorious country," while Mt. Pinatubo guarded the western frontier "half-way around the globe towards the setting sun." The Sierra Club publicized his boast: "I wanted to have the honor of being the first member of our Club to add this peak to our conquests."[84]

Overseas colonialism had always had detractors in the United States, and the bloody suppression of the Filipinos after the Spanish-American War cast shadows on American assumptions of beneficent conquest, but this disillusionment only enhanced the appeal of mountaineering. Even those who saw military suppression as obsolete, if not immoral, believed that men could not afford to lose the self-reliance, courage, and contempt for ease that colonialism and militarism had nurtured. Consider the virgin mountain to be scaled, suggested the AMC: "there is your adversary and a task to be accomplished which demands endurance, strength, sagacity, caution." No one can predict whether you will prevail against this phantom that lures you to the edge, but in the end you do prevail. The feat of "permissible conquest" was at once cognitive and physical, and hurtful of no one. The club argued that every man possesses powers he longs to exercise; if these longings are misdirected, a man became a jingoist; when wisely directed, he emerged a statesman, soldier, and citizen. At stake were prerogatives of manliness and class. The AMC portrayed the explorers of the North Pole as young men of "highest rank and enormous wealth," who in an age of comfort had risen above the temptations of leisure and subjected themselves to deprivation and struggle. Each was a "perfect physical specimen" possessing courage, judgment, and a sense of fair play. The

Arctic provided the ideal landscape for such heroes as Robert Peary, who for a time was believed to have conquered the North Pole in 1909.[85]

Both the "exotic" guide and the barren landscape presented ideal foils. A climber wrote that the thrill of the Tyrol was reinforced by the "wild, unearthly yells in a high falsetto key" the guides at the summit delivered to indicate to those below that "our ascent had been watched and we were being envied and admired." The guides possessed invaluable skills and a keen sense of their charge's need for recognition, but sportsmen dismissed them as, at best, "simple but honest" peasants. Of one such, making his twelfth ascent of Mont Blanc, an American wrote, "It was marvelous that a man could be so ignorant and take so little interest in the view."[86] Treating guides and porters as though they were anonymous was justified by their failure to take "the initiative as explorers," their failure to appreciate sublimity, and their pecuniary motives. American and European climbers prided themselves on recognizing the value of struggle for its own sake. True adventure required money, time, and a heart set on conquest.[87]

William Badè possessed all three. A biblical scholar, botanist, and archaeologist, he would later bring, to Berkeley's Pacific School of Theology, mounds of Palestinian artifacts; serve on the Sierra Club's board of directors from 1907 to 1936, and become editor of its bulletin. But in 1906 he was a young professor bent on playing the quintessential Victorian mountaineer, consuming time and danger with relish, and determined to collect his peak. Of the Matterhorn, he wrote that the guides were sent ahead "to prepare our supper and to look after our comfort for the night, while we came along more leisurely, enjoying the sublimity of the surroundings." He passed the night in a stone lodge enjoying the terror of a storm that sent rocks crashing down the slopes in trails of fiery sparks. He boasted of constant danger and the "supreme test of nerve and muscle," even as he noted that some guides, determined to collect their full fees, had dragged their charges to the top. On the descent, Badè contrasted his own bravery, as he looked down into the precipice that had claimed Whymper's companions, with the timidity of the "ignorant Swiss peasant" and the "simple folk of the mountains" who thought that demons guarded the "dizzy summit."[88]

The rule that he who paid the guide claimed the ascent assumed dark undertones when a Californian scaled a number of volcanic Mexican peaks in 1910—including 17,340-foot Ixtaccihuatl (Iztaccihuatl)—to place Sierra Club registers at the summits. He commended the adventure to others, impressed that native porters carried everything, walked (while he rode) through ice and snow on shoeless feet bound in rags, and did so cheaply and cheerfully. No heroes, these people seemed never to tire and invited you back with a smile.[89] Despite such callousness, most climbers reasonably viewed their sport as hurtful of neither place nor people.

Before and during World War I, the language of men's narratives swung away from the hypermasculinity of the 1890s, back toward the vision Muir had articulated after the Civil War. Perhaps tensions in Europe and war had made aggression less heroic. William Badè and Willis Jepson were among those who followed in Muir's footsteps as naturalists and climbers. A professor of botany at the University of California, Jepson began tramping the Sierra during Muir's last years, writing manuals that classified flowering plants and trees and listed their herbal uses.[90]

Even Badè and Jepson were concerned, however, as Muir had not been, about appearing effeminate, reminding those who read their natural history essays that they illustrated them with scientific photography rather than ornamental sketches, that their interests were bounded by Darwinian strictures, and that they had "conquered lofty summits."[91] They disavowed the sweetness of wild creatures, portraying butterflies of such apparent frailty that their existence appeared foreign to the summits. But no, they told readers, these butterflies represented the survival of the fittest; they were "descendants of the Glacial epoch, of long-dead species that now clung, with only seemingly delicate legs and tiny claws, to life." Watching their struggle, a devotee exclaimed: "I am part of all that I have met." One botanist, who defined the Alpine-Arctic zone of the Cascade Range as almost devoid of life, told of finding the remains of tiny creatures that had wandered into the zones to die "crippled, weak from hunger."[92] Mountaineering provided the opportunity for men like Badè to reconcile rival turn-of-the-century visions of nature. For men who drew, from Darwin's theory of evolution, the view that the world was violent and competitive, such a world required of them a combative spirit. For others, the natural world was beautiful, sacred, to be studied, loved, even worshiped. Climbing permitted sentiment while focusing on struggle.[93]

In the years before World War I, men wrote with particular ardor of gardens and birds "in their mountain homes." Poet Charles Keeler, whose mysticism echoed the domestic sublimity of his mentor Joseph LeConte, praised the maternal bounty of Yosemite and advised campers in the night-darkened valley to think of the russet-backed thrush: "of ten thousand mothers fondly brooding over their swinging cradles in the pines . . . each with her little lover close beside her, trustfully sleeping in all that wilderness. . . . Ah little mothers of the pines, you and your blessed mates are the world's most eloquent teachers . . . for you are forever preaching the eternal gospel of love."[94] Of the headwaters of the Kings River, a man recalled that "the song of the birds mingles with the whispering of the pines. . . . we climb the heights . . . then . . . return to camp and friends and—fall asleep."[95]

As war broke out in Europe, it seemed easier to emulate Muir, to argue that "Nature, like heaven, lies about us in our childhood,—and so do the intimations and interpretations of Nature."[96] Muir was by then well known in international mountaineering circles and was well received when he visited the AMC and London's Alpine Club.[97] Eleven years earlier he had begun the battle to block San Francisco's application to the U.S. Department of the Interior to harness the Tuolumne River in Hetch Hetchy Valley. Hikers frequented this small, deep valley in northwestern Yosemite National Park, and the Sierra Club had financed construction of its trail system. Nevertheless, few Americans had seen the Tuolumne River, and for most, there seemed little to debate when the city proposed to convert the valley into a reservoir. Muir's campaign, which reached its zenith between 1908 and 1913, represented the flowering of a domestic and religious sublime that would have made John Ruskin proud.

Muir sanctified the Hetch Hetchy Valley as a "Garden of Eden, . . . one of Nature's . . . mountain mansions," its walls glowing with life, its rocks "softly . . . adorned . . . [with] a thousand flowers leaning confidingly against their adamantine bosses, while birds, bees, and butterflies help the river and waterfalls to stir all the air into music, . . . into this glorious mountain temple, Nature had gathered her choicest treasures, whether great or small, to draw her lovers into close confiding communion with her."[98] Historians have noted Muir's success in precipitating a congressional debate over the project, despite national devotion to economic "progress" and the obscurity of the valley. His congenial fit with the gentler ethos of masculinity during these years explains much of his influence, as does the movement of women into the public and civic spheres. He solicited their concern and their activity.[99]

Despite his charisma and the timeliness of his appeal, Muir could not have generated a lobby without the local and national networks provided by the period's burgeoning social, educational, civic, professional, conservation, and outdoor associations. Active in the East were the American Civic Association, American Scenic and Historic Preservation Society, and the AMC, and in the West were the Mountaineers and Mazamas. The Sierra Club's own involvement, however, was fraught with difficulty. Some members argued that a reservoir on federal lands would assure San Francisco that its water supply would remain public. Muir's allies formed the California Branch of the Society for the Preservation of National Parks. In spite of all this effort, Congress

Figure 16. A photograph of the Tuolumne River as it flowed through Hetch Hetchy Valley in Yosemite National Park before the valley's inundation, beginning in 1914. Courtesy of University of California, Bancroft Library.

voted in September 1913 to harness the Tuolumne River. The reservoir filled slowly, permitting the Sierra Club to make final summer visits.

In August 1914, news of the European war came by pack train to the one hundred Mazamas camped in the Cascades. If men were particularly manly in the mountains, they also played in these uncommon places. The Mazamas passed the next days exploring and their evenings in "stunts of delicious foolery." On their last night, they staged a "wedding" of "Rube Sourdough" and "Spray Sliusjun." The bride and groom were John A. Lee and Rodney L. Glisan—"on the mountain, safe and stalwart guides; in town, serious men of affairs," but in this instance ridiculous. The bride was "a huge vision—of the traditional blushing variety of loveliness, with an elephantine grace"; the groom was a "frightened but otherwise Romantic figure in the costume of a gallant of 1830." Gasps of admiration met the arrival of the couple and their "Maids." Assorted gifts completed the frivolity, before John and Rodney returned down the slopes, back to their roles as "serious men of affairs."[100]

Muir died on Christmas Eve, 1914. Faced with war in Europe and a pacifist movement at home, America's mountaineers—men and women alike—took solace in his gentle aestheticism and androgynous relationship with nature—

his "glad caress" of her.[101] Badè became the guardian of Muir's writings, a literary estate that reconciled facets of his life that American culture had tried to make dichotomous. Described by friends as "child-like in his simplicity," Muir was a noted geologist. A master of the machine, he had rejected technology. He was husband, father, and rancher, but he remained a wanderer. A public man, he relished solitude. One who had faced sublime terror, he was also nature's lover. When he wrote of powerful cliffs glowing with life and adorned with flowers, he combined feminine and masculine sensibilities.[102] He collected and pressed wildflowers yet retained his manliness.[103]

Charles Keeler wrote: "Here was a real man, one who could get lost on the city streets, but could find his way through any unmapped wilderness."[104] Muir was without parallel in ascending peaks, often alone, first, and—in the spirit of efficiency that marked his early mechanical inventions—occasionally bragging of his speed. He was among Yosemite's first rock climbers, scaling Cathedral Peak without aid of a rope.[105] He dismissed King's terror by describing the ascent of Mt. Whitney as less dangerous than walking on "a cobblestoned street in a crowd." From 1908 to 1911 Muir was president of the American Alpine Club, an organization dedicated to Arctic and Antarctic exploration and open only to those who had ascended at least two thousand feet above the snow line. His writings made it clear that he had often faced down danger. His descriptions of such confrontations had served him well, as they had served King and Whymper. As achievements and literary devices, they proved the manliness of what might otherwise have seemed frivolous.[106] His geological studies and physical prowess balanced his fun and his loving words.

Climbers and conservationists eulogized him as a mediator between the presumably masculine sphere of culture and the feminine realm of the natural. He was a "protector of Nature uniquely gifted to interpret onto other men her mind and ways."[107] According to James Bryce of the American Alpine Club, Muir was the "patriarch of American lovers of mountains, one who had not only a passion for the splendors of Nature, but a wonderful power of interpreting her to men."[108] A fellow climber remembered "his tall, somewhat bent form, with the kindly face and gentle voice and the simplicity and virility of his speech. He seemed to me ... a true man of the mountains ..., a lover of nature and a scientist of mountain structure and glaciology." He had "penetrated the veil of nature," the AMC declared, and others could follow him there through his writings. Each of us is a "nature's lover," Muir had declared; an "ancient mother-love" is inherent in us all.[109]

As American men and women went to the European front, America's clubs took heart from the belief that the attention of their members to discipline on the trail, democratic simplicity, physical vigor, and individual sacrifice had prepared them to be effective soldiers, officers, and nurses.[110] Members wrote from the front describing landscapes that had inspired the European romantics. On a pilgrimage to Byron's "Monarch of the Mountains," one soldier shivered with delight as he looked down into a two-hundred-foot abyss laced with glistening icicles ready to impale him. Flickering lanterns held high by his guides cast weird shadows among the pinnacles and crevasses. In telling those at home of his triumph, he wrote simply: "We had conquered Mont Blanc."[111] A triumphant past was kept alive in the face of a fearful present and a problematic future. In war, as in peace, sport tied men to the memory of forefathers and to the future of sons.

Feminine Sublimes

The poet Harriet Monroe, later editor of the influential magazine *Poetry,* spent four weeks in 1908 on a Sierra Club High Trip through Yosemite Valley. Standing with her one quiet summer morning above Nevada Falls, John Muir described the valley's natural history and asked that she make of it a poem. Returning home to Chicago, she put to verse his description of fierce rivers, white-browed cliffs, crested forests, and ranged peaks on what he had called this, the morning of creation, but to these stanzas she added her own:

> Somewhere a babe is borning,
> Somewhere a maid is won.
> It is creation's morning—
> Now is the world begun.

"It was I," she ruefully confessed, "who dragged the human beings in." She admired Muir's commanding love not only for sublime scenery but for the "littlest thing that grows . . . , the mole, the beetle, the lily." Unlike him, however, she defined the Sierra as completed by the human presence.[1]

The convention that men achieved strength by confronting a natural world they visualized as barren and frightening, yet female, excluded women but also premised a powerful femininity. Embracing the metaphor, women climbers voiced intimacy with wilderness, as Monroe did when she wrote of Yosemite: "My little human life grew to its stature, throbbed with its force, sang its music."[2] By internalizing, yet modifying, aesthetic traditions and figurative language, these women addressed nature's power and their own spiritual needs. In the reproductive force of wilderness, they located sublime experiences similar to those men found in the abyss. By weaving Victorian notions of domesticity together with romantic conventions, and feminine customs with an understanding of the natural sciences, they inserted their voices into the conservation movement, enjoyed the mountains, and enhanced their own identities.

Their narratives described moral empowerment, aesthetic satisfaction, freedom, and spiritual pleasure in climbing. In the 1860s and 1870s, some claimed that their alpine skills proved them the equal of men, but even the most adventurous women occasionally professed to depend on men. The discrepancy between women's disclaimers and their actual accomplishments may have been due to their own ambivalence; perhaps their transgressions against gendered assumptions made even these outriders uneasy. Most hiked with husbands or in mixed-sex clubs and doubtless responded to men's heightened sense of masculinity, especially in the 1890s. Women used rhetorical devices, including, perhaps, their feminine perspectives, to deflect opposition to their activities, but the very use of such devices argues for the force of their interest in the wild.

Influenced by the nineteenth-century natural sciences, women employed a rich symbolism of fecundity. They rarely expressed the sublime as a mechanism of domination, claiming instead, consciously or not, a metaphoric entitlement. The power of the association was limited: industrial America denigrated the productivity of nature and of women (as opposed to that of technology and of men).[3] Nevertheless, women voiced feminine visions of sublimity that described their own spiritual and moral transformations. As they did so, they altered the American discourse on the place of nature in culture.

Women in the United States had begun climbing for sport in the 1830s, as early as did men. Julia Archibald Holmes was a Nova Scotia–born young bride who, arriving in the American West in 1858, promptly scaled Pike's Peak to prove that "a woman could take her place beside a man." She also told her "sisters in reform," who were promoting bloomers, that she had accomplished her feat in this "American Costume." As brash and able as most young men and well aware of sporting rituals, Holmes nevertheless identified with the natural world, finding the association nurturing and empowering. To bring humanity into wilderness, she found Ralph Waldo Emerson a more congenial muse than Henry David Thoreau. When she reached the summit, she quoted Emerson: "The landscape must always appear mocking until it has human figures as good as itself." She wrote of the moment, "This we call our home. . . . I possessed an ownership in all that was good or beautiful in nature . . . as if I had been one of the favored lords of creation."[4]

Figure 17. Sally L. Dutcher. "The First White Woman Known to Have Hiked to the Top of Half Dome in Yosemite National Park," 1875. Photograph by Carleton E. Watkins. Courtesy of Yosemite National Park Library.

While Clarence King was struggling in the Sierra and Edward Whymper on the Matterhorn, a group of New England women established the Alpine Club of Williamstown, Massachusetts, in 1863—perhaps the first such club in the United States—to study and explore the White Mountains. Over the next several years, the members made nineteen ascents of the highest peaks of the eastern United States. Except for the club's chronicler, all of its officers were woman: the secretary-treasurer, the surgeon, the bugler, and the trip leader. Soon American women made advantageous use of the popularity of British travelogues and their own growing literary presence to pen a wealth of mountain tales.[5]

Isabella Bird's *A Lady's Life in the Rocky Mountains* became one of the most widely known chronicles. Born in Yorkshire, her father an Anglican clergyman, Bird as a young woman cared for her ailing parents. After their deaths, she set out for the Sandwich Islands in 1873, pausing en route to climb in the Colorado Rocky Mountains. She wore what she proudly called variously a "Hawaiian riding dress" or an "American lady's Mountain Dress"—a half-fitted jacket, ankle-length skirt, and full Turkish trousers gathered into her boots—"thoroughly serviceable and feminine for climbing in the Alps or any

Figure 18. Captioned "Billy Goat-Nanny Goat," or "A Short Rest beneath Cathedral Rock." Photograph by Benjamin A. Gifford, August 15–16, 1896, during a climbing by the Mazamas of Mt. McLoughlin (9,495') in Oregon's Cascades. From Steel's Scrapbook #4. *Courtesy of the Mazamas of Portland, Oregon.*

other part of the world."[6] Together with trapper-turned-guide "Mountain Jim" Nugent—"a shocking figure," with his leather shirt, tawny, neglected ringlets, revolver, knife, and one eye—she rode horseback to Long's Peak, the first recorded ascent of which had been made only five years earlier. She echoed romantic conventions in describing the landscape as unspeakably awful, but, like Julia Archibald Holmes, she found spiritual catharsis in what she characterized as a newly created earth, saying simply: "I must worship here." She wrote, "Nature, rioting in her grandest mood, exclaimed with voices of grandeur, solitude, beauty, and infinity." After she and Mr. Nugent endured six hours of terror while scaling a perpendicular face of pink granite, they reached the top, where she felt "calm amidst the eternal silences, fanned by zephyrs and bathed in living blue, peace." This triumphant moment was in fact a stunning anticlimax. Bird unabashedly told her readers that had Mr. Nugent not dragged her to the top, sick and dizzy as she was, she would not have reached it. She faced a 3,500-foot precipice, but wrote that her feat would have meant nothing to a member of the Alpine Club of London.[7]

She was not alone in disavowing the power that might be found in confronting terror, asserting control over self, and mastering a rugged topography. Of a rigorous climb in the White Mountains, another woman wrote: "I . . . knew not the intention of my companion, for little was said; he took the lead and I followed blindly." Not uncommon was the climber who acknowledged that only the vigilance of male leaders had secured her safety on Mt. Rainier.[8] Renegotiating definitions of behavior appropriate for a lady required occasional bows to male superiority in necessary skills.

In the American West an ascent by the "first white woman," such as Holmes or Bird, became at once the self-advertised achievement of an assertive woman and the frontier benchmark of a racially defined civilization.[9] Their arrivals were considered as noteworthy signs of conquest, as were those of the official surveyors. The "first white women" to climb in the Sierra had arrived in the mid-1850s.[10] When Joseph LeConte joined a party of hikers in Yosemite in 1870, his daughter complained that "petticoats" had been excluded, but petticoats were soon seen in the Sierra.[11] In 1872, Bay Area botanist Jeanne Carr hiked the tortuous length of Tuolumne Canyon, "the first white woman" to do so. The press reported that she "practically asserts woman's rights by carrying her portion of the tent and provisions."[12]

In 1878 a young teacher from nearby Tulare County, Anna Mills, scaled Mt. Whitney and wrote an account for the Mt. Whitney Club. She called the peak "the handiwork of the Infinite" and described "places where the space between us and eternity could be measured by inches." Stepping near the eastern edge, she gazed down three thousand feet to a small lake and buildings below. Of the moment, she wrote, "Words fail to express the joy we felt when we reached the summit and looked down upon Little Kern Lake, a miniature of beauty, nestled so closely to the base of the mountain as if seeking protection." Years later the Sierra Club invited Mills to become a member. Her enthusiasm echoed across the country and was welcomed by men.[13]

Although the British established a tradition of single-sex clubs, very few clubs in the United States, New Zealand, or Canada restricted membership by sex.[14] In 1873 women helped found the White Mountain Club of Portland,

Maine. The Appalachian Mountain Club (AMC) admitted women in 1876, at its second meeting; eight promptly gained admittance. By 1882, 163 of the 474 members were women, as were most of those who had joined by the close of the decade.[15] Group climbs sponsored by these clubs offered planned itineraries, guides, reduced railroad fares, and inexpensive accommodations. Women participated in over one-third of the AMC's most arduous excursions in the 1870s, occasionally reaching the summits first, and constituted half of those scaling Mt. Washington in 1886.[16]

They embraced this sport at a time when middle- and upper-class Americans generally believed that the female physique was far weaker than that of the male. Women who chose to spend time outdoors were among the first to prove that their sex was not a disability and that they could transcend the norms of separate spheres. Their movements into wild places were facilitated by a liberalization of sexual mores, but long-standing assumptions of their affinity with the natural world also encouraged them to venture out.[17] This symbolic representation gained renewed credibility and greater power with the Victorians' heightened consciousness of the moral virtues of femininity and the elevated purpose of motherhood.

Historians call certain women born between the 1850s and 1890s representatives of the "New Woman." Most were of northern European descent, college-educated professionals who often did not marry.[18] Many who hiked boasted of not fitting society's narrow definitions of their proper place. One announced that "ladies now penetrate the wilderness, where a few years ago men would scarcely have ventured." Or, "No woman is so free as an American girl; if she uses her freedom in summer to build up her bodily strength and refresh her mental vision, if she tramps through the forests and over the mountain peaks." Sketching and bird-watching characterized the outdoor experiences of Victorian ladies, but their climbs were formidable and occasionally solo ascents. To the question, "Can a woman tramp alone?" came the answer in 1889: "*That* depends upon the woman." Americans bragged of one who scaled an eleven-thousand-foot Alpine peak alone.[19] Some men noticed this new freedom. With some unease, the Boston lawyer Philip Abbot called the Alps a "feminine Utopia," where ladies thought "nothing of going unattended," wore knickerbockers, and engaged men in conversation without having been introduced![20]

Muir, however, was unabashedly pleased in the summer of 1895 to meet young hikers in the high country behind Yosemite, many of them "girls, in parties of ten or fifteen, making bright pictures as they tramped merrily along through the forest aisles, with the sparkle and exhilaration of the mountains in their eyes." The following summer Theodore Solomons of San Francisco took four girls and one boy, all University of California students, through Tuolumne Canyon and up Mt. Lyell, calling the trek an experiment. They walked through heavy snows, swollen streams, and boggy meadows, and they were only the third group known to have climbed Mt. Lyell. The girls wore leggings and bloomers, describing themselves as hysterically funny as they crept, slid, and tumbled across the Sierra for seventeen days. Solomons pronounced women slower than athletic boys but as having a greater capacity to endure cold water, loss of sleep, snow, and muscular fatigue. He told the AMC that there was no reason why "college girls and home-wearied matrons" should not climb.[21] And they did, in parties of all sizes and types.[22]

Among the best-known women alpinists of the 1890s and early 1900s, however, were those who accompanied their husbands. The most widely publicized American husband-and-wife team was that of Fanny Bullock Workman, daughter of a wealthy Massachusetts family, and her reticent husband, physician William Hunter Workman. Having explored the White Mountains with the AMC, the couple went on six major Himalayan expeditions between 1899 and 1912. Bullock Workman reported the perils they faced in the Himalayas in a no-nonsense fashion: "One simply had to accept the circumstances of climbing a tight rope and not look to the right or left."[23] She made it clear that she was the driving force behind the couple's adventures. In voluminous skirts that swept the tops of her boots, she reached 23,400 feet, claiming and holding the female altitude record for eighteen years. She named a Himalayan peak Bullock Workman in honor of herself. According to one historian, she was the most "determined, uncompromising, and aggressive" of her contemporaries. A staunch supporter of women's suffrage, she claimed that her alpine successes proved sexual equality.[24]

Although women's narratives seldom expressed disdain of local residents, as men's commonly did, Bullock Workman's articles indicate that American women were not immune from "civilized" arrogance. In the Himalaya, she complained that her coolies preferred huddling around a fire and gossiping, instead of working; that they came only slowly when called; stood about eyeing their loads, instead of hoisting them; moaned piteously when faced with deeply crevassed glaciers; and proceeded only when their pay was increased on the spot.[25] Occasionally, climbers recognized that looks could be deceiving. In 1889 a young lady mistook, for a local hick, a suntanned, roughly dressed man. She later discovered him to be "a gentleman born and bred" and a suitable marriage prospect when he removed his hat to reveal a forehead "as fair as her own."[26]

Evidence of class and civilization, defined by complexion, may have been clear to this young lady, but evidence of femininity was less definitive. The women who shinnied up rocks and slipped down slopes were rebels. Mountaineering illustrated the independent attitudes of the "New Women" perhaps even more clearly than did bicycling and swimming, the other popular sports of the day. In alpine sport one courted danger in powerful and remote places. It is thus not surprising that, when women wrote of the quickening of body and spirit that they experienced, they often felt compelled to assure readers (and perhaps themselves) that their seeming divergence from other women did not threaten the ideology of domesticity or the institution of marriage. Men and women alike argued that mountains heightened sexual distinctions, a logical assumption given the common uses made of natural history's moral authority in social debates.[27]

Far from imperiling purity, one woman wrote, mountaineering sowed "the seed of white thoughts, the lilies of the mind," akin to the lilies that sit on the surface of unsullied alpine lakes. Others reassured readers that women could be pretty and modest even in flannel trousers covered with a scant skirt.[28] Male companions voiced pleasure that the ladies brought to camp their instincts for cleanliness and order. A man happily reported that, in the wild, people divided along natural lines. The women cooked, sketched, and collected flowers; the men fished and hunted.[29] Hiking with his son and daughter-in-law, the elderly Joseph LeConte found the mixed-sex team ideal after a lifetime of advocating separate spheres: "Nowhere more than in camp does true womanly refinement show itself."[30]

The presumed instincts of womanhood seemed to be agreed upon by both sexes. Even if women did something as audacious as killing and skinning a rattlesnake, they would continue to cook and clean. Adventure did not slacken domesticity. Turn-of-the-century women proudly carried out the commonplace in the wild—gathering wood, mending, cooking, washing, and scrubbing the pack animals. Some devoted whole days to making bread, detailing the triumph of baking in a Dutch oven at high altitudes.[31] One woman said that in such tasks "lies one secret of the keen joy of the gypsy way—there is enough of this contact of common things to make life sweet and wholesome. To walk with one's eyes forever fixed on the stars [was] just as narrowing to the field of vision as to never lift them from the ground."[32] Perhaps by arguing that wilderness enhanced, rather than threatened, sexual differences, women at least unconsciously protected their new autonomy.

Other mountaineers enjoyed the companionship that middle-class couples prized precisely because mountains freed them from separate social spheres.

Away from the business world that divided the sexes, they could forge the ideal spousal team. A man wrote that, "dressed alike," he and his wife ventured into the Sierra east of Lake Tahoe in winter. Their united strength was sufficient to pull a loaded sled. Priding themselves on an affinity with the Eskimos, they re-created on a mountainside a domicile with pretend tables, chairs, and carpets of snow. As they traveled, they lit signal fires to reassure their children in the valley. Ending the journey, he sighed, "How strong and rugged we have grown during the past week away from the nervous strain of the busy world!"[33]

Stanford Professor Bolton Coit Brown and wife Lucy Brown made an arduous trip with burros through the Sierra in 1896, ascending a number of twelve- and thirteen-thousand-foot peaks near Bubb's Creek Canyon and Kearsarge Pass. Brown bragged that Lucy had become so skillful a climber that he hesitated at nothing on her account. Her campfire served as his beacon of home. Traversing the Kings-Kern Divide, they entered the South Canyon, where she named Castilleja Lake for its flowers. Despite a day and night in a freezing rain at eleven thousand feet without a blanket or coat, Lucy remained so eager, her husband said, that they pioneered a route up 14,448-foot Mt. Williamson. In 1899 they took their two-year-old daughter for a two-month trip into the Sierra with burros. The child grew rosy and healthy, the father wrote, and, aside from a rattlesnake that slid too close to her, and once when an owl tried to carry her away in its talons, she had not so much as bumped her head all summer.[34]

Women re-created homes in the wild, but they also created opportunities to tramp without domestic chores or spousal escorts. Of 193 climbers who reached the summit of Mt. Hood in 1894 with the Mazamas, thirty-eight were women.[35] Nine women and twenty-two men ascended Mt. St. Helens in 1898. Four years later, a party of fifty-eight Mazamas—one-third of them women—roped together, made the perilous trek up Mt. Rainier.[36] Only eleven of the Sierra Club's 272 members were women by 1896.[37] When the club planned its first High Trips five years later, however, the language of its advertisement appeared to be directed to women. Recording secretary William Colby described what to expect:

The irksome duties of cooking, dishwashing, and provisioning will be turned over entirely to a commissary department. All transportation of outfits, etc. will be attended to by a committee, thus relieving the party of all drudgery and leaving their time entirely free for enjoyment of scenery and mountain life. The trip will be particularly attractive for women, and every effort made to secure comfort usually lacking in excursions to the high mountains.[38]

Figure 19. Members of Seattle's Mountaineers looking down into a glacial crevasse on Mt. Rainier in the early 1910s. Courtesy of Manuscripts, Special Collections, University Archives, University of Washington.

Colby also assured prospective participants that only members would be permitted to make the trip and, because membership required two personal sponsors and approval of the directors, the restriction guaranteed a "high class and tone." The ninety-six participants on the first High Trip in 1902 included college girls and experienced climbers, such as Helen Marion Gompertz LeConte, wife of J. N. LeConte and a working teacher.[39]

Despite amenities, the High Trips were arduous, requiring a minimum of two hundred miles of walking in rough terrains and at high altitudes. The ascents sponsored by the Mazamas were no less difficult, and women had come to outnumber men on its trips by 1907.[40] That year the charter members of the Seattle-based Mountaineers included seventy-nine women and seventy-two men.[41] Women helped to establish the Alpine Club of Canada in 1906 and the California Alpine Club in 1914.[42] Teacher Mary Cronin [Sabin] was one of two founders of the Colorado Mountain Club in 1912. She went on to ascend all of the forty-eight fourteen-thousand-footers then known in Colorado's Rocky Mountains.[43]

Figure 20. Line drawing from front cover of the Mazama: A
Record of Mountaineering in the Pacific Northwest
(Portland, OR, 1903).

Middle-class notions of probity prescribed long skirts and delicate blouses for ladies. Elaborate clothing was the most visible of consumer items. Wives were valuable goods, and well-dressed wives were particularly valuable. To dress unfashionably or immodestly was to risk the loss of social status.[44] In a day when garments made the man, such was certainly true of the woman. It is not surprising that, while a daring few wore bloomers in the 1870s, most scaled the heights in heavy, cumbersome clothing well into the twentieth century.[45] Some even worried about fashion. One counseled: "A costume for mountain climbing and camping ought to be selected like any other gown, for its adapt-

Figure 21. "Three Ladies Climbing" in skirts and bonnets in the Cascade Range, ca. 1890s. Courtesy of University of California, Bancroft Library.

ability and beauty." The color "must be becoming and it must fit into the color scheme which nature has tinted her mountains." She recommended "nearly every shade of green. . . . Black and white check also makes a stunning picture."[46]

The majority of women climbers, however, wrote of deliberately seeking mountains because they were places where they might escape artificial encumbrances, walk as equals of men, and dress comfortably.[47] This implies that women who climbed saw clothes as signifying confinement, subordination, and discomfort. Mountains were places in which to act "the fair barbarian," to indulge "Bohemian tastes," to "redefine the concept of necessities, and to trim skirts."[48] The growing acceptance of athleticism helped such women redefine their femininity. According to historian Sarah A. Gordon, "[T]he novelty and marginality of clothing for sports provided a space in which women contested notions of 'feminine' and 'appropriate' bodies, behavior, and appearances." The "new physical culture" of sports "infused and informed the emerging concepts of the New Woman."[49]

In the heyday of the French heel, of corsets, and of long dresses, however, even a shortened hem drew comment. Press attention to the Sierra Club's first High Trip in 1902 focused on what the ladies wore. Reporters quoted their views on the value of heavy-soled, hobnailed boots, bloomers, and shortened denim skirts. The women carried only one change of clothing, two of underclothing (one for warm days, the other for cool ones), and no corsets. Some readers of the *San Francisco Chronicle* may have compared these descriptions of unfettered comfort with an adjacent advertisement for Warner's Rust-Proof Corsets: "worn by the best dressers in town" and guaranteed to "stand the severest rust-proof test in the warmest temperature."[50] Such a comparison would have netted the message that accomplishment was difficult in corsets and voluminous fabrics but possible without them.

Seventeen women on the club's 1902 High Trip joined thirty-two men on a week-long ascent of Mt. Brewer. The front page of the *San Francisco Chronicle* showed photographs of happy ladies in skirts that revealed their boots on the 13,886-foot summit.[51] Hiking in trimmed skirts was a necessary and welcome first step in redefining womanhood. Even short skirts, however, swept loose rocks that occasionally went crashing down on climbers below. On later trips, some women wore close-fitting bloomers or denim knickerbockers on the slopes, although they removed their skirts only after they were in the mountains. Traveling into the wilderness, they literally divested themselves of society's layered trappings.[52]

These were concessions to lowland sensibilities. Traveling on public conveyances to and from the mountains, women continued to meet with shocked responses to their unconventional looks. They enjoyed the scandalized faces. High altitudes had released them, they said, from the requirement of being a consumer, from "clothes and vanities," from the corsseted, perfumed, and coiffured dictates of polite society. Of a trip into the Sierra's Kern Canyon in 1908, Harriet Monroe confided: "We learned . . . to wear our short skirts and high hob-nailed boots . . . as though we had been born to the joy of them . . . ; to be a barbarian and a communist, a homeless and roofless vagabond, limited to one gown or one suit of clothes; to lose one's last hat-pin . . . ; to make one's toilet on a slippery bank, after a brave plunge into an icy river—all these breaches of convention become commonplaces, . . . part of the adventure, a whispering in the ear of nature's secrets." She wrote, "We knew literally the emancipation of having 'only one dress' to put on."[53] Judging from their narratives, this emancipation encouraged more relaxed behaviors.

Women sought and found in mountains "joyous freedom" from social conventions. Escaping the constraints of a dainty appetite and a corseted midriff, they relished becoming very hungry and eating greedily. Given social assumptions that the female constitution was inherently weak, it is not surprising that women spoke of the joys of strenuous exercise, of becoming dirty, very tired, and sleeping soundly. They described as intoxicating the pleasure to be found in wearing loose clothing, in moving unfettered through space, and of geographic license. For those whose lives often confined them to the schoolroom, the house, the sickroom, or the office, mountains offered opportunities for motion that they had not dreamed could be so exhilarating.[54]

Some spoke of the relentless pressures they faced in their occupations and homes to serve others and of how much they prized the opportunity that climbs afforded for concentrating on their own spiritual rejuvenation.[55] One drew the analogy of a caged bird released to soar.[56] This emancipation was transforming. Mary Crawford of the Canadian Alpine Club said in 1909 that women gained self-assurance by facing danger and that this confidence would carry over into their ordinary lives. She suggested that the sport could make one a better nurse, teacher, or secretary, and more beautiful, to boot.[57]

Women wrote, then, of transcendence, awe, joy, pleasure, and occasionally of apprehension. They did not, however, say that they visualized peaks as personal antagonists or that they cultivated anger or sought mastery. Cultural expectations encouraged placid self-representation. Nor did women feel compelled by social conditioning to cultivate these strong emotions. So stark is the contrast between masculine and feminine narratives concerning wilderness that one might well conclude that expressions of fear, anger, and hatred were the primary definers of gender. Middle-class norms construed men's anger as manly, women's as hysterical. The masculine language of sublime landscapes that emphasized places made frightening by their size, austerity, or grotesqueness was only minimally evident in women's literature.

Of all creatures in western culture, perhaps the most disquieting has been the snake. Hated by man and—Freud might say—especially by woman, the snake has allegorical and symbolic significance in Christianity. In contrast to many men's narratives, women disavowed fear of snakes. A visitor to Yosemite reported that her "natural antipathy for killing any creature" overcame her initial misgivings, so that "no rattlesnake has had to wear mourning for any relation slain by me." Sanctifying the wild with Biblical allegories and symbolically defanging the reptile, she counseled readers that they could not have paradise without a serpent. In Tuolumne Canyon, Jennie Price encountered two large snakes that "seemed to stand on their very rattles, while, with heads erect, . . . twisted their long bodies around about each other, and sported in the most playful manner." Sensing her presence, they slipped among the rocks and vanished. Later she and her husband bedded down for the night, only to hear a warning rattle. "But, feeling that all efforts . . . to escape our unpleasant neighbors were useless, we calmed ourselves . . . and in a short time had forgotten our fears in quiet sleep." Others, too, disclaimed unease. One woman who dissected a rattlesnake, to see what it had in its stomach, said later that

Figure 22. Photograph caption in newspaper: "Wear Men's Garb on Mountain Hike." Edith Pawla and daughter Emily, with friends, August 8, 1911, coming down from a camping trip on Sugar Loaf in the San Bernardino Mountains. The women also went halfway up Grayback, now Mt. San Gorgonio, fishing and hunting. Courtesy of Shirley and Russell Coleman.

such creatures held "no terrors" for her.[58] Wilderness did not frighten. Bravado was not required.

This unwillingness of women to advertise courage was in part a response to society's reluctance to accord significance to their sporting accomplishments. A 1902 article in *Sunset* magazine described a climb of Mt. Whitney made by John Muir, the artist William Keith, C. Hart Merriam of the U.S. Division of Ornithology and Mammalogy, Henry Gannett of the U.S. Board on Geographic Names, and San Francisco lawyer and historian Theodore H. Hittel. A photograph of the party at the summit also shows four women smiling at the camera. Except for the grandniece of Josiah Whitney, whom the peak honored, none of the women were mentioned in the article, their identities seemingly irrelevant. The picture illustrates women's presence in the mountains at the same time that it records their near invisibility.[59] Even when alpine clubs recorded ascents in which they had participated, their exploits went at times unreported.[60]

Class and ethnicity could bestow privilege on women, but gender would not. The physically separate spheres that the middle class had inhabited throughout the early nineteenth century cast emotional shadows well into the twentieth century. Society continued to portray, as ideal feminine traits, passivity, beauty, domesticity, fecundity, and a willingness to be reflections of their husbands. By climbing, women defied bourgeois assumptions of male dominance and of the divergence between sexual roles. Some women climbers resolved the contradictions between social expectations of a lady's behavior and the exciting realities they lived by echoing visions of feminine sublimity.[61]

Wearing a long skirt that seemed to extend her five-foot height, Dora Keen scaled the Kennicott Glacier to reach the 16,140-foot summit of Mt. Blackburn in Alaska's Wrangell Range. Her feat demonstrated skill, endurance, and ambition—traits this graduate of Bryn Mawr had exhibited earlier in Europe, Mexico, and Peru. She financed the 1912 expedition, which lasted four weeks, and a previous one that had failed. She hired eight prospectors and a German ex-soldier as guides and porters, and John Benton, who drove the dogsled that transported two thousand pounds of supplies. Unlike many men, who often ignored or denigrated their guides and porters, Keen highlighted their roles in her tale of blinding snows, ice caves, glacial crevasses, ice fields, and avalanches on the southeast face of Blackburn. For three of thirty-three days, she and her guides had no bedding in temperatures varying from 16°F to 32°F. Only she and Benton reached the summit.

From the top, Keen described the Kennicott Glacier with deep joy: "The earth lay hidden from view and only the mountain tops appeared as the tints of the dawn added the last touch to the most superb view of my life. As we watched, the peaks took fire and in a moment over the snowy spires of Mt. Reynolds the sun crept forth." Looking back on what was the first recorded ascent of any Alaskan peak by an English speaker, she wrote even more simply: "I knew my men and I trusted their judgment and ability." From this generous statement, the reader temporarily forgets that all but one of her guides abandoned her on the ascent, turning back in the face of severe snow slides.[62]

The *Daily Alaskan*'s report on the expedition may explain some of Keen's reluctance to take sole credit. The newspaper acknowledged Keen's status as one of the "famous mountain climbers of the world" and lauded her for reaching Mt. Blackburn's summit to realize "everything she had set out to accomplish" despite cold and hardship. In contrast to this straightforward announcement, the editors employed the fulsome language of the masculine sublime to describe the ascent of the only slightly higher Mt. McKinley by three men that same August. The men had triumphed over "icy blasts of death," a cold that "drives one to madness," and a place that can be equated only to the "furies of hell." Although the newspaper attributed no geographical significance to Keen's "first ascent," it lauded the McKinley expedition as an exploration of "a blank space on the map."[63]

In spite of Keen's triumph, some mountaineering experts advised women to "take great pains to make themselves efficient seconds."[64] One confessed that she and her friends endured such lectures silently because "there was a pride and sense of responsibility in the fact that we were looked upon as comrades by the men, and we must in no wise fall below the standard by increasing their anxieties."[65] After thirty years of the sport, a woman warned that attempting to outdo men could produce "evil consequences."[66] The precariousness of her liberties may explain why one praised the men who led a treacherous, nineteen-hour descent in 1909 on Mt. St. Helens at night with the Mazamas, instead of speaking of her own control of nerves in situations where a misstep could mean death.[67] Such feats demanded strength and courage, yet only men were considered capable of the virtues of discipline, struggle, and transformation through fear. Women's prose defused the potential dissonance between the docility that society prescribed and their own vigor and competence.

They were impelled into North America's mountain ranges by impulses every bit as strong as those motivating men and not entirely dissimilar. Harriet Monroe described a sublime moment of spiritual transformation that she experienced in 1899. Traveling for days through a desert that "seemed to efface us from the earth," she arrived at the rim of the Grand Canyon one evening. "Terrific abysses yawned and darkened; magical heights glowed with iridescent fire," she wrote. Seeing "the earth lay stricken to the heart, her masks and draperies torn away, confessing her eternal passion to the absolving sun," Monroe felt grateful as the night covered the canyon's "awful secrets." In the morning, she returned to verify the "earth's revelation of her soul." At first she was comforted by the colors of the landscape—topaz, amethyst, opal, pearl—but soon "this vast unviolated silence" overcame her. "This was not earth—I intruded here," she exclaimed:

> Everywhere [was] proof of my unfitness. . . . The strain of existence became too tense against these infinities of beauty and terror. My narrow ledge of rock was a prison. I fought against the desperate temptation to fling myself down into that soft abyss, and thus redeem the affront . . . . So keen was the impulse . . . that I might almost have yielded but for a sudden word in my ear,—the trill of an oriole from the pine close above

me. The brave little song was a message personal and intimate, a miracle of sympathy or prophecy. And I cast myself on that tiny speck of life as on the heart of a friend—a friend who would save me from intolerable loneliness, from utter extinction and despair.

She asked the oriole the secret of his home, and he welcomed her "to the infinite" and gave her "healing and solace."[68] Empathizing with the earth's vulnerability, she experienced an immediate desire to surrender. Unlike Coleridge, who had claimed salvation by will and reason, hers was achieved by the life force that pulsed through both herself and the oriole.

The new fields of zoology, biology, paleontology, and geology generated and structured the interest of nineteenth-century women in the natural world. Above all, botany provided the foundation for the aesthetics and spirituality of the feminine sublime, much as geology underlay masculine responses.[69] Women echoed Muir's domestic sublime in which the flowers and dwarf trees growing on icy summits proved "conclusively the triumph of life."[70] For women, wilderness was preeminently wilding blooms. Having identified (and often named) a wildflower, gathered specimens and seed, and learned a plant's habits, they spoke of it as an old friend, describing "the special haunts and the special times of blooming of these children of the hills."[71] Whether as vocation or avocation, botany offered a singular avenue into leadership in outdoor and conservation groups; the only offices women held in the AMC were those charged with gathering plant specimens, arranging botanical exhibits, promoting alpine art, or serving as curator for the herbarium.[72] This pattern reflected lingering expectations about appropriate female behavior within scientific circles. Mathematics, astronomy, physics, and geology were decidedly masculine, while the life sciences were suitably feminine. Zoology and biology were manlier; botany was womanly. Even when men studied botany, they tended to focus on trees, leaving wildflowers to women.[73]

Women did not consider this a limitation, however. Their enthusiasm for botany reflected and extended definitions of womanhood. Wildflowers symbolized femininity while hinting at unusual freedom. Studying the primary organs of plant reproduction was popular and empowering at a time when motherhood defined the position where women's moral authority lay. One might dismiss the flower as a seemingly passive vehicle through which the force of life flowed, following pollination, rather than the site in which life originated. Flowers reproduce sexually, however, possessing organs analogous to those of human reproduction, thereby presenting a powerfully androgynous identity. A blossom holds the pistil, the seed-bearing organ containing the ovary and the stigma, which receives the pollen, and the stamen, the pollen-bearing organ located inside the floral envelopes. The word *flower* itself was early American slang for female genitalia and had been taboo for a lady to use. Climbing high in the Rockies or the Sierra to collect such specimens, at times alone, was more daring then than it may seem in retrospect.

Enthusiasm for native flora also complemented women's long-standing horticultural interest in propagating agriculturally and medically useful plants. Tending the family, women were repositories of practical (particularly herbal) information on health care. They grew and gathered plants for medical purposes.[74] By building on this tradition of domestic expertise in health care, especially at a time when male professionalism was contesting that expertise, women claimed authority for themselves, thus exercising agency in relation to their own lives and the natural world. A few women consciously conflated wilderness and womanhood, thereby deflating the profession of medicine. According to one woman: "Mother Earth seems to have intended the rovers in western woods, especially, to be their own doctors, for.... in Sierran Stretches, she offers him a cure for every ill," including sicknesses against which "[male] physicians' medicines have proved powerless."[75]

Late Victorian society also deemed women the standard-bearers of aesthetic and decorative sensibilities, the ones who tended the gardens and were responsible for floral arrangements. Such a common metaphor as "the full flowering of womanhood" captured the convergence of the decorous and life-giving functions, that moment when beauty and fertility coincided. The obituary for a young Sierra climber who fell to her death described her in the language of alpine lakes as "a flower in the wilderness, vivid with life, brilliant with color, responsive to winds from the heights."[76] Figurative imagery depicted women as beautiful, their responsiveness being that of water rippled by the wind. Women hikers wryly described their own reality as being swathed in grease to deflect bugs and sun, working hard, and perspiring profusely.

The association of flowers and femininity may seem to us to epitomize the restricted sphere of late Victorian and Edwardian gender roles, but it indicated to contemporaries much more than society's molding of sensibilities. Gathering floral specimens in the wild sanctioned women's entries into nondomestic space. Collecting was at once a justification for and an incentive to travel. "There is no peak so high, or valley so deep, but you see their lovely faces waiting to welcome you," botanist and watercolorist Emma Homan Thayer wrote of alpine blossoms: "They smile and nod as if inviting you to catch them. You reach up to pluck one, and you discover a bright-colored neighbor beckoning you higher, and so you climb to the very top, all unconscious of the dizzy heights, lured on by these bright-arrayed children of the mountains."[77]

Botany enabled women to push the boundaries of domesticity and yet remain within them, the process by which cultural spaces are expanded. Women took pride in tramping into the high country.[78] It became a place of freedom. "Public opinion has always esteemed a love of flowers a feminine quality," asserted Katherine Chandler, author of a 1903 book on California plants, but "in the past, only man could venture into new regions and explore unknown heights, for woman's place was in the haunts of home. So men discovered new plants and named them." But male botanists often made mistakes in describing floral colors because they were perceptually deficient, she added, and they had relied on dried specimens to identify living ones. "But to-day is the era of the amateur botanist. . . . Women now find themselves free to tramp anywhere. . . . They invade the most remote wilds and eagerly examine the flora in its native soil."[79] Through the 1930s, women were the most active of North America's botanical collectors, classifiers, and authors of wildflower identification books.[80]

From Boston to San Francisco, women encouraged climbing clubs to gather flowers and to mount floral exhibits.[81] In 1897, Alice Eastwood joined the Sierra Club, with Muir's sponsorship, and made the 1902 High Trip.[82] She had begun collecting flora as a child in Colorado; as a young teacher in Denver, she made summer research trips into the Rocky Mountains. On her first visit there, "she came upon mountain meadows covered in rich profusion with summer-blooming flowers. The experience partook of revelation." In 1892 Eastwood moved to San Francisco to assume the position held by Mary Katherine Curran as the Curator of Botany at the California Academy of Sciences, an institution known for promoting women in the sciences.[83] Because curatorships were closer to domestic work, required little in the way of formal credentials, and were less lucrative than academic posts, such positions proved more accessible to women than teaching or research jobs in universities and institutes. Through collecting and museum work, botanists such as Eastwood moved from amateur to professional status. She also wrote the first guidebook to the wildflowers of the Sierra, which the Sierra Club published.[84]

In the process of identifying and classifying plants, Eastwood had done a great deal of purposeful wandering. Traveling alone through North America in the 1870s and 1880s, she scaled peaks and walked deserts. Geographical liberties complemented her unconventional life and her casual disregard for social expectations, from marriage to fashion. Botanizing carried her seamlessly between urban and wild places. Her articles in *Zoe: A Biological Journal,* for the Academy of Sciences, focused variously on the wildlife of the Rockies, domestic geraniums, and the cliff dwellers of Colorado. Even as she helped plan and plant San Francisco's Golden Gate Park, she was an expert on mountain flora, worked as a conservationist, and was active in alpine and garden clubs. As president of the Tamalpais Conservation Club, she campaigned for the establishment of Mt. Tamalpais State Park. Through a long life, she pursued botany as diligently in the Bay Area as in the Sierra. She summed up the defining influence of this science: "I am not a true mountain climber as I go only for the flowers and views to be had from the lofty heights."[85]

Eastwood saw the natural world as nurturing and noncompetitive. Some women saw even the animal world as noncombative, but the botanical realm most readily lent itself to that ideal.[86] All ecological succession entails competition, yet evolutionary success in the plant world did not seem, to many female botanists, to require nature to be red in tooth and claw, as Alfred Lord Tennyson feared. Eastwood studied "plant communities." She highlighted the interconnected qualities in these communities that later social biologists would agree are characteristic of all ecosystems. She observed plants to be living in mutually supportive colonies, and, although she was aware of the arrival of foreign species in America, she cataloged all plants in a given landscape, rarely differentiating between native and alien. This form of presentation, common to wildflower guidebooks of the day, disregarded the intense competition between exotics and native plants in the western United States.

Eastwood saw no savagery in the competition among species, but she found the relationship between plants and their environments particularly nurturing. She detailed the life-zones that encircled western mountains, from the low ring of chaparral vegetation to the highest alpine communities, supplying data and specimens to C. Hart Merriam of the U.S. Biological Survey as he identified these zones. Eastwood embraced this ordered vision of nature; the earth seemed to her to offer each species a special niche in time and place. She saw seasonal succession, too, as giving each bloom its moment of color and aroma. The plants in turn nurtured the earth, she noted with pleasure, covering it in the wake of environmental catastrophes with a "soft and velvety . . . mantle of verdure." She cited the example of squaw grass, the seeds of which germinated only after fire swept the brush from California's coastal mountains. Squaw carpet served that function in the Sierra. She found self-sacrifice in the natural world, noting that, following wildfires, the wild lilac served as "a nurse to protect the young seedling trees from the wind and the sunshine that might destroy them." Although the lilacs grew to be small trees, they died in twelve to fifteen years, "when they are no longer needed to protect the other young trees."[87]

Many women found in John Muir a man who shared their experiences of the natural world. Like Eastwood, Muir averted his gaze from evidence of strife, evolutionary or predatory, in the wilderness. Michael Cohen wrote of him: "He did not want to think of any struggle in Nature at all. He even seemed put off by the appearance of the Sierran juniper, which reminded him, with its rocklike rigidity and fortitude, that life was tenuous on the granite slabs above Tenaya Lake . . . ; he was unable to look fully at the struggle or the pattern of eater and eaten."[88]

Although society encouraged women to restrict themselves to botany, Annie Alexander broke the rules to move into research on vertebrates. Her interest in nature had begun with plants, however, and her primary roles remained those of collector and patroness. A friend led her to the natural sciences by inviting her on a Sierra Club High Trip into the Sierra to collect wildflowers and to watch birds; the club recommended her for membership in 1900.[89] Over the course of a long life, she collected floral and fauna specimens from Africa to Alaska. She was largely responsible for founding the Museum of Vertebrate Zoology at the University of California in Berkeley.[90] Alexander, like Eastwood, found an active outdoor life to be an "avenue of escape from the conventional expectations defined by her wealth and social class, one that provided an opportunity to appropriate an additional cultural identity—that of field biologist-cum-amateur naturalist."[91] Also like Eastwood, Alexander's enthusiasm for fieldwork forced public recognition of the rapid disappearance of American flora and fauna, encouraging public commitment to conservation.

Many such women enjoyed the outdoors for its connection with animal and plant life, detailing in their narratives the sounds of the wild: the "lap or flow of the water, the hum of insects, the wing-flutter of a passing bird . . . ; no sound is too diminutive to lend voice to the mountain peace." One woman wrote of Tehipite Dome, "Here, in these lofty mountains, all nature teems with life."[92] Above all, however, the flora attracted women. Decades later, one woman recalled a trip to Glacier National Park that was made wonderful by the animals, but "the flowers were something to dream about."[93]

Few individuals more eloquently expressed the feminine sublime moment than Mary Austin, writer of fiction and nonfiction. Austin had left Illinois for California as a young teacher; she married and had a child while living in the Owens Valley, east of the Sierra. Her 1903 book of essays, *The Land of Little*

Rain, celebrating the valley and its Sierra boundary, reconfigured the aesthetics of the sublime. Like those following masculine conventions, Austin experienced the mountain storm as a spiritual epiphany. She recommended: "Choose a hill country for storms"; there one can gain "a sense of presence and intention in the storm process. Weather does not happen. It is the visible manifestation of the Spirit moving itself in the void." She found it telling that Muir, who knew high-country storms well, was "a devout man." Viewing a tempest from the splintered peaks of the Kern River and Kings River divide, she could see "the splendor of the apocalypse." From Kearsarge Pass, she loved to listen to thunder pealing over the lowlands, but she advised, as had Muir, that "to get the real effect of a mountain storm, you must be inside [it]."

The difference was that Muir wrote of transcendent ecstasy, while Austin wrote of transcendence in release: "Such rains relieve like tears." The long struggle of rearing a handicapped child led her to animate the stormy heights with maternal love, infusing the sublime with her own pain in life. She noted how certain blooms—the deep-throated, bell-flowered penstemons and the nodding pedicels of the columbine—guarded their pollen powder from the rain, and she watched "a bobcat mother mouthing her drowned kittens in the ruined lair built in the wash," identifying with the mother's seeming recognition of her own failure to have protected her progeny. It was not the strangeness of the storm that attracted Austin but its very familiarity. "You have to beat out for yourself many mornings on the windy headlands," she wrote, "the sense of the fact that you get the same rainbow in the cloud drift over Waban [a Sierra peak] and the spray of your garden hose. And not necessarily then do you live up to it."[94]

She saw deserts and mountains as sublime landscapes—mysterious, seductive, and feminine—but she felt empowered by her affinity with them rather than alienated. According to Vera Norwood, Austin admonished men, especially pioneers, to overcome "attitudes of dominance," and she urged women to move beyond "concepts of fertility and passivity."[95] In her life and climbs, Austin escaped the passivity that she knew society ascribed to women and the proclivities she faulted in men, yet fertility and reproduction remained central to her experience of wildness. The "high sharp regions," she wrote, "might be called desolate, but will not by me who love them." Her Sierra was rich in water ouzel, coyotes, scavengers, butterflies, and humanity.

Her life and her adamant voice set Austin apart from Victorian norms of female reticence, but the flowers lured even her above the timberline. Musing about who shall say what others like most about the mountains? she answered:

"As for me, once set above the country of the silver firs, I must go on until I find white columbine." She found no peaks "too high for comforting by succulent small herbs or golden tufted grass. A granite mountain does not crumble with alacrity, but once resolved to soil makes the best of it. Every handful of loose gravel . . . affords a plant footing." Rather than celebrating Clarence King's silent terra incognita, she said Sierra waters were her joy. She warned others to avoid that part of the range "uncomforted by singing floods. You will find it forsaken by most things but beauty and madness and death and God." Singing through narrow gorges and shouting in their falls, the rivers were her voices of the mountains; and the lakes, her eyes. She urged that they be protected.[96]

For Austin the attraction of the peaks included both the people who had once lived there and those who still did. When she called the trails of the Sierra "the streets of the mountains," she diminished the division of space between the wild and the cultivated. Mountains and deserts were neither "silent nor barren for her."[97] Lawrence Buell declares that she knew enough "to know that the sublime emptiness of the landscape is an artifact of the romantic westernizer's desire."[98] With an appreciation rare for her time, she was keenly aware of the range's natural history and its human histories, including those of Native Americans and Hispanic Americans. "There is always an amount of local history to be read in the names of the mountain highways," she said of local trails, "where one touches the successive waves of occupation or discovery, as in the old villages where the neighborhoods are not built but grow."[99] Your safe passage through the Sierra, she told readers, depended not only on your own powers but also on how many others had taken the road before you.

Austin preferred the Native American fashions of name-giving to those of English speakers, arguing that the native names expressed something of the land itself. Readers found place-names in her work that did not correspond with those on official maps. Coming upon a lake named for the man who had discovered it, she named it for its pine trees, staking her own claim to the site.[100] Literary critics have called her an early feminist who consciously situated her work "outside the confines of male authority," engaging places and people "outside of the institutional codes of patriarchy." She invested herself with the power inherent in place naming, but she identified her "Land of Little Rain" only as lying somewhere between the Sierra south of Yosemite and north of Death Valley.[101] She challenged codes of naming and mapping, and she deliberately rebutted the idea that the Sierra had ever been an unknown place.

Many women climbers were sensitive to evidence of human history. One, who pondered a narrow stand of piñon pine running down the canyon of the

Middle Fork of the Kings River, well outside the tree's natural zone on the eastern slopes, hypothesized that the strays marked an old trade route used by native peoples who were fond of eating piñon nuts and occasionally dropped them along the way. Women detailed encounters with mountain people— from Native Americans and placer miners from China, to Basque herders and Hispanic packers with their sombreros and red bandannas. Women added color and life to the vast size and monochromatic hues of the Sierra.[102]

Like men, women were fascinated by the varied topography of the range, its steep cliffs, deep-set canyons, shining peaks, and bowled valleys, yet they more often emphasized intimacies of scale, warmth, and touch. They celebrated "those wooded parks rich in meadows and flowers which Dame Nature loves to hide away in the heart of a grim waste of granite rocks." Of the Tuolumne River, one wrote, "It is a strange thing, standing beside one of these giant cataracts where . . . every voice of wind or living creature is silenced in the roar of the maddened waters, to see under what a delicate fabric this Titan's force is veiled—a billowing, gossamer texture, iris-tinted, with jeweled spray flying high upon the wind." Another wrote: "These overwhelming views might have weighed upon us but for the daily and nightly companionship of the friendly trees."[103]

Women valued the life above the timberline. A visitor to the Rockies loved the fragrance, color, and luxuriance of the summits; finding vegetation she had known from the White Mountains, she felt at home.[104] When Helen Marion Gompertz LeConte toiled up the final two thousand feet of the snow fields of Mt. Lyell, the "lifeless grandeur of the heights" frightened her so much that she delighted at the reappearance of every flower on her descent. Three years later, however, on thirteen-thousand-foot University Peak, she found the seeming barrenness "filled with arrested motion, ready to burst into life at the touch of the master's hand." Recalling that Muir had always regretted wasting a starry night in his bed at home when he might be on a mountain, she felt compelled to stretch out on the warm rock.[105] On Mt. St. Helens, another woman described feeling "almost lost in the sense of loneliness, of vastness," but she was reassured by the fading light of the reddened sun and the views "aglow with sunset light." She wrote of the silence as "significant not of death, but rather of the unborn ages yet to come."[106]

Western culture's feminization of nature encouraged women to verbalize their intimacy with wildness. They praised "the great mother," the "All Mother," or simply "Mother Earth."[107] Many emphasized the circumstances of the night, comforted by the luster of clear nights. "Before I slept," one wrote,

"I looked out upon the amphitheater of bare peaks, which, catching the last faint glow of sunset, took on a softer outline, and seemed to look down protectively upon us daring mortals."[108]

Harriet Monroe felt that the role of natural selection in biological evolution, which she assumed was independent of divine or manly forces, enhanced the female role in creation. Of "Mother Earth," she wrote:

> Oh what a grand old time has the earth
> In the long life she lives!
> Tiring not, pausing never,
> She labors and laughs and gives,
> Plains and mountains
> She slowly makes
> With mighty hand
> Slowly conceiving.

First she creates the plants, then the beasts. Finally, in an "arrogant plan," she winnows man "out of the bitter void."

> Oh a grand old time has the earth
> In the long long life she lives!
> A grand old time at her work sublime
> As she labors and laughs and gives!

Monroe's identification with nature was personal and nurturing. In the poem "Myself!" she wrote, "What am I?" answering: "I am Earth the mother, With her nebulous memories." In "High Places," she wrote: "My mountains . . . Oh speak to me, for you are mine as well—Drift of my soul. I built you long ago." In "The Climb" she advised men and women alike to find independence in the wilderness:

> Follow the trail. . . .
> High and more high! . . .
> Up, up the stony steep. . . .
> Then never look back, never more follow—
> Take your own way![109]

General histories have often overlooked feminine voices like that of Harriet Monroe, conceptualizing early conservation and sport as male endeavors having only masculine agendas.[110] Histories of the Sierra Club mention women only in passing.[111] Women climbers have complained that their successes were ignored, a perception that is confirmed by their absence from histories of the sport.[112] Women's contributions to the natural history essay, a genre that included the mountain narrative and one that did much to publicize the values of wilderness and the need for conservation, have traditionally been undervalued as well.[113] In sharp contrast, those writing special histories—the histories of women—have located their subjects in the center of outdoor sport and turn-of-the-century conservation. Between the mid-nineteenth century and World War I, women brought feminine perspectives to alpine sport and to conventions of landscape appreciation. When measured in numbers of participants and by the enthusiasm of their narratives, the sport of climbing has been strongly female. Even in terms of outstanding accomplishments, climbing has been far from exclusively male.[114]

In detailing the evolution of attitudes toward the natural world, historians have often looked exclusively at masculine perspectives.[115] Few general histories of landscape appreciation explore gender.[116] Women, however, have become keenly sensitive to its force.[117] While pioneering men fantasized about mastering the land, Annette Kolodny demonstrates that women visualized future gardens, homes, and communities. Vera Norwood and Janice Monk describe representations of the southwestern desert in women's art and literature that diverged from male cultural norms, and Norwood analyzes women's presence in and contributions to gardening, horticulture, and the biological sciences.[118]

Nineteenth- and twentieth-century experiences of mountains were heavily gendered, but American men and women held many attitudes and beliefs in common. The natural sciences fascinated both, and both profited from the rising levels of formal education that highlighted the sciences and literature in America. Outdoor sport drew strong, affluent, and influential members of the middle and upper classes. These classes in turn supported special-interest groups, such as alpine clubs, and the journals that published mountain narratives. Middle- and upper-class men and women alike enjoyed opportunities to celebrate leisure and the joys of what Thorstein Veblen called in 1899 "conspicuous leisure." Importantly, both shared a heightened "gender consciousness."[119] It is ironic that this intense consciousness, which created one strongly masculine culture and another strongly feminine culture, developed at a time when the spheres of the sexes were converging, and that men and women exaggerated their emotional differences just as they were beginning to act more like one another.

Mountains provided important arenas in which to renegotiate the meanings of femininity. Mountaineering served the same function for American women that globe-trotting did for Victorian English upper-class ladies; both were outriders. One historian has noted that the geographical liberties of the Victorian traveler "implicitly challenged the status quo in a way that even the suffragettes did not. She simply took the liberties that others argued about, and, knowingly or not, has been an outrider for the independent woman."[120] Like the British women traveling the far reaches of the British Empire, American mountaineers defied notions of separate spheres, the dictates of fashion, and assumptions of their inherent physical weaknesses. It is not surprising that they should have emphasized their own moral purity, filtered their descriptions of natural history through the prism of gender, and demythologized their feats. By doing so, they discouraged threats to their prerogatives. Their purpose was to increase their own liberties and their influence on issues of land use and wilderness protection.

San Francisco's 1906 earthquake destroyed records from the meeting at which the men of the Sierra Club decided to invite women to join. The issue probably elicited little debate, particularly given the presidency of John Muir. Women's presence was not only a logical extension of men's leisure-time aspirations but also politically expedient. In the fight for Hetch Hetchy Valley, Muir directed fellow campaigner and club director Edward T. Parsons to target "mountaineering clubs and in particular women's clubs." Muir advised Parsons to "stir up a storm of letters, filling the Senate chamber with the protesting leaves fathoms deep."[121] That Muir's descriptions of the valley mirrored facets of feminine visions of the sublime doubtless attracted the support of some women.

Defending Hetch Hetchy in 1909, Harriet Monroe wrote of "a little natural garden sunk between protecting mountain walls. . . , a level meadow of ancient oaks and cedars and flowery grasses . . . protected from severe cold and heavy winds, a little paradise where people will be happy—all the future generations of men and women. . . . You and I," she invited readers, "could then carry our blankets and frying pans into the valley any summer day, make ourselves comfortably at home under some tall cedar or broad oak," gather wildflowers, sleep under the stars, or climb a mountain. She told of communal fires, stories, songs, and operettas. (The club staged her play "Idyll of the Forest" at a campfire on its 1908 High Trip.)[122]

By the time the Hetch Hetchy battle became its most intense, one-third of the Sierra Club's members were women.[123] They were also active in single-sex organizations that campaigned to save Hetch Hetchy Valley from inundation.

When the valley's fate reached Congress in 1909, women's clubs across the nation were poised to strike. Their letters, Muir's "protesting leaves," poured into legislative offices and into the White House from every region of the country and every type of rural and urban community. Many women were affiliated with the General Federation of Women's Clubs, which, ten years earlier, had adopted forest conservation as one of its primary objectives. Women's literary and civic clubs, Jewish women's groups, singing groups, self-improvement clubs, and sundry impromptu collectives also lobbied for Hetch Hetchy. Between December 1909 and March 1910, these largely female constituencies sent thirty-nine petitions to Congress defending the valley.[124] Although the Sierra Club did not lend its name to Muir's battle, no such qualms assailed club women in Modesto, a small San Joaquin Valley town just east of Hetch Hetchy, or farm women who lived in Beatrice on the rural plains of Nebraska.

Part II
Outdoor Experiences and the Politics of Conservation, 1914–1944

In 1924 Bertha Rice, president of the California Wild Flower Conservation League, asked the Sierra Club to help save the state's native plants. Rice lived in the richly flowered Santa Clara Valley and, together with her husband, had written a popular guidebook to California wildflowers. A temperance fighter turned botanist, she pleaded with the club to save the wealth of species in the valleys and plains, where agriculture was threatening "the balance of nature." Although state laws protected game species, none protected native plants. California's burgeoning population was killing forests and draining marshes and had "all but erased our once bewilderingly beautiful gardens of wild blooms." If the red-belled toyon, or wild holly, bushes lining the highways should disappear, she warned, "the birds will miss the berries, and the bees will miss the flowers."[1] The increased presence of women in the Sierra Club may have encouraged Rice to request the club's assistance, but as she herself anticipated, most of the group's leaders were looking only to the mountains and took little action.

The masculine conventions of the sublime were particularly influential during the interwar years. The new wilderness areas and national parks established during that period were located in high and seemingly barren "primitive" terrains where men could exercise manly aspirations. Nevertheless, feminine perspectives were evident as well in broadened attention to birds, animals, and plants, a point of view that encouraged conservationists to fight for the preservation of biological communities.

Figure 23. Photo collage, 1930s. Woman looking down from the clouds. Photograph by Cedric Wright, who imposed a photograph of his wife, Ria Wright, over a photograph of the Sierra Nevada. Courtesy of University of California, Bancroft Library.

But "feminine" cannot simply be equated with women, nor "masculine" with men. During this period in particular, there were no absolute patterns in gendered roles. Many of the men who hunted saw wildernesses as places in which death flowed together with life. Naturalists such as William Badè kept alive the domestic sublime, celebrating the wildflowers even as he confronted terror on the peaks. Conversely, a significant number of women chose to lead climbs and to climb first ascents, speaking of these accomplishments as expanding their liberties and advancing the position of women in society. Feminine traits were thus shared by men and masculine by women, not only in sport but also within conservation. The wildflower protection movement fused feminine perspectives with the sensitivities of male and female naturalists; it also produced one of the earliest visions of wilderness as habitat and of ecology as a principle of land management.

Discussion of the histories of wildflower advocates, hunters, birders, and youth groups concludes Part II. Their activities, like those of mountaineers, display the ways in which gendered perspectives at once coalesced and separated. This interplay brought substantial progress in scenic, botanical, and wilderness protection. State and federal governments expanded systems of parks and reserves and provided legal guarantees for wildlife and native plants. Wilderness was translated from an imagined landscape into an administratively defined place, a shift that had profound implications for the mountains. All this progress was fueled by a synergy between the nation's nonprofit and public sectors. The successes realized by government agencies would not have occurred without the lobbying of organized citizens who wove a rich tapestry of influence out of their separate interests.

4

Mountains as Home and Garden

A few months after Congress voted in 1913 to dam Hetch Hetchy Valley, Muir learned of the death of his friend and ally Edward Parsons. Muir sent his condolences to Edward's wife, Marion Randall Parsons, who had long been one of Muir's many correspondents. The summer before her husband's death, Marion had spent a month with the Mountaineers on the peaks of the Pacific Northwest. Standing on the summit of Mt. Olympus, she looked across Puget Sound at Mts. Baker, Rainier, and Adams, which were glowing "with a lucent, vision-like beauty . . . as if they shone upon some borderland of the spirit, some coast of dreams where earth's beauty met the tides of things infinite and divine." She had traveled into a "summer world of light and laughter where seasons never change nor flowers die." The memory of this sublime, luminous, seemingly eternal landscape may have inspired her to seek her husband's seat on the Sierra Club's board of directors, taking the position shortly before Muir's own death and holding it for twenty-three years. She went on to edit Muir's *Travels in Alaska,* cultivating his memory and becoming a force in the wilderness campaigns of the John Muir Association. The legacy of Muir's "sweet, smiling face," his battles for the Sierra, and his articulation of what might best be called the "domestic sublime" resonated with women (and many men) and were among the factors that drew women into conservation long after his death.[1]

During World War I, Marion Randall Parsons served in France; afterward, she eagerly returned to America's mountains. She did not find herself alone among men. Women were increasingly making difficult climbs. Fourteen joined eleven men on the Mazamas' most

Figure 24. Left to right: Edward Parsons, John Muir, and Marion Randall Parsons on the front porch of John Muir's home in Martinez, California. Photographed by Herbert W. Gleason. The photograph was taken shortly before the death in 1913 of Edward Parsons and John Muir's death the following year. Courtesy of the Mazamas, Portland, Oregon.

challenging ascent, of Oregon's Eagle Cap, in 1918. Together with ten men, eleven made the Sierra Club's most difficult ascent in 1921, that of Mt. Ritter.[2] Some of these women strove to extend rights they won in the mountains into society at large. Their courage and daring advanced the public perception of female competence. A woman standing astride a summit, whether in the Himalayas or fourteen thousand feet above sea level in the Sierra, exemplified strength. Accustomed to seeing women only as helpmates to men, Americans began to revisualize women as capable individuals on their own.[3]

Women symbolized their new freedom by their dress. Historically, no means of identifying gender has been as visible as, or more controversial than, female attire. In the years after the war, women who climbed continued to clothe themselves in midcalf, heavy wool or denim skirts (often cunningly divided), at least as they began their climbs. Only on the slopes did they feel unconstrained, removing their skirts to reveal bloomers, donning skirts again when approaching villages or camps.[4] As they renegotiated the meaning of femininity for themselves, not only through sport but sporting attire, they had the help of the fashion industry. Sporting goods companies advertised "out-

Figure 25. Mountaineers on the top of a peak in the Cascade Range, late 1910s. Courtesy of Manuscripts, Special Collections, University Archives, University of Washington.

ing skirts" that on the slopes could be unbuttoned down the front and back, or a "Sierra hiking suit" with a skirt designed for easy removal and use as a cape. Modesty and decorum were thus preserved.[5]

By the early 1920s, however, skirts were being replaced by pants. Women of the Colorado Mountain Club satirized skirts as appropriate only for "Covered Wagons," not "Airplanes" like themselves.[6] Such women obviously thought of their participation in athletics and the wearing of sports clothing as making visible their modernity. Tailored-goods companies responded to the demands for liberating fashions by using images of women in their advertising who

Figure 26. A member of Seattle's Mountaineers is shown looking at the camera, ca. 1920s. Courtesy of Manuscripts, Special Collections, University Archives, University of Washington.

were jauntily attired in trousers, wide at the hip and fitted at the knees (much like those of American soldiers in the war). Publicity for the Union Pacific Railroad showed women striding off into the wild in snappy knickers, wearing middy blouses with ties. To sell rucksacks, "kook kits," Kodaks, maps, and boots, the San Francisco outfitters Spiro's and Leibold & Co. used the figures of young women in their advertisements, their short curls being ruffled by the breeze, often standing on a summit with crop, alpenstock, or camera in hand.[7] The 1920s became known not only for the flapper but also for the young woman who donned trousers to assail the heights.

Figure 27. Members of the Mountaineers on a crevasse in the
Nisqually Glacier, Mt. Rainier, Washington, ca. 1920. Courtesy of
Manuscripts, Special Collections, University Archives, University of
Washington.

The "New Women" also included those whose middle age coincided with
the interwar years and who already had a substantial voice in civic affairs as
well as in climbing. Parsons was one of them. When Parsons was elected a director in 1914, no women had ever held any office in the Sierra Club. Not until
1922, when the board of directors was enlarged from nine to fifteen, were two
more women added for two-year terms. Aurelia Harwood was one of them.
Between 1926 and 1928 and again between 1932 and 1934, three directors were
women. From 1925 to 1927, Harwood also served as a club vice-president and,
from 1927 to 1928, as president. A small woman, then in her fifties, she had long

climbed, often with the Mazamas, the Mountaineers, and the Green Mountain Club of Vermont. Nevertheless, she made an unusual president for the Sierra Club: a Southern Californian (the club was headquartered in San Francisco); a woman (a half century would pass before the next female served as president), and as well known for her philanthropy as her mountaineering. Born in Wisconsin, she had traveled with her family to Missouri, graduating from Drury College, which her father had helped found. After two years of graduate work at Wellesley College, she moved to Ontario, California, in 1887, where she cared for her parents. For forty years she gave time and money to conservation.

Shortly before her election to the club's board, Harwood had purchased Redwood and Wet Meadows in the Sierra. To connect Sequoia and General Grant National Parks and to protect the meadows, she donated the two meadows to the National Park Service. The gift increased her visibility within the club, as did her fight to save Mt. San Jacinto, which she called Southern California's "small wilderness." She chaired the Sierra Club Committee that lobbied for game preserves in the rugged San Bernardino National Forest, and she was active in the California State Park Council's campaign to establish a statewide park system.[8]

When Harwood became president of the Sierra Club, she brought a history of support for the protection of a wide diversity of scenic and wild places but also for the advancement of women. She believed that the causes were complementary. Women have an affinity with "the bird and bee and blossom," she said, and women could and should use it to empower themselves and to protect the natural environment. Perhaps in part in defense of her own voice in conservation, she argued that cultivating natural history was a way of nurturing children. Not herself a mother, she gave life memberships in climbing clubs to the children of others. The confluence of motherhood, women's rights, and conservation emerged in Harwood's work as one of the organizers of the Camp Fire Girls of America, a group that encouraged girls to hike and to work with community conservation projects. When Harwood died in 1928, on the eve of her second term as club president, Aurelia Reinhardt, dean of Mills College and a fellow board member, wrote, "Because of her, wild flowers lead a safer life, forests tower more grandly skyward and many learn again the ancient lessons as they look toward the mountains."[9]

Others in the Sierra Club kept alive Harwood's interests. In 1971 the club mailed a questionnaire to three hundred members who had joined before 1930. Eighty-two women replied, writing about their lives, suggesting how they envisioned wilderness, and describing their interest in the club. Such a sample may not have been representative (the more educated were probably more inclined to answer), but the results suggest a profile of educated, career women who had been born in the United States. Two-thirds of the eighty-two had been born in the 1880s and 1890s, almost half in California, and nearly all their parents were native to the eastern and midwestern United States. These were the daughters of pioneers—one was actually born on the Overland Trail—and they were descended from northern Europeans, mostly Scandinavians, Germans, and British.[10] Explaining why she had joined the club, one wrote simply: "I was already a nature lover and an admirer of John Muir." Most of the eighty-two were between twenty-four and thirty-five years old when they became members. They were interested in conservation and they were looking for new friends, but most of all they wanted to climb. One had been a young "newcomer to California from the mid-west, unacquainted. Always interested in the out-of-doors."[11] One who arrived in California from Iowa in 1921 recalled: "I wanted to put on slacks and . . . hike in the mountains."[12]

Membership required two sponsors and approval by the board of directors. The requirement seemed antithetical to diversity, and yet women of all classes were nominated. Wanda Goody had immigrated to San Francisco from her native Poland in 1915, aged thirty years, and immediately went hiking in the Sierra, where she encountered the Sierra Club. Within the year, while working as a mother's helper, she joined. She met her husband, a salesman, through the club. After their child was born, she remained active in the club. For fifty-six years, she worked as an office clerk in a tannery, later becoming a partner. At age eighty-five she wrote, "The Club gave me most of my social life."

Goody climbed beside Selah Chamberlain, born to wealthy New England parents in Rhode Island. As a representative of the Appalachian Mountain Club, Chamberlain joined the Sierra Club in the summer of 1913 to help blaze the John Muir Trail down the Sierra. Prepared for college by governesses, she held a B.A. from Smith College, a B.S. from Simmons College, and an M.A. from Harvard University. She had been a critic for a theater company, had taught for a year in Kentucky, passed that state's bar examination, and served as the assistant secretary for the *Christian Herald* and the Massachusetts Peace Society. The winter after she worked on the John Muir Trail, she married a wealthy factory owner. Well past World War II, she remained active in women's educational and industrial causes; established a wildlife preserve north of San Francisco; and managed her own lands in Massachusetts as wildlife refuges, keeping alive a complex of interests in natural history and in equity for women, comparable with the same interests that had inspired Harwood.

While Chamberlain and Goody illustrate the social extremes within the club, Ethelinda James characterized the norm. Born in 1889 in the upper San

Joaquin Valley to parents who had immigrated from England, James grew up on a ranch near Fresno. When she joined the Sierra Club in 1920, she held a B.A. from the University of California and earned her M.A. from Columbia University. She taught high school in San Francisco for forty years, during the first twenty of which she went on many club trips. Much as John Muir had hoped, the experience of the mountains encouraged James to become active in conservation. Like other women in the club, many of whom were determined to protect myriad forms of life, she worked with the Save-the-Redwoods League, the National Parks Association, the Audubon Societies, and the California Roadside Council, with its campaigns to protect native vegetation.[13]

James was representative of Sierra Club women not only by right of her conservation interests but also because of her high level of education and her career. A majority of the club's women had graduated from four-year colleges and had done graduate work. Forty-one had been teachers, nineteen were stenographers or other clerical workers, and five were businesswomen. The remainder worked in various professional and technical fields. Almost all were employed outside the home most of their lives. They had careers in city schools, state and federal institutions, and private corporations in oil, insurance, banking, or transportation. Only eight listed their vocation as "housewife." Almost half had remained single. Those who had married averaged two children, with one-third of the couples having no children.[14]

Most of the club's women had trained early for a career. Far more educated than the average American woman and less apt to marry and have children, these were the prototypic "New Women," although they married at a slightly higher rate than was generally true of this group. In the club they found the opportunity to balance travel and independence with companionship, a love of wilderness with social activism. Because teaching and clerical work offered only modest financial rewards, many enjoyed the club's month-long excursions at the reasonable cost of $100, or less if one worked with the commissary during the trip or went for only two weeks. Many who taught and remained single enjoyed unencumbered summers, but most were working wives, if not mothers, for whom mountaineering represented a significant commitment of scarce time. Some left family members behind to hike, sleeping in the women's camp on club trips; others traveled with husbands and children, sleeping in the section for married couples.[15] Such lives combined families, careers, a love of mountains, and social activism.

Indeed, these women had entered maturity with a commitment to a generally liberal and secular civic life, involving themselves in professional, cultural, college, and educational issues. Many became active in the American Civil Liberties Union and, later, the United Nations Association. Seventy-five belonged to single-sex groups that promoted the advancement of women, particularly the General Federation of Women's Clubs and the American Association of University Women. Few indicated an affiliation with organized religion. One said she had been christened in the Episcopalian Church and had joined the Presbyterians as a youth but reported that she was "neither now. I guess the Sierra Club was my religion for several decades."[16] Such responses suggest that mountaineering and its clubs met social, civic, and even spiritual needs.

Beyond the questionnaires, various other sources reveal elements of the feminine experience of mountains during the interwar years—travel narratives primarily, but also oral histories and an occasional diary. In articles she wrote for the club and in more personal sources, Marion Randall Parsons attributed to wilderness the distinctive values of home, family, and garden. Parsons had met her husband Edward on a Sierra Club High Trip; later, widowed and childless, she said that the club had become her family. Over the years she described ascents of more than fifty major peaks in the Sierra, Cascades, Rockies, and in Europe, her words savoring the physical attributes of these ranges.[17] She relished, much as Mary Austin had, finding an old Native American encampment in the Pate Valley, evidence of human habitation in the wild. Hieroglyphics were drawn in red on rock walls; mortar and pestle lay nearby, as did obsidian chips; and smoke from a cooking fire had blackened the rocks encircling it.[18]

A strong advocate of wilderness, Parsons warned the Sierra Club that something had been lost with the removal of the people who lived and worked in the mountains, that the club had neglected the human story—houses, churches, stores, and graves—finding history only in "stone and soil, vanishing glaciers, and ancient course of rivers." An encounter with a Basque herder moved her to "regretful consideration of the human contacts so frequent in Europe's mountain regions, which the Sierra, in these days, so signally lacks. For since Indian and trapper and miner, and even derelict old hermits like Lembert [a sheepherder] and his kind, have passed into history, there remains no group of men indigenous, so to speak, to the Sierra soil." She and other visitors saw climbers, rangers, engineers, construction crews, and agents of power companies, but they marked "the encroachments of civilization on the wilderness, while the men of old Lembert's type and day . . . were wilderness men, seeking refuge from cities."

She did not want her statement construed as endorsing the grazing of sheep but "rather as a groping, perhaps too personal expression of an uneasiness that must assail every loyal Sierra Club member with each new visit to the mountain regions his efforts have helped to preserve." Not blinded by mythic tropes of exploration, she was one of the first to recognize the damage that climbers and their pack animals were doing to the meadows of the Sierra. She recommended in 1930 that the club cease to encourage the building of roads in the Sierra, but the club did not change its policy of promoting access until after World War II.[19] Parsons, a recognized painter, expressed her apprehensions about the disappearance of inhabitants from the Sierra by painting the range's peaks towering behind reminders of departed people—the dilapidated shack of an Indian woman, abandoned mines, and cemeteries.[20]

The literary work of Anglo-American women in the Southwest exhibit a similar landscape appreciation. Vera Norwood and Janice Monk have concluded that, from Willa Cather to Sierra Club activist Nancy Newhall, women shared "male environmentalists' concerns," but "tempered those concerns with an ecological vision of a future in which natural and human worlds would be integrated." For southwestern women, "the American Indian and Hispanic populations constituted a part of the landscape which had to be preserved along with the natural environment." Such women interpreted landscapes as the settings of human life rather than as objects to contemplate or manipulate. Photographer, club leader, and climber Ansel Adams was fascinated with grand vistas, but there were no people in his photographs of the church San Xavier del Bac in Tucson. Newhall, his colleague and fellow mountaineer, "put the people back in the church" once she became familiar with the life of the Southwest.[21] In Colorado, where women were primarily responsible for establishing Mesa Verde National Park, their interest in the place of human history as part of the natural landscape became evident. While many men celebrated mastery of a virgin land, women often found human history compatible with wilderness.

Occasionally women expressed their discomfort above the timberline. One wrote: "After crossing a friendly meadow our trail led us up into a lost world— the sweepings of some glacial giant; ragged boulders, a few twisted trees, leafless, lifeless, as things that feed on granite. Here nothing lived, and it was with intense relief that we descended once more to meadows and pleasant forests." Most women, however, found life and warmth even at the highest elevations. Louise Hewlett wrote that the upper Kern Canyon was "a savage gorge, with the river thrashing angrily through its bottleneck.... The water here is so exciting, so turbulent, that one has eyes for nothing else—until he happens to glance up at the opposite wall.... High up in the granite wall ... an exotic garden has been slashed out. The lip of a hanging valley, with trees, a white thread of stream, the promise of hidden things—pools, meadows, flowers."[22] Disappointed by her first glimpse of the Sierra, "this great big hunk of granite . . . so stark and bare," a woman found reassurance in the lights below Mt. Whitney at night.[23]

Scaling a wall at thirteen thousand feet, one woman wrote: "There was the feeling of clean rough granite in my hands, . . . the corsage of polemonium on a gray granite wall. . . . There was the feeling of coming up out of the cold, drafty chute into the delicious warm sunshine. There was the serene stillness of the summit."[24] "Among the barren rocks within a few feet of the summit," another wrote, "were numerous patches of Polemonium eximium, a brave blue flower that makes its home on the rugged peaks of the Sierra above the timberline."[25] On Sierra Club High Trips in the 1920s, Ynes Mexia became interested in native flora. She completed a degree in botany at the University of California, then later traveled up the Amazon River, where in time she collected 150,000 specimens and identified 500 new species. For the Sierra Club she described the region's flora, fauna, and people, writing that she had "found a task where I could be useful and really produce something of lasting worth, while living out among the flowers."[26]

Women's narratives still introduced intimacies of scale to the heights. Seeing the Sierra, a Britisher delighted in the "incredibly detailed tiny life which finds a shelter in all this vastness." Women climbers found alpine flowers unusually brilliant.[27] In 1933 Ethel Boulware, an unmarried, forty-five-year-old teacher from the San Francisco area, joined the Sierra Club's High Trip; crossing Piute Pass, she took in the grand vista but focused on "a miniature garden hidden among the tall grasses. Lined with yellow *mimulus*, vivid *bryanthus*, and green sedges, a tiny stream fell clearly from pool to pool, then wandering off down-hill . . . leaving us to marvel at the grace with which Nature designs even her smallest areas." Thirty years later, answering the club's questionnaire, she recalled the lakes and animals of Glacier National Park but especially the "*Flowers*."[28] Another woman wrote, "From the top of the ridge we beheld . . . the deep gash of the Kern at our feet. . . . The rest of the trip that day was down through a little paradise of meadows clinging in brave gay ribbons to the ridge's westward fall, and full of the exquisite beauty of small things—miniature streams singing through the grass, footstools of plushing moss, unseen frogs dropping into pools with a plop-plop."[29]

Women continued to invoke an aesthetic of intimacy.[30] Sixty-five years later, one recalled a campsite at eight thousand feet as "warm and comfortable. It was all amongst green oak leaves, crumpled leaves. It was a very comfortable place. I washed my hair there."[31] Another wrote that the mountains were "so luminous with sound, . . . so sonorous with color" that they rang like bells.[32] Of Silver Pass, a woman exclaimed: "What a place! What a rare combination of exquisite mountain-snow beauty, springtime freshness, and warm bright sunshine; . . . it was not wildness or desolation, . . . only a wonderful shining stillness, . . . a feeling of being at the source of things." She watched threatening clouds build, yet she felt "as safe and secure—perhaps safer—than one does sometimes in a warm, dry house in town."[33]

Although women no longer bragged of their high-altitude housekeeping, they did draw domestic allusions.[34] One commented, "Everyone was the guest of nature here, and who can say which of nature's rooms is the most charming?" Another found home-sites among the aspens from which to "look at the sky so close overhead, snuggling down in the blankets."[35] The mountains were God's "house of peace," with "flowered carpets," "blue-tiled roof," and courts of "musical fountains," offering "shelter and sustenance and liberty."[36] A snowy camp on Mt. Lyell was "snugly tucked in among protecting albicaulis pines," allowing for a comfortable "boudoir." At Lake Garnet, a hiker found "miniature groves of white-bark pines for bedrooms, and polished rock pavements for dressing-room and bath." A diarist wrote that she had been a guest in "Mother Nature's choicest pent-house."[37]

Perhaps no representation of space more clearly symbolizes the continuum of urban and rural, human and wild, than does a garden. To these women, gardens were the natural within the urban and the intrusion of the human into the wild. Almost every woman who wrote of the mountains praised gardens.[38] The Sierra lent itself to the likeness. While men mentioned wild gardens only occasionally and in passing, women consistently praised them.[39] Of a climb up Kaweak Peak, one woman recalled being pinned down by the sun like "moths to the glaring mountain wall, . . . then suddenly an oasis! We rounded a bend and there it lay—a garden of unbelievable coolness slashed in the naked rock. . . . The flower gardens" were "a dip into Eden."[40] Another said: "The gardens along the trail filled us with 'delight, wide-eyed as a marigold.' Tall spikes of purple larkspur, blue monkshood, the lavender stalks of the wild onion, and the bright orange leopard lilies, the castillejas, and the masses of brown-eyed Susans, produced a color harmony difficult to rival in home gardens."[41] Yellowstone was for one woman an "enchanted wilderness [of] flower-gardens" that she equated with childhood innocence.[42]

Analogies of wilderness and garden came readily to those who cultivated the red-flowered columbine, not unlike the yellow mountain columbine, which is taller and wavy. Finding blooms like those in their gardens made the wild familiar, if not in some sense theirs. In elevations where vegetation was sparse, they found rock gardens and bonsai gardens. On a Sierra pass, one

Figure 28. Yosemite Wildflower Garden. View from the Museum Garden, July 7, 1933. Courtesy of Yosemite National Park Library.

woman sat in the shadow of "ancient timber-line pines, ... straining and con-torted as if dwarfed by artful gardeners of Japan." Another recalled that "rock gardens of rosy primrose, golden mimulus and all the rest against their gray granite were very exciting."[43]

Mountains were wild but not alien.[44] "By now, of course, the city had van-ished utterly," Marion Randall Parsons began her narrative of the club's 1929 outing; "our mountaineers were at home again." Mildred Thoren, born in Pennsylvania to Swedish parents, was an elementary school teacher in Pasadena when she took a Sierra High Trip in 1933 and declared herself at home.[45] Look-ing down from the twelve-thousand-foot Colby Pass toward the east rim of Cloud Canyon, Louise Hewlett described a "small enchanted world, ... a doll's garden." Anxious to reach "that lovely resting place," she descended the canyon wall, rounded a bend, and came "home."[46]

This word conveyed more than physical and emotional comfort. Home for the middle- and upper-class women in the United States who had achieved a significant degree of power within the family was a place of influence, con-trol, and autonomy. As they entered into reform efforts, civic clubs, and vo-cations, they extended their understanding of "home" beyond the confines of the house that they inhabited to other spheres of appropriate interest. In 1911, Marion Talbot, dean of women at the University of Chicago, delineated home thus: "It is as wide as the world into which the individual steps forth. The determination of the character of that world and the preservation of those interests which she has safeguarded in the home, constitute the real duty resting upon women." Talbot may not have climbed peaks, but her life resembled those of women who did. For such women, "home" had become "a code word," evoked when others challenged women's efforts to extend their prerogatives. It remained a well-used language between the world wars. By signifying feminine values, it established women's right to self-assertion.[47]

To claim the peaks between the wars, women also used with great frequency the code word that further denoted a sphere uniquely theirs—"garden." By extending the uses of the words *house* and *garden,* women defended their right to move freely and unencumbered through space, to be autonomous, to be with and like men, especially when parents or spouses challenged such adventures as dangerous, unwomanly, or neglectful of familial duties.[48] With such words that were quiet equivalents to men's language of territorial conquest, women laid claim to the mountains. Contact with an untarnished and powerful earth that was metaphorically female enhanced their pride in womanhood, as it would much later for modern ecofeminists.

Women still spoke of wilderness as a place of liberation and their pride still indicated a possession that was new and rare. Ethel Boulware found "utter naturalness and simplicity," freedom to do as one pleased.[49] Another declared that to be free—in this case in the Alps, alone with map and compass—was far better than the freedom of any city, because this "space seemed to unfold itself in great waves before me."[50] Climber Bertha Pope Clark wrote in 1925: "It is impossible to describe the pure and peculiar happiness one feels in the High Sierra, freedom from care and distractions, a natural life in the open." Turn-of-the-century women climbers escaped the demand that they function solely as consumers; now they spoke of release from the competitive workplace, from "thoughts of awards and tests."[51]

If mountain narratives are to be believed, women often, and with obvious pleasure, immersed themselves in icy streams and warm lakes, while men rarely bathed in the wild.[52] Dorothy "Dot" Pepper, an elementary school teacher from Los Angeles who left her workplace-bound husband each year to climb with the Sierra Club, said simply: "The women never used bathing suits."[53] But this right had been contested, as Dot's friend recalled. Pepper and a group of women had gone "skinny-swimming" on one trip. Within visual range of the camp's commissary, where the other men and women were at breakfast, Dot repeatedly dove down into the water, exposing her "biscuits" in the process. Mrs. Walter Huber, wife of the Sierra Club's president and attired in a khaki Norfolk jacket and knickers, objected strenuously. Huber was not to be dismissed lightly. A dispute followed. Virginie de Fremery, a "rather frail, patrician lady of an old San Francisco family," quietly went around to every person in the women's camp suggesting that they all go swimming in the nude at 11 o'clock the following morning. And all—except, one might assume, Mrs. Huber—"marched naked into the water," had a swim, came out, dressed, and went to lunch. Nothing more was said.[54]

Nudity was a valued form of emancipation. Bertha Pope told this story: "As a small child, I used to play with a boy named 'Bill,' who had an ill-concealed contempt for the weaker sex as he knew it. At the age of eleven, he wrote a poem setting forth the disadvantages of girls. I remember two withering lines: 'They cannot climb up trees for fruit. Nor bathe without a bathing-suit.' Across the years we salute you, Bill, and tell you times have changed."[55]

One woman said flatly that mountaineering should not be discussed in terms of success or failure, as she felt men too often did, but rather in terms of the gamine pleasures of sliding into dark lakes, diving into limpid rivers, or oozing gently into swampy waters. To her, "the joy of pool-plunging was atavistic, harkening back to a time when one was more truly part, not of a mechanized civilization, but of nature."[56] Another said: "Not least of all the pleasures of the Sierra Club trip is bathing in those mountain streams and lakes in green cold water that folds about one more soft than liquid silk."[57] One reminisced: "I did so enjoy mountain 'dips' every day in these ice-cold streams; . . . it always rested me."[58] Of the Sierra, a hiker recalled that "we sat above the ford washing our feet and making tea" and swam in a lake "supplied by springs, warm and tenanted by happy little watersnakes that felt no real objection to us."[59] Another woman exulted: "The rapture of mere solo bathing in soft cold mountain water has never been sufficiently sung, those aquamarine floods are soft and soothing as chilled velvet, exhilarating as sparkling light." One woman likened a stream to a tiled bathroom where "we all belong in this pure, natural, peaceful atmosphere."[60] By referring to their houses and their everyday lives, women used a language of sweet domesticity to cloak what society might have deemed deviant sensuality.

Teachers, secretaries, and housewives escaped into what amounted to mobile summer colonies characterized by similar tastes and background. They liked the balance between nature and humanity, freedom and socializing, that they found in solitary day-treks followed by campfires surrounded by as many as 250 hikers. One of them wrote of the fun of the evening campfire: "with all of us huddled closely together for warmth."[61] The communal and the co-educational aspects of American clubs impressed English visitors. Jessie Whitehead, the daughter of Harvard philosopher Alfred North Whitehead and familiar with the British system of sexually segregated alpine clubs, praised the integration she experienced while climbing with clubs in the United States.[62] According to another Englishwoman, you were accepted into a "family of mountain-lovers . . . an almost perfect society"; this society embodied in miniature "our dreams of what human relations in the Great Society of state and city might become."[63]

American women, too, enjoyed the familial aspects of these trips, and they associated wilderness with social equity.[64] They appreciated that rich and poor, men and women, were "garbed alike in rough clothes and dusty boots." Men, too, still found noteworthy the "frank equality" in dress and appearance between the sexes. In the 1930s women were delighted to find jeans a uniform, and they enjoyed wearing shorts.[65] Not everyone considered democracy a hallmark of these excursions. One recalled of the Sierra Club: "There were things about the club that were really undemocratic in those days," including signs posted for the climbs with "very exclusive" lists of the invited that often slighted women. "In those days," another remembered, "you climbed the . . . peaks—only if you were invited."[66]

Enough were invited, however, or found their own way, that in 1935 women made seventy (to men's one hundred thirty-two) of the notable climbs recorded for the Sierra Nevada, and twenty-one women joined forty-five men on the Sierra Club's most challenging ascents.[67] In their collective successes and those of high-profile individuals such as the American Elizabeth Knowlton, who accompanied the German-American Expedition up Nanga Parbar in the Himalayas in 1935, women defied the assumption of the world's alpinists as set forth by Tom de Lépiney: "Une femme, par definition, c'est quelque chose qu'on tire" [a woman, by definition, is something one drags along].[68]

Among their most dramatic gestures, women appropriated two symbols of masculine power: technology and leadership. Between the late 1920s and mid 1930s, American women began rock climbing with rope, piton, and the belay as quickly as their male counterparts. On occasion they also took the lead.[69] Marjory Bridge [Farquhar], a graduate in physical education from Berkeley's University of California, led several large parties on roped ascents in 1934. That year, she and two other Sierra Club women made difficult first-ascent rock climbs—without men. A new category had emerged in Europe and America— the "manless climb." The Sierra Club boasted: "Julie Mortimer and May Pridham added to their many fine achievements as 'manless climbers' by making

Figure 29. "Manless Climbers" in the High Sierra on the Sierra Club's High Trip, 1934. Left to right: Louise Hildebrand, Helen LeConte, and Marjory Bridge (Farquhar). Courtesy of Peter Farquhar.

a traverse of the West Tooth up the north side of the *arête* [narrow ridge of bare rock] west of the peak."[70]

Miriam O'Brien, the young graduate of Bryn Mawr who led the first all-women team up the Matterhorn in 1929, said that, contrary to common perceptions, women enjoyed leading, selecting routes, solving problems, and trusting their own judgment in emergencies. She also maintained that women could lead only when men were not present. If a male companion was more skilled, he might let a woman lead, but it would be no more than a "pleasant little fiction" offering only pale satisfaction and promptly dropped in the face of trouble. Nor could a woman lead with a man whose skills were inferior; either he would immediately resent being bossed by a woman—in which case it was war—or he would agree to follow but "revert to type" in even a minor crisis. According to O'Brien, the weaker the man, the less apt he was to accept female direction, in mountaineering as in life. It was traditional for male alpinists to claim that they had taken the lead and accomplished a "first ascent" despite the help of guides and porters, but the public saw the inclusion of any man, even a porter, as compromising a woman's achievement. O'Brien concluded: "It has been my experience that a woman cannot really lead if there is any man at all in the party. And so if she wants to lead, she must climb with other women."[71]

This new assertiveness met with much support but also subtle opposition, if not opprobrium. O'Brien encountered difficulty finding women who were sufficiently free of "hampering relatives." Her triumph in 1931 on the Grépon, which made all-women climbing parties famous (*en cordée féminine*, or women-only rope), elicited some incredulity and the following response from a Frenchman: "The Grépon has disappeared. Of course, there are still some rocks standing there, but as a climb it no longer exists. Now that it has been done by two women alone, no self-respecting man can undertake it." The remark played on a quip in 1881 by A. F. Mummery, the first to ascend the Grépon: "It has frequently been noticed that all mountains appear doomed to pass through three stages: an inaccessible peak—the most difficult ascent in the Alps—an easy day for a lady. I must confess that the Grépon has not yet reached this final stage, and the heading . . . must be regarded as prophetic rather than as a statement of actual fact."[72] O'Brien was not alone in encountering opposition to manless climbing or in finding the activity exhilarating. The British climber Nea Morin pioneered guideless and manless climbs—despite objections raised by her husband—arguing that if men were even nearby, "half the sense of adventure" was lost. "Alone at last!" she wrote of her all-women party as it prepared to ascend the Alpine Blaitière in 1934.[73]

In telling of their rock climbs and alpine ascents, however, women still did not use men's rhetoric of assault and attack, risk and mastery. Having practiced climbing in the Berkeley hills, Doris Leonard, a young secretary, went for her first Sierra rock climb on her honeymoon with her husband, climber and lawyer Richard Leonard, in 1934. At ten thousand feet, she wrote: "I was frightened. Great tears welled up in my eyes. I felt so small and overpowered as I looked at the tremendous heights around me"; then she remembered that there was someone there "who was thoroughly capable of taking care of me." Within a day or two, she lost her fear and enjoyed herself. After two weeks she observed that she and the mountains had changed and she now felt comfortable: "Springtime is short in such high altitudes, and the dainty cassiope-bells were turning brown with the change in the seasons." According to her known account of these experiences, no thrill of a determined assault coursed through her, and no sense of empowerment arose from her first and third ascents.[74]

In explaining their choice of peaks, women wrote less of challenge than of aesthetic attraction.[75] Morin chose the site for her first manless climb and said it was a formidable one as well as strikingly beautiful. In narrating her success, she adopted a breezy, assured air, explaining: "I was a 'natural' and climbing came easily. My body never let me down and because of this I was supremely confident, which in turn engendered strength and ease of movement." In addition to describing the thrill of scaling a sheer face, she wrote of sitting beside "the unruffled waters" of a lake, "soothed and engulfed by the timeless peace and strength of the hills." She admitted that her climbs were occasionally perilous, but the abyss did not prey on her prose. She and her companions "wound past crevasses hundreds of feet deep," she wrote of the Grépon, "admiring the range of colour in their depths where the clear ice is every imaginable shade of blue and green. We also peered into the unfathomable depths of the *moulins,* round openings like well-shafts, sometimes several yards in diameter, into which the melt-water from the glacier cascades and thunders." The rhetoric of the masculine sublime echoed only faintly as she wrote that if one were to peer into the "dreadful void," one would hastily draw back, "feeling dizzy and sick." Pondering the deaths of so many with whom she had climbed, Morin asked, later in her life, Was it worth it?, and she answered, yes, for all the "joy and comfort" the mountains had brought to her and to others.[76]

Even on organized group ascents, climbing remained hazardous. Making a traverse of a forty-five-degree pitch on Coe Glacier in 1927, for example, eleven members (four women) of the thirty-fourth annual Mazamas' climb of Mt. Hood fell and, tied together, all disappeared over the edge of an icy cliff.[77] One man was killed and the others seriously injured. Despite such risks, possible empowerment through control of fear, and the sense of accomplishment they might experience by getting to the top, women continued to avoid discussions of danger and the potential for conquest. They spoke instead of ease, joy, "laughter, and contentment."[78] Relating a hard ascent of Milestone Peak, one wrote that she and her companion moved ahead, "guessing all the way" on "a blissful day's journey."[79] Of the North Palisade, Helen LeConte offered that "the very simplicity of the climb is one of its greatest beauties."[80] Reviewing a leading English rock climber's book, an American woman praised her "delightful nonchalance in the recounting of hair-raising exploits, or near-accidents such as submergings in crevasses or putting the rope to the test in falls from cliffs."[81] Standing on the edge of a crevasse in one of Mt. Hood's glaciers, Pearl Turner of the Colorado Mountain Club looked down, she wrote in her album, into "blushing depths."[82] Perhaps such women felt no need to speak of danger, or perhaps they felt that their prerogatives were too new and too fragile to bear assertions of power.

Unwillingness to advertise courage also grew out of society's vision of femininity. The English language itself restricted women's presentations of self, prizing expressions of passivity and modesty.[83] Victorian notions that ladies should avoid doing anything that might generate in themselves hate and fear lingered well into the twentieth century. If emphasizing the difficulty of a task was an act of self-promotion for men, it was for women an act of self-deprecation, a sign of only-to-be-expected weakness. By not claiming bravery, women behaved as though it were natural to them. Perhaps echoing the quiet bravado of John Mallory (of Mt. Everest fame), O'Brien commented on her greatest manless feat: "Next day we climbed the Matterhorn. It was as easy as that."[84]

Ruth Currier, at age forty-five a competent climber, had graduated from the University of California, taught briefly, married a San Francisco businessman, and mothered a child. Now a civic leader who worked for the advancement of women, she was president of the California League of Women Voters, the Bay Chapter of the American Association of University Women, and the Century Club of California. She opened her description of the Sierra Club's 1933 High Trip by stating that all accounts of a climb "should begin with a rhapsody. No other word holds so well the joy of the out-of-doors, the sense of well-being, the thrill of mountain beauty, and the care-free weeks to come." She described her pleasure at being with others and the warmth of being "at home . . . under the stars."[85] Portraying a quintessential domesticity, she feminized the environment. She wrote of bathing in icy streams and peaceful lakes, lunching under low trees, and sleeping in quiet beauty.

Of the rigorous expedition, she recalled, "A few more miles over ridges and through meadows amid beautiful woods and flower gardens. . . . Below lay a long meadow that seemed to be landscaped like a park. . . . It was not long before we were in the midst of this park, where the shade of trees by the river invited rest and refreshment." She brought to the Sierra the commonplace. Crossing Tuolumne Canyon, she wrote: "The day came when we were at home in the highest timber at the head of the canyon near Matterhorn Peak and Sawtooth Ridge." After toiling down a steep wall into Big Meadows, she found a fawn, moved toward it so slowly that it did not stir, followed an Indian trail, swam, and slept. Her words echoed those of Jennie Price, who told of a morning in 1898 in which she walked across the Pait Valley through small gardens and followed bear trails into their feeding grounds and resting places under low sheltering trees.[86]

Glen Dawson and Marjory Bridge [Farquhar] wrote accounts of ascents made on the club's 1933 outing. A comparison of their narratives is telling. In both cases the peaks had long since been ascended, but the teams in question pioneered routes using new techniques. Of an ascent of 13,992-foot Mt. Humphrey with Jules Eichorn, Farquhar wrote that she had selected the peak for its beautiful "terra-cotta colored granite," and she recommended sleeping under its white-bark pines. She assured readers that the old peak had resigned itself to mastery and she described her pioneer climb as pleasurable and fun. She told of how, after enjoying the view, she had roped down for a swim.[87]

On the same outing, Glen Dawson climbed Devils Crags with Jules Eichorn. Helen LeConte, Julie Mortimer, and Farquhar herself had all climbed Devils Crags by various routes. But Eichorn and Dawson sought a new and particularly perilous angle, with Dawson observing: "The Devils Crags looked difficult . . . more difficult than we had anticipated. . . . The east cliffs seemed impossible." The south side was extremely precipitous, and the north was ragged. He shuddered as he looked down into the abyss between crags "black and defiant."[88]

The themes of feminine narratives had remained surprisingly consistent since the 1890s. Women emphasized the sensuality of nature, the pleasures of equity, and the desire to escape social strictures. Uncommon spaces still afforded uncommon freedoms. Their identity bound by conventions to the nurturance of others, women were not drawn to places they saw as barren or desolate. Instead they made the peaks theirs by using the words *home, garden,* and *family,* wrote of intimacy with such landscapes, and spoke of being comfortable and comforted in places neither savage nor alien. They saw wild mountains as places of life where humans belonged. Using everyday analogies, women domesticated wildness.

They laid claim to these places of life by virtue of their own maternal power. Most shared the sentiments of the young woman who wrote in 1921 of how she loved being in "the bosom of Mother Nature." From Jennie Price to Ruth Currier, they might well have concurred with her answer to why she climbed mountains: to find comradeship, to learn lessons from the flowers and from the rocks crumbling into fertile soil, to experience "the sanctity of life."[89] Women allowed themselves to be drawn into the natural world, rather than asserting control over it. By linking natural with domestic spaces and with fecundity, they continued to assert feminine rights to have challenging and sublime experiences and to have a say in the fate of rugged landscapes.

Despite their determined claim, however, women's climbing record declined abruptly in the late 1930s. Of the thirty-one Mazamas who made noteworthy ascents in 1939, only three were women. On the Sierra Club's trip that year, eighty-six men and twenty-one women made new or difficult climbs, but only three women were among the twenty-four climbers making first ascents. The decline in their climbing accelerated as the United States entered the war. Sixty men but only one woman were among those who made the 103 outstanding climbs in Yosemite in 1941. The loss was real but it was also a matter of record keeping. American clubs adopted the European system of classifying climbs on a six-point scale. A class I or II climb is the most difficult of rock climbs, a class III or IV is average, and class V or VI is the easiest. American clubs recorded only the most difficult. Women continued to make many class-III-through-VI climbs but fewer class I or II efforts. Thus did they disappear from the record.[90] As their profile in mountaineering declined, so too did their visibility within the sport's clubs.

Women had assumed leadership roles in these organizations only during World War I and the postwar years; few had held office before then. In 1903, for example, only two of the ten officers of the Mazamas, only one of nine members of the executive council, and none of its committee members were women. By 1915 three of its nine officers were women, as were sixteen of its forty committee members. At its founding in 1907, the Mountaineers had not elected a woman to its board, but by the 1920s women held five of eleven seats.[91] Despite these substantial advances in the Mountaineers, Mazamas, and even in the Sierra Club, women's leadership in organized mountaineering had come late and it had often remained minimal. Of the sixty-six whose ascents qualified them for active membership in the Alpine Club of Canada by 1914, for example, thirty-nine had been women, but there was only one woman among its eleven officers.[92] By 1935 only seven of the Sierra Club's sixty-one directors were women, almost all of them having been elected within the previous thirteen years.[93]

Within the Sierra Club the loss of power that was evident by the late 1930s resulted less from a closing of ranks at the top than from a lack of receptivity by the membership at large, at least one-third of which were women. Directors held office at the discretion of the membership. Women continued to have a strong presence on the nominating committee and to be well represented among those nominated to stand for election to the board, but they were disproportionately defeated. Even the most accomplished lost. Mary Yost, dean of women at Stanford University and a climber, was elected to the board in 1933, as was Ansel Adams's wife, Virginia Best Adams. Both served only one two-year term. Ruth Currier, author, climber, and civic leader, was defeated. Of the four who ran in 1936, all but Marion Randall Parsons lost, including Violet Newrenbert, a notary public; librarian Doris Rowland; and teachers Nora Evans and Ethel Boulware—climbers all.

On those occasions when women did win seats, they rarely held them for long. Their shorter tenure prevented them from developing authoritative voices. Male directors averaged fifteen years, and twenty to thirty years of service were common. Why women did not remain in office is unclear. Perhaps a directorship consumed too much time for Virginia Adams, who had small children and encountered difficulties finding child care.[94] Perhaps women felt uncomfortable on the board. By the late 1930s they were choosing not to run. Only Harriet Parsons ran in 1942 and was defeated. Nor was the Sierra Club unique; women's role in the Mountaineers declined to such a point that by 1939 only one remained on the board.

From 1939 through 1942 no women served on the Sierra Club's board of directors. In 1943 Harriet Parsons and Charlotte Mauk were elected. The daughter of a radical Berkeley minister, Parsons held a master's degree in landscape architecture, worked as an accountant, and wrote narratives that brought to the club a vision of warmth and life in the wilderness: "When it became too cold and lonely," she assured readers, "and one wondered if the night would ever end, a white-crowned sparrow sometimes broke the still air . . . and for a few moments the night seemed warmer." She loved Mt. Humphrey less for its soaring height than for its "mauve walls" and "brilliant lichens."[95] Mauk held a degree in chemistry and was an editor at Berkeley's Lawrence Radiation Laboratory. She brought a sublimely feminine enthusiasm to her mountain narratives; she described the Sierra as home and garden, praised the colors and forms, the sounds of Sierra water, wind, and life, the fragrance of pine and smoke, and the warmth and "friendly feel of granite."[96] Parsons served for only three years, leaving the gentle Mauk alone through the next two decades in what she called the board's "august company."[97]

Why had women become less visible on the peaks and in alpine clubs? Women had, of course, experienced difficulties in establishing leadership in any mixed-sex organization, but they had achieved a strong presence more readily and firmly in some groups, such as the Audubon Society. At issue was whether an activity fell within a properly masculine or a properly feminine cultural sphere. Men, it seemed, belonged in the mountains, but women could, even *should*, like birds and flowers. By writing chronicles that highlighted their accomplishments, men reinforced what would, in any case, have been their stronger role in a mixed-sex group. Perhaps women should have framed their exploits in the language of mastery rather than in terms of home, garden, and motherhood. It is more likely, however, that they had been correct in blunting their challenge. The decline in their climbing and in their leadership followed hard on the heels of their "manless" attempts and their efforts to win seats on club boards.

Perhaps American society had felt compelled to tame the manless climber, as some historians claim was the fate of the "New Woman."[98] Perhaps the Depression, which had cost many men their jobs, made competitiveness less seemly in women. One historian suggested that the "New Woman" had failed to base her autonomy on a restructured economic identity.[99] The women in the Sierra Club, however, had careers, and they appear to have retained them through the 1930s. Furthermore, they did not lose influence until late in the Depression. The reasons appear to lie more with the increasingly combative language of climbing and conservation than with economics. By the late 1930s the link between the masculine ideals evident in men's participation in the sport and society's vested interest in preparing men to be soldiers had become overt. Because few women joined the military at the time, their participation declined in civilian practices that had martial connotations.[100]

Although women certainly did not articulate the matter in such terms, they recognized the growing resistance to their achievements. An experienced female alpinist observed: "The feminine nature seems in general less adapted to the mountains than the feminine foot." She encouraged women to try, but she warned them that no matter how clumsy or inexperienced men themselves were, no man would be willing to "accept the fact that any woman is fit to go ahead of him, in this masculine world of the mountains."[101] Between the two wars, women of independent minds had become educated, had careers, were proud of leading and of making first ascents, and served as officers in mixed-sex organizations. If war had not followed the Depression, they might have succeeded in staking their claim as equals. As it was, they gave up leading. Few people in American clubs overtly retaliated against the self-avowed manless climber, but somehow she disappeared, and women lost much of their leadership role in the nonprofit sector that earlier had been their strongest base of power.

Miriam O'Brien's defection followed quickly upon her successes. After she and a friend claimed the "first manless" ascent of the Matterhorn in 1931, she was scheduled to return to Chamonix, where friends had prepared a reception at the railway station with flowers, a band, and orations. Instead, she joined Robert Underhill, one of the best technical climbers in the United States, in the Eastern Alps for some "guideless climbing." Her friends predicted that her "manless" days were over, and they were correct. She announced her engagement to Underhill simultaneously with the appearance of her article, "Without Men," in *Appalachia*. They married and reared their family in New Hampshire, where she became an expert on the mountain flowers of New England.[102] She continued to climb for nineteen years with Underhill. "Manless climbing is fun for a while," she wrote, "but this other arrangement is better!" She recalled, "I liked climbing with Bob. We made a good, harmonious, efficient team." On one occasion he allowed her to take the lead coming down a glacier, a gesture she called "out of the ordinary, as men go! . . . Only a man of considerable ability himself would so generously recognize ability in someone else."[103] The Sierra Club's Doris Leonard and Marjory Bridge Farquhar, too, had married accomplished climbers, had families, and continued to climb but made no more "manless" ascents. Like Miriam Underhill, both remained very active in climbing clubs and in conservation for decades after World War II.

Few college girls assumed the all-women mantle. "Taking the lead" was increasingly coming into conflict with society's emphasis on the family and with its narrowing expectations of what constituted masculinity. The physical ideal of the athletic young woman gave way to a more curvaceous figure. Nevertheless, the feminine and naturalist sublimes, using the language of home and garden, had become and would remain central to the wilderness movement.

Mountains as the Measure of Men

Delivering the keynote address at the Sierra Club's annual meeting in 1921, Chester H. Rowell, newspaper editor, journalist, and a leader in progressive Republican politics, compared what he called the earth's "two symbols of the Infinite—the great mountain and the great sea." The first was of timeless, self-defined certainty, the other of ceaseless fluidity. On a mountain, he said, a man could believe in a personal God and individual immortality; "the mountain's life is a man's life multiplied by billions." Men could learn a peak's history and stand on its summit "as if we had grown to its height." "The mountains call us," he declared, "not to rest, but to work. A great peak is a frowning challenge, until we have scaled it; a strong and trusted friend thereafter." In contrast, the sea "has no past, no future"—it offers no measure of men. "Individuality, separateness, are illusions in the sea.... Its language ... is the occult speech of the Orient. Its creed is not Christianity.... Its God is the Inscrutable; its destiny Nirvana."[1] One might well imagine the members of Rowell's audience, who later elected him to the club's board of directors, nodding in agreement at his association of physical environment with racial identity, of self-actualizing manliness with the genius of western civilization, and of alpine triumphs with success in life, if not with spiritual salvation.

During the years between World War I and World War II, men found new venues for celebrating exploration: the study of the American West, the sport of rock climbing, and the fine art of photography. The period opened with naturalist and outdoorsman John C. Van Dyke crying: "Was there ever a time in human history when a return to Nature was so much needed as just now?" How shall the nations be rebuilt and "the race live again"?[2] By the period's close, North America's heights had become landscapes appropriate to the forging of comradeship, the deploying of alpine technologies, and the designing of military strategies. In the interim, American men drew reassurances from nature, from their own climbing successes, from the triumphs of alpinists throughout the world, and from the history of the exploration of the American West.[3]

The same year that Rowell gave his speech, the United States National Bank advertised its headquarters in a new San Francisco skyscraper. The caption under a sketch of the bank's skyscraper read: "Climbing to Success: The climb to financial independence was rough going. It's a climb on which more have failed than any other known—but a strong banking connection has been the Alpine-stock of everyone who has made it to the top." Hard work and self-control exercised in outdoor sport would translate into professional and financial accomplishment.[4] A Mazama carried the parallel further: in wilderness "we work hard and fare hard and sleep hard, sweating and shivering by turns, toiling to exhaustion." His answer to the query, Why do it? was: to try "powers of achievement and endurance" in arenas where only natural talent counted.[5] Men spoke of eluding the cult of success, but in fact they imposed its language on their encounters with rugged terrains.[6] Outdoor sport was, they claimed, "our task and pleasure."[7] America's climbing clubs agreed that their members were well-rounded, civic-minded, hard-working men.

The men of the Sierra Club were, in fact, well-educated, generally white-collar professionals. Of the sixty-seven men who responded to the 1971 questionnaire sent to those who had joined the Sierra Club before 1930, almost all said they had attended, if not completed, a four-year college program. A substantial number reported graduate work in medicine or law. A large percentage were employed in the corporate or public sectors, but many worked in their own small firms or partnerships. The wide variety of their vocations included a barber, a firefighter, a retail lumberman, an insurance salesman, and a realtor. There were, as well, artists, clerks, and machinists. Far more common, however, were doctors, dentists, and attorneys, with engineers the most numerous group—they were representatives of the progressive era's "New Middle Class," now in their maturity. Nearly all belonged to fraternal, business, and professional groups and were active in a wealth of forestry and park associations; alpine clubs; scouting groups; botanical, garden, and native plant societies. Very few noted an affiliation with organized religion, suggesting that the experience of mountains offered them spiritual and moral sustenance.[8]

Two-thirds had been born in the 1880s and 1890s, nearly half in California, the other half in American places as diverse as rural Nebraska and New York

Figure 30. Francis P. Farquhar on the summit of Mt. Whitney. Courtesy of Peter Farquhar.

City. Few of their parents had been born in California but almost all had been born in North America; members who were foreign-born, or whose parents had been, were of British, northern, or central European descent. Men's reasons for joining the Sierra Club varied, from the "botanical interest" of a professor trained at the University of Berlin to the man who cited "a young lady," and another who "hoped to find influential friends." The overwhelming majority mentioned a "love of the mountains," adding that their involvement in conservation had grown out of that love.[9]

Francis P. Farquhar had come to California as a young Harvard graduate and taken a position with a publishing house. As a boy he had climbed in Maine's Rangeley region, but shortly after coming west and hearing of the Sierra Club's outings from a young man in his boardinghouse, Farquhar joined the 1911 High Trip to Yosemite. He became obsessed with the process by which a man was "matched against the resistance of the mountain." A thin,

*Figure 31. Francis P. Farquhar and Marjory Bridge Farquhar in
their study in San Francisco, together with their climbing
equipment (piton, carabiner, ice picks, and topographic map),
October 1935. Photograph by Gabriel Moulin. Courtesy of Peter
Farquhar and Moulin Archives.*

agile individual, he eventually climbed every fourteen-thousand-foot peak on
the West Coast. "As one would expect," a fellow climber wrote, "Francis was
successful in many other fields." Together with his own accountancy practice,
he became president of the California Society of Certified Public Accountants,
the State Board of Accountancy, the California Academy of Sciences, the California Historical Society, and the Save-the-Redwoods League. He was a Sierra
Club director, president, and editor of its *Bulletin* from 1926 to 1945. For Farquhar, climbing, the telling of the tale, and conservation were merely different expressions on the face of one fascination.[10]

He chronicled his own bids for increasingly elusive "first ascents," claiming
them on California's Milestone, Midway Mountain, and Mt. Haeckel. He

explained his obsession: "A first ascent of a high mountain has a thrill . . . that can never be duplicated . . . on that particular peak." In 1921 he and Yosemite National Park naturalist Ansel Hall set their sights on California's Middle Palisades. Clearly linking mountaineering with conservation, the two had both a political and a personal agenda: they were lobbying to convince Congress to add the peaks of the Palisades to Sequoia National Park. They also hoped to claim personally the Middle Palisades, considered the last unclaimed fourteen-thousand-foot peak in the Sierra. When they actually reached what appeared to be the highest of its serrated ridges, however, they discovered that someone had already been there. Only the glimpse of a nearby ridge unmistakably higher revived their spirits. As they pushed on, however, Farquhar found himself unnerved, unable to go up or down. Only gradually did he recover: "I pulled myself together, subdued my fears, and began to concentrate." He and Hall made the summit. Finding no evidence of a prior claimant, "with a shout we greeted the summit as its first visitors" and built a monument.[11]

The sublime moment of terror, mastered by will and reason and bringing spiritual transformation, remained a strong motif in men's narratives. On a snow slide down a peak that he named The Thumb, located in the Sierra's Palisades group, a man from the Sierra Club found he had lost control. As he fell he caught a glimpse, out of the corner of his eye, of the peak "solemn and unmoved above its glacier. A feeling of helplessness came over me. I struck a rock and could in a far-off way hear myself utter a feeble groan." Only at the critical moment did he regain his composure and his footing. Men shuddered as they wrote—or even as they read—of being suffocated by vertical cliffs, rocks, ice, and snow, and of experiencing fatigue that reduced them to impotence.[12] Peaks could induce such feelings of failure that it was painful to look at them. Climbing was "the conquest of fear and triumph over the weakness of the flesh in a united assault on the ramparts of nature."[13] A man said of Mt. Goddard, "The country is rough and the trials are many, but once you have been there, your moral fiber and make-up have been changed and strengthened."[14] The vision of salvation remained the summit, while hell remained the abyss, with its Biblical and existential allusions to immeasurable evil and to a bottomless darkness that threatened to obliterate identity. The panic that haunted high places was demonic, and was to be overcome by spiritual strength.[15]

Men faced a natural world that was at best indifferent to their fate, but the terror they experienced was "not in her [nature] but in yourself." "Have we vanquished an enemy?" a climber in the Rockies asked; he answered his own question: "None but ourselves."[16] When George Mallory and a companion died on Mt. Everest in 1924, climbers in England and the United States elevated him to the status of a hero, mourning him as a man whose spirit had dominated his body, a man for whom "mountaineering . . . was a spiritual necessity," which, "like any other religion, had its moments of ecstasy, of worship, of abasement."[17] Of Mallory and his companion, Farquhar wrote: "One can almost see through the mystery of their death and behold them rise, clasped by the friendly hands of Captain Scott of the Antarctic tragedy and Sir John Franklin of the frozen north." Poetic license, perhaps, but Farquhar was a devout Christian for whom self-abasement, discipline, and the proximity of death gave alpine exploration spiritual meaning.[18]

Along with their own transformations, men visualized themselves transforming the landscape. Determining the distance a peak soars above sea level was an exacting science that preoccupied mountaineers, yet most climbers also indulged in imaginatively reshaping the landscapes to their desire. Their fancies suggest that a peak's elevation was a human construction: the beholder defined it and so it was mutable in the hands of a man. Reaching the Sierra summit of Black Kaweah, a climber repaired the flagstaff, replaced the flag, added his name to the Sierra Club's canister, and built a rock monument that made "the Black Kaweah two feet higher than its imposing mate to the east." He fantasized that topographic maps might thereby need revising.[19]

Born in Philadelphia in 1885, Norman Clyde had studied the classics at Geneva College in Pennsylvania. After reading Muir's descriptions of the Sierra, Clyde went west, enrolled at the University of California, and in 1914 followed Muir into the mountains. He spent the next twenty-seven years climbing, earning his living by teaching classics in an Owens Valley high school. A restless, often impatient man, Clyde was fired from his teaching position in 1927, working thereafter as caretaker, writer, and guide for the Sierra Club. The Sierra Club dismissed him for poor judgment on a climb in 1941. But no one ever questioned his skills as a mountaineer. Said to possess "almost superhuman endurance," he made fifteen hundred climbs, of which two hundred were considered first ascents. An alpine machine, he set a speed record in climbing Mt. Shasta; climbed Mt. Whitney more than fifty times, using every conceivable route; and scaled thirty-six peaks in as many days in Glacier National Park.[20]

Making a first ascent of Glacier National Park's Mt. Wilbur, Clyde constructed a seven-foot cairn to memorialize a friend who had died there. The next morning, Clyde noted with satisfaction that "the monument could be seen with the naked eye from the veranda of Many Glacier Hotel, and the precipitous form of Mount Wilbur did not seem to tower so defiantly across the lucid waters of lovely Lake McDermott." He had conquered Mt. Wilbur by literally raising its height while figuratively making that height less awesome.[21] Today, maps of the Sierra include Norman Clyde Peak as well as Clyde Minaret, Clyde Glacier, and Clyde Meadow. Men such as Clyde were "forever seeking new problems of ascent against which they may match their skill and strength."[22] Nature was still an obstacle to be mastered.

Echoing the masculine conventions of romanticism in which he was well schooled, Clyde praised Mt. Humphreys for "its peculiarly forbidding, almost sinister aspect, as it towers in solitary grandeur above the desolate basin at its base [and] seems to hurl a challenge."[23] Men like Clyde coveted places they called chaotic, barren, even forlorn.[24] They imagined themselves confronting landscapes of "unrelieved waste," vast, shattered upheavals of "pale granite and frowning cliffs," places alien to the largely cultivated landscapes of everyday life.[25] A climber wrote of the Minarets, "When seen from the distance, they wear a black and sinister look. Precipitous walls rise to the sky-line, where beetling crags cut raggedly against the horizon . . . ; the scowling sheerness warns one off. The spirit of the mountain is the spirit of defiance, and in every aspect there is a challenge to the climber."[26] Visiting Enchanted Gorge near Mt. Goddard, another found "weirdly shaped fields and grotesque tongues of snow—the gaunt black ribs giving these peaks a savage, hungry look." His campfire became "a weird lantern, burning in the blackness of the gorge." The following day he and his companions caught a large rattlesnake and cut off its head and rattlers. He related with relish how the snake then wiggled its body over to its severed head. In a last venomous lunge, the head embedded its fangs in its own decapitated torso. Such grotesquery provided "unalloyed pleasure."[27]

The men of America's alpine clubs, much like early romantics, remained obsessed with history. They used the past to mold their own collective and individual identities and to establish a sense of place. Members of the Sierra Club, the Mazamas, and the Mountaineers were generally first-generation westerners eager to concretize, if not to rationalize, their right to a new land through the stories of their heroic forebears who had claimed the West's "mapless, trailless wilderness."[28] Their fascination with this history also afforded them the aesthetic experience of a past that was seemingly more exotic and, for men, more heroic than the settled present. Recalling Clarence King's description of Mt. Tyndall in the 1860s, a climber told with obvious sensual pleasure that "a strong desire seized us to discover . . . the precipices and the ice tongues which were the occasion of his [King's] thrills."[29] Norman Clyde was lauded as "a man of the wilderness in the mold of Daniel Boone," though his admirers were quick to add that he had been "schooled in the classics" and carried copies of Homer, Virgil, and Dante in his backpack.[30]

Each of the major clubs had its own climber-cum-historian who celebrated the conquest of America's mountains. Edmond Meany, president of the Mountaineers and a professor of history at the University of Washington, catalogued the origins of the largely Anglo-American surnames of the peaks of the Cascade Mountains. The Colorado Mountain Club's president, John L. Jerome Hart, chronicled for publication the early ascents and the naming of Colorado's fifty-four peaks higher than fourteen thousand feet. Clubs also published exploration narratives; the Colorado Mountain Club printed an edition of William H. Brewer's letters from the Rockies.[31] Farquhar edited and published Brewer's journal, narrated John Frémont's travels, wrote a history of the Sierra Nevada, and documented the origins of mountain place-names. Farquhar also edited the logs of Juan Rodriquez Cabrillo's 1542 explorations of California and Gabriel Moraga's 1806 expedition into the Sierra. The extent to which English-speaking alpinists now deemed the Spanish sufficiently European to be accorded a place in civilizing the west was thereby apparent.[32] For the most part, however, the clubs of the United States recorded Anglo-American history; after all, a Mountaineer explained, it had not been "until the Englishman appeared on the scene, enforced the Pax Britannia on the turbulent mountain races and opened the country, that real knowledge of the mountains and the climbing area began." The divide between themselves and "mountain races" was clear to those who still viewed Alpine and Himalayan peoples as superstitious and fearful of the heights of their own mountains.[33]

Meany, Hart, and Farquhar assembled substantial private libraries documenting the global history of alpine exploration. Hart's collection later formed the nucleus of the Mountaineering Library at the University of Colorado, in Boulder. The Sierra Club maintained libraries in San Francisco and Yosemite Valley; the Mazamas, in Portland; the Mountaineers, in Seattle; and the Appalachian Mountain Club, on the Boston Commons. The American Alpine Club kept a room in the New York Public Library while it completed the construction of its own building and library.

Stories of strong men echoed in these clubrooms. John White of the Sierra Club told of how, sitting by a campfire near the Kern River, he reminisced about years with the foreign legion in Greece, where he had first experienced "lust for the smell of wood smoke at twilight," squatting in a circle with men "like hungry dogs." He recalled: "We were meat-hungry warriors." He remembered hunting in British Columbia in 1898 and chasing "fanatical outlaws" into the mountains of the Philippines in 1902. Few of the men of the club who heard or read White's reminiscences had chased outlaws, but doubtless many enjoyed the analogies of legionnaire and camper, military action and sport, imperial successes and masculinity, especially when related by one who had been active in the club, had once been a colonel in the Philippine constabulary, and had served as the superintendent of Sequoia National Park.[34]

With their collections of maps and narratives, clubs and climbers also celebrated the stories of Anglophile conquests, old and new, in places as diverse as the Alps, the Caucasus, and the Himalayas. On the eve of Brigadier General C. G. Bruce's third assault on Mt. Everest in 1924, the Sierra Club told its members: "A world whose chief mountain is still unclimbed surely is not yet old and the little northern island which sends forth men to meet this challenge cannot have passed the meridian of its prowess and power."[35] According to the Appalachian Mountain Club, those who attempted Everest demonstrated that the British still possessed the spirit that had made the empire.[36] Everest's was the story of "the great deeds of great men" and offered models for young men to emulate.[37]

Not surprisingly, young men pursued unexplored country with unrelenting determination, finding it most often in the seeming barrenness above the timberline.[38] Then, too, one could always ignore evidence of life.[39] The narrator of an attempt on Mt. Everest was praised for not having mentioned the land and people of Tibet, for "such considerations are merely incident and introductory of the great epic."[40] The newly popular sport of mountain skiing also presented chances to act the explorer.[41] The Sierra in winter was pleasingly barren and inhospitable; a man wrote that "the majestic mass of an unnamed peak . . . bade [him] attempt its summit," where he experienced the "unique thrill in standing, the first . . . in midwinter and alone."[42] Another saw in the Sierra a "new wilderness of white," a landscape much "as it might have been a thousand years ago"; it was "easy to fancy yourself the first white man to tread this wilderness."[43]

Most importantly, however, new techniques of rock climbing presented opportunities to claim first ascents. People had long used ropes to lasso peaks or to tie themselves together and then attach the ropes onto a mountain. They had driven bolts and nails into cliffs, sometimes constructing roped paths up almost vertical planes. These systems had limitations. Nails might loosen, and climbers tethered together would be pulled down when someone fell. Technical rock climbing did not become a distinctive sport until Europeans perfected the piton, a flattened spike that could be driven into cracks, with an eye on the side through which a rope would be threaded. A secured piton made it possible to move up and down almost any surface, no matter how smooth or vertical. In 1930 Robert Underhill of the AMC demonstrated for western climbers how to use the piton and the carabiner, a steel, oval-shaped snap ring

Figure 32. Man on mountaintop recording an ascent in the Cascade Range, Washington, ca. 1920. Courtesy of Manuscripts, Special Collections, University Archives, University of Washington.

that could attach the rope to the piton without threading it through the eye. Since the rope is passed through the carabiner, steel connects the climbers with the piton, which joins them to the rock.[44] These technologies opened new geographies in the Canadian Rockies, but they also made first ascents possible even in familiar sites.[45] As Underhill, Clyde, Glen Dawson, and Jules Eichorn demonstrated on Temple Crag in the Sierra in 1931, objectives were now faces, pinnacles, rocks, towers, and spires.[46]

Figure 33. First ascent of Higher Cathedral Rock, Yosemite National Park, by Richard Leonard, Bestor Robinson, and Jules Eichorn in 1934. Photograph by Marjory Bridge Farquhar. Courtesy of University of California, Bancroft Library.

Rock climbing realized masculine and imperial expectations by bringing men into intimate physical contact with barren surfaces, where they could execute dangerous, measurable, and often delightfully visible feats. Yosemite Valley's two Cathedral Spires were assumed to be unconquered when in 1934 Jules Eichorn and Bay Area lawyers Bestor Robinson and Richard Leonard decided to scale the higher spire. They began with a reconnoitering trip. Using a microscope and protractor, they examined possible routes on maps and in photographs. They estimated the average slope of the spire's four faces at 81° and identified a massive overhang. One morning they finally started up. Wives and friends stood below, cheering and taking photographs. Inching upward, the climbers tackled the overhang, locating a crack too small for fingers or toes but large enough for a piton. They drove in twelve pitons and roped up to the top. As the sun set, they snapped pictures, raised the American flag, and built a cairn. Whymper and King would have been proud.

Eichorn, Robinson, and Leonard altered the terms of manly sport, however, when they announced afterward "that by the proper application of climbing technique, extremely difficult ascents can be made in safety."[47] They spoke of the strategic value of planning and of engineering spectacular feats with safety.[48] Using piton and carabiner not only to reach inaccessible heights but also to reduce risk, the Sierra Club's Rock Climbing Section perfected the technique of belaying the leader. With the belay, the fall of a leader could be gradually broken by others who were on the rope and who were firmly anchored to the rock. The men of the section practiced jumping off cliffs up to thirty feet high in order to test their skills.[49] The older practice had been to cut the line of a falling leader, partly to save others on the rope and partly because the force exerted on a falling body tied to a rope that was stopped quickly was deadly. Using the belay and nylon rope, which was more elastic than hemp, the momentum of a fallen leader could be slowed and finally stopped—a life could be saved.

The *Alpine Journal* of London initially dismissed the climbs made by Americans who used pitons for safety. British alpinists argued that, while it might be acceptable for a guide to use the piton, it was wrong for an amateur to do so. The Americans retorted that the mortality rate of Europeans was unacceptably high, not only because many of them did not use proper belaying techniques but also because they in fact too often climbed solo. This first generation of the Sierra Club's Rock Climbing Section generally favored small teams of three to seven members, each selected for a particular place on the rope according to his or her specific strengths, so that they functioned as one organic machine. Pitons and the belay made the sport remarkably safe.[50]

David Brower touted the American safety record and criticized the high fatality rates of German climbers, accusing them of deliberately flirting with death as though they were defying the authoritarianism of their state. Brower epitomized a new ethos during the 1930s, one every bit as masculine as earlier ones but with a more stoic face. Fear was dealt with in a matter-of-fact fashion, anticipating the demeanor of the World War II soldiers that Brower and his friends would soon become. They reduced risk by careful planning, technological aids, and efficient teamwork. Masculinity was now defined as the ability to foresee and manage all exigencies, even terror.

Brower began hiking in 1933 with Hervey Voge, of the Harvard Moun-

Figure 34. Sierra Club climbers, 1930s, left to right: Lewis Clark, William Colby, Richard Leonard, and David Brower. Courtesy of University of California, Bancroft Library.

taineering Club. Voge persuaded Brower to join the Sierra Club. Not much later, a close call on the northwest face of The Thumb prompted Brower to join the new Rock Climbing Section the club had established and to take instruction from Norman Clyde. The following summer Voge and Brower spent ten weeks in the Sierra, making sixty-five ascents—thirty "first ascents"—and correcting the Sierra Club's maps. Brower's long arms made him a good climber, and he took quickly to the new technologies of rope and piton.

In 1935, Brower offered five answers to the question, "Why do we climb?" In descending order of importance, the first was the satisfaction "of beholding a panorama from a vantage point, access to which had cost something in effort and training; of knowing that here is a frontier still; of being aloof, and yet in close communion" with others. The second was the pleasure of geological and biological inquiry. The third was the intrigue of topographic inquiry. Mocking Whymper, Brower listed the fourth as "the sport of rolling rocks down upon no one." The fifth he called "the esthetic enjoyment of the pictures of harsh cliffs, towering clouds and graceful trees."[51] By placing aesthetics last, Brower suggested the extent to which struggle remained central to the wilderness experience for men. His priorities were those of the masculine conventions of hard work, which incorporated a frontier ethos, and of a sense of separateness from nature that made possible human ascendancy over it.

Brower was one of eight men who in 1935 traveled to British Columbia to attack one of the great unconquered giants. Mt. Waddington's thirteen-thousand-foot vertical face, its glaciers, and its unpredictable weather had defeated a team of ten British and Canadian climbers. The new team included Voge, men from the British Columbia Mountaineering Club, and Eichorn, Leonard, and Robinson of the Sierra Club. The "Mt. of Mystery had cast her irresistible spell," and the climbers hurried on. With Mt. Waddington soaring six thousand feet above their base camp, they made Spartan-like preparations. They calculated caloric intake, shared sleeping bags, and plotted strategies, only to be forced into retreat by a blizzard and avalanches. The following year they returned, spending two weeks on snow and ice two thousand feet thick—only to have the Sierra Club's men lose to the two members of their own team from British Columbia, who raced to the top.[52]

The club's men decided to forsake the lost virgin in favor of the nearby Mt. Ball (named for the president of the Alpine Club of London). "Evil-looking seracs" lined the three-mile route to the second mountain. Dominating its surroundings in "majestic isolation," Mt. Ball was a worthy protagonist at 11,750 feet. This time they claimed their trophy, standing for a moment at the top. Beginning their descent, they found a "mysterious glacial world, a region cold, remote, vacuous. Dead walls sculptured from gray rock enclosed the scene. . . . Now and then a stone rattling down into the abyss punctuated the silence. A pallid moon hung in the leaden sky; no living thing was in sight." They basked in the monochromatic landscape; conquering this desolation was "a spiritual pleasure, . . . a stimulus to consciousness." They felt the peak's strength transmuted into themselves.[53] By using the techniques of the belay, climbers literally placed their lives in each other's hands. While the sport thrived on a "desire for solitude," as one man explained about climbers—both as fellow workers and as comrades in arms—it depended on "the exercise of comradeship."[54]

While small teams choreographed trajectories on the peaks, American clubs continued to sponsor collective climbs of one hundred or more men and women. Participants wrote of a natural order surfacing within the group, once it was away from the "veneer of conventions and artificialities." Wilderness purged one of greed and selfishness, making humanity as good as when God had created it. Referencing Kipling, a climber maintained that when "one's own personal qualities count," people learn "to know one another's naked souls."[55]

In 1929 a train equipped with "colonial cars" for horses, feed, and dunnage

Figure 35. Virginia Best (Adams) on Mt. Dana in the High Sierra with 16-mm movie camera and telephoto lens. Courtesy of Yosemite National Park Library, RL-14-361.

transported the Sierra Club, Mountaineers, and Mazamas into the Canadian Rockies to assault the forbidden peak called Ramparts, with the help of Swiss guides. Now, however, the expedition began with an Indian prayer. Clubs incorporated pseudo-Indian practices and language that western culture had long used to describe primitive peoples: *mystical, clan, tribe,* and *chief.*[56] Photographer Ansel Adams wrote to future wife Virginia Best, describing a Sierra Club outing in the Sierra and how much he had loved "the primal song of the wilderness . . . and the sympathy of ideals among members of the party—the simple food and glorious pagan activity—it is all a delicious procession of unearthly experiences discounting civilization and chronological time."[57] He called these "tribal treks" relics of prehistoric culture, staged in "a wild world of stone and snarling brush and raging waters."[58] The search for a harmonious communal state brought halting reappraisals of what climbers had earlier dismissed as primitive cultures

Since the mid-nineteenth century, when Edward Whymper had engraved ghastly scenes of the Matterhorn, climbers had used images to illustrate sublime landscapes and to memorialize the act of taking physical possession of them. Now climbing clubs, with their outing programs and high-quality publications, provided institutional settings in which landscape photography thrived. Mills College professor Cedric Wright vied with Ansel Adams to be chosen as the Sierra Club's photographer of the year. Wright frequently won.

Figure 36. Ansel Adams with his Brownie Box Camera on his first visit to Yosemite National Park, 1916. Courtesy of Yosemite National Park Library.

Wright's most popular photographs showed climbers encircling the evening campfire, the surrounding darkness being relieved only by their faces illuminated in the flames. Adams praised Wright's images of the campfire for recalling not just frontier days but "archaic vistas," writing: "There is a long history of man and fire. Something from the past descends and flows down silently on firewatchers like the dim racial memory of rain." Beyond the "chosen group of comprehending friends," few humans appeared in Wright's work and fewer still in Adams's photographs.[59] From J. N. LeConte and James McBride to Walter Huber, Philip Hyde, and David Brower, the men whose photographs appeared in the Sierra Club's publications showed barren landscapes. Only rarely did even birds or flowers relieve these images that celebrated the allure of desolation and the mythic virginity of the heights.

Figure 37. Members of the Sierra Club around a campfire in the Sierra Nevada, 1930s. Photograph by Cedric Wright. Courtesy of University of California, Bancroft Library.

These photographers followed the romantic conventions set in the heyday of American imperialism by landscape artists such as Thomas Moran and Albert Bierstadt, in whose paintings people were absent or insignificant and the topography was rendered in heroic proportions. Ironically, Wright himself urged photographers not to be obsessed with the "*big mountain* and the *big tree,* and with what *they* [themselves] *did.*" "When we see the exquisite charm of little intimate rivulets, their moss gardens and little separate worlds, is it any wonder to feel the need of being closer in spirit to this sort of thing, to collect into ourselves all the intimate touches of a mountain trip . . . and to try to translate the phrasings of mountains into the phrasings of music and human life?" Yet most of Wright's photographs showed stark panoramas in the style of nineteenth-century landscape painters. Even his studies of the swirling texture of tree bark, the arrested motion of glaciers, and the ripples of rivers were intense, dramatic, almost spiritual in import. When Wright, who played the violin for the High Trips' nightly campfires, translated his Sierra into "mountain music," he heard the strains of Beethoven and the words of Walt Whitman.[60]

Figure 38. Cedric Wright with his violin on a Sierra Club High Trip in the Sierra Nevada in the 1930s. Courtesy of University of California, Bancroft Library.

Adams described Wright's photographs as "dominated by a mystical symbolism of wilderness images, seen warmly and dramatically," rather than by the "impressionistic symbolisms of human images." Praising Wright's images of the club's campfires, Adams asked, "Must we be content with static compositions of landscapes and minutiae and occasional interpolations of humanity in appropriate minor situations?"[61] Adams was questioning the very traditions evident in his own most powerful and popular images. From those of the Palisades to the Sawtooth, his camera recorded topographic irregularities, places "vast, powerful, touched by the hand of God" but not by man. Even his intimate studies, such as those of the Sierra Juniper, were Ruskin-like portrayals of what he called a "magical union with beauty," a communion with the "great Presence."[62]

The conventions evident in the work of Wright and Adams differed from those women used when they described wilderness. Narrating the Sierra Club's 1934 High Trip through Tuolumne and Virginia Canyons, into Benson Lake, and up Matterhorn Peak, Ruth Currier wrote of joy and freedom, of warmth, of being "at home," and of the pleasure of companionship with 150 others.[63] In contrast, Wright narrated the identical 1934 trip as being a solitary, mystical jaunt. He spoke of penetrating the veil of the Sierra, a passage that soothed a self "long harassed by the insolent hammering" of the world of advertising and newspapers. He found himself "face to face with something quite different." Nature "invites analysis of herself." She was his partner in "a dreamlike communion," a "world-consciousness" that man did not share but from which he might learn. In nature "there is no veneer, . . . nothing but the real growth out of itself." Men there were "not troubled with the thought of other people's disapproval, the stamp of clique and caste, or the attainment of place and power." He looked to Whitman's "Leaves of Grass": "To her children the words of the eloquent dumb great mother [nature] never fail." This cosmic consciousness offered psychic liberation.[64] The earth's femininity continued to define her allure, as did her alien and palliative virtues.

The metaphor encouraged men to conflate territorial and erotic conquest. Novelist Thomas Wolfe portrayed the ascent of a mountain as the coming of age for his fifteen-year-old small-town character Mark Joyner. Moving through a winter landscape of desolate and savage bareness and stormy wind that seemed "to be the very spirit of the joy, the sorrow, and the wild desire he felt," the boy finally reached the top, finding there, "as nowhere else on earth some strange and powerful catharsis," a sublime moment portrayed by Wolfe with tender exaggeration:

> He was a child of fifteen no longer. He was the overlord of this great earth, and he looked down from the mountain top upon his native town, a conqueror . . . ; and he knew that everything on earth that he desired was his. Saddled in power upon the wild back of that maniacal force, not less wild, willful, and all-conquering than the steed that carried him, he would hold the kingdoms of the earth in fee, inhabit the world at his caprice, swoop in the darkness over mountains, rivers, plains, and cities, look . . . into a million rooms, and know all things at once, and lie in darkness in some lonely and forgotten place with a woman, lavish, wild, and secret as the earth.[65]

Imagining a similar sensual pleasure in her novel *Other Gods,* Pearl Buck depicts an alpinist she called Bert, intent on conquest in the Himalayas. Reaching the top of Pangbat Peak, Bert "stood, dizzy and panting," but as his head cleared, he found: "She was under his feet, this mountain! He was on her where nobody had ever been. He was doing something nobody had done before."[66]

These fictive characters, however, also offered glimpses into darker sides of masculinity and sport. Bert's wife asks of her husband's obsession, "What magic was there on a mountaintop? What satisfaction in the mere achievement of its height?" She conceded that her husband was not fearless, but "it was only that he saw nothing to achieve except, physically, the tops of mountains." Beyond that he was shallow, self-absorbed, and cruel in his indifference to all else but the mountain. Strong, agile, and handsome, he was as empty as his desire to reach the summit. Wolfe's boy, Mark Joyner, speaks with loathing of his own father's sexual lust and selfishness.[67] These ulterior faces of masculinity were evident to Buck and Wolfe by the mid- and late 1930s, but wilderness enthusiasts had for years written of men's need to exorcise demons.

Federal forester and Alaskan explorer Robert Marshall claimed that wilderness was essential to physical and psychological health. In wild places a man could develop "a body distinguished by soundness, stamina, and élan unknown among normal surroundings." Marshall hinted at the "terrific harm caused by suppressed desires," in his influential 1930 essay, "The Problem of Wilderness," published in *Scientific Monthly.* Modernity had brought choking monotony; the suppression of men's natural desire for adventure made them amenable "to the suggestion of any lurid diversions. Especially in battle, they imagine, will be found the glorious romance of futile dreams. And so they endorse war with enthusiasm and march away to stirring music, only to find their adventure a chimera, and the whole world miserable." In the 1906 essay "The Moral Equivalent of War," William James had argued that, while militarism was to be rejected, it did provide an outlet for violence and it preserved manly virtues of competence and hardihood. A moral equivalent that served the same purpose without bloodshed, James proposed, was for young men to enlist in an army of miners, fishermen, and road builders, not battling one another, but to subdue nature. After World War I, Marshall was in an even better position to advocate "peaceful stimulation," and he echoed Bertrand Russell: "Many men would cease to desire war if they had opportunities to risk their lives in Alpine climbing."[68]

Although others agreed that wilderness could safely channel dangerous impulses, by the late 1930s more men saw outdoor sport as preparation for combat. Their repetitive use of the word *attack* suggests that many men associated climbing with battle. *Attack* is indeed synonymous with words describing acts of grasping and gripping that are essential on steep grades and vertical walls, but constant repetition of the word brings to mind acts of aggression almost by reflex, as do other words commonly used: *assault, mastery,* and *conquest.* After one world war, and by then watching turmoil build in Europe, American society was placing a stronger emphasis on masculine identities in civic life and in outdoor sport.

Political scientist R. Claire Snyder tells us that citizens engage in rituals and behaviors that are important components of a republican state. She concludes that when war was seen as the most important function of a state and men alone engaged in war, society thought of men as the only true citizens.[69] According to society's expectations, particularly evident by the late 1930s, the purpose of mountaineering was to prepare men for war. Participants in the sport were encouraged to define masculinity according to the virtues of the warrior, from courage to comradeship. This reasoning by society in the 1930s may help explain why women lost visibility within outdoor sport and conservation.

While the darker sides of manliness and war were forgotten and "commissary sergeant" Florence Robinson stayed below, three young men in the desert made one of the most spectacular climbs that the Sierra Club had yet sponsored. Shiprock Peak rises 1,450 feet out of the New Mexican desert, an eroded, basaltic, volcanic skeleton, visible from Colorado to Arizona. Once considered an eerie parody of the arrival of the Europeans on the American shore, the monolith was named for its likeness to a frigate, with sails unfurled, entering the Navajo nation. Its "fantastic shapes and weird setting," barren walls, and seeming impregnability attracted climbers. Located on the Navajo reservation, the peak had already defeated the Canadian Alpine and Appalachian Mountain Clubs when the Sierra Club team of Brower, Bestor Robinson, storeowner Raffi Bedayan, and chemist John Dyer began charting their "offensive plays."[70]

The men arrived at their desert base in 1939 with one thousand feet of rope, dozens of pitons and carabiners of varying sizes, four anchor bolts, and drills. Sitting around a campfire and looking up at the rock silhouetted against the summer sky, they conjured up the analogy between their sport and a military action. "Like an army staff," they developed their "plans of attack deliberately and in detail," as was appropriate to an effort to conquer "a mountain which had repulsed dozens of previous attempts." Having completed "military preparations," they determined that "the attack would have to be along the lines of methodical siege tactics, instead of the now famous blitzkrieg,"

Figure 39. Shiprock, 1876. Lithograph by J. J. Young, entitled "The Needles, Looking South-Westerly," made from a sketch by J. S. Newberry and attached to the 1859 Geological Report by Professor J. S. Newberry (Washington, D.C., 1876). Courtesy of Museum of New Mexico.

maximizing the use of technology and minimizing risk. They rejected a chain of command, saying they were thereby honoring the United States as a free nation and their sport as an amalgam of camaraderie and individuality; the "composite mind" formed by competent individuals would make better choices than even a "brilliant leader." From intelligence officer to quartermaster, they were soldiers in a democratic army.

Their attack lasted four days. Bivouacking at night on the "battle front" high on Shiprock's face, they were surprised to see campfires dotting the surrounding desert below. They did not wonder at the purpose of the vigil but at what the Navajo "must have thought of their campfire just beneath the invincible summit of Shiprock." On the second day, Brower echoed the cry of World War I trench warfare: "We've gone over the top." Sitting on the mainmast of Shiprock, he and two comrades built a cairn to house a Sierra Club canister and yodeled at the joy of being in a place where only crows had landed previously.

The climbers were unaware of the implications of their action, but the ascent of Shiprock, because the peak was located on reservation land, was one of the last imperial adventures in the lower forty-eight states. Recognizing the covert territoriality of the ascent and the intrusiveness of piton, bolt, and drill,

Figure 40. "On the Mainmast." David Brower on Shiprock, New Mexico. Photograph by John Dyer, taken on the 1938 ascent of Shiprock. Courtesy of John Dyer.

Navajo authorities closed Shiprock and their other sacred mountains to out-siders. A month later, as the four conquerors penned their narratives, Ger-many invaded Poland, and Great Britain and France declared war.[71]

It had been clear to climbers as early as the turn of the century that their sport, if properly imagined, had as great a potential to prepare men for war as it did to sublimate aggressions. The civic spaces created by alpinism, in fact, helped meet the need of the American republic to ready an army of citizen soldiers. According to Snyder, "The Citizen Soldier functions as a prescriptive ideal that calls for male individuals to engage in the civic and martial prac-tices that constitute them as masculine republican citizens."[72] Rock climbing

Figure 41. Soldiers, headed by Col. Ray W. Barker, of the 30th Field Artillery, from Camp Roberts, on the 10 Mile Trail, Yosemite National Park, October 22, 1941. Photographed by R. H. Anderson. Courtesy of Yosemite National Park Library.

promoted the virtues of fraternity, camaraderie, sacrifice for the common good, control of fear, and participatory citizenship that could prepare American men to be soldiers.

When the United States declared war in 1941, many climbers entered the service, bringing valuable knowledge. Richard Leonard introduced the technology of the piton and carabiner to the U.S. Army and perfected the use of nylon rope. He familiarized the Army with the Sierra Club's experiences of surviving in the snow at temperatures below zero. Working under General George S. Patton in the California desert, Leonard helped prepare soldiers for survival in arid places. Using principles formulated on Sierra Club High Trips, Leonard also advised the army on jungle survival skills.[73]

The War Department saw that wilderness could serve as a practice battlefield. Much like the British, who prepared combat troops in the mountains of Wales and India, the United States trained its ski troopers, alpine fighters, paratroopers, and saboteurs on public lands. National parks and forests became defense installations, aircraft warning posts, and grounds for troop maneuvers. Robert Marshall's contention that wilderness built warriors rang true

Figure 42. Two howitzers in the inner parking area of Yosemite National Park, 30th Field Artillery, from Camp Roberts, October 22, 1941. Photograph by R. H. Anderson. Courtesy of Yosemite National Park Library.

when the South Rim of the Grand Canyon became a training ground, and troops readied combat skills on Mt. Rainier. The American Alpine Club and the U.S. Army collaborated on an expedition to the summit of Mt. McKinley in 1942 to secure Alaska against invasion and to test men and equipment under conditions of Arctic warfare. Drawing climbers from many clubs, the U.S. Army's Tenth Mountain Division fought in the Italian Alps. One soldier remarked in 1946 that fighting in Italy and Albania proved the truth of William Blake's line: "Great things are done when men and mountains meet."[74]

Historian Jackson Lears identifies a secular project he finds pervasive within the American upper and middle classes of this period and that he calls "the managerial ideal of personal efficiency." Men's tales of working with, while competing against, each other, nature, and themselves call this project to mind. According to Lears the project was part of a movement away from an evangelical religious ideal toward a liberal model of Protestant self-development. Religious longings were reincarnated in an "ethos of personal efficiency." For the men of the Sierra Club, for whom conventional religiosity appears to have played little role, mountains provided places that were appropriate to the exercise of this secular, yet strikingly spiritual, project—one that extended the ethos of personal efficiency into the possibility of salvation.

Interpersonal cooperation stood together with self-reliance as a distinctly masculine virtue. In their lives as engineers, lawyers, and professors, most clubmen were situated in organizations: universities, partnerships, corporate firms, and public agencies. They found congenial a leisure-time activity that fostered an identity defined by individual success, but was exercised within a context of teamwork that was as well suited for work as it was for war. Even the sublime moment of spiritual transcendence was personal yet rarely solitary. The sport provided an outlet for the tension that Lears identifies between a modern "managerial ethos," with its emphasis on strategies of control, and the desire for a personal, ecstatic experience of conversion.[75]

The seeming incompatibility of the needs that the masculine sublime served lay at the heart of its appeal. It defined yet reconciled tensions between masculinity and femininity—no matter that it erected new tensions between men and women. It also reconciled love and hate, freedom and belonging, pride and shame, courage and fear, independence and interdependence, control and release, war and peace. Mastery of mountains seemed to correlate with success in life and in battle; climbers set goals that they realized only against great odds, garnering tokens of accomplishment in their contests with nature, self, and others. They honed habits of self-discipline that they anticipated would make them powerful in the competitive marketplace of commodities and ideas, as well as in the military arena if need be. Climbing afforded men the opportunity to learn when to wield, and when to sheathe, the metaphoric swords of love, fear, and hate. At all levels, the sport forged a powerful vehicle for formulating and perpetuating masculine identities.

6

In Fire, Blossoms, and Blood

Speaking of wilderness, Aldo Leopold asked, "Wherein lies the goodness?"[1] Americans gave varied answers: companionship around an evening campfire, the enjoyment of wildflowers, the sport of hunting. Diverse and often gendered enthusiasms, many dating to the nineteenth century, influenced public policies during the period between the wars. Organizations led primarily by men lobbied federal agencies to preserve landscapes that reflected the masculine sublime, describing these places in the language of hunting grounds, frontiers, or battlefields. Groups in which women were influential also campaigned for wilderness but conceptualized it instead as redolent with life. Both women and men, particularly those who were naturalists, came together to study communities of life and to advocate ecology as a principle of land management. Although public officials were aware of feminine and of scientific perspectives, they found the masculine more congenial.

Nowhere were the divergence and the convergence of gendered identities clearer than in organizations that promoted outdoor sport for children. The number and success of such groups grew dramatically in the early twentieth century. In the United States, the Sons of Daniel Boone, founded in 1900, was followed in 1902 by the Woodcraft League of America, sponsored by Canadian naturalist Ernest Thompson Seton. Lieutenant-General Robert Baden-Powell, a hero of the Boer War, founded British scouting in 1908, which was shortly followed by the Boy Scouts of America. In 1911 the Girl Pioneers of America and the Camp Fire Girls were established by experts in recreation eager to capitalize on the widespread interest in scouting for girls. Prominent among the organizers were Luther Halsey Gulick and his wife, Charlotte Vetter Gulick; and Charlotte J. Farnsworth, preceptor of New York City's Horace Mann School. Gulick was head of the Department of Child Hygiene at the Russell Sage Foundation in New York City, and his wife operated a summer camp for girls in Maine. The Gulicks, Farnsworth, and other organizers believed that gender was biologically determined, but their rhetoric betrayed a fear that gender might be socially constructed. To reinforce the presumably essential nature of gender, they targeted adolescence as a period of psychological and physical rebirth during which it was critical that young people experience supervised play. Also active in the Boy Scouts, Luther Gulick denounced effeminacy in boys as rigorously as he denounced masculinity in girls.[2]

The beliefs and interests expressed by the Gulicks and other leaders of youth groups echoed themes common to early-twentieth-century mountaineering. The ideology of Boy Scouting reflected the assumptions of adult men. The Camp Fire Girls were instructed about nature in the manner of women who called the mountains "home." These parallels owed much to overlapping leaderships; patrons and organizers of youth groups were often climbers.[3] As well, the similarities were a result of shared middle- and upper-class social norms. Just as men and women usually described differently their experiences while engaging in the same sport, girls and boys were taught to attribute different meanings to outdoor life. Activities designed for children had the purpose of perpetuating physically separate spheres. The leaders of youth groups viewed natural settings as valuable for preparing each sex to fulfill its distinctive role in society. Middle-class expectations of appropriate masculine and feminine behaviors were shifting dramatically, however, making gender a near obsession for youth group leaders.

Charlotte Farnsworth told the *New York Sun* in June 1911: "We felt from the first that although this organization was to be a movement affiliated with the boy scouts it should be distinctive in its character and radically different in its point of view, just as girls are fundamentally different from boys in their instincts, interests, and ambitions." She continued, "The founders of the boy scouts recognize that hero worship is one of a boy's strongest incentives. They know that one of the ways to make a boy manly and courageous is by encouraging him to imitate the lives led by the pioneer heroes he admires. They know too that military regulation and organization make a peculiar appeal to a boy." Girls, on the other hand, were taught to be womanly. Although a girl was to experience rigorous outdoor sport and learn natural history, she would also be encouraged in her "love of beauty" and her appreciation of "form rather than speed or endurance in what she undertakes to do and in her ideals of service and helpfulness."[4]

In a similar vein, and even more bluntly, Luther Gulick told the fourteen women and six men gathered in 1911 for the first organizational meeting of the Camp Fire Girls:

> Some twenty years ago I was compelled to discover if possible what was meant by womanly and manly. . . . I followed the investigation through anatomy, physiology, psychology, ethics and religions. I believe that the keynote to the organization which appears to be before us is a clearer vision of this question. . . . I believe the keynote is here—that we wish to develop girls to be womanly as much as we desire men to be manly . . . ; to copy the Boy Scouts would be utterly and fundamentally evil. . . . We hate manly women and womanly men, but we all do love to have a woman who is thoroughly womanly, and then adds to that a splendid ability of service to the state—anything else you please, *on that foundation*.[5]

The two groups nevertheless developed much in common, perhaps because Luther's influence was offset by others. Independent-minded women who saw outdoor life as vital to liberating girls were active in organizing the Camp Fire Girls. Charlotte Gulick's presence continued to be strong after Luther's death in 1918. Until 1943 all of the executive directors were men, but most of those who served on the board of directors were women. Boy Scout and Camp Fire Girl leaders alike practiced social engineering and preached a secular gospel of the well-lived life. They depicted outdoor living and sport as essential to the formation of adult identities and told parents to send their children out of unhealthy cities and into the countryside for the summer.[6]

Perhaps the parents of boys heeded the experts' warning because they feared that families and schools had become bastions of feminine society. One historian asserts that the impetus behind the Boy Scouts was men's wish to remove boys from the "stifling atmosphere of the Edwardian home, where the feminine atmosphere would be all too likely to make a boy soft."[7] Only if boys were taken away from mothers, sequestered in the wild with other boys, could they become men. Although this explanation is persuasive, it ignores the parallel logic of the girls' groups: girls, too, were considered isolated, cloistered, and even smothered in the Edwardian home, rendering them unprepared for modern life. For the Gulicks, Charlotte Farnsworth, and other youth leaders, boys and girls alike needed to elude both mothers and fathers, to escape not only female-dominated institutions but the crippling bonds of a dying Victorian culture.

Turn-of-the-century child psychologists argued that only under professional supervision, in the open air, and under circumstances that integrated work and play could boys and girls be properly socialized to become efficient and fulfilled men and women. Youth groups offered regimes of physical fitness, outdoor sport, moral guidance, and instruction in natural history. Reflecting the "whole child" movement, experts preached the value of camping and hiking with peers for as long as ten weeks as the best path to character development. Across the nation, from the White Mountains to the Sierra, young people trekked up mountains and crossed rugged terrains.

The leaders of the Camp Fire Girls and the Boy Scouts acknowledged the importance of individualism as well as of teamwork. They spoke of freeing children from the mores of home and city, but they also fostered discipline. Both groups were hierarchically structured, almost authoritarian. Regimentation was designed to prepare boys for military service and the industrial workforce and to prepare girls for motherhood and service to the community. According to Luther Gulick, women had acquired the undesirable trait of independence because they had been sequestered in their homes; not having been trained in collective obedience, as men had, women lacked the habits necessary for functioning within organizations.[8]

Camp counselors taught girls the values of routine, punctuality, self-control, patriotism, and interpersonal skills. The militarism of the Boy Scouts was apparent in their uniforms, salutes, and drills; but the Camp Fire Girls also had uniforms, rituals, mottoes, and code words, and they received physical training. The honorary badges given to the boys were paralleled in the colorful wooden beads awarded to the girls, which they wore around their necks or sewed onto their uniforms. The girl's creed was: "We glorify work because through work we are free." The motto was selected to train girls for gainful employment, efficient homemaking, and public service.[9]

Although boys and girls were assigned similar activities, the camping, handcrafts, hiking, and nature study they shared were given different meanings. The campfire lay at the heart of the communal rituals of both. The boys, however, were told that fire stood for the camaraderie of the battlefield, factory, and office, and the girls learned that fire represented hearth and home. The two groups diverged as well in their uses of history. Hoping to produce citizens suitable for soldiering, Boy Scout leaders portrayed the outdoors as a frontier, if not an imperial adventure, with the natural world a stage on which to rehearse manhood.[10] For the Camp Fire Girls, there were no fantasies of territorial conquest, no colonial heroes to emulate, no Daniel Boones or Boer Wars. Although Seton's Woodcraft League proved short-lived, native crafts and lore were an enduring part of the Boy Scouts of America. It was the Camp Fire Girls, however, who did the most to incorporate a vision of Native American lore. The girls memorized pseudo-Indian words and took symbolic names, such as "Warchahwashtay," meaning "pretty flower." They sewed leather ceremonial dresses, paddled canoes with oars marked for the seasons of the moon, and erected encampments of the "Maiden chiefs of many nations." On the eve of World War I, the organization adopted the uniform of a white middy blouse, red necktie, and blue bloomers, but it retained its "Indian" rituals.[11]

The analogy between young women and Native Americans seemed appropriate. In retrospect, the similarity is logical given their shared history of political disenfranchisement. Dominant cultural assumptions ascribed both to the Native American and to other women an innate affinity with the earth; the leaders of the Camp Fire Girls may well have visualized women and Native Americans as "natural ecologists." In the hands of club leaders, the "Indian" maiden became a model for instructing girls of all social classes in the "naturalness" of what amounted to Victorian prescriptions of feminine behavior, including vows of purity and pledges of service. In the end, the values girls were to take from nature were those of the purity of the mountain lakes, of duty, and of sacrifice. The biological imperative of motherhood dictated that "the bearing and rearing of children has always been the first duty of most women, and that must always continue to be. This involves service, constant service, self-forgetfulness and always service."[12] Good health groomed boys to be workers and fighters; girls were to value their bodies for reproduction and nurturing.

Even though the Camp Fire Girls emphasized traditional values, the organization also liberally defined women's sphere. The Camp Fire Girls worked to promote and channel feminine liberties "to prove that girls and women could be independent of men when need arose," as happened during a war.[13] By learning survival in the wild, girls were to grow in self-confidence and physical prowess. The group's motto, WO-HE-LO, called for mastery of themselves and their environments through work, health, and love. By blending the language of autonomy with that of domesticity, the organization, its girls, and their parents negotiated changing expectations of womanhood, as did those women who donned pants in the mountains and found home there.[14]

Camp Fire Girl leaders urged their charges to pattern themselves after Jane Addams, a member of its board of directors and founder of Chicago's Hull House. As a person to emulate, Addams served the group well; according to one historian, she was a "living link between past and present, embodying the

Figure 43. Line drawing from frontispiece of Jane L. Stewart's Camp Fire Girls on the March *(Akron, Ohio: Saalfield, 1914).*

virtues of Victorian womanhood while simultaneously providing a model of female leadership in public life."[15] Combining their new physical mobility with conventional feminine values, the girls could defend natural environments and improve those that human beings had constructed. Girls were to campaign for sanitation and health reforms and to offset with amenities the drabness and lifelessness of modern cities. By helping to provide areas for outdoor recreation, they could make Americans who grew up in cities more aware of natural history.

The girls learned domestic skills in the wild: nature lore, woodcraft, cooking, mending, and preparing campsites. Integral to this message was their presumed role as tender of the campfire. Without fire, that primordial "preserver of life," a house was dark and cold; flames were the heart of a "woman's home and woman's happiness." Fanning these flames on outdoor hearths was a feminine duty, one that sanctioned women's right to be in the wilderness and have a voice in its fate.[16]

Sierra Club president Aurelia Harwood and its director, Aurelia Henry Reinhardt, were both patrons of the Camp Fire Girls, viewing the organization as empowering for women by associating them with nature and as

protecting nature by exploiting its affinity with womanhood. Nurturing society and the natural world, women and girls would themselves be nurtured.
Harwood and Reinhardt encouraged girls to participate in tree planting programs, to build birdhouses, and to construct small check dams to improve
fish habitats. The Gulicks, too, endorsed the "conservation of streams, birds,
trees, and parks," calling it an act of patriotism. As the Gulicks's daughter
Frances said, the group stood for "Ye who love . . . the thunder of the mountains." Such organizations encouraged appreciation of landscapes and promoted conservation. The Boy Scouts and the Camp Fire Girls lobbied for the
establishment of national parks and forests, including wilderness areas. The
groups also promoted public receptivity to conservation by reaching large
numbers of children as well as their parents. By 1923, the Camp Fire Girls alone
had 160,000 members. In the mere dozen years since it had been founded, it
had influenced the lives of 600,000 girls.[17] Their voices combined with those
of other special-interest groups to promote state and federal conservation during the interwar period.

The association between "gendered consciousness," outdoor sport, and
conservation was not unique to youth groups. Organized hunters drew upon
masculine identities in the manner of Boy Scout leaders and male climbers.
Sportsmen had been one of the earliest groups to champion the conservation
of game and of forests, and they had lobbied for the establishment of national
forests, parks, and wildlife refuges.[18]

Convinced that these established public areas could not offer men the true
wilderness experience, however, Aldo Leopold set out in the 1920s to marshal
sportsmen to urge the Forest Service to protect some of its wilderness.
Leopold had for years managed logging operations, mining, and grazing in
the national forests of the Southwest. He also enjoyed hunting, riding horseback, and studying natural history. He became aware of the growing tide of
visitors and the burgeoning of new roads curving around and through the
mountains. In the national forests alone, which held the highest western
ranges, thirty-five thousand miles of roads were built between 1919 and 1927.

"What shall we do with our mountains?" became a popular debate in the
heyday of the Ford. Even those interested in protecting nature gave differing answers. Some liked the automobile because it facilitated public use of public land,
democratizing America's scenic and wild sites and gaining political support for
preservation. The National Park Service also favored increased vehicular access to parks and did not look askance at the idea, promoted by automobile
clubs, of a national-park-to-national-park highway that would slice through
mountain ranges of the eastern and the western United States. Leopold's own

agency, the U.S. Forest Service, considered constructing a Sierra Highway to fol-low the Muir Trail north from the Kings River, with laterals at Piute Pass and Mammoth Pass. Federal officials entertained proposals for a road to the top of Mt. Whitney and for a tramway and a cableway up Oregon's Mt. Hood.[19]

A few Forest Service rangers, notably Colorado's Arthur Carhart, urged that portions of national forests in the Rocky Mountains, the Quetico-Superior Boundary Waters Canoe Area, the Cascade Mountains, and the Sierra Nevada be designated as roadless areas. In 1924, Leopold asked the Forest Service to set aside half a million acres of national forest lands in the headwaters of New Mexico's Gila River as "wilderness hunting grounds," with a similar reserve in the Rockies.[20] His "wilderness hunting grounds" were to be "a continuous stretch of country preserved in its natural state, open to lawful hunting and fishing, big enough to absorb a two-week pack trip, and kept devoid of roads, artificial trails, cottages, or other works of man."[21] He visualized these grounds as serving the small minority of men who stalked game species that required space and seclusion: grizzlies, mountain sheep, elk, turkey, and grouse.[22]

Leopold's wilderness was the landscape of frontier America. "Who shall say that the diamond hitch and the tumpline are not as much worth conserving as the black-tail buck or the moose?" he asked.[23] In Leopold's "The Romance of the March of Empire," race and environment played equal roles. Describ-ing how "our fathers" had won the West, he quoted his poem:

> We pitched our tents where the buffalo feed,
> Unheard of streams were our flagons;
> And we sowed our sons like the apple seed
> In the trail of the prairie wagons.[24]

Men of strong thirst were Leopold's forefathers. He echoed Theodore Roo-sevelt's talk of a virile young race, of ancestors who had been great hunters, fight-ers, and breeders. Leopold wanted America's sons to experience in full meas-ure that which had nourished their sires. Like Roosevelt, Leopold believed that the primary criteria of civilization had been its "ability to conquer the wilder-ness and convert it to economic use." Hence the pioneer environment had de-termined the character of national development for three centuries; coupled with "our racial stocks, it is the very stuff America is made of." Should we now, he asked rhetorically, "exterminate this thing that made us American?"[25]

Following the reasoning that historian Frederick Jackson Turner had put forward in the 1890s, Leopold argued that the pioneer environment had pro-moted individualism, the ability to organize, intellectual curiosity, practicality, "a lack of subservience to stiff social forms," and "an intolerance of drones." Leopold wanted the mountains saved to perpetuate the "social value in primitive modes of travel and subsistence, such as exploration trips by pack-train or canoe." Unless some mountains remained wild, he feared the day when "the diamond hitch will be merely rope, and Kit Carson and Jim Bridger will be names in a history lesson. Rendezvous will be French for 'date,' and Forty-Nine will be the number preceding fifty. And thenceforth the march of empire will be a matter of gasoline and four-wheel brakes." The instinct to hunt, once used for survival, now served social and ethical ends. Because he was aware of the ethical and historical significance of his actions, the modern hunter was superior to the pioneer. Leopold valued outdoor sport, as alpinists did, for the deliberate attention it demanded and because people undertook it without thought of remuneration. He warned that if we cannot balance the expansion of industry with the protection of recreational resources, "then surely there is an impotence in our vaunted Americanism that augurs ill for our future."[26]

Embedded in Leopold's rhetoric were assumptions about manhood, race, and lineage. In his effort to promote wilderness protection, he appealed to men, ignoring women alpinists, women hunters, Native Americans, frontier women, and non-Nordic pioneers. He wrote, "Anthropologists tell us that we, the Nordic, have a racial genius for pioneering, surpassing all other races in ability to reduce the wilderness to possession."[27] Leopold assumed that the sport of hunting was uniquely and historically characteristic of the British and their North American descendants. In Leopold's wilderness, Anglo-American men would be able to realize a racial imperative to emulate their fathers. "Saturday morning," Leopold wrote of the American man of the city, "he stands like a god, directing the wheels of industry that have dominion over the earth. Saturday afternoon he is playing golf on a kindly greensward. Saturday evening he may till a homely garden. . . . And if, once in a while, he has the opportunity to flee the city, throw a diamond hitch upon a pack-mule, and disappear into the wilderness of the Covered Wagon Days . . . , [he is] much more civilized . . . , one more kind of a man—a pioneer." Wilderness was the antidote to the tame landscapes of golf links, home, and garden. The biggest threat to men was what Leopold called the "soft 'improvements'" epitomized by the motorcar; he quoted Shakespeare: "For virtue, grown into a pleurisy / Dies of its own too-much."[28]

Like outdoor enthusiasts from Edward Whymper to Theodore Roosevelt, Leopold feared ease produced effeminacy in men that could cripple western civilization. Leopold looked to the remedial force of physicality and savagery. He echoed the imperial language of Baden-Powell and Rudyard Kipling, who had asked, "Are we men of The Blood?" For Leopold, "The well-to-do sportsmen go to Alaska, or British Columbia, or Africa, or Siberia in search of the wilderness and the life and hardy sports that go with it." Each man pushed to the "Back of Beyond" and returned to tell of the "Great Adventure" with zest, not because of his trophy ("the tusk of an elephant or the hide of the brown bear"), but because he had "proved himself to be still another kind of man than his friends gave him credit for." He had "met the test. He has justified the Blood of the Conquerors." American men of "moderate means" required the opportunity, available to the British Empire's big game hunters, to test themselves in the mountains of New Mexico, Colorado, or Wyoming.[29] Leopold echoed the admiration for British imperialism found in the Boy Scouts and in climbing clubs, but his language also represented a distinctively American nostalgia.

For Leopold, saving wilderness areas addressed a problem that the narrative of western history raised: the American people were destroying the very frontier condition that had defined them.[30] Americans of European descent had long assumed that their personal and national identities had been forged in the process of conquering uncivilized, if not uninhabited, lands. As early as the seventeenth century, a few thoughtful individuals had recognized the paradox inherent in admiring the creative force of a frontier. Advocates of wilderness conservation believed that they could resolve this dilemma of national genesis. Men could continue to act as frontiersmen, at least on occasion, despite what Frederick Jackson Turner had persuasively written of as the closing of the western frontier.

Although Leopold spoke of his longing for "a blank spot on the map," his vision was not truly that of a terra incognita. Roads had not yet penetrated the box canyons of the Gila, but cattle grazed there. Leopold reasoned that the presence of livestock was compatible with recreation "because of the interest which attaches to cattle grazing operations under frontier conditions." The experience of wilderness was threatened not by cows, but by the tourists, who "want all the automobile roads, summer hotels, graded trails, and other modern conveniences that we can give them." His hunting grounds were for the minority of men who were not Babbitts, who sought something other than "roads, Fords, and summer boarders."[31] Leopold urged those who enjoyed the pack country experience to lobby the Forest Service for a national system of hunting grounds. "Unless the wilderness idea represents the mandate of an organized, fighting and voting body of far-seeing Americans . . . ," it would fail.[32] Local hunting clubs and national groups—the Boone and Crockett Club, among others—seconded his proposal, as did some Forest Service officials.

In June 1924, two years after Leopold first made his plan public, the Forest Service set aside 755,000 acres in the upper watershed of the Gila as a primitive area and began considering other sites. Historians have viewed this action with a jaundiced eye. The upper Gila had little economic value beyond grazing, which continued despite the "wilderness" designation. The only use that was categorically outlawed was the roadway. Moreover, the service had been motivated to establish the area out of fear that Congress would transfer such scenic sites to the jurisdiction of the new National Park Service. On the other hand, the American Forestry Association and many Forest Service rangers were receptive to Leopold's cause. The service's chief, William Greeley, agreed that men needed wilderness, defining it as "God's country . . . exactly as it was when Jim Bridger discovered it."[33]

Hunters had preferred the status of "national forest" to that of "national park" even before Leopold proposed his wilderness hunting grounds, because hunting was permitted in the forests. Not all outdoor groups, however, shared this preference. The nation's alpine clubs initially said little about the Gila Primitive Area or similar proposals, although they should have found appealing Leopold's nostalgic declaration: "I am glad I shall never be young without wild country to be young in. Of what avail are forty freedoms without a blank spot on the map?"[34] In fact, they came to support the designation of primitive areas slowly.[35] Hunting held little interest for most climbers; mining, grazing, and dams held even less. To protect the most scenic sites of the high ranges from grazing, mining, and waterpower developments—all of which were permitted in the primitive areas that the U.S. Department of Agriculture's Forest Service controlled—alpine groups looked to the small but growing system of national parks administered by the U.S. Department of the Interior.

A young, energetic California businessman, Stephen Mather, had become interested in the national parks on Sierra Club High Trips, first up Mt. Rainier in 1905 and then through the Kern Canyon of the Sierra in 1912. Dismayed at the minimal upkeep of the parks, Mather complained to the secretary of the interior, who responded by challenging Mather to come to Washington to assume responsibility for managing the parks. When Mather accepted in 1915, one of his first actions was to ask climbing clubs to help federal officials construct trail systems and to lobby Congress to establish an agency within the Department of the Interior to administer the parks. He recognized that these clubs possessed unique knowledge of the mountains and valleys where the parks were located, but he also knew that two years earlier, Congress had barred federal agencies from using public funds to lobby in their own behalf.

Courting friendly constituencies was the obvious path for Mather to pursue. Congress finally established the National Park Service in 1916, responding to the many interest groups that lobbied legislators, including women's groups, conservation organizations, and outdoor clubs.

Climbers had long pressed for parks to protect the scenic wonders of their regional mountains: the Appalachian Mountain Club had lobbied for the White Mountains; the Oregon Alpine Club and the Mazamas, for Crater Lake and Mt. McKinley National Parks; the Mountaineers, for Mt. Rainier National Park; Muir, for Yosemite National Park; and the Sierra Club, for Sequoia and General Grant National Parks. When Representative Frank Barbour of California introduced legislation to expand Sequoia National Park in the 1920s, Mather turned to, and received help from, all these clubs. He also had the support of the National Parks Association, a nonprofit advocacy group he had established in Washington in 1919 to create a national network of supporters. Among its forty-five-member governing council, three were women, from garden clubs and the General Federation of Women's Clubs, and forty-two were men: hunters, naturalists, Boy Scouts, and climbers.[36]

In 1924 the Sierra Club drew up a map that would accompany Barbour's bill to enlarge Sequoia National Park by including the headwaters of the Middle and South Forks of the Kings River and the Kern River. Club leaders maintained that this was "the most stupendously impressive scenery to be found," with the highest peaks, the most jagged rocks, the sheerest cliffs, and the deepest abysses. The canyons of the Kings and the Kern Rivers were the types of sublime wilderness that club members had long enjoyed.[37] The Mazamas, the Mountaineers, the Appalachian Mountain Club, the National Parks Association, women's organizations, naturalists, wildlife activists, and youth groups, together with the Sierra Club, pressed for the enlarged Sequoia National Park.

In 1926 Congress passed, and President Coolidge signed, the legislation that added to the park the High Sierra region at the head of the Kaweah and Kern Rivers and the summit of Mt. Whitney, more than doubling the size of Sequoia National Park.[38] One side of Mt. Whitney, the Kings River Canyon, and the watershed of the Middle Fork of the Kings River, however, had remained with the Forest Service. The opposition of stockmen, herders, waterpower interests, and some hunters had been telling. At Barbour's suggestion, the Sierra Club had persuaded the Forest Service to accept ninety-seven acres of merchantable timber in the Sierra in exchange for 953 acres of mountainous and commercially less valuable forest for the park. Despite this concession, the Park Service, fearing it would nonetheless lose the bill, had wired an eleventh-hour query asking the Sierra Club and other groups for approval to delete

Kings Canyon and the headwaters of the Middle Fork of the Kings River. The club reluctantly agreed, and Congress passed the bill.[39]

Endorsing the idea of wilderness and supported by a Forest Service apprehensive of losing more land in the Sierra, the Cascades, the Rockies, and the Southwest, some district rangers established classified areas similar to the Gila Primitive Area. In 1929 the Forest Service established an administrative mechanism to facilitate the designation of such areas. Generally vast and roadless, these areas seemed to some conservationists to offer a more genuine wilderness experience than did parks. Because Forest Service regulations did not ban grazing, mining, or waterpower developments, however, other wilderness advocates still viewed "national park" status as preferable to "classified" status in the national forests. Climbing clubs endorsed the Forest Service's classified areas while continuing to campaign for additional national park lands. Youth groups, some conservationists, and even some sportsmen added their support.

While men controlled the governance of the Boy Scouts and the alpine and hunting groups that advocated wilderness protection, women had a substantial voice in other associations that also lobbied for wilderness areas and parks. Naturalists and wildflower protectionists were prominent among them. Elizabeth Gertrude Knight Britton founded the Wild Flower Preservation Society in 1902. Anchored by the New York Botanical Garden, the society flourished nationally until the mid-1920s, when the garden developed financial troubles and Elizabeth's husband, Nathaniel Lord Britton, resigned as its director.[40] In 1917, E. Lucy Braun, a young professor of botany at the University of Cincinnati who had just completed her dissertation at Ohio State University, created an Ohio chapter of the Wild Flower Preservation Society. By the mid-1920s Braun had assumed national leadership of the society.[41] Other states, most notably Wisconsin and Missouri, soon established chapters as well and met annually in Cincinnati to coordinate strategies.

Determinedly preservationist and political, Braun's Wild Flower Preservation Society established headquarters in Washington to lobby Congress and state legislators for laws protecting plant life. The society published its objectives in 1924: "(1) To encourage by every possible means the preservation and protection of native plants; (2) To secure the better enforcement of existing laws governing such preservation; (3) To introduce such further legislation" as necessary. According to the founders: "One of our purposes is to study the flowers in their native homes, to know them, to love them, and to search out their habits and life histories, but our greater purpose revolves around the central idea of preservation (or conservation, if you prefer), a purpose we should never lose sight of." Although the Wild Flower Preservation Society advanced a distinctly feminine perspective, its constituency was mixed. Women founded the society and were well represented among the members, but men also played vital roles in the movement.[42]

In their campaigns, wildflower leagues and societies were joined by other groups that reflected feminine perspectives, whether or not their memberships were mixed: the General Federation of Women's Clubs, the Garden Clubs of America, the California Roadside Council, native plant societies, and the Camp Fire Girls. California, Vermont, Connecticut, Massachusetts, Maryland, and Wisconsin responded to these voices by enacting legislation in the 1920s to protect wildflowers. The members of these organizations also lobbied for native plant sanctuaries, state parks, and roadside protection for native vegetation, and they lobbied against hydroelectric developments that threatened flowered valleys. The new understanding that many plants were becoming endangered made compelling the need to save habitats, whether human or wild.[43] These naturalists, many of whom were women, shaped a vision of the natural landscape that favored plant life, and they helped to formulate a conservation ideology that prized not only wilderness but also the countryside where human beings and wildlife coexisted.

The Wild Flower Preservation Society was one of the first organizations to nationally endorse the Forest Service's plans for primitive and wilderness areas. Wildflower protectionists understood that these areas would be sizable, that human influence would modify them as little as possible, and that only primitive modes of travel and of outdoor life would be permitted. They emphasized, however, that the areas were important primarily as places where "representation[s] of the wealth of wild life with which this country was originally endowed may be preserved for all time." Their wilderness was the ideal native plant sanctuary.[44] Their vision differed from that of most hunters, most men who climbed, and most foresters. The desire to protect wildflowers impelled naturalists toward an ecological perspective rare even among conservationists. Wildflower literature drove home the message that every plant requires soil, moisture, and associations with compatible plants and that even a subtle alteration in any of these was detrimental to its survival. The society pointed out that nothing had been studied "of the ecology of most of our wild flowers and their response to changing soil and moisture conditions." As early as 1925 the society argued for "complete ecological studies of the flowers themselves."[45]

Ecology has become such a pervasive field of study that it is difficult to remember its relatively recent origin as a discipline within biology that studies communities and that treats the relationships among organisms and their environments. Ernst Haeckel is credited with first suggesting, in the late 1860s, that a science was needed to study organisms in their environments. In 1873 he called it "*Oekologie*," translating the Greek into his native German. The principles of ecology were first explored fully in connection with plants because they were so clearly based in the specifics of soil, topography, and community. At the turn of the century, Henry C. Cowles studied the sand dunes of Lake Michigan and the ecology of the Chicago area, the causes of vegetative cycles, and the influence of underlying rocks on vegetation. Others examined discrete plant zones. Perhaps the best known of the early ecologists was Frederick Clements, who, during the second decade of the twentieth century, detailed plant formations, plant succession, and biological climax. Ecology reached a broader scientific audience in the 1920s with Charles Elton's *Animal Ecology* and Herbert Stoddard's studies of quail.[46]

Women were among the first ecologists. Trained in chemistry at the Massachusetts Institute of Technology, Ellen Swallow Richards built upon her analyses of water pollution to campaign in the 1870s for an accredited, interdisciplinary science of environment. Tracing Haeckel's "*Oekologie*" to the Greek word *oik*, for "household or family," with "*oe*" making it universal, she understood him as having suggested a science of "everyone's house environment." In 1892 she publicly proposed the discipline of Oekology as a science of life. Her efforts were foundational for the field of "home economics." Few displayed more readily the compatibility of the natural sciences and feminine perspectives than Richards, with her vision of the human body operating within the physical environment.[47]

Edith Schwartz Clements, wife of Frederick Clements and one of the first women to receive a doctorate in ecology (from the University of Nebraska in 1904), went on to work with the Carnegie Institution in the 1920s. She wrote scientific articles and guides to the wildflower communities of differing regions of the United States, including the Sierra Nevada.[48] Ohio State University published Federica Detmers's *Ecological Study of Buckeye Lake* in 1912 and E. Lucy Braun's dissertation, *The Physiographic Ecology of the Cincinnati Region*, four years later.[49] Well aware of the work of Cowles, the Clementses, and the Detmers, Braun emphasized the intimate relationship between plant geography and topographic, soil, and geologic formations.

Women's interest in botanical studies, gardening, and mountaineering led some to become early advocates of the principles of ecology and to campaign for the application of its scientific principles to wildflower protection. The word *ecology* held a special meaning for women. Its Greek roots in the words for "household" and "study" helped shape their views of their work.[50] Braun herself argued for the connections among ecology, domesticity, and biological reproduction. She recognized that all environmental factors were essential to wild plants: soil conditions, weather, degrees of slope, and tree canopies. She urged people to consider the long-term implications of "disturbing nature's balance." If you clear vegetation off one slope of a ravine, she said, but leave the other undisturbed, even the plants on the untouched side will be adversely affected: the heat of the sun will not be well buffered, the soil will become drier, humus will form more slowly, and less snow will blanket the plants during the winter.

> The plant cannot be separated—successfully—from its environment. It is a part of it. The air which bathes its leaves, the air which enters its pores, is vital to the plant's continued life. Existence, under unnatural and uncongenial surroundings, is not life. Life must include reproduction; and it is only under congenial surroundings that plants reproduce—that is, that the community continues to flourish.

She framed her cause in a language of domesticity that reflected her own identity and that of the audiences she anticipated would be receptive to her message: women's clubs, mothers, and children. "If we wish to keep our wild flowers," she warned, "we must keep their homes. We must save homes large enough to keep home conditions congenial. It is only thus that we, and the future generations, may continue to enjoy nature's inimitable groupings."[51]

Decades would pass before the idea that nature had rights would become pervasive within mainstream movements in behalf of wilderness and wildlife.[52] As early as 1924, however, the General Federation of Women's Clubs and the Wild Flower Preservation Society had asked: "Has the wild flower any rights? Can it not call upon the state for legal protection?" Members answered their own question angrily, "Wild flowers have no legal rights. For trees the protection of the state may be invoked because with the loss of tree cover, the whole state will suffer. Otherwise the plant is the property of the owner of the land in which it is rooted, and this ownership is established by federal laws."[53] These members grasped the need to save representative plant communities and to safeguard ecosystems as diverse as those of desert and prairie.

These groups recognized, too, the limitations of existing national forests and parks. The multiple uses practiced in the forests, particularly logging, destroyed communities of life, but heavy recreational uses—roads, hotels, gas stations, souvenir shops—also damaged wild plants in the national parks. They advocated that state and federal sanctuaries truly be dedicated to protecting communities of life in their natural state and that previous damage to the sanctuaries be repaired. Wildflower advocates recognized the need for remedial human intervention in natural landscapes, and they urged that research be undertaken into the propagation of wild species, the reconstruction of ecological systems, and the regeneration of plant communities.[54]

Movements to save other elements of wildlife also developed an acute consciousness of the importance of the "balance of nature" in public policy. Here, too, gender played a role, but interest in natural history was the strongest factor. Advocates of nature sanctuaries and state parks included John Campbell Merriam, paleontologist and president of California's Save-the-Redwoods League, an organization that was led by men but that depended heavily on the support and participation of women. Both sexes fought on behalf of birds. George Bird Grinnell established the Audubon Society in the 1870s to campaign against the female fashion of wearing feathers. His group languished, but a loose network of state and local Audubon Societies sprang up across the country. Separate from this network and more powerful, the National Association of Audubon Societies was established in New York City in 1901. It acquired thirty-two sanctuaries nationwide, lobbied for the protection of wild birds and animals, sponsored educational programs, and cooperated with federal and state officials and private groups. The national association and its state and local affiliates were successful because they appealed to men (most of its officers were male) as well as to women. Women had begun to organize state and local Audubon Societies in 1896, and they remained strong leaders at those levels.[55] By 1939 the president emeritus, president, first and second vice presidents, secretary, and curator of the Audubon Society of Los Angeles were all women.

The Audubon movement drew support from naturalists, animal rights activists, birders, and hunters. Given its diverse constituencies, a schism was perhaps inevitable. Hunters and fishermen fought to protect game species, but the involvement of others, particularly women, often grew out of a more humane impulse. Some naturalists emphasized the need to preserve all species (not just game species) and opposed blood sports; others were themselves sportsmen.[56] In the early 1930s, Rosalie Edge, a New York member, accused the National Association of Audubon Societies of mismanaging its wildlife sanctuaries. She charged it with killing 289,940 mink, muskrat, raccoon, opossum, and other small mammals in the Rainey Sanctuary in Louisiana alone within a five-year period. She accused it of using steel traps to do so and of quietly pocketing profits from the sale of the pelts. The steel trap killed and maimed indiscriminately, and its use "brutalizes the trappers, men and young boys who use it." She maintained there was no proof these mammals were the enemies of birds, that sanctuaries were their home, and that it was not sound wildlife management to eliminate predators. She also denounced the association for slaughtering hawks, owls, and other birds of prey on its sanctuaries, claiming that dedicated wildlife areas should protect all species.[57]

In her battle with the national association, Edge was caught between a masculine vision of the natural world common to hunters in the Audubon movement and a more feminine perception of nurturance that included caring not only for game species but also for species with which human beings competed for game. Audubon's leaders reacted indignantly to her charge that killing birds and mammals that preyed on game species and songbirds was immoral and unscientific. Echoing an old law against nagging wives, they called Edge "a common scold." By the late 1930s and early 1940s, the new field of wildlife management would emphasize the role of predation in controlling game species and protecting habitats, but until then, most sportsmen found it acceptable to kill creatures with which they competed for prey.[58] Many birders distinguished bad from good birds on the basis of their behavior, beauty, and eating habits. Certainly the American public tended to divide wildlife into desirable and undesirable species, useful and destructive, if not morally good and evil.

Edge brought together a sympathetic advisory board of naturalists that included men. She drew on the work of Vernon Kellogg of the U.S. Biological Survey, who had invented a humane box-trap. Her allies also included the editors of *The Auk*, published by the American Ornithologists' Union, which focused on endangered species; and Henry Fairfield Osborn of the New York Museum of Natural History, who championed the cause of the muskrat. The animal rights groups, however, which were largely funded and governed by women, were her most valuable supporters: the Anti–Steel Trap League, headquartered in Washington and led by Lucy Furman and Mrs. Edward Breck; Sue Farrell's Anti-Vivisection Investigation; and the Western Federation of Animal Crusaders, of Everett, Washington. Among Edge's supporters, as well, was Linnie Marsh Wolfe of the John Muir Association, whose admiration for Muir was shared by Edge.[59]

Edge established her own organization in 1929, the Emergency Conservation Committee (ECC). She remained its chairperson and executive secretary for over thirty years, working out of a small office on Lexington Avenue in Manhattan. She also made a bid to oust the National Association of Audubon Societies' board of directors. Failing to do that, she sued the board, alleging financial improprieties. Some members called her simply ill informed and indiscreet, even militant; she angered many. A few accused her of "domestic irregularities" (she was divorced) and of having worked with suffragists. Edge and the society negotiated a settlement, but the association changed its practices only fractionally. She remained emphatic in her disdain of what she called "the so-called sportsman," condemning "the modern gunner who has the effrontery to prate of the manliness of 'sport.'" For Edge, hunting raised issues of gender as well as of class. She called sportsmen "rich club men" who made it difficult for working-class men to hunt for food. In 1937 she reproduced a cartoon from *Punch* picturing a room decorated with stuffed trophies, heads especially, and a portrait of a hunter who resembled Theodore Roosevelt. The cartoon was captioned, "Yes, Mr. Featherstonehaugh. The Major was passionately fond of all living creatures."[60]

A humane impulse, an ecological perspective, and the faith that all species had legal rights guided Edge. Common law in the United States defines wildlife as the property of the citizens of a state, but, to Edge, wildlife "is not our property. Creatures of the wild belong to themselves alone. They, too, like humans have their inalienable rights to life, liberty and the pursuit of happiness that should command respect from us." Man should not treat them with cruelty and should protect them from unnecessary destruction. She declared that the global loss of wildlife was unparalleled in history. Direct killing of wild creatures—and, indirectly, environmental changes—were destroying hundreds of species of animals and plants and threatening thousands more. She fought for wildlife sanctuaries, which she called sacred places, but argued as well that all nature should be held "sacred from interference." The ECC argued for the preservation of all species in numbers sufficient to prevent their extermination.[61]

Edge campaigned against hunting except if it was done under careful regulation, against the indiscriminate scattering of poisons—especially sprays and powders—and against the killing of creatures accused of destroying game, crops, and livestock. She lobbied against steel traps, criticized scientists for collecting rare species, and opposed the introduction of foreign species. She argued that biologists had impeccable evidence that the successful introduction of any alien species brings the disappearance of native species with which they compete. She called national attention to the impact of oil pollution on harbors and rivers and of overgrazing on the national forests.

Despite the prescient quality of her thinking, historians are only now coming to recognize Edge's role in conservation; even today her fight with the Audubon Association overshadows her later contributions. Over the course of the following three decades, she participated in a reappraisal of the environmental role of predators. She established Pennsylvania's Hawk Mountain, the first sanctuary for birds of prey in North America. She lobbied through the 1950s, often single-handedly, out of her New York City office. She was particularly effective in pressing public officials and enlisting women's groups to act in behalf of enlarging national parks so as to include key plant and animal habitats. Along with the Sierra Club, especially its mountaineer and director Richard M. Leonard, she was largely responsible for having a tract of sugar pines restored to Yosemite National Park. She campaigned for the enlargement of Crater Lake, Sequoia, and Yellowstone National Parks to include crucial biological zones. She fought for the addition of the Douglas fir and hemlock forest to Mt. Olympus National Monument, the absence of which had threatened the Roosevelt elk. She pressed the Forest Service to expand its wilderness areas, and she pleaded for private, state, and federal sanctuaries where wildlife might "remain unmolested by man."[62]

In the mid- and late 1930s women maintained strong voices in the nation's many Audubon Societies and in Edge's ECC, but these organizations were becoming the exceptions. The wildflower movement, in particular, went into sharp decline. The General Federation of Women's Clubs remained civic-minded but turned its attention to issues of social equity and unemployment.[63] Women's leadership in conservation and climbing clubs weakened. During the Depression years, when sites for wild, primitive, and wilderness areas in the national forests were under consideration, hunters and climbers had far more influence within the nonprofit sector of conservation than did wildflower or animal rights advocates. Only the desolate mountain summits were protected from exploitation.

A masculine vision of goals and methods dominated federal conservation in the 1930s. For hunting and alpine groups, cooperation with federal officials offered them a voice in the management of places in which they had an abiding interest, while land managers sought regionally powerful groups as friendly lobbyists. This clientele relationship and gentlemanly politics dominated wilderness politics well past the end of World War II.[64] Reciprocity was based on common perceptions of class, gender, and the outdoor experience.

Forest Service officials articulated this shared perception in 1933, when they established eighteen "primitive" areas in California. Almost two million acres, or 10 percent of the state's national forests, were so designated. Most of the acreage was in the High Sierra Primitive Area. The service's regional forester for California, S. B. Show, told the Sierra Club that the primitive area contained that portion of the High Sierra that the club had "made its own." To the pleasure of the climbing clubs of the Pacific Northwest, the service also established, in the Cascade Range, a primitive area along the Canadian border, in a region that agency officials described as "practically unknown mountains" extending east and west of the continental divide. The service made similar designations in the highest reaches of the Rocky Mountains. Show said that because these sites contained little or no usable timber, they would not require fire protection and could be left roadless. Historian Alfred Runte has convincingly argued that the quality of economic "worthlessness" was decisive in selecting the lands that the government ultimately saved.[65]

Nevertheless, according to Show, these lands had also been chosen because foresters understood wilderness to be the place where Americans could replicate the struggle whereby they had come to dominate their country. This view resonated with hunters and male climbers. "The older generation of mountain travelers know," Show said, "that personal contest with Nature and conquest of her difficulties—no matter how stern or kind she might be—was typical of the self-reliance, durability, and hardihood of the genuine pioneer." Riding up a mountain in an automobile could hardly "increase one's self-reliance or self-respect. But conquest of the same mountain on foot . . . added something . . . to the individual and to society. . . . Conquest of her—beating her at her own game by his own efforts—is rather the quality that counted."[66] The Sierra Club welcomed the announcement that the High Sierra would remain theirs in some sense. They concurred with Show's assessment of the proper relationship of human beings to the natural world.

Robert Marshall, for whom wilderness was as an outlet for manly aggression, was the director of forestry in the Department of the Interior's Office of Indian Affairs. He had been a forester with the Forest Service and a mountaineer. In an effort to encourage the Forest Service to designate additional wild, primitive, and wilderness areas, Marshall and eight others, including Aldo Leopold, organized the Wilderness Society in 1935 to oppose the fashion that wanted "to barber and manicure wild America as smartly as the modern girl." Within two years, the society had 576 members and a council of thirteen. Only one of the thirteen was a woman. For decades its council and officers remained almost exclusively male, its rhetoric reflecting a masculinity that was defined by the urge to conquer.[67]

The Wilderness Society, based in the nation's capital, followed Leopold in describing wilderness as "the primeval environment" that should be free of "mechanized transportation." It denounced roads, automobiles, airplanes, beacon towers, radios, ski lifts, railroads, and motorboats more strenuously than it did logging, dams, and grazing.[68] The wilderness experience demanded travel on foot or by animal and total self-reliance. Isolated and isolating, mountains still provided the "environment of solitude."[69] By the time the society was founded, however, Leopold had altered his vision of wilderness as hunting grounds. Populations of deer—the favored game animal—were exploding on the Grand Canyon's Kaibab Plateau, destroying their own range. It became clear to Leopold that predation was vital to an ecological balance. He lost his enthusiasm for hunting predators, dating his unease to the moment he had watched the dimming of the green fire in the eyes of an old wolf he had helped to kill. He came to see this fire as symbolizing the mystery and wisdom of wilderness. He urged people to see the world from the perspective of an overgrazed mountain. He called that "thinking like a mountain."[70]

The Wilderness Society followed Leopold in defining wilderness in terms of ecological wisdom as well as offering the experience of primitive conditions. The society opposed ski facilities in New York's Adirondack State Forest, parkways in the Green Mountains, logging in Olympic National Park, dams in Yellowstone National Park, the Big Thompson tunnel and river diversion project in the Rocky Mountains, and mining in Joshua Tree National Monument. It tried to have Thoreau's Mt. Katahdin designated a national park, and it pressed for primitive areas in Idaho's Selkirk Mountains and in Arizona's Superstition Mountain. The Forest Service, with its vast mountain holdings, was the society's natural enemy and its strongest potential ally.

Forest Service chief Ferdinand Silcox was well aware of the society's interest. In 1937 he invited Robert Marshall to address the agency's regional foresters and to propose the establishment of twenty-one wilderness areas, averaging two hundred thousand to four hundred thousand acres each. The audience welcomed the proposal, as did the American Forestry Association, in which many Forest Service rangers were active.[71] That same year, Silcox appointed Marshall to head the Forest Service's Division of Recreation and Lands.[72] Two months later, the service established a national system of primitive, limited, wild, and wilderness areas.[73] Advocates for wildflowers and native plants applauded, as did naturalists, birders, hunters, and members of women's organizations, youth groups, outdoor clubs, and other conservation associations.

These groups also appreciated the opportunity of playing off the Forest and Park Services against each other. Their political leverage made the difference for Kings Canyon. Stephen Mather had taken up the canyon's cause a month after Muir's death. After the canyon had been cut from the bill that enlarged Sequoia National Park in 1928, various members of Congress had introduced legislation calling for a Kings Canyon National Park. The Forest Service, which now administered the canyon as a primitive area, asked the Sierra Club to lobby against transferring the site to the national parks. Hesitant about the

Park Service's penchant for promoting tourism, club members debated the proposal. Secretary of the Interior Harold Ickes visited California to assure them that the Park Service would keep Kings Canyon free of roads. He promised wording to that effect in the bill, its title, and its legislative history. The club planned its 1938 annual outing into Kings Canyon in the company of a park official and shortly thereafter threw its weight behind the park, as did the California Alpine Club, the Mazamas, and Seattle's Federation of Western Outdoor Clubs.[74] The Wilderness Society, Audubon, and the Save-the-Redwoods League continued to support the Forest Service, but the National Parks Association, the John Muir Association, and the American Planning and Civic Association of Washington decided for the park.

Garden clubs and naturalists lent their weight to the park. Women's groups offered the largest base of support: the General Federation of Women's Clubs, the Federation of Church Women, Edge's Emergency Conservation Committee, the Daughters of the Golden West, the Daughters of the American Revolution, the Hollywood Women's Club, San Francisco's Legal Secretaries Association, the League of American Pen Women, and the Garden Club of America. Endorsements also came from local and county chambers of commerce, California newspapers, and hotel associations. In 1940 Congress established the park. A last-minute amendment robbed it of the beautiful Tehipite Valley and part of Kings Canyon; nevertheless, the park now held 454,000 acres. Appropriations were subject to the provision that the Park Service not extend the road up the South Fork of the Kings River beyond Cooper Creek. The secretary of the interior's commitment to wilderness as a principle in park management, recorded in the legislative history, was unprecedented.[75] Public pressure persuaded Secretary Ickes to heed the call of the wild in the management of other parks as well.

There is no more sublime place than Kings Canyon National Park. On the whole, however, the greatest success in capturing landscapes that epitomized the romantic conventions of the masculine sublime lay with the Forest Service. The agency's "classified" areas held the rugged, unpeopled vastness that men had long sought. Most of the areas varied in size between one hundred thousand and five hundred thousand acres—by design, too large to be crossed on foot in a single day; some sizable enough for a person to explore for at least ten days, perhaps two weeks. These lands incorporated the highest and most remote portions of the Rocky Mountains, the Cascade Range, Aldo Leopold's southwestern mountains, California's Trinity Alps, and the summit of the High Sierra. They also included Aurelia Harwood's "small wilderness"—Mt. San Jacinto. By 1940 most of the highest portions of the western mountains were located either in national parks or in national forest wilderness, wild, or primitive areas.[76]

For people such as Aurelia Harwood, wilderness areas and national parks were places of life; this vision was common to wildflower protectionists, animal rights advocates, and leaders of the Camp Fire Girls, all of whose social and scientific expectations predisposed them to appreciate plant communities and rugged landscapes as home. For those who shared this perspective—naturalists such as Muir, botanist Willis Jepson, paleontologist John Campbell Merriam, and biologist Vernon Kellogg, in particular—the human presence was problematic because it compromised other forms of life. Men and women who shared this view—those in the Audubon Society, the Wild Flower Preservation Society, Camp Fire Girls, and native plant groups—championed the Forest Service's wilderness regulations. Support also grew out of the masculine perspective of those who climbed, hunted, and led Boy Scout troops. Here, wilderness was the unknown, as much a place as an experience, one most often rooted in gendered, class, and ethnic identities. Such places attracted those who defined themselves by their high levels of education, their manhood, and their role in American history. The masculine view would continue to prevail in the 1940s and 1950s, as the voices of women and naturalists were quieted in the national quest for the ideal family and a mythic frontier. But the concerns of postwar Americans for the future added impetus to the search for a past, and public support for wilderness would grow.

Part III
In Wildness Is the Preservation of the Nation, and the World, 1945–1964

David Brower came into national prominence in the 1950s. Working to mold Americans' enthusiasm for the outdoors into a lobby for the protection of wild places, he transformed wilderness conservation from a recreational perspective into an issue of human health and safety. "The connection between the ability of civilization to protect wilderness, and the ability of civilization to survive is not so tenuous as we might think," he warned students at Reed College in 1959.[1] His metamorphosis from mountaineer into a citizen fighting to save the world drew not only on long-standing tenets of conservation, but on mid-twentieth-century developments. Brower's life and career illustrate the ongoing influence of mountains on the formulation of a wilderness aesthetic, the central place of outdoor sport in conservation, and the importance of notions of masculinity and family to both.

When asked to identify the origins of his dedication, Brower highlighted the influence of California's landscapes and offered his own boyhood as a parable for conservation, much as had John Muir, Aldo Leopold, and William O. Douglas. Brower recalled hiking as a child with his family and being relieved to see that the hills behind Berkeley, his birthplace, stretched beyond the horizon and that drinkable water "came for free out in the hills." His family vacationed in Yosemite in a 1916 Maxwell outfitted for camping. He was too frightened to climb the cliffs but he did enjoy camping. "There in the Sierra, on little trips we would take nearby, and in my experiences . . . on a farm in Two Rock Valley where my mother had been born, I learned to appreciate what was going on out-of-doors, and I never got over it." Describing forms and colors to his mother, who had lost her sight, sensitized him to nature. He recalled natural history as a haven. Fearful his enthusiasm for chasing butterflies was "not a manly thing to do," he had deliberately whistled "popular tunes of the time."[2] He came to see the experience of wilderness as crucial to the normal process of male maturation.

Coming of age during the Depression, Brower earned money wherever he could, delivering newspapers, gardening, and clerking. He learned to use a calculating machine and to type by the hunt-and-peck system. The temptation to flee the city, however, led him back into the Sierra. In 1930, at age eighteen, he made his first important scramble, down the face of Echo Peak near Berkeley, picking the peak because his father had done it years before, mysteriously disappearing from home one day to make the climb. Brower went up the Sierra's Mt. Lyell in 1931 with his father and older brother and felt elated at the top. He began technical rock climbing in Yosemite Valley, chronicled his triumphs and those of fellow climbers for the *Sierra Club Bulletin,* and joined its editorial board.[3] Photographs show a tall, thin, good-looking young man, fair, with light blue eyes.

Brower later asserted that it was climbing that had prepared the members of the Sierra Club to assume controversial roles in conservation. Recalling the ascent of Shiprock in particular, he said, "I took my share of risks. I possessed a certain amount of boldness, a key trait for leaders, and one that served the Club well in the early decades when nearly all who guided the organization were accomplished mountaineers."[4] Brower hinted at this boldness as early as 1935, when he reviewed *Men Against the Clouds: The Conquest of Minya Konka,* a book by well-known climbers describing their ascent of one of the highest points in eastern Tibet. Brower cataloged "certain departures from sound practices," several of which resulted in serious injuries.[5] Some club members were outraged at his "negative destructive criticism of an acknowledged authority on the subject,"[6] but others felt that the attack brought the organization "national recognition."[7]

Still restive in the Bay Area, Brower moved to the Sierra, where he became publicity manager for the Yosemite Park and Curry Company. There he met Ansel Adams. Working out of the rustic Best Studio, which his wife's family operated in the valley, Adams provided photographs for the company's press releases. As Brower went to the studio to select photos, the two men formed a friendship and launched an editorial collaboration that would in time publicize wilderness nationally. Late in the 1930s Brower began working part-time for the Sierra Club, and in 1941 he joined Adams and Bay Area lawyers Richard Leonard and Bestor Robinson, also climbers, on the Sierra Club's board of directors.[8]

Within the year Brower had enlisted in the U.S. Army and was assigned, as he had hoped, to the Tenth Mountain Division. Drawing on his own and the club's experiences, he helped to train troops for combat and was soon sent to the Italian front. Like George Perkins Marsh a century earlier, Brower came to recognize the fragility of the Mediterranean mountains. Marsh's 1863 book, *Man and Nature,* had warned of man's capacity to endanger the earth. As Marsh saw it, Rome had destroyed itself by allowing grazing, logging, and plowing to erode the slopes of the Mediterranean. Marsh's hypotheses, together with Brower's own observations of how roads disrupted soils, convinced him that there was a parallel between the ways in which technologies of war were killing men and technologies of transportation were destroying the environment.[9] He returned home to argue that road construction and logging in the nation's mountains threatened the survival of American civilization.[10]

After the war, Brower took a position as an editor for the University of California Press in Berkeley, and he volunteered as outing leader for the Sierra Club, soon becoming the assistant to its president. In 1952 the club's board of directors appointed him as its first executive secretary. For the next twenty years he traveled throughout the United States, representing the group, and commuted daily to its San Francisco office from Berkeley, where he and his wife Anne reared four children. Critical of organizational life in America, he drew evidence from his own conflicts with federal officials and the club's board of directors. When he urged parents to take their children camping, he described his family vacations. When the Forest Service increased logging in regions of the Cascade Range and the Sierra Nevada in which he, as a mountaineer, felt a proprietary interest, he became what some sociologists call a prototypic "movement intellectual." In tune with liberal skepticism toward government in the 1950s, he explained: "If you have to choose between being naive or paranoid—I don't think there are any other choices—I guess I would rather be paranoid."[11]

Brower was part of a national cadre of intellectuals and conservationists whose liberal critique of American culture included an environmental perspective. Prominent among them were photographer and club activist Ansel Adams; Howard Zahniser, executive secretary of the Wilderness Society; Joseph Prendergast, executive director of the National Recreation Association; Olaus Murie of the Wilderness Society; Aldo Leopold, by then professor of wildlife management at the University of Wisconsin; Nancy Newhall of the

Museum of Modern Art in New York; and biologist Rachel Carson. These individuals translated Thoreau's "In wildness is the preservation of the world" into recommendations for public policy. They developed their love for nature into a perspective that was global, antimodern, and concerned with the impact of commercial and technological change on humanity. Although the emergent environmental perspective can be traced to early efforts to improve public health in the cities, it flowed as well out of an ideology that described Burke's "sublime and beautiful" as the belled canary of civilization.[12] It was World War II that sharpened the focus on wilderness and survival.

7

Mountain Conquest—Family Style

In *Michael and Ann in Yosemite Valley*, published in 1941, Ansel Adams and his wife Virginia Best Adams described in fiction their own family life. His photographs and her text showed their children romping in Yosemite's meadows, fishing its streams, and sleeping under the protective walls of Half Dome and El Capitan. A benign vision of national history unfolded as the children befriended the dignified Indian Tabuce, the Spanish cowboy Uncle Don, and his horse Don Juan. Ann learned to grind the acorn meal that had sustained the valley's indigenous people, and Michael pretended to hunt with bow and arrow. A thunderstorm brought nothing worse than the chore of removing the laundry from the clothesline—and a rainbow. In the evening father returned from work to put Michael and Ann to bed, with the promise of a climb the next day. As the moon rose over Yosemite, the children dreamt "of a future summer happiness, of camping with daddy in the High Sierra."[1] This was a story for children, but even accomplished mountaineers were coming to describe the Sierra as "a gracious, gentle, inviting mountain range," a place of innocence, congenial to the rituals of family life.[2] During the postwar years, men like Adams reconciled John Muir's domestic sublime with other conventions of the sublime to forge new and nurturing, but no less aggressive, visions of mountains.

World War II had cast a patriotic glow over America's landscapes and conflated them with the family. Leaving for war, young men and women had glanced back with nostalgia at their own landscapes. Transported from one installation to another, soldiers, airmen, sailors, nurses, and wives became familiar with arresting places. After the war, they and their grateful families sank back into the hills of home.[3] Returning to his farm, a soldier said: "Behind and above the house was the mountain. It looked just the same—the blue sky in back of the high granite peak."[4] Another wrote, "In this world that has so much of chaos, it is comforting to know that the mountains are there, mountains that have stood while dynasties have risen and fallen." Climber, ex-serviceman, and lawyer Richard Leonard described Little Lost Valley in the Yosemite High Country as "a bit of fossil scenery ante-dating the origin of man. . . . Now it is a national park, protected by man from himself, so that future generations of our civilization may be able to see what a segment of the earth was like long ago." For Leonard, Adams, and other Americans, mountains had become places of permanence in a turbulent world.[5]

The years following World War II were at once exhilarating and sobering. The automobile made national parks and national forests accessible, and the nation turned to these places out of joy but also out of unease. An anxious peace followed unimaginable horror. Americans looked for moral guidance to the family, to the natural world, and to history. Armed with the conviction that the physical environment shaped human development, experts in conservation, mental health, recreation, and education imparted a seriousness of purpose to outdoor life. Children's summer camps prospered, as did the sport of climbing, but it was the family camping trip that best fit the social order to which Americans now aspired. Under a photograph of the Sierra's Mt. Hoffmann, the 10,921-foot height reflecting the placid waters of May Lake, named for Hoffmann's fiancée, *Sunset* magazine announced the heyday of "Mountain 'conquest' . . . family style."[6]

The meanings often attributed to wilderness in the 1940s and 1950s were shaped by society's determination to foster manly aggression, self-discipline, and teamwork. Cultural arbiters urged on women self-sacrifice, motherhood, and service. Evidence of the authenticity of distinctly gendered identities remained located in natural landscapes, as men continued to name alpine lakes for women. Americans interpreted their experience of nature as teaching that families should be hierarchically structured. Boys and men were to be nurtured in a rigidly defined domestic order. By encountering wilderness, they would learn to defend the republic. Federal agencies funded alpine expeditions during and after the war.

The armed forces suggested that nature was also a healer when it sent injured and distressed service personnel into the national parks for rest and recuperation. While staying in the Eastman Hotel, veterans recovered in the waters of Hot Springs National Park. Wounded and weary servicemen recuperated, as well, in the fresh air around the McKinley Park Hotel. In the

Figure 44. Sailors at the Wawona Tunnel, looking out over the Yosemite Valley, May 19, 1944. Photograph by R. H. Anderson. Courtesy of Yosemite National Park Library.

summer of 1943 the U.S. Navy converted Yosemite's elegantly timbered Awahnee Hotel into a convalescent hospital. Over a two-year period, 6,752 patients were trucked into the valley for a physical rehabilitation regime that included hiking in the summer and skiing in the winter.[7] Under a commission from the U.S. Department of the Interior, Adams photographed the convoys of injured entering the valley. Other federal agencies similarly promoted patriotism by invoking Americans' love of their countryside.[8]

Military interests looked to the public lands for training and recovery, but commercial interests sought the resources of these lands. When they pressed for the timber and minerals of the national parks and wilderness areas, most conservationists balked, sensing particular threats to Kings Canyon, Yosemite, and Olympic National Parks. Rebuffed during the war, timber interests tried again after the war, citing the need for veterans' housing. Wilderness advocates defeated these attempts by claiming that parks and wilderness were vital to national security and that "eternal vigilance" was needed to defend "the freedom of the wilderness." According to the Wilderness Society, once you instill in a man "a deep love for his country's mountains, you have sown the seed of patriotism so deeply that [it] cannot be uprooted."[9]

As Americans took to the hills in the postwar years, membership in outdoor clubs and wilderness groups grew. Applications for hunting and fishing licenses soared, empowering wildlife and sportsmen's associations.[10] Exemplified by those midwestern women who campaigned to protect the yellow lady-slipper of the prairie, native plant, garden, wildlife, and women's clubs added their voices to the cause of nature preservation. Of all the nation's groups, however, it was the Sierra Club and the Wilderness Society that capitalized most effectively on public enthusiasm for the outdoors, appointing new and dynamic executive secretaries. The Wilderness Society retained Howard Zahniser, a former information specialist for the U.S. Biological Survey and the Bureau of Plant Industry. David Brower soon became Zahniser's West Coast counterpart. Each man was a skilled publicist who captured the hopes and fears of the American public.

According to historian Curt Meine, "The war and its aftermath had only underscored the importance of wilderness in the minds of the leaders of the Wilderness Society. As they prepared for their annual meeting [in 1946], they planned to revise their by-laws and reconsider the role of wilderness in the nuclear age." In June 1947 the society announced a campaign for a national wilderness system. It circulated a map of the wild, limited, primitive, and wilderness areas that the Forest Service had established before the war and sought a congressional guarantee that the agency would not log these areas.[11] To implement these strategies, the society elected a federal forester and the founder of the Appalachian Mountain Trail, Benton McKaye, as its president. McKaye announced that the society's "bedrock strategy" was to defend the classified areas of the national forests, but that it planned to save undesignated wilderness as well: "We need to do some invading of our own."[12] McKaye said that the society was going to "infiltrate the nation," called the society's map "the ground plan of a military fortress," and identified public lands as "strategic theaters" that needed to be "held against all comers." He vowed to protect the "wilderness frontier against invasion by illicit herdsmen, insidious lumbermen, and machine-succored skiers."[13] The language of the frontier proved, as Patricia Limerick tells us, "a simple and attractive metaphor for challenge, struggle, and mastery."[14]

When the Wilderness Society was established, it had defined wilderness as the vast roadless terrains that the Forest Service had classified as primitive, limited, wild, or wilderness. Now the group argued that a true wilderness system had to include examples of all the nation's original ecosystems. Anything could be wilderness, McKaye asserted—speaking of his beloved Appalachian Trail—"from the little accidental wild spot at the head of a ravine or . . . vast expanses of virgin territory." In addition to the influence of McKaye, who focused his energies on the eastern United States, where only pockets of wilderness could be realized, the society's shift owed much to Aldo Leopold's revisualization of wilderness as any piece of original land, be it a bit of prairie, a ravine, or a clean stream.[15] Wilderness was now understood not only in the traditional language of the masculine sublime but increasingly as the community of life—not only as the unknown but also as home.[16]

Increasing numbers of men came to refer to wilderness as home. With its historical connotations, their understanding of the word, however, differed substantially from that long embedded in the feminine sublime. By "home," these men meant "the place to rediscover the vast, harmonious pattern of the natural world . . . , an escape—from turmoil and doubt, from war and the threat of war, from the perplexities and sorrows of the artificial world we have built ourselves to live in. . . . but . . . an escape not *from* but *to* reality." The primordial home remained alien even as it enticed men to test their bodies, provoking in them "weakness and [the] will to master it."[17]

As vice-president of the Wilderness Society, Aldo Leopold had moved toward a new understanding of wilderness as community and as home. In the late 1930s and early 1940s he reconceptualized his "wilderness hunting grounds" as places of ecological truths, a "common home" for man and beast in the vastness of time and space. He wrote of learning to think like an overgrazed mountain overwhelmed by the voracious appetites of wildlife populations, such as deer, lacking in natural predators. Leopold, however, had also come to love modest landscapes. His wife Estelle Leopold and their children arranged for the publication, after his death in 1948, of Leopold's essays from this period as *A Sand County Almanac*. The *Almanac* described the family's efforts to restore an abused prairie farmland to ecological health. For over a decade, while Leopold taught wildlife management at the University of Wisconsin, the family had spent their free time living in a dirt-floored shack, planting thousands of trees, and watching life return to their Sand County farm. Leopold's essays described "what my family sees and does at its weekend refuge from too much modernity: 'the shack.' On this sand farm in Wisconsin, first worn out and then abandoned by our bigger-and-better society, we try to rebuild, with shovel and ax, what we are losing elsewhere."[18] The young forester who had gone west to rope, ride, hunt, and harvest trees had returned home to make restitution to the land.

Leopold's sense of intimacy with place, his family's presence, and his fascination with the habits of wildlife gave the *Almanac* a decidedly domestic tone. Leopold still unraveled mountain mysteries, but he found as many answers in the landscapes of home. The hunter had become a father; his sympathies widened. Listening to the spring migration of geese, he heard a "disconsolate tone to their honkings," suggesting that they might be "brokenhearted widowers, or mothers hunting lost children." He recognized that biologists resisted such anthropomorphic interpretations of bird behavior. An analysis of the populations in Sand County, however, compelled Leopold to conclude that "goose flocks are families, or aggregates of families, and lone geese in spring are probably what our fond imaginings had first suggested. They are bereaved survivors of the winter's shooting, searching in vain for their kin. Now I am free to grieve with and for the lone honkers."[19] His essays echoed familiar chords in family-centered America.

Even during the war, despite shortages of gas and park facilities, overburdened soldiers and their sweethearts had taken outdoor vacations. After the war, advertisers urged couples to hike—in the Cascades, the Sierra, Colorado's mountains, or Maine's Katahdin.[20] Veterans and their spouses brought along their children. Postwar Americans had babies at a rate unparalleled in the previous one hundred years, and the sheer force of demographics transformed public lands. No longer were the heights the seemingly exclusive domain of the very adventurous. Camping reflected the budgetary limitations of young families and the luxury of middle-class leisure. A sizable portion of the nation's labor management contracts provided vacations with pay by the mid-1950s. The federal government built interstate highways, improved park and forest roads, and promoted recreational use of public lands, while commercial interests advertised travel. Middle-class leisure and wealth democratized outdoor sport and enlarged the potential constituency for conservation.

Lest a Puritan-like conscience dampen adult play, conservationists capitalized on popular versions of psychological theories. Most middle-class Americans were vague about the separate dynamics of Gestalt, Jungian, behaviorist, and Freudian theories, but they grasped the association of development, environment, and personality. The cold war presented the federal government and citizens alike with a reason to examine the mental well-being of future soldiers. Servicemen had experienced combat fatigue or "shock disease" in World War II. Captives in Korea, "away from home and mother" (the Sierra Club's phrase), had experienced physical and mental anxiety. When asked how the United States might reinforce the resilience of its future soldiers or reduce the stress of citizens living under the threat of nuclear attack, preservationists answered, "Wilderness."[21]

The first vigorous efforts of American society to cultivate a home that would fulfill all of its members' personal needs were made in the 1950s. "Amid a world of uncertainties brought about by World War II and its aftermath," historian Elaine Tyler May writes that, "the home seemed to offer a secure private nest removed from the dangers of the outside world."[22] Wilderness advocates agreed: "A national emergency changes the structure of the very foundation of our society—the family." As men marched off, families moved, and mothers worked outside the home; "great numbers of children are burdened with the insecurities of a nation in the midst of an emergency," insecurities nature would soothe.[23]

The number of professionals in the public and nonprofit sectors grew dramatically in the 1950s. Coordinated by Joseph Prendergast of the National Recreation Association, professionals in recreation lobbied for new national parks, outdoor programs, and wilderness designations. The association fashioned a national network of public agencies, educational institutions, and citizen groups. Colleges and universities established curricula to train students to become physical education teachers, camp directors, and park superintendents. States, counties, and cities created divisions of youth services, park districts, and public health agencies. Organizations as diverse as the American Psychiatric Association and the Family Camping Association promoted outdoor life.[24]

Parents' Magazine and *Consumer Reports* told parents that youngsters, particularly those with the misfortune to have working mothers, required substantial contact with the natural world. Alpine clubs counseled: "Pack up the Kids and Go Camping" or take "A Family Outing." Narratives appeared in print with such titles as "A California Family in the Alps" and "The Children Loved Them."[25] The nuclear family and a frontierlike wilderness seemed to represent a stable, cleanly structured social order.

Popular perceptions of psychology, of the psychic strain of the cold war, and of frontier history located national security at the intersection of wilderness and childhood. Seen as synonymous with primitivism, wilderness conjured up a continuity stretching back to the beginning of time, at once youthful and ancient, with a presumably correct alignment of father, mother, and child. Ansel Adams simply said that families grew better in the mountains. Each member found his or her place, so that the whole functioned as a team. After several weeks in the Sierra with his young children, walking seven miles a day and scaling one of the highest peaks, a father wrote: "We found our family was really a family once again," operating as "a working unit." Of his son, the peaks were now "in his blood." Taking teenagers into "the wild places of the mountains," a father wrote, forged a personal history rooted in a special sense of place.[26] In a tent or around a campfire, a family seemed safe from outside nuclear threats. The routines of primitive living seemed to reassure children who cowered under their school desks during air raid warnings. Outdoor life afforded them "opportunities to *be* children or youth, to enjoy life, fun and activities, to gain a sense of security in a world of insecurity."[27]

Opinions varied as to what constituted a primitive experience. During the war, to the horror of Ansel Adams, national advertisers had urged Americans to fight for what Jackson Lears has called "a revitalized vision of 'home' colored by pastoral memories and fantasies but surrounded by modern creature comforts."[28] The 1950s brought trailers and the station wagon, hailed as "the greatest thing since the covered wagon." Tent and trailer towns mushroomed in the national parks. A father told *Parents' Magazine* of his family's vacation: "While camping, we ate steak regularly. . . . We bought Navajo and other trinkets, gallons of soda pop . . . [and] clothing as needed, stayed in an occasional motel to wash, and visited lots of national parks."[29] Most wilderness advocates, however, saw such blatant consumerism as antithetical to their cause. Nevertheless, new technologies—like air mattresses, kelty packs, better sleeping bags, kerosene camp stoves, freeze-dried foods, and nylon tents—made mountaineering much easier, especially for families.[30]

The Sierra Club invited families: "If you have wished you could take your children with you to the High Sierra, why not consider the Family Burro Trip this year?" Earlier, the club had provided supplies, pack animals, packers, and the commissary for the more than one hundred people on each High Trip. With the burro trips, however, each family provisioned itself, cooked for itself, and cared for its own pack animals on the trail. In 1951 Brower edited, and the club published, a how-to book of essays entitled *Going Light—With Backpack or Burro*.[31] The experiences of climbers-turned-fathers inspired these trips and the essays in the manual. Brower told readers that no child was too young to hike—not infant, toddler, or adolescent—and that a child's capacity for appreciation grew at each stage. With the very young, he thought it best "to recapture childish joy in aimless wandering and delight in all the wonders of the trail, great and small, from the loveliest, longest vista down to the queerest bug or the smallest flower." He said children should be permitted to take along their favorite blankets. He also cautioned parents that adolescents might develop "ambitions to perform feats of endurance such as the scaling of high mountains in conscious competition with their elders."[32]

Joel Hildebrand, the Sierra Club president who initiated the burro trips and a professor of chemistry at the University of California, Berkeley, and members of his family wrote some of the book's chapters. Hildebrand said of his wife Louise and their children: "We have had lots of fun, you see." He

Figure 45. Children's burro trip. This photograph was taken by Alfred Dole in the Sierra, in 1947. Courtesy of Helen Dole.

explained his philosophy—that camping with burros made families independent—in "the introductory chapter on *Going Light—With Backpack or Burro.* Son Milton and I wrote together the chapter on travel. He wrote the chapters on burro management. . . . Son Alex wrote [about foot travel], drawing from his experience with the family. Louise wrote on women and children's problems." This father believed that you could do more for people by introducing them to the joys of the wild and its "attendant moral lessons than you do by trying to convert them to your particular religion."[33]

The Sierra Club sponsored a prize for the best essay describing such a trip. California philanthropist and eugenicist Charles Goethe donated the prize money in the belief that reenacting the frontier bolstered the family. Take your children to the mountains, the winning essay counseled.[34] Hiking was a lesson in self-sufficiency, in paying one's own way: "children learned that in order to enjoy life you must put up with the inconveniences." Hildebrand maintained, "If you want to catch trout, you must put up perhaps with mosquitoes. If you want to have comforts in camp, you must carry them with you on your back during the day, etc. You take pride in meeting emergencies and overcoming difficulties."[35] What better return was there, a man enthused, than "the kind of companionship that emerges between father and son in the woods?"[36]

Howard Zahniser of the Wilderness Society suggested, however, that outdoor living taught a boy skills that families had overlooked: "an ability to care for himself," to provide his own fuel, prepare his own food, and make his own bed.[37] Authorities as diverse as the American Medical Association, the National Recreation Association, and the editors of *McCall's* recommended supervised experiences away from home. Fathers and mothers responded eagerly. *Parents' Magazine* announced in its spring 1948 issue: "Summer will soon be here and then about one and one quarter million boys and girls will be on their way to camp, to a thrilling experience against a background of woodlands, mountains, lakes and streams."[38] The illustrated cover for the *Saturday Evening Post* captured the day of departure at New York's Grand Central Station. Under the sign on track 11, "Camp Beechwood Meet Here," trains waited, as parents, conductors, and porters, carrying water skis, teddy bears, bats, balls, and suitcases, escorted somber kids onto the platform.[39]

Youth camps became big business. Most were sponsored by groups dating to the turn of the century: the National Recreation Association, Boy Scouts, Girl Scouts, and the Camp Fire Girls.[40] Their message to postwar parents differed only in emphasis: psychological health, along with physical health, mattered now, and discipline was important to the survival of the family as well as the nation. Living with a "camp family" was "practice in democracy," teaching boys and girls the laws of community essential to representative government.[41]

Summer camps were not for the faint of heart. Camp Beechwood may have provided cabins, commissaries, and water skiing, but most camps prized ruggedness. Boy Scouts climbed Mt. Whitney. Camp Fire Girls slept in the forest. Bugs, snakes, and poison oak or ivy plagued Girls Scouts. *Recreation* magazine endorsed "*real camping,* that is, an experience in outdoor living in which the camper has some responsibility for his shelter and self-occupation." Organizers strove to prepare campers to survive "a state of emergency," such as a nuclear attack, through self-reliance and self-discipline. With activities like planting trees to control erosion and protect wildlife, young people were told they could contribute to national defense.[42]

According to Zahniser, wilderness stimulated patriotism, because it was the land "as it was. It is this civilization, this culture, this way of living that will be sacrificed if our wilderness is lost." Wilderness was "a piece of the long ago that we still have with us." By emphasizing and embedding that need for wilderness in history, Zahniser plowed fertile ground. The frontier loomed large in public perceptions of American history. Commercial culture pro-moted frontier heroes: Disney celebrated Daniel Boone and Davy Crockett, and John Wayne starred in Hollywood westerns.

Americans understood Zahniser's remark that wilderness was "so much our past that it has shaped our very bodies and minds." It is "our nature"; away from it, "we degenerate into the squalor of slums or the frustration of clini-cal couches. With the wilderness we are at home."[43] For Zahniser the word "home" meant the primordial site of the origins of the human species, but his use of the word also referred to the frontier as a racialized place of national origins. There, according to historian Frederick Jackson Turner, writing in the 1890s, Americans had broken with European traditions, becoming primitives themselves, subduing nature, and infusing their collective character with in-dividualism, self-reliance, and a love of democracy. To Zahniser and other men, the word "home" meant a place and a time in the social evolution of human civilization and national development. The millennia separating Pa-leolithic man and the nineteenth-century West were thus bridged in a single intellectual leap. Turner described the frontier as the crucible that had turned the civilized into the savage and then the savage into the civilized.[44] Although professional historians were already challenging Turner's theory, conserva-tionists drew heavily on the belief that the survival of a people hinged on the opportunity to replay this evolutionary drama in perpetuity.

According to the Wilderness Society, "the ultimate health of the race" re-quired that primeval influences be equal in acreage to the urban and civilized. Olaus Murie, wildlife biologist and now the society's president, said that wilderness was the "optimum environment for modern man who seeks in-spiration of various kinds from his original habitat."[45] It was important that boys, in particular, replay those early evolutionary stages when men had de-pended on their physical prowess.[46] Discipline unfolded naturally on the trail and in camp, real places far from social artifice. It appeared "important for children to have the opportunity to live through some of the more primitive experiences of their earlier ancestors in contact with the elements and natu-ral forces if their personalities are to develop fully and wholesomely." A boy seemed to deserve the opportunity to "escape from the sheltered and mecha-nized existence imposed upon him by modern urban life, with its unnatural emphasis upon respect for man-made material property."[47]

Brower claimed that American society let the love that small boys had of pioneering in the wild die as they matured, so that they grew "afraid of wild places." He told of a colonel training an infantry group from a large eastern city: "The first time a field exercise required them to spend a night out in the woods an amazing number of them wept." An Air Force officer had a "sadder story . . . of a pilot who was forced down an easy day's walk from civilization in the north woods but who, for fear of the unknown of the wilderness, shot himself in the few hours before rescuers reached him."[48]

Primitive landscapes seemed conducive to what some Americans firmly believed was a society in which gender was naturally structured. Boys were simply more boyish in the wild. According to the Sierra Club, "The average mother finds the veneer of civilization on her small boy remarkably thin." Boys as young as ten or twelve rode their own horses and considered themselves "blends of the Lone Ranger, Red Ryder, and the Northwest Mounted." On river rafts these boys became "shades of Tom Sawyer and Huck Finn."[49] Of family camping, *Parents' Magazine* wrote: "You're together most of the day and all night. You suddenly are aware that your ten-year-old son, whom you have sometimes viewed as an elaborate accessory to a television set or a financial wellspring for the orthodontist, is a remarkably large, capable, intelligent, self-sufficient and handsome young human. You turn around and find your five-year-old daughter is, on her own initiative, washing the dishes with unsuspected skill. The seven-year-old son develops into an expert woodsman and a skillful gatherer of wood and builder of fires. He also proceeds to out-fish you two-to-one."[50]

Published in 1960 and titled *This is the American Earth,* the Sierra Club's first exhibit format book began with Brower's voice:

A mile of mountain wall spills out of the Wyoming sky, beyond a wide meadow, a meadow edged with wonder this morning when a small boy's excited cry *moose!* woke us and we watched a mother and calf leisurely browse their way downstream, ford, and then disappear. . . . A moose needs a lot of wild space and here she found it, in a place that was just about as much the way it was when trappers first saw it as a place could be and still be part of a national park.

The boy would grow up but the "image fixed well, as wild images do, on that perfectly sensitized but almost totally unexposed film of his mind." Any small boy, given the chance, would see the same, Brower said, "and the composite image of a thousand such experiences would enrich his living in the civilized world so thinly separated from the wildness the boy was designed to live with." When the child was himself a father, "how much of this magic, the American earth," would remain?[51]

Men and boys alike required ongoing exposure to primitive circumstances.[52] Zahniser quoted Robert Marshall from 1930: "It is difficult to over-estimate the importance adventure assumes in the longings of innumerable vigorous people. Lack of opportunity to satisfy such longings undoubtedly is responsible for much unhappiness, for a considerable portion of the crime which is so often committed as a means of self-expression, and . . . even for war. . . . I wonder sometimes if we could long survive, a final destruction of all wilderness."[53]

What were Americans to make of the enthusiasm for natural history that had characterized pre–World War II Germany, the recklessness of continental climbers in the 1930s, and the ways in which the National Socialists had used the youth movement and nature to fuel patriotism? Some postwar Americans pointed to parallels between the promotion of outdoor recreation by the United States and the propaganda of fascists, Nazis, and even communists.[54] For others, the language of democracy, family, and frontier, and the safety records of American climbers, made it clear that the purpose of wilderness was to channel, if not discourage, human aggression.

When the 1950s brought rising wages and increased time off for the average worker, most observers agreed that wilderness was needed. A representative of the American Psychiatric Association told the National Recreation Congress that the nation was embarking on a "great adventure in free time," an opportunity to use our biological capacity for athletics and our innate affinity with nature to offset the industrial world's capacity to induce compulsive behavior. A member of the New York Academy of Sciences used the ambivalent phrase "leisure stricken" to describe the middle class. Others worried that Americans were physically unfit and that a mechanized, sedentary lifestyle threatened adolescents who might one day be required to defend the nation.[55]

Men who had learned seafaring skills in sport had saved Great Britain at Dunkirk, according to the editors of *Recreation.* Outdoor activities would permit Americans to remain true to the traditions of freedom without falling behind in the production race with the Soviet Union. Alluding to explanations of the rise and fall of Rome, Joseph Prendergast of the National Recreation Association warned that "too much leisure with too much money has been the dread of societies across the ages. That is when nations cave from within."[56]

For Zahniser, humans were "dependent members of an interdependent community of living creatures . . . " Without knowledge of our place in the world, the future would be human-centered, machine-based, lonely, jarring, stressful, and violent.[57] By the 1950s fears about dark human impulses resonated with a middle-class audience that had been influenced by vaguely Freudian ideas of the danger of repression. Zahniser thought of wilderness, much as Turner had, as a social and psychological safety valve. If parents failed to give their sons opportunities to release pent-up impulses, they invited mental instability, juvenile delinquency, and criminality. Zahniser wrote: "This wilderness is a need. The idea of wilderness as an area without man's influence is man's own concept. Its preservation is a purpose that arises out of man's own sense of his fundamental needs."[58]

What of women's needs? In this postwar enthusiasm their presence was assumed to be incidental to those of men and children. Women were counseled to be patient and nurturing. A 1948 article for the Colorado Mountain Club parodied an advice column: "Dear Mrs. Mayfield, I have lost my husband to the Colorado Mountain Club. I put up quite a fight—but I lost. On week-ends and Sundays my husband had to take part in mountain club activities. He had no time for us at home. As a result I bitterly opposed his Mountain Club contacts— and my husband in turn bitterly opposed me. So, we got a divorce. That's the long and short of it. If I had named a corespondent in the suit I would have named the Colorado Mountain Club. This club just as surely stole my husband from me as though it had been 'the other woman' in the case." "Mrs. Mayfield" replied: "Dear Disillusioned: What a sad mistake you made. . . . Your mistake was in being unwilling to share your husband"; a good wife should have been more tolerant.[59] Masculinity required exposure to wilderness and history seemingly sanctioned that. The "manless climber" was forgotten, as was the young college girl in the middy blouse, scaling the heights. In her place was the young lady eager to wed.

In the mountains, romance was seen to flourish naturally. Summer camps for single adults were popular. At Camp Karamac in Pennsylvania's Delaware Water Gap, young women were instructed to lose their inhibitions. The result: "Many a stenographer has grabbed a husband at Karamac, where it's every girl for herself!" On their first evening, campers were initiated into the Leni-Lenape tribe at the Wigwam, tom-toms throbbing. To summon Chief Karamac from "his long sleep," a figure appeared in a skull mask, headdress, and black garment on which a skeleton had been painted. Chief Karamac in turn launched the Potato Dance, won by the couple who, holding a potato under their chins, danced the longest without dropping it. After a "baby-bottle race," the six finalists in the Little Mothers Club burped the six winning men. The message of the evening was: "Inside every wolf is a husband . . . if you hold out long enough."[60]

Historian Peter Stearns argues that, by the 1950s, the perception that men and women were emotionally different had faded.[61] Nevertheless, those women who resisted the demand that they function only in the traditional family could still assert a powerful claim on the wilderness through, for example, their abiding interest in wildflowers. In 1944 the University of California Press issued a series on the natural sciences in North America. The books that men wrote focused on alpine geology, mountaineering, and large mammals. Only *The Wild Violets of North America* was written by a woman, Viola Brainerd Baird. Roderick Peattie edited a 1947 anthology on the natural history of the Sierra, most of the contributors to which were men, including the author of the essay on climbing; but women contributed the essays on wildflowers and trees.[62] By the end of the 1950s, however, even women's hold on cataloging wildflowers had diminished. They claimed neither a place of equity within the natural world nor an empowering association with it.

Women held little formal authority within many of the nation's conservation organizations. In 1953 all of the Wilderness Society's officers and the eleven members of its council were male, as were the National Parks Association's officers, executive secretary, editor, and all its trustees. The association's council represented twenty-seven organizations, primarily outdoor clubs, conservation groups, and scientific societies; of these, only two garden clubs and the General Federation of Women's Clubs sent female representatives. Women remained leaders within groups that were either exclusively female or traditionally feminine in their interests. Although Oregon's Mazamas elected a woman president in the 1950s specifically because of her dedication to conservation, most outdoor clubs were similar to the Sierra Club, which had only three women directors during the 1940s and 1950s. Sierra Club president Aurelia Harwood's civic activism, feminist perspective, extensive climbing, and unmarried status a decade earlier no longer accorded with what Americans considered to be natural for women.

Perhaps to offset their minimal formal authority, women were active volunteers at the grassroots level in the Sierra Club. At the national and local levels they exerted a strong influence within the conservation movement through garden clubs, the General Federation of Women's Clubs, and Audubon societies, all of which had large national memberships that could wield money and influence. As Glenda Riley has noted, "Given the 'back-to-the-home' movement that followed World War II, women's commitment is even more remarkable."[63] As long as society encouraged the family, as a unit, to experience the outdoors, women could effectively address public land issues by capitalizing on their right to defend home and family. Nevertheless, the road to formal authority was rocky. A "manless climber" of the 1930s, Marjory Bridge

Farquhar led Sierra Club trips in the 1950s and was elected to its board of directors in 1951. But she left the board briefly for family reasons in 1955 and was not asked to return.[64]

The work of Charlotte Mauk, the only woman to serve on the club's board besides Farquhar between the late 1940s and 1960, demonstrates the pressure that women were under to serve as volunteers rather than paid professionals. Mauk had long been a conservationist, wilderness photographer, writer, and editor for the club. She had organized the club's first national Wilderness Conference in 1949, bringing representatives from around the nation to discuss the need for greater federal protection of wilderness. Her narratives of the Sierra Club's High Trips had long described experiences of "human community, anthropocentric and interdependent"; her wilderness was home. When the club decided to hire a full-time executive secretary in 1952, however, the directors chose David Brower, appointing Mauk to the volunteer position of secretary to the board. The choice was far from unreasonable; Brower was an outstanding rock climber, a capable outing leader, and a creative editor. But when contrasted with Mauk's extensive conservation experience and higher level of formal education, the decision in his favor hinted that a masculine perspective had triumphed.[65]

Early discussions in 1958 about employing a staff person to serve as the Sierra Club's Pacific Northwest representative involved Polly Dyer, president of the Mountaineers, conservation chairman of the Federation of Western Outdoor Clubs, and an alpinist. When she applied for the position, her longtime friends in the club interviewed her, asking questions such as, "Do you have administrative ability? Do you think you can use a Dictaphone?" They hired a young man from Montana, who quit within a month.[66] Both Mauk and Dyer were important members of the club's board of directors in the 1960s.

The club continued to advertise a democratic wilderness where no group was too young, too old, too rich, too poor, or "too frail a sex." "Women and girls can cope with weather, bugs, bears, and topography with perfect confidence and success," Brower assured women, "even when they go on hen parties without the aid of any male horse-sense or muscle at all. What it takes is know-how, and precisely the same advice that applies to men and boys should be assimilated by women and girls." The latter were nevertheless warned to test themselves first so as not to get in over their heads and "thereafter be classified as a ball-and-chain." Brower cautioned women against bringing too many things: "Most women will be sorely tempted to take more changes of clothing than they really need." He admonished them to resist the unreasonable "modern urge to cleanliness." He conceded that cleanliness for the sake of comfort was fine, but insisted that hygienic and aesthetic "requirements vanish when you hit the trail. The dirt you will encounter in the wilderness is perfectly sanitary." The club advised women to bring their own feminine products (as "there are no rest rooms with vending machines"), to wear jeans, and to do without cosmetics, "even though you may shudder now at the thought of wearing a nude face."[67]

Elizabeth Cowles, a Vassar graduate and Colorado Springs resident, scaled more than two hundred major peaks in the Rockies, Alps, Andes, and Pyrenees, and she was on the board of American and European alpine clubs. She modestly attributed her interest to her father's Alpine exploits. In 1950 she joined an expedition attempting the southern approach to Mt. Everest. In lauding this "first Western woman to penetrate so far into that high, wild country," *American Magazine* assured its readers that Mrs. Cowles was a mother and "so completely feminine that one would never suspect her stamina and spirit of adventure. But it's as much a part of her mountaineering equipment as her climbing shoes, or the lipstick she carries in her knapsack. That's important, too, says Betsy, 'I've never been one to feel that the rough life became more delightful the worse you looked.'"[68]

Writing for the *Sierra Club Bulletin* in 1949, under the title "Have You A Mountain Widow in Your Home?," Cowles suggested that when men introduce their wives to climbing, they follow certain rules: (1) "Don't let her get tired. 'Take it easy.'" (2) "Don't let her get scared," take real climbing slowly, with simple chimneys, slabs, and ledges. (3) "Praise her endlessly! . . . do NOT condescend!" (4) "Don't let her get bored." She added: "I don't mean to say the little woman will necessarily be able to wave the American flag beside you on K-2, but the probabilities are she'll grow to love the mountains and share your joy in wild country." Cowles urged women to make themselves essential as helpmates by learning to cook on the trail.[69]

Women had become less visible, but they had not in fact disappeared from the mountains. In spring 1955 three made what was called the first women's Himalayan Expedition, an arduous and perilous, if underreported, trek into Jugal Himal.[70] Barbara Washburn joined her husband Bradford on the 20,320-foot summit of Mt. McKinley, enjoying especially, she said, the comradeship of the expedition. Women made many rope-and-piton climbs, claiming first ascents on Mt. Confederation in the Rockies, for example, in 1939, 1940, and 1948.[71] On the Sierra Club's 1953 High Trip, men made fifty-seven notable ascents, and women made seventeen, leading two. But in 1955 only one woman made a noteworthy climb.[72] Women made no recorded outstanding climbs with the Mazamas between 1941 and 1949, but between 1950 and 1960 they came back to complete sixteen notable ascents compared to men's thirty-eight.[73] European women were more visible: in 1951 two manless climbers ascended the twenty-thousand-foot Andean peak, Quitaraju, and in 1959 an all-women team made an attempt in the Himalayas.[74]

Nevertheless, many European alpinists disparaged women's accomplishments. Pioneer of the *cordée féminine*, Nea Morin climbed throughout the 1950s and 1960s, often with widows like herself, whose husbands had died in World War II. She wrote: "Sometimes I have found myself sighing for the golden age" of the 1920s, when men were more gallant and concerned with the welfare of the ladies whom they took climbing, a time when little prejudice existed, and women made great strides in leading. Despite their presence in the British hills, the Alps, and the Himalayas, no great number "of notable fresh ascents [were made] by women's parties in the Alps and the tremendous increase in the standard of climbing achieved by men has now widened the gap between men and women. The golden years of female ascents were between the wars when women's parties climbed the Matterhorn, Meije, Grépon, Verte and Drus."[75] Pointing to a new prejudice on men's part, Morin translated the French alpinist and artist Samivel's *L'Amateur d'Abîmes:*

Well do we know them, *les Malheureuses Dames de Pic!* [the *Dame de Picques* is the Queen of Spades], lonely crows who, aping men, haunt the huts and great mountain faces and ply the harsh tools of the mountains, baring their faces to the winds in ecstasy and straining to their bosoms the unfeeling rock with the ardour of lovers. . . . No! True women are too tender for the rigours of the mountains, and men will not accept that they should penetrate their domain—in their own interest of course— and after all we all must have some occasion to show ourselves (oh! so) superior.[76]

Explanations for women's diminished visibility are obvious yet elusive. In the United States, prejudice against women in well-paid jobs was growing; men were invariably the first employed in the professional ranks in conservation. As well, the postwar domestic ideal of motherhood was antithetical to alpine conventions. Morin herself was active in the Outward Bound movement for girls, but she thought that the movement's policy of using climbing "as a test of courage in others is unfair and futile"—whether for boys or for girls. She continued, "The aim of the mountaineer who takes novices climbing should surely be to awake in them a love of the mountains, to teach them to climb safely and to enjoy climbing, so that they will return on their own." The sport was aggres-

Figure 46. Line drawings of a man with a fig leaf and a man in a cage done by Samivel (the pseudonym used by Paul Gayet-Tancrède), L'Amateur d'Abîmes *(Paris: Delamain et Boutelleau, 1940).*

sively competitive in the 1950s, and men's dominance was as unchallenged on the peaks as it was in the home, where women were urged to be supportive.[77]

During this period technical climbing became popular. Women had participated in early rock climbs, using pitons and ropes. Men's often greater upper-body strength facilitated shoulder belays, and their height and longer arms offered advantages, but the sport does not necessarily favor men. Women vary in strength and agility, and teams routinely mixed physical types, often placing the lightest member as the leader. Women's diminished visibility owed much less to their physical limitations than to a growing reliance on alpine technologies, assumptions that men had a greater affinity with technology, and the escalating costs of expeditions. Men's increased use of mechanical aids became clear in Yosemite Valley, with some of the most inaccessible rock formations in the world. Mastery of the South Buttress of El Capitan, for example, required fifty days, elaborate logistics, the stamina of the alpinist, and the aerobic skills of the rock climber.[78]

Standing free from the valley's rim, near the top of Yosemite Falls, the granite spire Lost Arrow was considered by some "the last difficult unclimbed summit in America." Brower attempted it in 1937 and in 1941. After the war, the club's Rock Climbing Section resumed the assault, but their attempts floundered on the final pitch. Four of the section's men decided on a daring strategy. By casting ropes from the rim onto the top of the spire and then down its side, they could surmount the final unclimbable pitch by climbing

Figure 47. "The Arrow and the Clark Range" shows Jack Arnold
on the top of Lost Arrow in 1947. Photograph by Mark Zaepfle.
This picture appeared in the Sierra Club Bulletin *in 1948,*
illustrating an article narrating the 1947 ascent, written by Anton
Nelson, "Five Days and Nights on the Lost Arrow." The Arrow is
located between Yosemite Falls and Yosemite Point.

up the rope itself and then returning to the rim with an aerial traverse. After hours of casting, they finally placed the rope over the top of the rock.

While two men remained on the rim, Jack Arnold and Anton Nelson moved up the ledges of Lost Arrow, intending to reach the end of the rope dangling above them. The pitches required a 90 percent use of direct mechanical aids. At one point, Nelson, in the lead, found himself unable to continue; earlier attempts had damaged the few existing cracks and the angle was too steep to balance on and the rock was too smooth for his nails to dig into. Only ten inches from his face, however, he suddenly found a small, round hole that an earlier climber had drilled. He jammed a bolt into it. The bolt fit only

Figure 48. Tyrolean traverse on Lost Arrow. This photograph by Henry W. Kendall appeared in the Sierra Club Bulletin *in 1962, illustrating an article, "Climber's Camera," describing the 1947 ascent of Lost Arrow. The photograph shows Paul Delancy, the last man on the climb to leave the summit of the Arrow for the rim.*

loosely, but he relied on it to free his hands to drill another hole. The strain caused his leg muscles to quiver uncontrollably, and his temples pounded. Twenty minutes later he had secured the bolt, and his partner took the lead. They reached the bottom of the final pitch and the end of the rope. Positioned in a sling attached to the fixed line, Arnold pulled himself up. There were no cracks in which to secure pitons, and the rope might well have pulled free, but he reached the top, yodeling his success. Cheers went up from the audience on the rim. Park rangers below announced "to comfortable tourists seated at the evening campfire program at Camp Curry" that the top had been realized.

In the dusk, Nelson followed; the two men more firmly anchored the rope at the top of the Arrow. Nelson looped a sling around his body and snapped it to the fixed ropes with a carabiner to form a little trolley. Backing off the edge, hand over hand, head first, and crossing his legs over the heavy line, he slipped out over "a black, forbidding abyss," on ropes spanning one hundred feet between the anchors. The drop was twelve hundred feet to the base of the Arrow. After recording their conquest of the Arrow, Arnold followed Nelson to the rim, where the weary men paused to reflect: "The three days of unforgettable adventure have forged a comradeship like that of a bomber crew coming through the perils of war. In the starlight we look back. There looms the Lost Arrow . . . , silent, implacable, a phantom in the night."[79] Thus did men reach new heights in Yosemite. The techniques used in the climb were highly innovative. Nevertheless, the narrative reiterated long-accepted male conventions: battlefield analogies, the sublime moment, the implacable foe, and the frightening abyss.

Beginning in the mid-1940s, American men also claimed high-profile first ascents on alpine expeditions, finding Samivel's "*La Sublime Horreur*" in conventionally romantic environments.[80] Alaska's St. Elias Range was one such location. Bradford Washburn led his second and third scientific expeditions up Mt. McKinley.[81] The Himalayas, in particular, fascinated Americans with their unnamed peaks, unmapped topographies, uncataloged plants, and an ethnographic frontier of "paleo-mongoloid tribes," including "strange savages and dwarflike people."[82]

Makalu rises 27,900 feet in the Himalayas and is the world's fifth highest peak. On the Nepal-Tibet border, Makalu is southeast of Everest. British climbers had tried to reach the summit before World War II, but had failed. Ten young San Francisco Bay Area men, led by research physicist William Siri, tried again in 1954, with funding from the Sierra Club, the American Alpine Club, the National Science Foundation, and the Air Force's Department of Research and Development. The expedition required four base camps and fourteen Sherpas, 153 Nepalese village porters, and 90 porters from Dhahran. For four rupees per day, or eighty-two cents, each porter carried seventy pounds (sixty pounds, plus their own clothing and food). "A strong Nepalese coolie [male or female] without shoes can carry nearly two mauds—164 lbs.—for days along a rocky track, subsisting on little more than a small sack of rice."[83]

Makalu provided the quintessential alpine adventure. Men of European descent competed in national teams against nature at her worst. The climbers voiced the satisfaction that "derived while fighting for the top. It is a battle between man and nature." They recorded moments of near death and failure, "saturated moments" of intense concentration on staying alive. They called Makalu their enemy, a savage that guarded a land of avalanches and crevasses

Figure 49. "*Mountaineers at Base Camp, Rest Day.*" *The first California Himalayan Expedition and the first reconnaissance of Makalu (27,790'), in 1954. The expedition's photographers were Allen Steck and William Siri, both of whom appear in the front row of this photograph. Courtesy of the Sierra Club.*

with greenish innards. As the *Saturday Evening Post* said of such mountains, they "hate people." Makalu won with an early monsoon. Waiting it out, the men watched their funding run out. Their wives, who had packed the provisions and typed the inventories, now raised $3,000 to pay for their husbands' transportation home. (A sidebar to the expedition narrative asked, "Why Aren't More Women Naturalists? The answer was: "They're apt to blither.— At things that slither.") The California men took heart from the conviction that they had served science. They had recorded information on men's performance under conditions of cold and fatigue, collected materials on the animal and plant life of "the unknown parts of Nepal," and mapped the peak so that others could follow. They had fulfilled their roles as citizens, soldiers, and explorers. A French team reached the top in 1955.[84]

While alpinism thus retained its racial, national, gendered, and combative overtones through the 1950s, and while its practitioners still courted and mastered fear, the conventions of the sport no longer allowed men to express these emotions. American climbers described themselves as closed-mouthed, self-contained, and self-controlled, a composite of the traditional British alpinist, the GI of World War II, and the hero of western movies. These were soldiers of the wilderness, the strong and the brave, disciplined to solve technical problems of survival. Reminiscent of Whymper, they claimed that they had to coax their Sherpas across crevasses and teach them how to handle ropes.

American climbers read Maurice Herzog's narrative of his French team's conquest of 26,493-foot Annapurna.[85] They particularly relished, however, the Englishman Sir John Hunt's account "of how, on May 29, 1953, two men . . . inspired by an unflinching resolve, reached the top of Everest." Hunt described the allure: "The possibility of entering the unknown; the simple fact that it was the highest point on the world's surface—these things goaded us on." He called the effort symbolic of "man's struggle to come to terms with the forces of nature . . . ; the opponent was not other parties, but Everest itself." One man who read Hunt's narrative concluded that there was "no time in human history when mountains and mountaineering have had so much to offer to men."[86] Despite Hunt's conventional rhetoric, those who led the expedition grappled with their own assumptions about their superiority as civilized men. When Sir Edmund Hillary and Sherpa Tenzing Norkey reached the top, they planted British, Nepalese, United Nations, and Indian flags. Tenzing left chocolate, biscuits, and candy. Hunt called the gesture "a token gift to the gods that all devout Buddhists believe have their home on this lofty summit." When an Asian student asked him "what the point was of climbing Everest," Hunt replied that danger forged "comradeship, regardless of race or creed."[87]

Some Americans also questioned the assumptions they held about other peoples, if only in relation to the "primitives" of the past. The Wilderness Society explained why its 1949 meeting was being held in the wilderness: "No place . . . could offer a more appropriate environment . . . than this natural setting of Indian Pow-wows . . . in the heart of the vast continent. Here is the place of places to emulate, in reverse, the pioneering spirit of Joliet and Marquette. They came to quell the wilderness for the sake of civilization. We come to restore the wilderness for the sake of civilization." By opening the meeting with tales of an "aged Indian Squaw," the society sought, it explained, not to "supplant urbanity by pan-primevaldom," but to reinstate "the complete, though not continuous, aboriginal American landscape . . . ; to reclaim the civilized unto a resplendent savage dignity."[88] Praising a map of areas that the Forest Service had classified as wilderness, the society also extolled "man's primitive environment." As the original "home of the genus Homo, its influence is essential to his well being."[89]

As Hillary and Tenzing were starting up Everest, the Sierra Club was honoring the life (and death twenty years earlier) of Totuya (who later took the name Maria Labrado), considered the last Native American to have been present when the Mariposa Battalion invaded Yosemite Valley in 1851. The club

Figure 50. Maria Labrado, or Totuya, was considered the last survivor of the Ahwahneechee present when her people were driven from Yosemite Valley in the early 1850s. This photograph of her was taken in 1929 by Joseph Dixon, behind the Yosemite National Park Museum, on the occasion of a return to the valley. Courtesy of Yosemite National Park Library.

praised her dignity and expressed regret at losing the innocence that her life represented. After years of refusing to do so, Totuya had revisited the valley in 1929. Park Service officials accompanied her in and showed her their collection of native artifacts. Totuya had reportedly smiled at seeing these reminders of her people and at having been treated with "warmth and understanding" by a "white woman"—the museum librarian. To the Sierra Club, that smile signaled a "change of heart," perhaps forgiveness.[90] Climbers who had once assumed that the significance of the summits had been invisible to the eye of a Totuya now found in her a natural reverence they hoped to emulate; civilized man needed to "discipline his possessiveness."[91]

In 1954 Ansel Adams mounted an exhibit of his landscape photographs on panels in the Sierra Club's LeConte Lodge. Located on the floor of Yosemite Valley and named for geologist Joseph LeConte, the lodge had housed club gatherings since 1902 and served as the northern terminus of the John Muir Trail. With its Tyrolean architecture, peaked roof, great fireplace, and library of classics that included Edward Whymper's *Scrambles* and Sir John Hunt's narrative, the lodge evoked Anglo-American alpine traditions. The exhibit, entitled "This is the American Earth," invited visitors to see their surroundings through the lens of Adams's camera. Most visitors doubtlessly assumed that Adams's magnificent images of empty landscapes showed Yosemite much as it had looked when Totuya's people had been forced out of the valley.

Adams's images reflected long-standing aesthetic conventions that made wilderness a place in which humans were either absent or afterthoughts, and even animals were rare. Bears, deer, and people had no place in the fine art of landscape photography. Although his heroic black-and-white images evoked the seemingly barren Sierra, Adams also brought new dimensions to the traditions of the masculine sublime. His mountains were vast but not forbidding; their symmetry, grace, and sublime beauty invited lingering attention. The observer entered the wild by passing through the frames of his photographs. In the body of his work, he addressed the paradox of wilderness as a place without humans, yet defined by humans. Yosemite remained the abyss, but Michael and Ann played there. Adams depicted the desolate Sierra, so expressive of the masculine sublime, images that would have thrilled Clarence King. But children also belonged in the mountains that Adams loved.[92] The primitive was a place of rebirth—for men, for the family, for the nation, and for humanity. The nurturing mother, the helpmate-in-training daughter, the self-reliant man-child, and the strong father flourished in the mountains. As long as family and wilderness held steady, as long as men surmounted peaks, women were supportive, and families camped together, the nation, it was assumed, would survive.[93]

Prominent among the couples who were active in conservation in the 1940s and 1950s, and who found comfort in seeing the parks and forests as at once wild and home, were Estelle and Aldo Leopold, Ann and David Brower, Joel and Louise Hildebrand, Ansel and Virginia Best Adams, Francis and Marjory Bridge Farquhar, and the Alaskan wildlife conservationists Olaus and Margaret Murie.[94] Psychological and historical paradigms had prompted these and other conservationists to call mountains home. In the outdoors, as in the home, women often handled the logistics. Most American men took for granted not only spousal help but the porters and guides who toiled beside them. They believed that the family outing, the rock climb, the alpine expedition, and even the heights themselves affirmed the naturalness of social hierarchies that placed women and minorities in supportive roles. The sport prospered as it drew on conventions of territorial mastery well suited to the global sway of the American way of life.

There were inconsistencies in this vision. First, conservationists were nostalgic for a frontier that had destroyed the native cultures they now idealized. Second, by making summits the sole domain of men, they misrepresented the sport's own history and slighted women's achievements. Third, the very act of exploration destroyed the unknown, such that by the mid-1950s, it was clear to the Sierra Club that its own pack animals were badly damaging the meadows of the Sierra.[95] Even as wilderness advocates came to recognize problems of recreational overcrowding, however, they found it necessary to broaden their base of political support in order to protect America's mountains from logging.

Mountains Made Wilderness

In the summer of 1960 resource managers from sixty-five countries gathered in Seattle for the Fifth World Forestry Congress. The chief of the U.S. Forest Service, Richard McArdle, opened the proceedings with words of praise for his agency's own foresters.[1] His remarks should not have surprised his audience. In the popular imagination, forest rangers were a blend of mythic western lawman and cowboy—American heroes, patrolling the national forests on horseback, vigilant with trespassers yet helpful to the public and friend to Smoky the Bear—a manly image that the service cultivated. Nevertheless, during McArdle's speech, climbers from the Mazamas stood out in the hall distributing copies of the Sierra Club's *Outdoor Newsletter* showing photographs of lush mountain forests next to slopes that had been clear-cut, their soils exposed, and strewn with downed logs and slash, their creek beds maimed. The *Newsletter* likened the agency's management of the Cascade Range, the Sierra Nevada, and the Rocky Mountains to the poor land-use practices that had caused the collapse of the classical civilizations of the Mediterranean. That day, the rangers at the conference confiscated all the copies of the *Newsletter* that they could find.[2]

Assuming that the Sierra Club's executive secretary, David Brower, was responsible for the literature, the chief asked the club's directors whether they had approved this "vicious propaganda." Brower accused McArdle of trying to get him fired and of attempting to abridge his freedom of speech. Brower, however, was not fired. He represented people like club director Ansel Adams, who said simply: "I trust no Government Bureau." To Adams, Brower, and others, the forest ranger had become the organization man.[3]

The episode in Seattle illustrates the pivotal role that mountains and mountaineers continued to play within the conservation movement. The old-growth forests of the western ranges had borne the brunt of a national housing boom. Hiking into their high-altitude destinations, the Mazamas, the Mountaineers, the Federation of Western Outdoor Clubs, and the Sierra Club were among the first to observe the accelerated pace of logging operations on public lands. Familiar with the terrain, conversant with officials, and accustomed to working together, these clubs became the vanguard of environmentalism, fighting the united strength of the logging, mining, grazing, and waterpower interests. In the immediate postwar years, wilderness defenders had relied on the language of family and patriotism. A decade later, a general revitalization of liberalism nationally made advocates bolder as they undertook their chosen task of defining for Congress and the public the values that wilderness represented.[4]

At stake were not only specific wild places but also what writer Wallace Stegner called "the wilderness idea."[5] Western outdoor clubs joined with eastern groups, such as the National Recreation Association, the Appalachian Mountain Club, and the Wilderness Society, to become a major lobby critical of federal policies.[6] They presented wilderness as a solution to the social ills that liberal critics William H. Whyte, Vance Packard, and John Kenneth Galbraith were describing, and identified with the concerns for human survival expressed by George Orwell, Julian Huxley, Bertrand Russell, and others. Nancy Newhall and Rachel Carson brought feminine perspectives into these broad critiques of American society. Nevertheless, "the idea of wilderness" was framed primarily by and for middle-class men, with David Brower at the forefront. During the 1950s and early 1960s, middle-class society defined masculinity in terms of domestic and military obligation, locking men into roles as breadwinners, fathers, husbands, and soldiers.[7] Advocates of wilderness described places in which men could escape these roles while holding out wilderness as a place where men could also validate the authenticity of these roles.

Climbers and hikers enjoyed the areas that the Forest Service had classified as wilderness, primitive, roadless, limited, or wild prior to World War II. In 1952, however, the Forest Service made public its intention to review the status of the seventy-nine sites that it had so classified. Comprising fourteen million acres in the western mountains, these areas contained much of the nation's last old growth forests. The agency claimed that the review process would ensure long-term protection, but wilderness advocates soon realized that the boundaries were being redrawn so as to exclude commercially valuable timber in the national forests of the Sierra Nevada, in Aldo Leopold's Gila Primitive Area, and on the slopes of Southern California's tallest peak, Mt. San Gorgonio. They also foresaw that the forests of the Cascades of Washington and Oregon needed protection.

The seven-hundred-mile length of the Cascades is dominated in west central Oregon by a chain of volcanic domes running from Mt. Jefferson in the north through Three-Fingered Jack, Mt. Washington, Mt. Hood, and the Three Sisters south to Diamond Peak and Crater Lake. The Mazamas prized these peaks, particularly Mt. Hood, on whose summit the club had been founded. As World War II had drawn to a close, these glacier-tipped "shining mountains" still loomed over clear lakes, fresh streams, waterfalls, abundant wildlife, and ancient stands that were nearly rain forests.[8] Anticipating that the Forest Service intended to log these areas, Brower urged the Sierra Club's board of directors to establish a chapter in the Pacific Northwest. To concerns that creating such a chapter might offend the Mazamas, the Mountaineers, and the Federation of Western Outdoor Clubs, Brower responded that competition was required in order to "increase in wisdom, stature, and favor." In the summer of 1952, the directors agreed.[9] Brower's audacity in taking from sport the spirit of productive rivalry suited them. That December, as the nation waited for Dwight D. Eisenhower to assume the presidency, the Sierra Club hired David Brower as its first executive secretary.[10] He immediately headed for Seattle to establish the new chapter and then traveled east to discuss Dinosaur National Monument with leaders of the Wilderness Society, the Izaac Walton League, and the American Planning and Civic Association.[11]

The U.S. Bureau of Reclamation had applied to Congress to locate one of the dams of the Upper Colorado River Storage Project in Dinosaur National Monument, a sublime landscape of deeply fissured, warmly colored sandstone situated in the high intermountain plateau on the border of Colorado and Utah.[12] From Washington, D.C., Brower telephoned the Berkeley home of Richard and Doris Leonard, prompting an emergency meeting at which members of the Sierra Club sat on the Leonard's living room floor to plan a defensive strategy for a place they knew only dimly. First they visited the park, the traditional exploratory step that club strategists had taken since the nineteenth century. Richard Leonard made the trip and stayed in the fight, as did, among others, the Mountaineers' Polly Dyer, manless climber Marjory Bridge Farquhar, landscape architect Cicely Christy, and Kathleen Goddard Jones, a southern Californian for whom Dinosaur launched a career of grassroots activism with the club, the Audubon Society, and the Native Plant Society.[13]

The high point of the battle came in 1954, when Brower told a House committee that the Bureau of Reclamation's calculations of how much water a dam in the monument would conserve were incorrect.[14] He denounced the entire project as an engineering mistake. He was convinced that the engineers "knew they were lying."[15] Opposition to the dam also came from the five-million-member General Federation of Women's Clubs and the three-million-member National Wildlife Federation, both of which deluged Congress with letters.[16] The House dropped Dinosaur from the Colorado Water Project. The battle had broadened the wilderness movement's agenda to include the intermountain plateaus of the west.[17]

Meanwhile, the Forest Service had reclassified its Three Sisters Primitive Area in Oregon's Cascades as a wilderness area, eliminating fifty-two thousand acres of timbered lowlands known as "French Pete."[18] By releasing French Pete for logging, the service hoped to fend off pressures to privatize the national forests and to meet the Eisenhower administration's call for full utilization of public resources, a policy aimed at stimulating the national economy.[19] The areas excluded from the Three Sisters Primitive Area were eventually logged, but not before preservationists put up a fight. In an address delivered that year to the Society of American Foresters and introduced into the *Congressional Record*, a professor at the Oklahoma Agricultural and Mechanical College, James P. Gilligan, charged that the Forest Service had never intended to protect the wild, primitive, and wilderness areas for the long term.[20]

The charge of hypocrisy seemed borne out when McArdle announced the following year that the boundaries of all seventy-nine classified areas would be adjusted, beginning with Oregon's Diamond Peak and Mt. Washington Limited Areas, both of which would become smaller, isolated "wild" areas.[21] The Forest Service had always held discretion over such designations, and five years earlier wilderness advocates had begun to address the need for stronger guarantees.[22] They now looked for a legislative sponsor to introduce their bill for a National Wilderness Preservation System and found one in Senator Hubert Humphrey.[23] Humphrey's 1956 bill defined places that would be roadless, where mining, logging, and grazing were limited, and where humans would be only visitors.[24] For the next eight years, advocates lobbied for the bill, and for eight years logging, mining, and grazing interests blocked it. So did the Forest Service's foresters, who did not want their professional discretion limited. In the interim, the agency was already reevaluating areas in the State of Washington.

Dams on the Skagit River bisected Washington's Cascades, but glacial peaks towered above unbroken conifer forests north and south of the river. A North Cascades Primitive Area extended from Hart's Pass to Canada; this had been the territory of the Mountaineers, presumably safe with the Forest Service. Dominating the range to the south of the river was Glacier Peak, a 10,528-foot volcanic cone known for its glaciers, lakes, meadows, and forests. Before the war, the Forest Service had designated the peak a limited area, identifying its natural values for future study. In 1957, however, the service announced that the Glacier Peak Limited Area would be reclassified as a wilderness area and its size significantly reduced.[25] The Mountaineers, the Federation of Western Outdoor Clubs, and the new North Cascades Conservation Council, among other local groups, activated a national network to lobby for a North Cascades National Park, and redoubled their support for the wilderness bill.[26]

The campaigners publicly portrayed the new Glacier Peak and Three Sisters Wilderness Areas as little more than treeless lava flows, barren zones of "perpetual snow," their thin fingers stretching along rocky ridges, their forested corridors, valleys, and slopes slated for logging. Brower called the Glacier Peak area "a Rorschach blot designed to bring out the worst in a highly guilty subconscious." He predicted a "symphony of destruction." The new areas represented the essence of sublimity: still as death, barren, and desolate. The service justified this literal interpretation of wilderness, but climbers were angry.[27] When the service held public hearings on the Glacier Peak plan in 1959, Brower testified that he and his allies had not reached their "conclusions second-hand, nor out of fear of the government. . . . We have tried . . . to see for ourselves," he said, pointing to a four-year study of Glacier Peak by the Mountaineers. He called federal foresters "medicine men" who spouted clichés they paraded as science.[28] Calling himself a working conservationist, Brower argued against professional specialization. "To 'leave these things to the experts' [was] to resort to absentee citizenship."[29]

Brower was applying the lessons he had learned long ago from the Yosemite Park and Curry Company and newer ones that federal agencies, nonprofit organizations, and private corporations had taught him. "To enlist disciplined belief," he targeted "the urban conservationist."[30] Sharing his determination, the Sierra Club's board readily agreed when the press asked to attend its meetings in 1956. The board also supported Brower's hectic rounds of speaking, where he presented 16 mm films: the "Wilderness Alps of Stehekin," showing a family exploring Washington's Cascades; and "Two Yosemites," which contrasted the part of the national park that remained wild and the lost Hetch Hetchy Valley.[31] He traveled by train to address the National Geographic Society in the nation's capital and the National Council of Churches in California. Taking to the air in 1958, he spoke to the Harvard Travelers Club in Boston, to students in Oregon, oil executives in Washington, agricultural engineers in Santa Barbara, the Lions Club in Fruitvale, California, and to conservationists in Montana.[32]

Eager to prove his case to his generally well-educated audiences, Brower referred to scholarly and popular works, including James Gilligan's address to the Society of American Foresters; Herbert Kaufman's study *The Forest Ranger;* and the then widely popular book *Parkinson's Law,* which derided bureaucracies for empire building, mediocrity, inertia, and waste.[33] Using Vance Packard's recently published exposé of advertising, Brower called federal foresters "hidden persuaders" who manipulated public opinion by labeling preservationists as "extremists" or "members of the daffodil wing of bird watchers," and who called an old-growth stand "a decadent forest" that should be cut down to make room for "tree farms." He accused the service of giving schoolchildren "posters heralding the togetherness of recreation and logging." He held up slick, four-color advertisements in which the service invariably used paintings; photographs, he said, told "a different story," the true one, and that was why the club used them.[34]

Mastering "before" and "after" images, the club showed scenes of clear-cut operations, undoubtedly surprising the average American who may have thought that the service permitted only selective logging. Club publications carried Ansel Adams's photographs of great forests skirting what the club called "the frozen violence" of Glacier Peak, following these images with those of stumps on a brushy slope that had been logged in 1942 and had yet to reforest itself. Glacier Peak appeared in the background, its fierce visage compromised. Aerial photographs recorded entire mountainsides on which every tree had been felled, the land laced with the tracks of heavy machinery.[35]

Calling wilderness "the pressure of man's conscience," Brower warned Americans that their "tranquilized future" would not match their dreams.[36] "We see the world coagulating, slogan by slogan." He told citizens to resist "destructive developments for the sake of present ease" if they wanted "a 1984 different from Orwell's Big Brother and brainwashing." He urged college students to establish "public interest groups" to fight pressures for conformity.[37] Echoing David Riesman and other contemporary critics, Brower told Americans that they were too concerned with being liked, and he attacked the complacency engendered by wealth, referring his listeners to John Kenneth Galbraith's then new book, *The Affluent Society.* "It is our mission to identify fault, place blame, urge change," Brower harped; he called himself "the consumer" who demanded high levels of performance from the expert.[38] His words capitalized on the faith that postwar social critics placed in nonprofit organizations and in pluralism.

The club spoke of middle-class needs to middle-class audiences, evoking that class's potential for moral reform. Although affluence brought deterioration in the quality of public life, affluence also afforded amenities.[39] Brower quoted Laurencot from Romain Gary's *The Roots of Heaven:* "A utilitarian civilization will always go on to its logical conclusion—forced labor camps." Next to a publicity photograph of a multiterraced highway cut into a mountainside in Yosemite National Park, the club's caption quoted Galbraith's *The Liberal Hour:* "A poor society may ask only that its products be well engineered. But a richer one is certain to require that they have beauty as well."[40]

In 1956 the Eisenhower Administration launched Mission 66, a ten-year, billion dollar program to finance new structures, services, and roads in the national parks. Eager to protect the roadless portions of the parks, the framers of the wilderness bill had already incorporated the national parks into their legislation. Events surrounding Tioga Road, a steep, high-altitude, trans-Sierra route that ran east out of Yosemite Valley, soon confirmed their fears concerning the potential of Mission 66. A twenty-one-mile stretch of this road, which had been built in 1883, remained only ten feet wide, but now the service was asking the Sierra Club for recommendations on how it might be widened to two lanes. The club recommended a narrow, slow-speed road, and for two years it was under the impression that the service had agreed.[41]

When construction began in 1958, however, the engineers blasted across a beautiful slope of granite polished by ancient glaciers to construct a wide, high-speed road around Tenaya Lake in the upper valley. According to Conrad Wirth, the director of the Park Service, Brower and Ansel Adams became "violent protesters."[42] The club accused the service of hypocrisy, and Brower charged Wirth with having ties to the American Automobile Association and to road construction people, of coveting a large budget, and of ignoring objections from his own superintendent of Yosemite Park. Adams labeled the Tenaya Road a desecration by the "bulldozers of bureaucracy," and he charged that "nothing but disdain, evasion, and sometimes downright duplicity" had resulted from the club's efforts to maintain friendly relations with the Park Service. Club literature showed Adams's elegant photographs of beautiful granite walls next to photographs that Brower had taken of dynamited slopes and a bulldozed roadbed.[43] The club strongly recommended against new roads in the parks and outlined standards for reconstructing existing routes.[44]

Figure 51. Photograph of David Brower. Courtesy of University of
California, Bancroft Library.

The Forest Service's administration of its multiple-use areas—the largest
portion of the national forests—also angered the club. The service claimed
that it managed each such area for at least two of six uses: logging, livestock,
mining, watershed, wildlife, and recreation.[45] In 1956 the agency released a
multiple-use management plan calling for the construction of a dense system
of logging roads into the timber regions of the Kern Plateau. According to the
club, the plateau was a "gentle wilderness" of half a million acres of granite
domes, timbered basins, and high forested flats.[46] Located on the hot, dry, east
slopes of the southern Sierra, the plateau was important to climbers and hikers; as well, the plateau protected the headwaters of the Kern River. The club
asked that the region be classified as a wilderness area.[47] The service issued a
second multiple-use plan for the Kern Plateau in 1959, this time proposing numerous access roads for recreational developments.[48] Brower charged
hypocrisy again. On a tour of the plateau, a local ranger showed Brower

exemplary logging along approach roads, meadows, and streams, but in other parts of the watershed, Brower jotted in his diary, he was "sickened" by what he found. Predicting that the Sierra and Cascades would be "riddled" with roads, he set out to prove that multiple-use management was nothing more than a public relations ploy.[49]

He asked audiences to visualize camping in a multiple-use area where "the whole complex biota of the virgin forest floor, born of aeons of growth and death, . . . cool, exquisite" had been replaced by a "simplified, dried out and warmed up" land with a few commercial species of trees. Visitors would enter on logging roads, camp in clear-cuts, and burn logging debris in their campfires. "Ecological recreation" in a complex natural community differed dramatically. For Brower, wilderness was the place "where man could be alone, where you could rescue your *self* from what Ortega calls the *other*—all the extraneities that pile on you too deep." But the value of old growth went beyond freedom for individuals; wilderness conservation was "humanity fighting for the future."[50] He predicted that Americans would eventually realize that "growth without end" was "soon monstrous, then malignant, and finally lethal." Monstrous because human and nonhuman resources were being devoured; malignant because "incessant growth" represented a "chain-letter economy" with handsome early returns but with empty mailboxes for our children. As proof that growth would also be fatal, he held up photos of two billboards next to each other. One announced, "Your future is great in a growing America!" The other urged, "Protect yourself from Fallout."[51]

To the Harvard Travelers Club, he said that America was "a society out of control." He asked: Was it "timidity to wonder" how nations could "rush pell mell through their natural resources without colliding with the neighbors whose resources they covet?" Was it "Malthusian to wonder if a world bent on doubling its population every century" could survive? Was it "pessimism to doubt that Science will rescue us, once the clean H-bomb and space hardware have been perfected and there's money for other research?" He called "the present-day rivalry in resource development an international exploit in the game of chicken, wherein . . . 'juvenile delinquents' approach each other at high speed on a highway and the first guy who turns to avoid the head-on crash is chicken." He quoted anthropologist Ashley Montagu: "War must be outlawed." If we do not, "a few blind flashes can destroy all that mankind has dreamed in all millenniums."[52]

When the Soviet Union's Nikita Khrushchev hinted at a de-escalation of the cold war during his visit to the United States in 1959, the *San Francisco Chronicle* warned of the adverse economic impact of three million fewer men in the military and cutbacks in orders to every major industry.[53] Brower used the editorial as his foil for a speech in Chicago. He predicted that de-escalation of the cold war would mean the end of "tithing" to aid military preparedness, the end of $50 million for plants to build obsolete bombs. He foresaw more time off from work and echoed Bertrand Russell's prophecy of global happiness. Logic should instead tell you, he said, that de-escalation promised a better life; "so did your heart" when you saw "your six-year-old playing air-raid drill, lying prone with his arms protecting his head." Seconding Linus Pauling's opposition to nuclear testing, Brower asked how people could ignore the "radioactive hazard to man's future" as they watched their children practice responding to "air raids" by diving under their desks. He said, "No environment" could "produce a gene that can shield itself from unnatural radiation."[54]

The Sierra Club targeted another explosion, warning that wilderness would not be the only casualty of uncontrolled human population; "the population explosion has severely disturbed the ecological relationship between mankind and his environment." The several hundred delegates attending the club's 1959 Wilderness Conference had passed a resolution that supported "desirable population controls." Linus Pauling, Julian Huxley, Aldous Huxley, Lewis Mumford, and William H. Whyte were all quoted as calling overpopulation the most serious threat to the future of our species.[55]

How had the desire to protect mountains become a population issue? The housing boom generated by the postwar demographic spike and rising affluence had encouraged the timber industry to look to the old-growth stands of the mountains; and burgeoning numbers of American families, eager to camp outdoors, were destroying the very quality of desolation that was central to experiences of the masculine sublime. Recreational use of the national forests and parks had become equally problematic from feminine and naturalist perspectives. Climber Phoebe Anne Sumner offered a wilderness parable of "the last citadel" deep in the Sierra, so inaccessible that it had never been explored. Discovered by a few climbers, the canyon now spoke to them, urging them to go away, to tell no one of its existence, and to leave hidden this "self-sustaining world" with its animals, birds, plants, and trees all "in perfect equilibrium, requiring nothing from outside their granite home" except the sun and the rain.[56] This was the lesson of the mountain meadow: that peoples and resources, like pack animals and pastures, must be kept in balance.[57]

To Brower, global conflict and the destruction of wild places were the products of selfishness; conservation meant practicing everywhere the self-restraint and sacrifice that climbers learned in the mountains.[58] The club reprinted Robert Marshall's 1930 article arguing that men became violent without wild places into which they can retreat.[59] Although the resources of the high range had once appeared beyond the reach of the industrial world, they were now being used to fuel the arms race. Activists highlighted the connection by calling "Operation Multiple Use" "an assault" or "invasion" of the nation's public lands. The association became clear with the State of California's plan to build a trans-Sierra highway near Mammoth Lakes to move military equipment and to evacuate citizens in the event of war. Brower countered: "The kind of national defense the Mammoth Pass Road could serve is rapidly becoming more obsolete. . . . Even Detroit's fleetest set of tail fins cannot outrace an ICBM, nor escape wind-borne fallout . . . on a panic-packed highway. The Mammoth-for-national-defense argument is a phony."[60]

By linking war, population, and wilderness, the club was bringing up to date Aldo Leopold's declarations that wild places were the yardsticks against which to measure the health of ecosystems, that only in wilderness could we find the pieces with which to repair damaged ecosystems. This was the meaning of Thoreau's "In wildness is the preservation of the world" and of physicist Benjamin Rush's warning, "If man obliterates wilderness, he is in a terrifying sense on his own." Brower urged attending to the wisdom of what he variously called God, the Creator, the Teacher, Deity, or simply Nature. He had "infinitely more confidence in what evolutionary force—the stream of life— has built into your chromosomes and mine than I have in any scientist's conclusions from his incomplete research." Wildness was for those "willing to accept what God has done," he told listeners. Again quoting Laurencot: man must have "a sanctuary . . . from his own cleverness and folly."[61]

The Sierra Club published an article by Yale botanist Paul Sears, who, like Julian Huxley, warned that science and industry were creating a dangerous illusion of limitless abundance. Sears and Huxley argued that because resources are in reality finite, human survival requires struggle, and the lessons of struggle are most readily learned in the wilderness. Moreover, limited resources must be used wisely. In a world where millions are hungry, Sears asked, why does American industry concentrate on the mass production of "toys for adults"? Why should we "worry so much about the other side of the moon when our cities . . . are erupting into unplanned chaos?"[62]

The Sierra Club produced "an exhibit format book" using the photographs that Ansel Adams had exhibited in the Sierra Club's LeConte Lodge in 1954. The book's title, *This Is the American Earth*, played upon themes of our national landscape in peril, but the book located this landscape within a story of the fall of western civilization. Adams's black-and-white images and Nancy Newhall's blank-verse text captured themes of a liberal social critique by portraying history as a story of moral decline and environmental degradation. The reader's eye moved from pristine scenes of wilderness to suburban rows of ticky-tacky houses and jagged skylines of television antennas. Newhall analyzed modern abundance and technology: "Now by machines we are torn loose from the earth—too soon, too suddenly, surrendered, the arts, the skills, the strength that were our pride as man. Confined by our own artifice [that is] borne up on vast abundance and colossal waste." The pall of radioactive fallout hung over the book's final pages. Next to ominous images of thunderclouds and of children in a trailer camp, the text read: "Today in the 20th Century . . . , death rides a ray, an atom . . . dooming . . . how many forms of life to cancerous corruption and to monstrous births?" Newhall evoked crowds in the billions, their hunger multiplying, their needs driving "nations to madness," while the affluent few blasted, strangled, choked, drilled, and grabbed the precious land. Only in the highest of America's mountains, she added, could pilgrims still tread "light and silent."[63]

Contemporary images represented stages in this history. Adams's photographs of agriculture in California's Salinas Valley stood for the rural past. His scenes of the Sierra captured the terra incognita of the masculine sublime: geological irregularities, portentous clouds, black ridges erupting against brittle ice fields, granite walls nude and pale in full sun, barren peaks spiking above the timberline, and glaciers that dropped off into the abyss. Images in black, white, and grays presented places as vast and empty as Americans wished to visualize their continent at the moment before European settlement. The book was a critical success, and the club used this story of cultural and environmental decay in lobbying for passage of the wilderness bill.[64]

In its campaign the club also drew on its familiarity with how federal bureaucracies operated.[65] Brower cited budgetary figures to prove that the Forest Service was biased against wilderness, attributing the bias to the absence of internal dissent within the agency. He warned college students against William Whyte's "organization man."[66] Claiming that all foresters held their pipes "in the same hand at the same angle," Brower called them "the organization man's organization man." He detailed the strategies that the Forest Service used to defeat internal dissent, but also adding that its foresters were so socialized by the agency that they did not feel that they were simply obeying orders.[67] For years the club had criticized schools of forestry for focusing exclusively on timber management.[68] Now it denounced decisions "by expert technicians" who were trained only in "saw log" forestry.[69] The club further noted that neither Congress nor the secretary of agriculture exerted external control on the Forest Service, and Brower quoted Wallace Stegner's description of the chief of the Forest Service—a "benevolent dictator" and "more powerful than the President himself."[70]

To Brower, the Forest Service's multiple-use management was "a political device" that enabled the service to determine "the balance of power between the various user groups, with minimal control imposed upon it by law, regulation, or by difficulty of discipline within the organization."[71] The club relied on the work of political scientist and climber Grant McConnell, whose expertise lay in organizational behavior. McConnell saw multiple-use management as "the disguise for an absence of policy and for the arbitrary exercise of large-scale discretion."[72] The club warned that the Forest Service was using the rationale of multiple use to block proposals that would transfer to the Park Service some of the nation's most magnificent national forest sites in the North Cascades, the Great Basin-Wheeler Peak country of Nevada, the Ritter-Minarets country in the Sierra, and the Sawtooth Mountains of Idaho.[73] Brower and the rest of his organization lobbied for the transfer of Forest Service lands to the jurisdiction of the Park Service.[74] Urging Congress to assume control over the management of all federal lands, especially the national parks and the national forests, Brower said that the real intent of bureaucratic policy was to "never let go of authority."[75]

In the middle of these controversies, the delegates to the 1960 World Forestry Congress had arrived in Seattle and the Mazamas had distributed the Sierra Club's *Outdoor Newsletter* that charged the Forest Service with "infesting the deepest recesses" of the western ranges. The president of the Society of American Foresters, Henry Clepper, told President Nathan Clark of the Sierra Club that airing domestic controversies at a global meeting was "in shocking bad taste."[76] Clark replied that "some serious citizens do not agree with all things that our government is doing . . . , a fine proof that our people are free to speak their minds—even in opposition to their officials. . . . Perhaps we should be proud of our freedom and let the rest of the world see that we really have it." As Clark described the conflict, it was between those with "vocational interests in the forests" and "volunteer citizens."[77] Historians have found this antithesis suggestive. According to Samuel P. Hays, modern environmentalism is consumer-led, unlike the earlier conservation movement, which was led by such professionals as foresters.[78] The wilderness lobby employed the rhetoric and the reality of democracy; its leaders, however, built a democratic base by relying on public relations campaigns as well as on the work of professionals in conservation, health, recreation, psychology, and the arts.

Brower's combative style and his broad reform agenda attracted Americans to his cause and shaped diverse interests into a powerful movement.[79] As the club became larger and more socially and geographically diffuse, well-delineated enemies sustained a common purpose. Acting as what sociologists now call a "movement intellectual," Brower turned "the organization man" into a common enemy whose existence forged a unity of purpose within the Sierra Club and within the wilderness movement.[80]

Between the wars, mountaineers who took time from careers as lawyers, teachers, engineers, and academics had led the Sierra Club because they wanted to protect mountains they knew well. Now volunteers and staff pursued a broader agenda. Their annual budget had grown from $10,000 in 1956 to $280,000 by 1960. The club was no longer the social organization it had been even a decade earlier. The requirement that two members attest to a prospective member's character was dropped, because many people were joining solely out of an interest in conservation. "Intangible objections to the personality of the applicant for membership" had long been regarded as "sufficient bar in view of the close social nature of many of the club's functions and trips into the mountains." Now only one sponsor need attest simply to a prospect's interest in conservation.[81]

Fifty members from the Los Angeles chapter protested the implication that the club was now "ONLY A CONSERVATION CLUB." Citing the "intimate fraternal association" of mountain trips, they petitioned the board to have applicants swear that they supported the purposes of the club and had never advocated the overthrow of the United States government. They also asked the club to require once again two sponsors to attest to a prospective member's character. As members prepared to vote on the petition, the *Christian Science Monitor* assured them: "If some would-be exploiter of park lands occasionally calls the club 'socialist' . . . , it need not hasten to prove its loyalty." The petition was defeated by a large margin.[82] Although the club still sponsored mountain trips, conservation had become the primary reason people joined. Knowing no one who might vouch for them, some people wrote directly to the club's San Francisco office and the staff sponsored them sight unseen. The late gasp of McCarthyism in its Los Angeles chapter emphasized the transformation of the club, much as the discrediting of McCarthyism nationally had earlier opened new horizons for social reform.

Although no more than 4 percent of the American population may have been aware of the pending wilderness bill, letters pouring into Congress were fifty to one in favor of the legislation, many sent by the members of mountaineering clubs. Nevertheless, Brower correctly claimed that the letters had been written not only by "rugged hikers" but also by those questioning the value of unconstrained economic growth. He said that support came from those who had never climbed a peak but had read Sears, Stegner, Galbraith, Packard, Whyte, Gary, Julian Huxley's *Brave New World Revisited,* or John Keats's critiques of suburbanization, *Insolent Chariots* and *The Crack in the Picture Window.*[83] The "idea of wilderness" had become part of the liberal social critique.

The wilderness movement exemplified the critique's strengths and weaknesses. Reasonably prosperous, well-educated white Americans belonged to the movement's nonprofit organizations. Their perspectives were informed by scholarly and intellectual debates. In trusting to the nonprofit sector to redress problems and by emphasizing the potential of the nation's wealth to improve the quality of life for all, they overlooked, according to the New Left, the realities of poverty, discrepancies in wealth, and issues of class. Structural reforms were less the focus of their attention than were shifts in values and in laws. Nevertheless, even its critics to the left concede that the wilderness movement of the 1940s and 1950s did lobby the federal government to address environmental problems; did question unbridled economic growth, consumption, and technology; and did challenge the assumption that foreign communism was the primary threat to the United States. Brower's speeches from the 1950s may sound tame to some, but as Galbraith noted, those were "days in which even the mildly critical individual" seemed "like a lion in contrast with the general mood." Activists searched for a less exploitive relationship with nature and a greater voice in public policy.[84] The sport of mountaineering had developed into environmental activism, a prototype of what sociologists now call "the new social movement," distinguishing it from older movements such as labor unionism.

Scholars date the "Environmental Revolution" to the 1960s and define it as a form of consumerism that centered on human vulnerability, "reactive and antiestablishment," a "social and political movement."[85] This definition suggests antecedents in the 1950s, when activists recognized that the shift from an economy of producers to consumers had the potential for building a constituency that could challenge the hold of privileged users of resources on the nation's public lands. These activists emulated Whyte's ideal man who sought personal liberation by challenging authority and promoting communal needs. Determined to engineer consent, Brower preached individual, cultural, and ecological redemption.[86]

Drafting its 1960 platform in Denver, the Democratic National Committee invited conservation groups to speak. Brower accepted, urging a broadly liberal agenda that would deploy the resources of a growing economy in defense of rivers wild and free of sewage, and in favor of mass transportation, better education, world health, pesticide-free habitats, parks, and wilderness. "These are issues to be faced honestly in man's own interest, if survival interests him. Other species—and wilderness, too—will survive as a happy coincidence." He told audiences that Congress was appropriating hundreds of thousands of dollars for roads while failing to pass a pollution-abatement program or a wilderness bill. Meanwhile, "our kids sit in old, temporary classrooms."[87]

That winter found Brower meeting with the Kennedy Administration's Secretary of the Interior Stewart Udall. Facetiously or not, the Sierra Club's executive director suggested National Park Service appointments for himself and William Whyte.[88] The club was also seconding the suggestion of Galbraith's *The Liberal Hour* that Americans spend their new wealth improving people's lives.[89] Like Galbraith, Brower praised extremism as "the indispensable ingredient" of change. To an audience in Chicago, Brower said that there was nothing wrong with "good, red-blooded, nonobjective, challenging advocacy of issues." We need to disregard "the vile myth that emotion is unseemly." He fought government propaganda with his own, arguing that "militance" generated visibility.[90] By emphasizing public concerns about affluence, the cold war, consumerism, overpopulation, and bureaucratization, Brower, Ansel Adams, Howard Zahniser, Paul Sears, Nancy Newhall, and others had transformed wilderness conservation into a broad program for reform.

By the early 1960s many women were campaigning for wilderness and against environmental pollutants. They addressed these issues by assuming the authority of their traditional right to protect home and family.[91] Too often discouraged from acting in professional capacities within conservation organizations, women became a formidable volunteer presence, particularly as editors and organizers. At the instigation of Charlotte Mauk, for example, the Sierra Club had begun in 1949 to hold biennial Wilderness Conferences that forged the national network essential for passage of the 1964 Wilderness Act. Women activists often formed new organizations in which they played leadership roles. Polly Dyer, who, like Mauk, had been turned down for a paid position within the Sierra Club, established the North Cascades Conservation Council and went on to serve with Mauk on the club's board of directors through the 1960s. Although few women held even unpaid positions in the Sierra Club, they felt that the club was no less receptive to assertive women than was society at large. Certainly the club still encouraged family trips, and women remained among the most active, if less noticed, climbers.[92]

Women continued to be nominated for the club's board more often than they were elected. Dorothy Varian, who was defeated in 1964, joined with climber Doris Leonard in Conservation Associates, a small activist group in

San Francisco. Varian and Leonard were responding to the limitations on women in larger, well-established groups. In the fashion of Rosalie Edge and Polly Dyer, they created their own venues. Cicely Christy, a volunteer in the club's Bay chapter and editor of the chapter's magazine, recalled that there was some tendency "in the minds of those voting" to cast their ballots against women. "It was just a holdover from the time when they automatically voted for men many years ago . . . ; on the whole the men got elected a little bit better than the women." Women's role was "the committee work, the social work."[93] They also influenced the movement through large single-sex organizations, such as the League of Women Voters, and through interest groups operating within feminine cultural spheres, such as the Audubon Societies.

Rachel Carson's background lay with the Audubon Society, in the predominantly female nature study movement, and in her profession in the biological sciences. Her book *Silent Spring* lent immediate credibility to the wilderness conservation movement. On April 3, 1963, speaking on CBS television, she told Americans: "We still talk in terms of conquest. We still haven't become mature enough to think of ourselves as only a tiny part of a vast and incredible universe . . . ; we have now acquired a fateful power to alter and destroy nature. But man is a part of nature, and his war against nature is inevitably a war against himself." Carson warned of the dangers of chemical pesticides and herbicides to all life—plant, animal, and human—telling Americans not to trust government, industry, or technology. She targeted the women in her audiences and thereby cultivated a female network receptive to her message.[94] Carson's perspective mirrored the traditions of the feminine sublime. She emphasized the sounds and warmth of wildlife over the silence of desolation, and she challenged the masculine rhetoric of conquest. She also brought suburbs and oceans into one vision and linked humans and birds in a single chain of life—a spatial continuity that had long been characteristic of feminine visions of the sublime.

Traveling west in the summer of 1963, Carson hoped to attend the Sierra Club's Seventh Wilderness Conference, but she was too ill. Her regard for the club was made clear in a substantial bequest at her death. The group had welcomed her message, having long challenged the use of pesticides and herbicides in wilderness areas and parks. Carson's apocalyptic vision echoed its own ideology; she had, the club explained, exposed the Department of Agriculture as "an entrenched, proliferating, government bureaucracy" that was allied with private industry. Carson's message contributed to passage of the Wilderness Act,[95] which became law in the summer of 1964 on the crest of liberalism in national politics.[96] Although bipartisan support enacted the legislation, sponsorship had depended on the liberal wing of the Democratic Party. President Lyndon Johnson signed it into law as part of his program of broad reforms involving civil rights and issues of poverty.

The act established the National Wilderness Preservation System, placing all national forest "wilderness," "wild," and "canoe areas" in this system. The legislation outlined procedures by which other federal lands—de facto wildernesses destined for multiple-use management, primitive areas, as well as undeveloped portions of the national parks and wildlife refuges—could be added to the system over the next decade. These areas to be reviewed represented a significant portion of the nation's public "roadless" lands, for which the fight had just begun, and the legislation laid out laborious procedures for deciding their fate. The legislation did, however, formalize the public's voice in the administration of public lands, and it protected much of the nation's highest mountains from logging.[97]

Central to the act's passage had been the Wilderness Society, the Sierra Club, the National Recreation Association, the National Parks Association, the National Wildlife Federation, the Izaac Walton League, the Wildlife Management Institute, Audubon and Native Plant Societies, and garden clubs. The Mazamas, the Mountaineers, the Federation of Western Outdoor Clubs, the Appalachian Mountain Club, youth groups, naturalists, and women's groups added their voices. These organizations dated to the early twentieth century, if not the nineteenth century, and the act's language bore witness to the cultural heritage that they had fostered.

Indeed, the act was the culmination of processes that had begun when Samuel Coleridge, Clarence King, Edward Whymper, Isabella Bird, Henry David Thoreau, John Muir, and others had first looked to the mountains. Such individuals had prized the heights because they seemed so "real"—savage, adamant, and specific. Peaks could be triangulated, named, mastered, and marked. Through the 1960s, climbing clubs continued to detail topographic and geographic singularities. Mountain narratives remained central to climbers' efforts to convey a sense of the immediacy of place. Increasingly, photographs and films concretized scenic sites for the broad public. Despite the vivid reality of mountains, however, much of their value still resided in their presumably natural moral authority. The cultural meanings of "the idea of wilderness" remained as important as the land itself.

That "the idea of wilderness" brought together varied perspectives is illustrated by a key word in the 1964 Act: the act would save nature "untrammeled." Howard Zahniser, who wrote the definition of wilderness that appeared in the act, used the word *untrammeled* because Polly Dyer had done so, often. This uncommon, if not archaic, word was particularly appropriate because it described the different faces of wilderness. For Zahniser the word conjured up spaces of personal freedom, places without societal restraints, while it also implied places not walked by others where one might tramp on foot for long periods of time. The word also referred to the idea of plants and animals untrod by the human foot.[98]

In its effect and in its language, the 1964 act saved the quintessentially romantic landscape. Men still spoke of sublimity as the highest aesthetic standard and the experience of it as the antidote for effeminacy. Echoing the conventions of the masculine sublime, anthropologist Ashley Montagu told a Wilderness Conference held in the mid-1960s: "The esthetic life and the enjoyment of the merely picturesque often lead to a sybaritic self-indulgence rather than to spiritual exaltation."[99] Justice William O. Douglas wrote: "It takes peaks to lift the heart—peaks that thrust sharp rocks into the blue, or snow domes against the sky. . . . They are exhilarating in part for their challenge to the climber in us."[100]

Speaking before the Sierra Club's Wilderness Conference, Sigurd Olson, the champion of the Quetico-Superior Wilderness Area, spoke of his own experience of the sublime moment, "the supreme climax of spiritual revelation." He described it as that moment when "everything glows as if impregnated with the essential flavor of the absolute, showing our ascension . . . to a different and higher sphere, a new spirituality . . . when life was suddenly illuminated, beautiful, and transcendent, and we are filled with awe and deep happiness." He told of one evening "when I had climbed to the summit of Robinson Peak in the Quetico to watch the sunset; the flaming ball trembling on the very edge of a far ridge—fluid, alive, pulsating. As I watched it sink into the dusk, it seemed to me I could actually feel the earth turning away from it, sense its rotation." It was "a moment of fusion with the country," the moment in which he felt "an overwhelming sense of completion in which all my hopes and experiences seemed concentrated in the moment before me."[101]

To afford men opportunities for such sublime moments, "*real* wilderness" had to be, Brower said, "big enough to have a beyond to it and an inside." Boyhood and horizon remained linked in Brower's mind. "Where as you start up a trail and your nine-year-old Bob asks, 'Is there civilization behind that ridge?' you can say no and share his 'That's good!' feeling."[102] The automatic inclusion of areas that had been classified before World War II and the suggested minimum of five thousand acres for inclusion meant that the 1964 act implemented desires for landscapes vast and desolate.

Premising masculine conventions, the legislation read: "A wilderness, in contrast with those areas where man and his own works dominate the landscape, is hereby recognized as an area where the earth and its community of life are untrammeled by man, where man himself is a visitor who does not remain." Wilderness was that place that "(1) generally appears to have been affected primarily by the forces of nature, with the imprint of man's work substantially unnoticeable; (2) has outstanding opportunities for solitude or a primitive and unconfined type of recreation; (3) has at least five thousand acres of land or is of sufficient size as to make practical its preservation and use in an unimpaired condition and (4) may also contain ecological, geological, or other features of scientific, educational, scenic, or historical value." Wilderness remained the primeval "other" that defined civilization, the land on which western man could formulate his identity, and locate God and country.

What had happened to the habit of equating nature with femininity? Few men in the late 1950s and early 1960s spoke readily, if at all, of nature as Mother or lover, of her allure, or even of her stern presence. But the symbolism remained. Men fulsomely quoted Coleridge, William Wordsworth, Alexander Pope, John Keats, and James Fenimore Cooper. Perhaps they were nostalgic for the time when the earth had been "woman," when men's relationship with wild areas had been one of "patronizing and romanticizing" nature, when Washington Irving "waxed eloquent over the American scene: 'her mighty lakes, . . . her mountains, . . . her valleys.'" The natural world retained its metaphoric femininity, if only as a wistful memory.[103]

The Wilderness Act, however, was also a statement about mid-twentieth-century culture. Its passage came on the cusp of a transformation of the nation's social topography. Most of its supporters were not strong harbingers of the new realities of feminism or of demands for racial equality, economic equity, and other challenges to traditional authorities. The eagerness with which white middle-class men embraced "the wilderness idea" in the 1960s reflected the realization that the sites of their childhood were being irrevocably altered. Their eagerness also reflected a sense of how much American society appeared to be changing and how much the changes threatened the presumably traditional preeminence of middle-class men. What motivated them to act in defense of wild places? One man answered, "In the last analysis man acts to preserve himself. He must and he will . . . ; it is in man's self-interest to protect wilderness . . . ; it relates to our preserving ourselves."[104]

Evoking the presumed closing of a landed frontier seventy-five years earlier, the act was designed "to assure that an increasing population, accompanied by expanding settlement and growing mechanization, does not occupy and modify all areas within the United States and its possessions, leaving no land designated for preservation and protection in their natural condition." A. Starker Leopold, a Berkeley professor of zoology and Aldo Leopold's son, said that wilderness should be the land "as nearly as possible in the condition that prevailed when the area was first visited by the white man."[105]

The overwhelming trope men used in the 1960s when discussing wilderness was that of the frontier, a simple and powerful metaphor for then and now. It was a word that women rarely employed, but mid-twentieth-century men spoke frequently and with nostalgia of the American West, by then an exotic story of white, male heroes locked in relentless struggles with each other, society, death, landscapes, and themselves. Men spoke of re-creating their own frontier on which they could realize male camaraderie, become a man, recall their youth, and remember their forefathers. Frontier wilderness was defined as free of mediating conveniences, where one functioned on instinct and muscle.

What advocates saw destroying the frontier was no longer simply automobiles but the burden of a growing population, material affluence, a culture of conformity, a lack of manly restraint, and nuclear threats. Men spoke now of two frontiers: the old one that nurtured masculine values; and the new one of science and technology, which they said threatened those values.[106] Olson explained, "We have substituted science and technology for the intuitive wisdom of the ages. As a result, within many of us is a sense of insecurity and a gnawing unrest that somehow the age of gadgetry and science cannot still." Did these men, many of whom were themselves engineers and scientists, actually feel threatened by science and technology? Or should one read into their anxiety a replay of "the crisis of masculinity" experienced in the 1890s? Grant McConnell spoke of a "cultural heritage" debased and he declared the battle for wilderness to be men's way of taking charge. One can read "cultural heritage" as a code phrase for middle-class, white, masculine values and preeminence.[107] The repositioning of women and others in society had generated a century of anxieties, leaving those who still moved to "ancient rhythms" feeling out of place, Olson said. Wilderness advocates were "trying to bridge the gap between our old racial wisdom, our old primeval consciousness . . . and beliefs of the new era of technology."[108] It is also true, however, that many of the fears for the future that plagued men were shared by women, including Rachel Carson and Nancy Newhall. Not only social issues but truly environmental issues, such as atomic radiation, were presenting themselves with particular force by the 1960s.

Although the Sierra Club ceased to run articles on mountaineering in its *Bulletin* in the 1960s, it launched the magazine *Ascent* and expanded its program of High Trips. In 1967 alone, the Sierra Club offered ninety-eight wilderness outings as compared to twenty-eight in 1957. This $400,000 operation relied on 270 trip leaders and 3,600 participants. Even with the displacement of mountaineering at the club's core, men's vision of outdoor sport, particularly rock climbing, changed little in the 1960s. Rock climbers found the camera a marvelous adjunct to their adventures. Their images recorded the essence of the masculine sublime, showing figures suspended on vertical faces over deep voids and silhouetted against grainy cliffs. Technical climbing was an increasingly popular sport of young men (as well as young women) who made singular conquests from Mt. Everest to El Capitan, with explanations that echoed King, Whymper, and Mallory: "There is no reason. It is all reason. The rock is cold. The rock is hard. The rock is me."[109]

For over a century and a half, men had written of forging identities, spiritual and secular, in contests with mountains that they gendered with feminine metaphors. By the early 1960s, however, men were less sure of the womanliness of nature, less eager to concede the power of femininity, and more ambivalent about their own relationship to nature. Were they still the conquerors, like those who had discovered the Americas, subdued the West, and mastered the world's greatest peaks? Did they remain the outsiders, able to enter that realm only in moments of sublime fusion? Or were they merely, as the ecological and evolutionary sciences suggested, part of the web of life, totally and utterly dependent for their survival on the natural world? And if they were part of this web, was that not more frightening than comforting? Most of the men who endorsed the idea of wilderness spoke with longing for the nineteenth century as a time of clarity and of male ascendance; they also suspected that they were part of a "chain of life" and that it was dangerous to think otherwise.[110]

Almost as an afterthought, the Wilderness Act mentioned the ecological significance of wilderness. Howard Zahniser, who was responsible for the language of the wilderness bill, had incorporated into the legislation his belief that a terra incognita was vital to the perpetuation of masculinity and the nation, publicly joking that "wilderness is a place where the hand of man has never set foot." Nevertheless, he also praised wilderness as evidence of the "interdependence of all life," the "sense of ourselves as a responsible part of a continuing community of life."[111] This language of the community of life had reflected visions of the domestic sublime described by men like John Muir and William Badè as well as feminine champions of the sublime—naturalists all.

Few women had public voices in the cultural debates swirling around wilderness in the early and mid-1960s, but feminine perspectives remained distinctive.[112] Shortly after passage of the 1964 act, the Sierra Club held a Wilderness Conference at which more than twenty men spoke and only two women: Peggy Wayburn, the organizer of the conference; and Margaret W. Owings, long active in the Audubon Society and in protecting California's redwoods, its coastline, and its sea lions. Owings noted that for two days debaters had been turning over in their hands and passing on to one another a treasured rock with many facets. The rock, she said, was wilderness. "Each facet is one variety of this wilderness, and the reflection from each facet is a human response to that experience. There are those of us who look at wilderness primarily as a dimension—an immensity, a grand proportion—the horizon large in outline against the dark mountain range. These may be people who work by expansion and think by expansion." On the other hand, there were those, among whom she included herself and Rachel Carson, "who turn primarily to the intimate savor of landscape: the detail, the scent of nettle and mint, the lazy buzz of a mountain fly, the careless grace of a flower opening. These people are selective and concentrate their attention, finding their reward in infinite detail."[113]

Owings referred to Sigurd Olson's description of achieving "animal oneness with the earth" on a mountaintop, but she had experienced this oneness on the sidewalk of 55th Street in New York City, surrounded by the noises and confusion of a constructed world of buildings. "At that moment, as if by a signal," she recalled, "every city sound about me was suddenly hushed . . . as if the power had been shut off. And in the silence of that instant, I heard but one thing—the delicate honking of geese high overheard." She looked up to see a V-shaped wedge of geese flying south, calling to one another as they passed out of view. "One world had given way to another." "Burning instances of truth," when "everything stands clear," could be had even in the city.[114] Owings's reflections on the sublime moment and the multiple facets of wilderness would have pleased Harriet Monroe, Mary Austin, Marion Randall Parsons, Bertha Pope, Lucy Braun, and Rosalie Edge.

The history of mountaineering makes it clear that even the highest peaks of North America were never truly unknown or devoid of people, but it also illustrates the deep resonance that narratives of exploration had for Americans in the nineteenth and twentieth centuries.[1] Ignoring indigenous people and local users eased the potential for guilt among newcomers. Behind the pervasiveness of such narratives, however, lay more than exoneration; even when carried out within national boundaries, the enactment of rituals of discovery had a purpose and an outcome: shaping the identities of the self-proclaimed explorers and the fate of the lands "discovered." That it did so for the United States is obvious, but it served a purpose as well for those public agencies and private organizations intent on creating forest reserves and national parks. By mapping, naming, climbing, and lobbying, recreational climbers, scientists, and federal employees determined the fate of North America's summits. These activities illustrate the political power inherent in control over geographical and topographical data, as well as the cultural and psychological processes by which people invest a land with their own memories.

The concept of wilderness developed as climbers, hikers, scientists, and tourists wrote their histories, imagined and real, onto North America's heights. It grew out of broadly transatlantic cultural traditions and a sensitivity to established literary forms and romantic tropes. In the mid-nineteenth century, many Americans, particularly within the educated, middle, and upper classes, became interested in pristine and rugged landscapes. They visualized these places as at once uncivilized and feminine, places in which they sought to locate personal and collective identities—primarily gendered ones, the seemingly unsullied virtues of which they hoped to protect. The most sublime of landscapes elicited the most protective of urges. With its original meaning of "elevated," the word *sublime* well suited the exaltation of mountains. The highest became wilderness as a result of philosophical assumptions current in nineteenth- and early-twentieth-century western thought.

These patterns of thought were characteristic of climbers throughout Europe, the British Empire, and the United States. Consciously and deliberately, alpine sport was a transatlantic exchange. Yet it was in the high western ranges of the United States that these assumptions left their most definitive imprint. Mountains came to define wildness; they also became "wilderness," legally and politically, as climbers and other visitors inscribed their social beliefs on formal maps and lobbied for the recreational, scientific, and aesthetic uses of these areas. The idea of wilderness conservation, along with other forms of land preservation, was rooted in notions of what was properly civilized and naturally savage, properly masculine and naturally feminine.

These expectations revolved around traditional portrayals of nature as analogous to the feminine body. Working in relation to a nature visualized in feminine terms, men defined manhood as a counteridentity to both, seeing nature as simply alien, if not adversarial. The language of attack and conflict was common in climbing narratives throughout the nineteenth and twentieth centuries. Echoing across continents and centuries, the conventions of the romantic sublime encouraged men to measure themselves against peaks, as well as in relation to the opposite sex and what they deemed to be the less enlightened indigenous people they encountered in the heights.

Mountaineering celebrated the occasions when one first came face to face with the frightening unknown. These were moments of open-ended possibilities, of terror and struggle, of seduction and mastery, of navigating and mapping; their success in such encounters seemed, to Anglo-American men, to demonstrate their right to possess the land. Indeed, most men who climbed consciously conflated discovery with taking possession—naming the peaks, building rock cairns at the summits, mapping the topography, and advertising their "first ascents." Often denigrating local people for failing to appreciate the sublimity of the surroundings, mountaineers found in exotic places and peoples perfect foils for constructing their own identities. Even after "first ascents" on North American peaks became sadly elusive, climbers found new routes to pioneer and imagined new circumstances, with the sport of rock climbing opening dramatic frontiers on the cliffs, pinnacles, and ledges of even familiar places like Yosemite Valley.

American climbers thought of their adventures as "permissible conquest." Despite the overuse of alpine meadows by pack animals, the intrusiveness of mechanical aids hammered into rock, and the potential to exploit local packers, twentieth-century mountaineering has in fact generally been a low-impact, if not benign, activity. Yet in the years between the mid-nineteenth century and the mid-twentieth century, outdoor sport did much to shape the history of North America's mountains. Not all travelers described why they were drawn to the heights, but many did, leaving rich records for the historian to ponder: narratives, maps, and photographs. In such documents can be found much of the history of mountains and conservation.

Central to the romantic conventions of the masculine sublime was the mastery of self. Men from Samuel Taylor Coleridge to John Muir, from William O. Douglas to David Brower, with various degrees of purposefulness, placed themselves in positions of mortal danger that demanded of them, if they were to survive, instant command of mind and body. Often powerless to control their fate or even their bodies, in a moment of blinding clarity—of transcendence that united body and spirit—reason and will were restored. Men spoke of mountains in the language of love and lust, of transport, and of rebirth, with intensely spiritual moments often coinciding with the process of maturation.

Reflexive fear was reinforced by the cultivation of hatred and anger. Mountains were personal, malevolent, and feminine enemies. Learning how to invoke and to control anger and hate was seen as correlating with manly success in life, especially in the competitive marketplace of ideas and commodities. That men learned to confront and control fear seemed essential, as well, to the need of a democratic society for citizen-soldiers. In the years preceding each of the world wars, however, some wilderness advocates suggested that these strong emotions threatened the social order and required release in savage places. Even as men enacted the roles that society had prescribed for them, they spoke earnestly of escaping into the wild in an effort to distance themselves from the competitive social order. American men climbed and hiked and wrote of their adventures as ways to simultaneously fulfill and contest complex and contentious ideas of what it meant to be a man. What they sought—variously, the cultivation, the sublimation, the escape from, or the release of, strong emotions—sprang from society's expectations that they struggle with each other and with the natural world. They imaged sublime and frightening landscapes suitable to their agenda of conflict and catharsis.

Given the overwhelming prevalence of symbolic and linguistic representations of nature, it is not surprising that feminine visions of the sublime differed substantively from masculine ones. For women, as for men, the love of mountains centered on experiences of transcendence concentrated in the sublime moment. What men found in barren rock and in the abyss, women located in the life of the mountains, from the wildflowers to the birds. The feminine sublime coalesced in moments of almost overpowering intimacy with place, moments of keen awareness of the life forces that flowed through the physical world and themselves, verifying the values of nurturance and reproduction that society expected of women. These moments, no less intense and spiritual than men's, comforted through a sense of affinity with places that seemed at once strong and nurturing. By interpreting western aesthetic conventions and figurative language, the feminine sublime addressed the natural world and realized participants' spiritual needs. By weaving together Victorian notions of proper womanhood with masculine conventions of romanticism, and feminine customs with the natural sciences, many climbers enjoyed the mountains, and as they did so, they constructed their own sense of self.

Botany served as a wellspring for the feminine sublime, much as geology laid a foundation for the masculine. Natural selection seemed, to some botanists, to enhance the role of the physical or maternal environment (rather than otherworldly forces). They tended to see natural history as characterized by cooperation and sacrifice rather than by competition and struggle. Collecting and identifying botanical specimens sanctioned women's right to wander in wild places, to indulge and extend the traditions of womanhood, and to enjoy the androgynous power of the flower. Building on their traditional domestic and horticultural interests, botany offered women a position of authority from which to influence the conservation movement, a stepping stone into positions within traditional organizations; it also motivated them to form their own, often female-led, groups aimed at affecting public policy. The feminine sublime and ecology proved congenial. The principles of this science that would define the modern environmental movement were first made evident in the fragility of the wildflowers that so attracted naturalists, male and female.

Women mountaineers shaped their lives through high adventure. Scaling peaks from the Sierra to the Himalayas, they challenged assumptions about the limitations of the female physique and the Victorian logic of their exclusion from public spaces. Some spoke of their alpine prowess as proving their equality with men; there were those women in conservation who cultivated their relationship with the natural world, hoping for mutual empowerment. Women relished the freedom they found in uncommon places. Even as they looked for release from the constraints of polite society, however, they found opportunities to engage in quintessentially feminine behaviors: collecting wildflowers, bathing in outdoor waters, and feeling comforted by the sounds, smells, and colors of even the highest peaks. Although American audiences were more willing to embrace heroic men, alpine sport altered the ways in which society visualized women's bodies, their judgment, and their determination. Collecting wildflowers liberated them while it domesticated the mountains. The blossoms provided a satisfying sense of spatial continuity between these rarified landscapes and the familiar ones below. As climbers and as conservationists, women proved highly receptive not only to the natural history of the mountains but also the human history.

Masculine conventions emphasized the emptiness of wild places and feminine conventions gave them life, but all enthusiasts, first imaginatively and then politically, represented these places and gendered them female. That which was considered most threatened by the modern industrial and commercial orders was not the masculine but the feminine. The expectation that one should love one's wife and children encouraged men to express love for the natural world and to lobby for its protection. Much as the Victorian home had been presumed to offer men solace and rejuvenation, they sought spiritual and physical transformation in wild places. The analogy of femininity and nature encouraged the idea of the wilderness parks and reserves, bounded femininity, analogous to the walled gardens of home. Women called wild places "home" and "garden," finding in these words affirmation of their own and nature's virtues. The growing political power of women advanced conservation and scenic preservation, much as did the desire of men to enjoy female companionship. The protective instincts of both sexes flowered logically out of the earth's feminine identity—the enactment of women's socially constructed need to nurture and men's desire to love (if also to challenge and fear).

Although history reveals the strength of gendered expectations, actual patterns in the social fabric were complex and varied over time. In the mid-nineteenth century, many women deliberately stepped outside of their proper spheres to tramp unchaperoned while wearing bloomers. At the same time, men like John Muir, perhaps made wary of manly aggression by the horror of the Civil War, articulated a domestic vision of sublimity. In the 1890s, the parameters of masculinity narrowed, and the imperial connotations of climbing were clearly evident in the period's narratives. Men described triumphing over alien places and people, while women wrote of carrying domestic arts into the wild as they hiked beside their husbands. On the eve of World War I, however, men and women were strongly drawn to John Muir's domestic vision of the sublime. Well known as a climber, Muir had ascended some of Yosemite's steepest rock faces and had analyzed powerful geologic forces and narrated classic moments of fear and self-discipline—all assumed by contemporaries and followers to be manly activities. Muir also described a love of wildflowers, a sense of affinity with nature, and a disavowal of mastery. Throughout his life and after his death, Muir's ability to mediate between the masculine and the feminine, between man and nature, brought his writings and the story of his life continuing attention and influence.

In the 1920s and 1930s a more secular agenda prevailed; alpine accomplishment was highlighted as integral to being a successful, self-actualizing man. At the same time, the vigor of women, their sporting attire, and their determination to lead climbs and go "manless" challenged traditional social expectations. As Americans watched World War II develop in Europe and Asia and then joined in that war, mountains became training grounds for the citizen-soldier. The value of the outdoorsman as a potential warrior seemed to encourage women to be helpmates on the trail and volunteer workers. As the safety to be found in the family and wilderness became paramount during the cold war, women were less visible but no less influential. The sounds of distinctive feminine voices were quieter for a time; meanwhile, men moved toward an understanding of wilderness as the primordial home of mankind.

Powerful forces of organized citizenry had marshaled a lobby for nature—from Muir's "protesting leaves" to the missives of those who, fearing much in the modern world, sent letters to Congress in support of the Wilderness Act. The language of the Wilderness Act of 1964 reflected a century of complex gendered cultural history. The conventions of the masculine sublime encouraged the formulation of desolate wilderness, but the act also gave voice to the feminine and domestic sublimes by calling such places communities of life.

Conservation, ecological thinking, and environmentalism had in significant part grown out of an appreciation of the mountains and assumptions as to the proper relationship between men, women, and nature. However, by the late twentieth century, some Americans were questioning these relationships, seeing them as both less absolute and less natural than had most Victorians. In the late 1960s and the 1970s, some women, prepared to establish control over their own lives, chose to scale icy peaks and granite walls; they expropriated the conventions of the masculine sublime. By consciously bringing their physical and intellectual powers into play and overtly defying norms of female passivity, they built confidence in themselves and gained it from others. They were determined "to perform as well as a man."[2]

The all-women climb of 26,545-foot Annapurna in 1978 coalesced much of this energy. For biochemist Arlene Blum, the expedition's leader, and her team members, their attempt was simply a glorious adventure, but at the same time, it was a self-conscious effort to establish the principle of equal abilities. The expedition, which was deliberately sexually exclusive, echoed the traditions of the *cordée féminine*. A lack of institutional support for women's sport and the expense of such an alpine expedition made it necessary for the leaders to find novel methods for acquiring funding. They marshaled a national community of boosters who raised money through the sale of T-shirts. A storm of publicity swirled about the ascent. Interviews, sponsors, and narratives appeared in such traditional venues as the *New York Times* and *National Geographic*.

The Sierra Club published Blum's inspiring and poignant description of the climb. Attention also came from new venues like *Seventeen* and *Glamour*. *People* magazine listed Blum as one of the twenty-five notable Americans of 1978, along with "Pretty Baby" Brooke Shields, President Carter, and Miss Piggy, who revealed "how she balanced love and a career." Such publicity portrayed the attempt on Annapurna as a reach for "gender equity."[3]

Two members of the team—Irene Miller, a physicist from California; and Vera Komarkova, a plant ecologist from Denver—along with two Sherpas, reached the summit of Annapurna, despite unusually heavy snows. They placed a Nepali flag and a flag of the United States at the summit. They also raised a banner reading, "A woman's place is on the top." But when two British women in the expedition, moving up without their guide, slipped on the ice and fell to their deaths, some critics excoriated Blum, claiming that she should never have allowed the women to go on unassisted. Some commentators implied that the deaths showed Blum's failure to establish gender equity, if not a weakness in the very premise that women could be equal to men in everything. Feminists around the world were stunned by the implication, because terror and the imminence of death have always been integral to alpine sport.

The criticism of the Annapurna disaster suggested that the ways by which men have created such heroes as George Mallory remained for women elusive. Climbing tragedies had long elicited criticism. But censure was generally directed at methods rather than at premises. Finding the body of a fellow professional guide, Rob Hall, on Everest, David Breashears realized that Hall had died attempting to rescue a client, yet questioned the arrogance of Hall that had prompted him to lead so many such clients to the summit so late in the day. In the end, Breashears recorded the mixed emotions of "sadness, anger, and admiration." The faulting of Blum's Annapurna expedition failed to dampen the enthusiasm of other women for dangerous climbs, however.[4]

As some women were asserting themselves as climbers, some men flirted with less adversarial relations with the earth. In 1968, David Brower, having moved far from his youthful search for "first ascents," arranged for the publication of a full-page advertisement in the *New York Times* calling for the establishment of an "Earth National Park," with mankind as the endangered species and the planet as humanity's only refuge. The ad marked a moment of clarity in the Sierra Club's metamorphosis from a mountaineering club into an environmental organization. The sense of isolation captured by the satellite photograph of the earth floating alone in space had first come to men in the mountains, as had their desire to protect these places that had dramatized their vulnerability, At the same time, however, the advertisement suggested that wilderness was less a terra incognita than a home. And that suggestion had been made earlier by naturalists and by women.

The geographer Yi-fu Tuan, writing in 1974, saw evidence of a "counter-cultural" ethos and "a gentle, unselfconscious involvement with the physical world" emerging among men in response to broad cultural changes in American society.[5] Mountaineering was, for many men during these years, a continuum—from strolling to scrambling to scaling—with minimal sense of contest. The outpouring of public and scholarly attention to John Muir indicated that his domestic sublime still resonated with men and women alike. Some climbers doubted that there ever were such things as "first ascents" and were embarrassed by the rhetoric of conquest, even while they perpetuated the metaphor by writing of the rape of Mother Earth.[6] Writing later in the century, historian William Cronon suggested that it was time for Americans to abandon the romantic vision of wilderness as a place without humans, building on a process clearly begun by men like Aldo Leopold, to find it more appropriate to call wilderness "home."[7]

Even in the 1960s and 1970s, however, climbing remained dominated by men, its language sexualized and combative. Wilderness was still the terra incognita to be navigated with the objective of facing danger. This was especially clear with rock climbing in the Yosemite Valley, where skilled young men were permitted to stay the summer in exchange for participating in rescue operations for hikers who inadvertently became stranded on the walls of the valley. Describing a heyday of Yosemite rock climbing during these decades, the young men of the Sierra Club's Camp 4 basked in the history of climbers like Richard Leonard, who had preceded them on those walls, and in the camaraderie of the sport. "Wives and girlfriends tried climbing, of course," Steve Roper wrote of his young adult years in Yosemite, "but they usually did it because their men were doing it—not for any particular love of the sport."[8]

By the 1980s and 1990s the tenets of the masculine sublime, so clear in Clarence King's narrative of the Sierra, still seemed highly relevant to men. The practice of free climbing (without technical aids for safety or assistance), although far from unknown among women, became particularly common among young male climbers in locations like Yosemite Valley. Free climbing has brought a sobering death rate and a renewed celebration of risk. Federal regulations limiting the use of mechanical climbing aids such as pitons, bolts, and drills served to undo much of the attention to belaying as a safety measure that Leonard had brought to the sport in the 1930s. Climbing remained largely the prerogative of young men. A 1983 book on the psychology and sociology of outdoor sport began: "Why do men climb?"[9] For some, the best ascents remained the most athletic—those where, as their enthusiasts quipped, the first step could be taken off the bumper of one's car, thus obviating the need to walk, cherished by others, through lowlands, forests, or meadows.

A 1996 issue of *National Geographic* featured the Wyoming "cowboys" who stormed Trango Tower ("Nameless" Tower) in the Himalayas, the tallest sheer drop in the world. The men reveled in their mastery of a vast, barren landscape, voiced a personal animosity toward the tower, cultivated fear, and exercised self-control when faced with the abyss. They visualized themselves reenacting, with their hands and feet, a "frontier" experience while traveling through a militarily controlled region near a disputed border. When one participant was asked if he were ready to cross an ice field that lay above a drop of fifteen hundred feet, using crampons for the first time, he answered, with a bravado that would have warmed the heart of Clarence King, "Heck, yes. Let's give her a shot."[10]

Alpine expeditions and rock climbing soared to popularity in the 1990s as Americans continued to find relevant an Anglophilic narrative that began in London with the Alpine Club. The death rate soared in what was now often referred to as an "extreme sport," as the number of untrained climbers determined to reach the summits of the highest mountains grew. David Breashears's book *High Exposure* vividly illustrates the ongoing engagement with death as he describes the upper reaches of Everest as "an open graveyard"—a "hallowed ground"—and much of his life as a guide an exercise in body retrieval and photographing the dead.[11] The continuing appeal of outdoor sport is clear in the large numbers and the national and ethnic diversity of those who attempt Mt. Denali every year and in the numbers who die on Mt. Everest, Mt. Hood, and Mt. Rainier. The historical resonance of the sport was evident in the efforts by Breashears to retrace George Mallory's route up Everest in 1924. It was evident in the poignant drama of those who filmed their search for Mallory's body, in part to determine whether he had in fact made it to the summit before his death.

Mountaineering's continued ability to attract outstanding authors and grab public attention is evident in the presence on the bestseller lists of Jon Krakauer's 1997 book *Into Thin Air: A Personal Account of the Mount Everest Disaster*, followed two years later by Breashears's *High Exposure*. This American fascination, as the century closed, defied both political correctness and the postmodern deconstruction of notions of gender, primitivism, wilderness, and imperialism. The enthusiasm for this very Victorian sport and the conventions of the sublime thrived at a time when many were questioning those very conventions.

As the masculine sublime survives, so does the feminine, preeminently among ecofeminists who argue that women should capitalize on separate spheres and on their affinity, natural or constructed, with the earth.[12] By situating themselves as mothers defending families and their communities, many women, ecofeminists argue, have tried, with notable successes, to hold public and corporate sectors accountable on issues from open space and wilderness to toxic dumps and clean water. Ecofeminists themselves have vigorously challenged patriarchal, racial, and class-based assumptions.[13] Historian Carolyn Merchant calls for a "radical ecology," a new social ethic, with no one group free to exploit the natural world at the expense of the others.[14] Sharing Merchant's concern for women's lives and many of her premises, other feminist scholars, such as Indian activist and philosopher Vantana Shiva, see a parallel between violence against women and that exercised by modern societies against nature; these scholars look to improve the lot of women by implementing sound ecological practices and to protect nature through a stronger voice for women, thus forestalling the victimization of both. Such feminist scholars, writing from a broad understanding of modern global developments, echo the thoughts of those mountaineers and conservationists from the nineteenth and twentieth centuries who consciously employed the symbolism that linked women and the natural world to invest themselves with authority, to protect wildlife with the power of their nurturance, and to improve the position of women in society.[15]

The feminine and domestic sublimes continue to be heard, especially from women who write natural history today; they talk of wildflowers and gardens in the wilderness, of being at home even in rugged landscapes, and of walking through lands that are wild, yet rich in human history. They bring feelings of intimacy, domesticity, and life to the mountains, after dismissing the alpine dance with death.[16] Ruth Anne Kocour's *Facing the Extreme* describes her 20,320-foot ascent to the summit of Mt. Denali. Kocour climbed "for the visual feast. I climb because the challenging situations thrill me. I climb, too, because I love being in the vertical environment." As for danger, "I simply never think that I am risking my life when I head off on a climb."[17]

How shall this history of mountaineering and of the sublime experience address suggestions that the wilderness areas that the United States government maintains today are "unnatural" places premised on a "profoundly mistaken fantasy"?[18] What would Lucy Braun, botanist and leader of the Wild

Flower Preservation Society, have replied to such suggestions? She might have emphasized the ecological and feminine concerns that shaped public policies designed to save native plant communities. She could fairly have pointed to the influence that she, Aldo Leopold, and other naturalists had in translating ecology into a guiding principle of land management and a reason for creating wilderness.

How would Howard Zahniser of the Wilderness Society have contributed to the discussion? Although he embraced narratives of discovery and frontier, Zahniser was strikingly postmodern in his thinking. He recognized the constructed quality of wilderness: that it is at once a place that humans try not to influence, yet is a human creation.[19] The postmodern perspective may have brought us to see what he saw: wilderness has been the crucible in which identities—national, class, gendered, and racial—have been formed, for better or for worse. Victorian culture did much to produce the modern industrial environment, but it also provided an antidote to it, as Frederick Law Olmsted noted with satisfaction. Coming from Olmsted, architect of Manhattan's Central Park but also an intimate of Yosemite Valley, this summary by antithesis bears remembering if Americans are tempted to rewrite the history of wilderness in the United States. Wild places offer at least the illusion of resistance to toxic and pervasive technologies, population pressures, and war. These places bridge everyday life and whatever we may find of the spiritual in natural realms.

Given that American society and law have constructed a great many aspects of these landscapes, they have come to represent a cultural heritage. Wilderness is, in many senses of the word, a strange place. Americans speak of it as both historical and natural. Much as Ansel Adams's landscape photographs, it represents for many people an important, if misleading, vision of this continent before its despoilment. In such places Americans have sought not only a historical past but also an ecological truth honed by evolution, the world (as David Brower maintained) as God made it. But like all myths—part truth and part fantasy—wilderness is essentially ahistorical; it is a space that allows people to deny change. It represents the impulse to stay in touch with something strange yet deeply familiar. Just as our uses of myth and history shift with time, so do the meanings we attribute to the mountains, even when we are oblivious to these alterations and their irony.

It is appropriate that the people of the United States, who have witnessed unrelenting transformations of their landscapes, who measure time in the smallest of increments, and who have otherwise sold their souls to technology, have done so much to cultivate the idea of wilderness. As industrialization sweeps the globe, people in nonwestern cultures increasingly find compelling the rituals of nineteenth-century alpine sport. Nineteenth-century Americans possessed a peculiarly keen sense of historical discontinuity, a sensitivity that was evident in their faith in their own modernity, in their conviction that civilization had developed out of the primitive, and in the theory that humans had evolved out of other species. When faced with abrupt alterations in their environments, they told themselves stories that explained the discontinuities of global colonialization and industrialization and inscribed those stories on the mountains, making them places where presumably nothing had changed or ever would. By recognizing that humans have had a hand in creating wilderness, however, we see, in its very artificiality, a fragility impelling us to defend it well against not only those who wish to exploit it but against our own trampling feet of pleasure.

In my mind's eye, Gilroy's Christmas Hill has never changed and never will. This hill, with its wild iris and strange sounds in the grass, its sense of privacy and adventure, unlike almost everything else in my life, remains unaltered, much as the sharp contours of Yosemite, the bulky presence of Mt. Whitney, the icy summit of Glacier Peak, and the forested ridges of the Adirondacks all remain reassuringly familiar to me and to many other Americans—unfailing sources of inspiration and challenge, occasions for exploration, freedom, spiritual catharsis, and emotional solace. Perhaps, above all, these places of seeming permanence continue to encourage us to explore who we are, as a people, as a nation, and as individuals—women and men.

NOTES

INTRODUCTION

1. The 1894 climb of Mt. Hood was reported in local papers along with news of labor discontent and violence throughout the United States and appeared beside long lists of those in Portland whose property was being sold at public action for nonpayment of taxes. "Smoking Mountain: The Mazamas Will Soon Climb Mount Hood," *Sunday Oregonian* 13, no. 7 (July 8, 1894): 6. "Hood's South Slope," *Sunday Oregonian* 13, no. 28 (July 15, 1894): 6. In newspaper files, University of Washington Library, Seattle; C. H. Sholes, "President's Address for 1896," *Mazama* 1, no. 2 (1897): 279.

2. Yi-fu Tuan, *Topophilia: A Study of Environmental Perception, Attitudes, and Values* (Englewood Cliffs, NJ: Prentice-Hall, 1974), 70–74, 109, 112; Donald W. Meinig, ed., *The Interpretation of Ordinary Landscapes: Geographical Essays* (New York: Oxford University Press, 1979), 2; William Cronon, "The Trouble with Wilderness; or, Getting Back to the Wrong Nature," in *Uncommon Ground: Toward Reinventing Nature*, ed. William Cronon (New York: Norton, 1995), 74–75; Vera Norwood and Janice Monk, eds., *The Desert Is No Lady: Southwestern Landscapes in Women's Writing and Art* (New Haven: Yale University Press, 1987), 3.

3. Charles E. Fay, "The Annual Address of the President," *Appalachia* 2, no. 1 (June 1879): 6–7; see also Arnold Lunn, *The Exploration of the Alps* (New York: Henry Holt, [1914]), 208; John Tyndall, *Hours of Exercise in the Alps* (New York: D. Appleton, 1899), 190.

4. On mountaineering and its narratives as "rhetorical conquest" and participants' behaviors and motivations as extensions of a "new imperialism," see Reuben Ellis, *Vertical Margins: Mountaineering and the Landscapes of Neoimperialism* (Madison: University of Wisconsin Press, 2001), 177. Reuben brilliantly describes three famous climbs, including a 1908 ascent by Annie Smith Peck in Bolivia, as forms of American and British neoimperialism.

5. http://www.shef.ac.uk/~cm/jwb/ewwuahcd.htm; accessed October 7, 2003.

6. Carolyn Merchant, *The Death of Nature: Women, Ecology, and the Scientific Revolution* (New York: Harper and Row, 1980).

7. On romanticism, see Roderick Nash, *Wilderness and the American Mind*, 3rd ed. (New Haven: Yale University Press, 1982), 146; Robert Gottlieb, *Forcing the Spring: The Transformation of the American Environmental Movement* (Washington, DC: Island Press, 1993), 15–36; Cronon, "Trouble with Wilderness," 74–75; Thomas Weiskel, *The Romantic Sublime: Studies in the Structure and Psychology of Transcendance* (Baltimore: Johns Hopkins University Press, 1976), 3–33.

8. Peter France, "Western Civilisation and Its Mountain Frontiers, 1750–1850," *History of European Ideas* 6, no. 3 (1985): 299; Simon Schama, *Landscape and Memory* (New York: Knopf, 1995), 449–61.

9. For "pathway," see Josiah Dwight Whitney, *The Yosemite Guide-Book: A Description of the Yosemite Valley and the Adjacent Region of the Sierra Nevada, and of the Big Trees of California* (Cambridge, MA: University Press, Welch, Bigelow, 1870), 24; for "master narrative," see Krista Comer, *Landscapes of the New West: Gender and Geography in Contemporary Women's Writing* (Chapel Hill: University of North Carolina Press, 1999),

127–53; Aldo Leopold, "Conserving the Covered Wagon: Shall We Save Parts of the Far Western Wilderness from Soft 'Improvements'?" *Sunset* 54, no. 3 (March 1925): 21.

10. Roderick Nash, "The American Cult of the Primitive," *American Quarterly* 18 (fall 1966): 517–37; Peter G. Filene, *Him/Her/Self: Sex Roles in Modern America*, 2nd ed. (Baltimore: Johns Hopkins University Press, 1986), 138, 147, 153; Michael S. Kimmel, "The Contemporary 'Crisis' of Masculinity in Historical Perspective," and Michael Messner, "The Meaning of Success: The Athletic Experience and the Development of Male Identity," in *The Making of Masculinities: The New Men's Studies,* ed. Harry Brod (Boston: Allen and Unwin, 1987), 196, 148–49.

11. Margaret Marsh, "Suburban Men and Masculine Domesticity 1870–1915," in *Meanings for Manhood: Constructions of Masculinity in Victorian America,* ed. Mark C. Carnes and Clyde Griffen (Chicago: University of Chicago Press, 1990), 112, 114–17.

12. On women in environmentalism, see Gottlieb, *Forcing the Spring,* 207–34; Carolyn Merchant, *Earthcare: Women and the Environment* (New York: Routledge, 1995); Polly Welts Kaufman, *National Parks and the Woman's Voice: A History* (Albuquerque: University of New Mexico Press, 1996), 6; Vera Norwood, *Made from This Earth: American Women and Nature* (Chapel Hill: University of North Carolina Press, 1993), xiii.

13. Barbara Claire Freeman, *The Feminine Sublime: Gender and Excess in Women's Fiction* (Berkeley: University of California Press, 1995), 45.

14. "U.S. Seeks to Limit Logging in the Sierra Nevada," *New York Times,* January 14, 2001.

15. "What is the Nature of Nature?" *New York Times,* July 1, 1998, front page; Cronon, "Trouble," 74–75; Michael Cohen, "Resistance to Wilderness," *Environmental History* (1996): 26–46; Comer, *Landscapes of the New West,* 127–53. On loss of use rights resulting from conservation measures and the establishment of public parks and reserves, see Mark David Spence, *Dispossessing the Wilderness: Indian Removal and the Making of the National Parks* (Oxford: Oxford University, 1999); Louis S. Warren, *The Hunter's Game: Poachers and Conservation in Twentieth Century-America* (New Haven: Yale, 1997); Karl Jacoby, *Crimes Against Nature: Squatters, Poachers, and the Hidden History of American Conservation* (Berkeley: University of California Press, 2001).

PART I: (EN)GENDERING THE WILDERNESS, 1860S–1914

1. Josiah Dwight Whitney, *The Yosemite Guide-Book: A Description of the Yosemite Valley and Adjacent Region of the Sierra Nevada, and of the Big Trees of California* (Cambridge, MA: University Press, Welch, Bigelow, 1870), 102, 114, 123; Francis P. Farquhar, *Up and Down California: The Journal of William H. Brewer, Professor of Agriculture in the Sheffield Scientific School from 1864 to 1903* (Berkeley: University of California Press, 1966), 407–8, 518, 520–21.

2. Clarence King, *Mountaineering in the Sierra Nevada* (London: Sampson Low, Marston, Low, and Searle, 1872), 49–51, 78–79, 274, 276–77, 281; reviewed in *Proceedings of the Alpine Club,* 1872, 394.

3. Edward Whymper, *Scrambles Amongst the Alps in the Years 1860-69* (Cleveland, OH: Burrows Brothers, [1871]), 9–10, 118, 161; John Tyndall, *Hours of Exercise in the Alps* (New York: D. Appleton, 1899), 155–56; C. H. Sholes, "President's Address for 1896) *Mazama* 1, no. 2 (1897): 276.

4. Whymper, *Scrambles,* frontispiece, 152–57, 42–43, 95; for "Alpine warfare," see "Reviews," *Proceedings of Alpine Club,* 1872, 395. On the belief in dragons, see Edwin Bernbaum, *Sacred Mountains of the World* (San Francisco: Sierra Club, 1990), 123.

5. King climbed Mt. Langley. King, *Mountaineering,* 280–81; for King's explanation of his error and his expedition to correct it, see Clarence King, *Mountaineering in the Sierra*

Nevada (New York: Charles Scribner's, 1907; rev. ed.), 345–61; see also Francis P. Farquhar, *History of the Sierra Nevada* (Berkeley: University of California, 1965), 148, 173–74; Donald Keith Anderson, "Legacy of the American Frontier: A History of the John Muir Trail" (MS thesis, School of Social Sciences, California State University, Fresno, December 1997), 43–44.

6. Quote from James D. Hague, "Mount Whitney," *Overland Monthly* 11, no. 5 (November 1873): 463.

7. Francis P. Farquhar, "The Story of Mount Whitney," *Sierra Club Bulletin* (hereafter *SCB*) 14, no. 1 (February 1929): 39–52; W. Storrs Lee, *The Sierra* (New York: G. P. Putnam's Sons, 1962), 250–56; W. A. Chalfant, *The Story of Inyo* (1922; reprint, Bishop, CA: Chalfant Press, 1975), 318–19.

8. Quote from Sholes, "President's Address for 1896," 281. For Cooper's critique of American place naming, see Susan Fenimore Cooper, *Rural Hours* (Syracuse: Syracuse University Press, 1968, 299–308.

9. Edward W. Said, *Culture and Imperialism* (New York: Knopf, 1993), xii–xiii.

CHAPTER 1. PLACE NAMING IN THE HIGH SIERRA

1. The Sierra is defined here as extending from the northern border of Alpine County and Lassen Peak south to Walker Pass, Lake Isabelle, and Tehachapi Pass. See Peter Browning, *Place Names of the Sierra Nevada: From Abbott to Zumwalt* (Berkeley: Wilderness Press, 1986), [iii]; Francis P. Farquhar, "Naming America's Mountains: The Sierra Nevada of California," *American Alpine Journal* 14 (1964): 131. On recent history, see Timothy Duane, *Shaping the Sierra: Nature, Culture, and Conflict in the Changing West* (Berkeley: University of California Press, 1999).

2. Erwin G. Gudde, *California Place Names: The Origin and Etymology of Current Geographical Names* (Berkeley: University of California Press, 1962), 293–94; J. D. Whitney, *Names and Places: Studies in Geographic and Topographic Nomenclature* (Cambridge, MA: University Press, 1888), 21; Browning, *Place Names,* 198.

3. [Theodore Solomons], map of Mt. Goddard region, n.d. [mid-1890s], Bancroft Library, 71-295 c/243: 48; Francis P. Farquhar, "Place Names of the High Sierra," *Sierra Club Bulletin* (hereafter *SCB*) 11, no. 4 (1923): 394; Nellie Van de Grift Sanchez, *Spanish and Indian Place Names of California: Their Meaning and Their Romance* (New York: Arno Press, 1976, from A. M. Robertson's 1922 ed.), 209–34.

4. Browning, *Place Names,* 117, 163, 32; Frémont named features for Edward Kern, Richard Owens, and Kit Carson. See J. C. Frémont, *Report of the Exploring Expedition to the Rocky Mountains in the Year 1842, and to Oregon and Northern California in the Years 1843-44* (Washington, DC: Gales and Seaton, 1845), 248; Gudde, *California Place Names,* 385; Vincent Gianella, "Where Frémont Crossed the Sierra Nevada in 1844," *SCB* 44, no. 7 (October 1959): 62.

5. Quote from "Notes, Lil' Winchell's accts of early history of Fresno County—mts etc. Told me at Mill, Ockenden, July 25, 1896," Bancroft Library, Lil' Winchell Papers, 243: 46. See also Lilbourne Alsip Winchell, *History of Fresno County and the San Joaquin Valley, Narrative and Biographical* (Fresno, CA: A. H. Cawston, 1933), 155–58; W. A. Chalfant, *The Story of Inyo* (Bishop, CA: Chalfant, 1933, rev. ed.), 140–43; C. King and J. D. Gardiner, "Map of Portion of the Yosemite Valley from Surveys Made by the Order of the Commissioners to Manage Yosemite Valley and the Big Trees," in J. D. Whitney, *Yosemite,* inside back cover; Jeronima Echeverria, "Basque 'Tramp Herders' on Forbidden Ground: Early Grazing Controversies in California's National Reserves," *Locus* 4, no. 1 (fall 1991): 42.

6. Henry David Thoreau, *Walden, or Life in the Woods* (New York: New American Library, 1960), 134.

7. Alison Blunt and Gillian Rose, "Introduction: Women's Colonial and Postcolonial Geographies," ed. Alison Blunt and Gillian Rose, in *Writing Women and Space: Colonial and Postcolonial Geographies* (New York: Guilford Press, 1994), 9; for maps as "weapons of imperialsm," see J. B. Harley, "Maps, Knowledge, and Power," in *The Iconography of Landscape: Essays on the Symbolic Representation, Design and Use of Past Environments*, ed. Denis Cosgrove and Stephen Daniels (Cambridge University Press, 1988), 282–312; see also Gregory H. Nobles, "Straight Lines and Stability: Mapping the Political Order of the Anglo-American Frontier," *Journal of American History* (June 1993): 15; John F. Sears, *Sacred Places: American Tourist Attractions in the Nineteenth Century* (Oxford: Oxford University Press, 1989), 123–27.

8. Josiah Dwight Whitney, *Geographical and Geological Surveys* (Cambridge: Welch, Bigelow, 1875), 3, 29; "Geological Survey," *Overland Monthly* (hereafter *OM*) 12, no. 1 (January 1874): 88; Albert Williams Jr., "Geological Surveys," *OM* 12, no. 3 (March 1874): 261–65; on the surveyors, see William H. Goetzmann, *Exploration and Empire: The Explorer and the Scientist in the Winning of the American West* (New York: Norton, 1966), 355–89.

9. Alan Trachtenberg, *Reading American Photographs: Images as History, Mathew Brady to Walker Evans* (New York: Hill and Wang, 1989); Kevin Starr, *Americans and the California Dream, 1850-1915* (New York: Oxford University Press, 1973), 172–91; Ted Orland, *Man & Yosemite: A Photographer's View of the Early Years* (Santa Cruz, CA: Image Continuum Press, [1985]), 30–42; Alfred Runte, *Yosemite: The Embattled Wilderness* (Lincoln: University of Nebraska Press, 1990), 19–21.

10. Josiah Dwight Whitney, *The Yosemite Guide-Book: A Description of the Yosemite Valley and Adjacent Region of the Sierra Nevada, and of the Big Trees of California* (London: H. Milford, Oxford University Press, 1930; Welch, Bigelow, 1870), 9–12; Act of June 30, 1864.

11. Whitney, *Yosemite*, 15–18, 60; Lafayette Houghton Bunnell, *Discovery of the Yosemite and the Indian War of 1851 that Led to that Event* (Los Angeles: G. W. Gerlicher, 1911), 212; Francis P. Farquhar, ed., *Up and Down California in 1860-1864: The Journal of William Brewer* (Berkeley: University of California Press, 1966), 404.

12. Whitney, *Yosemite*, 15; Clarence King, *Mountaineering in the Sierra Nevada* (London: Sampson Low, Marston, Low, and Searle, 1872), 36–40; Clarence King, "Bancroft's Native Races of the Pacific States," *Atlantic Monthly* 35 (February 1875): 169, 163.

13. James M. Hutchings, *In the Heart of the Sierras: The Yo Semite Valley and the Big Trees Groves*, ed. Peter Browning (1886; reprint, Lafayette, CA: Great West Books, 1990), 389.

14. Brewer, *Up and Down*, 525–32, 540; Whitney, *Yosemite*, 113, 133; for "California conglomerate," see William H. Brewer, "Tenth Anniversary of the Appalachian Mountain Club," *Appalachia* 4, no. 4 (December 1886): 368; on prospectors, see Thomas Keough, "Over Kearsarge Pass in 1864," *SCB* 10, no. 3 (January 1918): 340–42.

15. Brewer, *Up and Down*, 519–39; Francis P. Farquhar, "Early History of the Kings River Sierra," *SCB* 26, no. 1 (February 1941): 32–41.

16. King, *Mountaineering* (1872), 51, 75; Goetzmann, *Exploration and Empire*, 375–76; Arnold Lunn, *The Exploration of the Alps* (New York: Henry Holt, [1914]), 111–84.

17. John Ruskin, *Sesame and Lilies: Two Lectures* (Chicago: C. McClure, 1889), 94–95; Simon Schama, *Landscape and Memory* (New York: Knopf, 1995), 506–10.

18. E. C. Winchell, *San Francisco Morning Call*, September 11–12, 1872, reprinted in *SCB* 12, no. 3 (1926): 245, as "Kings River Cañon in 1868"; see also Winchell, *History of Fresno County*, 156–57.

19. J. M. Hutchings, *Hutchings' Tourist's Guide to the Yo Semite Valley and the Big Trees Groves for the Spring and Summer of 1877* (San Francisco: A. Roman, 1877); see also Charles Nordhoff, *California: For Health, Pleasure, and Residence* (New York: Harper & Brothers, 1878), 22, 34–83; Trachtenberg, *Reading American Photographs*, 139.

20. Nordhoff, *California*, 69, 75; Earl Pomeroy, *In Search of the Golden West: The Tourist in Western America* (New York: Knopf, 1957), 15–30; Emma Homan Thayer, *Wild Flowers of the Pacific Coast* (New York: Cassell, 1887), [52]; Mark David Spence, *Dispossessing the Wilderness: Indian Removal and the Making of the National Parks* (New York: Oxford University Press, 1999), 101–13.

21. Sixty English names blanketed the valley by 1905. See U.S. Geological Survey, topographer F. E. Matthes and geographer E. M. Douglas, "Map of Yosemite Valley, Mariposa County, California," July 1907, reprinted June 1909. I have a copy of this map.

22. Peter Browning lists only approximately thirty that are even indirectly indigenous in *Place Names*. See also Henry Sicade, "Aboriginal Nomenclature," *Mazama* 5, no. 3 (December 1918): 251–54; Hazard Stevens, "The Ascent of Takhoma," *Atlantic Monthly* 38, no. 229 (November 1876): 526. For Native American names recorded and then lost, see "Notes, Lil' Winchell's accts," Bancroft Library, Winchell Papers, 243:46; "Guide to the Scenery of the Sierra Nevada," map by J. W. A. Wright, in *History of Fresno County, California, with Illustrations* (Fresno: Valley Publishers, 1973, reprint of Wallace W. Elliott, 1882), 231. On Spanish names lost, see N. F. McClure, "Map of the Yosemite National Park, 1895"; Frémont, "Report" (1845), 53, 154–55, 220; Sanchez, *Spanish and Indian Place Names*, 205; Phil Townsend Hanna, *The Dictionary of California Land Names* (Los Angeles: Automobile Club of Southern California, 1946), 56; Solomons, "Contour Map—Tehipite Valley," Bancroft Library 71-295c/243: 48.

23. Edmond S. Meany, *Origin of Washington Geographic Names* (Seattle: University of Washington Press, 1923), 173–80, vi; Robert Hitchman, *Place Names of Washington* (Tacoma: Washington State Historical Society, 1985): 194–200.

24. C. F. (Constance Frederica) Gordon-Cumming, *Granite Crags of California* (Edinburgh: William Blackwood and Sons, 1886, new ed.), 201, 69–170; Mary Roberts Rinehart, *Through Glacier Park: Seeing America First with Howard Eaton* (1916; reprint, New York: Doubleday, 1928), 66–69; Polly Welts Kaufman, *National Parks and the Woman's Voice: A History* (Albuquerque: University of New Mexico Press, 1996), 6; Spence, *Dispossessing the Wilderness*, 27–40; Pomeroy, *In Search of the Golden West*, 153–54. See also Stanford E. Demars, *The Tourist in Yosemite, 1855-1985* (Salt Lake City: University of Utah Press, 1991), 38.

25. Susan Fenimore Cooper, *Rural Hours* (Syracuse: Syracuse University Press, 1968), 307; on Cooper, see also Lawrence Buell, *The Environmental Imagination: Thoreau, Nature Writing, and the Formation of American Culture* (Cambridge: Harvard University Press, 1995), 47–49; and Vera Norwood, *Made from This Earth: American Women and Nature* (Chapel Hill: University of North Carolina Press, 1993), 24–41. There were men, like Starr King, who objected as well.

26. Elizabeth Cady Stanton, *Eighty Years and More (1815-1897); Reminiscences of Elizabeth Cady Stanton* (New York: European Publishing, 1898), 293–94. University of Michigan microfilm, reel 606.

27. Wright, *History of Fresno County, California*, 245–46; Francis P. Farquhar, "The Record on Mount Young," *SCB* 20, no. 1 (February 1935): 108–9; Farquhar, "The Story of Mount Whitney: Part IV," *SCB* 32, no. 5 (May 1947): 78–81; Browning, *Place Names*, 99, 244.

28. John Muir, "A Rival of the Yosemite: The Cañon of the South Fork of King's River, California," *Century Illustrated Magazine* 43, no. 1 (November 1891): 77, 80–84; John Muir,

"The Yosemite," in *The Wilderness World of John Muir*, ed. Edwin Way Teale (Boston: Houghton Mifflin, 1954), 99–101; John Muir, "Snow Banners of the Californian Alps," *Harper's New Monthly Magazine* 55, no. 326 (July 1877): 162–64; John Muir, "Explorations in the Great Tuolumne Cañon," *OM* 11, no. 2 (August 1873): 139; John Muir, *The Story of My Boyhood and Youth* (Boston: Houghton Mifflin, 1913).

29. Samuel Merrill, "Personal Recollections of John Muir," *SCB* 13, no. 1 (February 1928): 29.

30. First quote from Shirley Sargent, *Solomons of the Sierra: The Pioneer of the John Muir Trail* (Yosemite: Flying Spur Press, 1989), 26, quoting Theodore S. Solomons, "The Muir of the Nineties," May 16, 1935, *Mariposa Gazette*, reprinted in the May 1936 *Yosemite Nature Notes*; "bestowing no names" from Solomons, "The Beginnings of the John Muir Trail," *SCB* 25, no. 1 (February 1940): 31.

31. For "I care little," Muir to Johnson, April 30, 1895, University of the Pacific Library, Stockton, California (hereafter UOP), Muir Papers, reel 8. "On any mountain," see letter from Muir, *Mt. Whitney Club Journal*, May 1903, in Richard Leonard, "Mountain Records of the Sierra Nevada" (San Francisco: Bancroft Library, 1936), 105; see also Thurman Wilkins, *John Muir: Apostle of Nature* (Norman: University of Oklahoma Press, 1995).

32. Muir, "By-Ways of Yosemite Travel," *OM* 13, no. 3 (September 1874): 271–72; Muir, "Rival of the Yosemite," 96–97.

33. Muir, "The Hetch Hetchy Valley," *OM* 11, no. 1 (July 1873): 42–50; Muir, "The Kings River Valley," San Francisco *Daily Evening Bulletin*, August 13, 1873, in *SCB* 26, no. 1 (February 1941): 8; Muir, "Rival of the Yosemite," 4, 93.

34. Muir, "Kings River Valley," 8; Chalfant, *Story of Inyo*, 318; J. M. Hutchings, "Journal (YNP [Yosemite National Park]) August 23–24, 1877," cited in Francis P. Farquhar, "A Revival of Interest in Mount Starr King," *SCB* 17, no. 1 (February 1932): 117–18; Lilbourne Alsip Winchell, *History of Fresno County*, 155–58.

35. Muir's address, "Proceedings of the Meeting of the Sierra Club, Held November 23, 1895," *SCB* 1, no. 7 (January 1896): 275–80; Lembert homesteaded Tuolumne Meadows in the 1880s, grazed Angora goats, and mined the site; see interview with William E. Colby by Hal Roth on February 27 and 28, 1961, in Big Sur. Bancroft Library, SC Papers, 58–59; see also Runte, *Yosemite*, 54–56; Holway R. Jones, *John Muir and the Sierra Club: The Battle for Yosemite* (San Francisco: Sierra Club, 1965); Michael P. Cohen, *The Pathless Way: John Muir and American Wilderness* (Madison: University of Wisconsin Press, 1984).

36. Allen H. Bent, "The Mountaineering Clubs of America," *Appalachia* 14, no. 1 (December 1916): 5–18; Ronald Clark, *The Victorian Mountaineers* (London: B. T. Batsford, 1953).

37. The AMC purchased peaks in the White Mountains, promoted state and county regulation of private lands in New England, and called for state acquisition of the region's mountains. The Oregon Alpine Club organized in 1887 to lobby for Crater Lake National Park. John D. Scott, *We Climb High: A Thumbnail Chronology of the Mazamas, 1894-1964* (Portland: Mazamas, 1969), 1; E. Fay Fuller, "Historian's Report for 1894," *Mazama* 1, no. 1 (1896): 18–19.

38. Robert L. Wood, *The Land That Slept Late: The Olympic Mountains in Legend and History* (Seattle: The Mountaineers, 1995), 94–95.

39. Armes to Muir, May 15, 1891; Muir to Armes, May 26, 1891, University of the Pacific, Muir Papers, ser. 1A; Starr, *Americans and the California Dream*, 189–90, 208; Michael L. Smith, *Pacific Visions: California Scientists and the Environment, 1850-1915* (New Haven: Yale University Press, 1987), 4.

40. "Members of the Corporation," *Appalachia* 2, no. 1 (June 1879): 84–87; Schama, *Landscape and Memory*, 502.

41. J. N. LeConte's maps: "That Portion of the Sierra Nevada Adjacent to the Yosemite and Hetch Hetchy Valleys" and "A Portion of the Sierra Nevada Adjacent to the Kings River," University of California, Berkeley, Bancroft Library Map Room. Francis P. Farquhar, "Sierra Club Mountaineer and Editor," oral history conducted by Ann and Ray Lage (Sierra Club History Committee, 1974), 55–56; interview with William E. Colby by Hal Roth on February 27 and 28, 1961, in Big Sur, California. Transcript in Bancroft Library, SC Papers; Nathan C. Clark, "Sierra Club Leader, Outdoorsman, & Engineer," oral history conducted by Richard Searle (Sierra Club History Committee, 1977), 14–15.

42. Senger and Armes to Muir, May 25, 1892, Muir to Senger, May 22, 1892, Armes to Muir, September 18, 1892, UOP, Muir Papers, reel 7; "The Story of the Sierra Club," *SC Handbook* (San Francisco: Sierra Club, 1947), 3–10. Olney to Senger, January 14, 1892, Bancroft Library, SC Member Papers, box 172:2.

43. Colby to Whymper, January 12, 1911, Bancroft Library 71–295, Colby Papers, Box 38: 2; Elizabeth Parker, "In Memoriam," *Canadian Alpine Journal* 4 (1912): 126–36.

44. Elliott McAllister to members, May 22, 1893, UOP, Muir Papers, doc. 0704135. David Starr Jordan, *The Days of a Man, Volume 1: 1851-1899* (Yonkers-on-Hudson, NY: World Book, 1922), 258–64; F. H. Chapin, "Ascents of the Breithorn and Mont Blanc," *Appalachia* 5, no. 1 (December 1887): 39–42; Charles E. Fay, "Up to the Crags of Sir Donald," *Appalachia* 7, no. 2 (December 1893): 157–64; J. B. Henck Jr., "A Visit to Milan," *Appalachia* 3, no. 1 (June 1882): 13–14; "Proceedings of the Club," *Appalachia* 4, no. 1 (December 1884): 88–89; "Report of the Corresponding Secretary for 1884," *Appalachia* 4, no. 2 (July 1885): 156.

45. Of the 480 who joined by May 1900, 91 lived near the Sierra. See "Records of Proposal for Membership and Ballots," Bancroft Library, SC Papers, ser. 12, cartons 309–10.

46. J. M. Stillman, "Our Sister Societies," *SCB* 2, no. 1 (January 1897): 56–58.

47. See, for example, the Club Alpine Francais to SC, January 24, 1896; Section Todi to SC, July 4, 1895; W. Douglas to Scottish Mountaineering Club, Bancroft Library, SC Member Papers, 4:37. Senger arranged (1892–96) exchanges with European geographical societies. Bancroft Library, SC Member Papers, 172: 2.

48. Charles E. Fay, "Annual Address of the President," *Appalachia* 2, no. 1 (June 1879): 6–7; see also C. H. Sholes, "President's Address for 1896," *Mazama* 1, no. 2 (1897): 276, 280; Hazard Stevens, "Ascent of Takhoma," 513–30; Paul Schullery, ed., *Island in the Sky: Pioneering Accounts of Mount Rainier, 1833-1894* (Seattle: The Mountaineers, 1987): 50, 65.

49. H. Nichols, "Back Ranges of the Selkirks," *Appalachia* 7, no. 2 (December 1893): 102; E. Fay Fuller, "Historian's Report for 1894," 18; "Reports," *Appalachia* 4, no. 2 (July 1885): 163–66, no. 3 (March 1886): 256–57; Charles E. Fay, "The First Ascent of Mount Dawson," *Appalachia* 9, no. 3 (April 1901): 258.

50. Armes to Muir, September 25, 1892, UPO, Muir Papers, ser. 1A; Noble to Armes, January 4, 1893, in "Letters from Our Honorary Members," *SCB* 1, no. 2 (June 1893): 25.

51. "Run mad" from "Proceedings of the Meeting of the SC," November 23, 1895, *SCB* 1, no. 7 (January 1896): 270; see also M. M. Pychowska, "Two in the Alpine Pastures," *Appalachia* 5, no. 3 (December 1888): 189.

52. Fay, "Annual Address of the President" (1879), 5–7; Fuller, "Historian's Report for 1894," 16–20.

53. Whitney, *Yosemite*, 2, 28–29; King, "Bancroft's Native Races of the Pacific States," 169. Charles E. Fay, "The Mountain as an Influence in Modern Life," *Appalachia* 11, no. 1 (June 1905): 27; Frederick Law Olmsted, "The Yosemite Valley and the Mariposa Big

Trees: A Preliminary Report (1865)," in *Landscape Architecture* 43 (1952): 20; Nordhoff, *California*, 80. On separation of work and nature in environmentalism, see Richard White, "'Are You an Environmentalist or Do You Work for a Living?' Work and Nature," in *Uncommon Ground: Toward Reinventing Nature*, ed. William Cronon (New York: Norton, 1995), 171–85.

54. Whitney, *Yosemite*, 29; Charles Fay, "Annual Address of the President" (1879), 7; Hazard Stevens, "The Ascent of Takoma," 522–23, 527; Francis P. Farquhar, "The Literature of Mountaineering," *California Library Association* (1930s), Bancroft Library, University of California, Berkeley, SC Papers, 44: 13.

55. Roderick Nash, *Wilderness and the American Mind*, 3rd ed. (New Haven: Yale University Press, 1982), 44; Charles Fay, "Mountain as an Influence," 27; Pomeroy, *In Search of the Golden West*, 88, 92.

56. Harold K. Steen, *The U.S. Forest Service: A History* (Seattle: University of Washington Press, 1976), 26–30; "Proceedings of the Sierra Club, First General Meeting, September 16, 1892," in *SCB* 1, no. 1 (January 1893): 23–24.

57. William Russell Dudley, "Forest Reservations; with a Report on the Sierra Reservation, California," *SCB* 1, no. 7 (January 1896): 254–67.

58. Theodore S. Solomons, "Among the Sources of the San Joaquin," *SCB* 1, no. 3 (January 1894): 62; C. Mulholland, "Mt. Barnard," *SCB* 1, no. 3 (June 1894): 85–89; Cornelius Beach Bradley, "Exploration of the East Creek Amphitheater," *SCB* 2, no. 5 (January 1899): 270–77; Theodore S. Solomons, "Explorations in the Sierra Nevada During the Season of 1896," *Appalachia* 7, no. 3 (July 1897): 240.

59. Theodore S. Solomons, "A Search for a High Mountain Route from the Yosemite to the King's River Cañon," *SCB* 1, no. 5 (January 1895): 221–26; Solomons, "Mount Goddard and Its Vicinity—In the High Sierra of California," *Appalachia* 3, no. 1 (January 1896): 45, 51; [T. S. Solomons], map of Mt. Goddard region (mid-1890s), Bancroft Library 71-295 c/243: 48; J. S. Hutchinson, "Goddard and Disappearing Creeks—The Enchanted Gorge," *SCB* 12, no. 1 (1924): 20.

60. [T. S. Solomons], "Contour Map—Tehipite Valley," January 1897, Bancroft Library 71-295c/243: 48; [T. S. Solomons], map of Mt. Goddard region (mid-1890s), Bancroft Library 71-295c/243: 48.

61. Solomons, "Among the Sources of the San Joaquin," 74, 79; Solomons, "Search for a High Mountain Route," 221–26; Solomons, "Mount Goddard and Its Vicinity," 47–57; [Solomons], "Contour Map—Tehipite—Valley," 1897; see also Theodore Seixas Solomons, "After Forty Years," *SCB* 18, no. 1 (February 1933): 22; George R. Stewart, *Names on the Land: A Historical Account of Place-Naming in the United States* (New York: Random House, 1945), 334; Charles Norman Fiske, "First Ascent of Mount Fiske," *SCB* 11, no. 4 (1923): 417; "Notes and Correspondence," *SCB* 1, no. 7 (January 1896): 287–89; Shirley Sargent, *Solomons of the Sierra*, 43–44. Twenty-nine years later the club and the State of California built the John Muir Trail approximating Solomons's summit route as it passes west of the main crest and crosses high passes and lateral ridges.

62. Vernon L. Kellogg, "A Stanford Party in the Kings River Canyon," *Sunset* 4, no. 1 (November 1899): 17–18; W. W. Bradley, "Exploration of the East Creek Amphitheater," *SCB* 2, no. 5 (January 1899): 273; R. M. Price, "Through the Tuolumne Cañon," *SCB* 1, no. 6 (May 1895): 204, 206; Farquhar, "Place Names of the High Sierra," *SCB* 12, no. 1 (1924): 60–61; Church to McArdie, March 18, 1905, in *SCB* 5, no. 4 (June 1905): 316–17; William Russell Dudley, "Forestry Notes," *SCB* 2, no. 5 (January 1899): 290–93; 4, no. 1 (January 1902): 71–75; 4, no. 2 (June 1902): 173–74; 4, no. 4 (June 1903): 319–23; 5, no. 1 (January 1904): 84.

63. William Russell Dudley, "Forest Reservations: With a Report on the Sierra Reservation, California," *SCB* 1, no. 7 (January 1896): 265; "Report of the Acting Superintendent of Sequoia and General Grant National Parks," September 1, 1895; A. E. Wood, "Report of the Acting Superintendent of the Yosemite National Park," August 31, 1891, 4; Alex Rodgers, "Report of the Acting Superintendent of Yosemite National Park," August 22, 1895, 6; Geo. Gale, "Report of the Acting Superintendent of Sequoia and General Grant National Parks," August 31, 1896, 748; "Report of the Acting Superintendent of the Yosemite National Park," August 15, 1896, January 6, 1899, and September 15, 1900; Bolton Coit Brown, "Three Days with Mt. King," *SCB* 1, no. 7 (January 1896): 243, 252.

64. Reports of the Acting Superintendent of the Yosemite National Park, August 31, 1891, 4–6; August 28, 1894, 4–6; January 6, 1899, 3–5; October 28, 1899; Sargent, *Solomons of the Sierra*, 19.

65. Quote from Howard Longley, "From Fresno to Mt. Whitney by Way of Roaring (or Cloudy) River," *SCB* 1, no. 6 (May 1895): 196, 192; see also Joseph N. LeConte, "The High Mountain Route Between Yosemite and the King's River Cañon," *SCB* 7, no. 1 (January 1909): 8; Howard Longley, "From Fresno to Mt. Whitney," *SCB* 1, no. 6 (May 1895): 187–98; J. S. Hutchinson, August 20, 1896, to Editor, *SCB* 2, no. 1 (January 1897): 57.

66. *United States v. Grimaud*, 170 *Federal Reporter* (1908), 206–13; "Judicial Amendment," and "Ruling Against Grazing Penalty," *Fresno Morning Republican*, May 4, 1909; Steen, *U.S. Forest Service*, 88–89.

67. Francis M. Fultz, "The Mt. Ritter Knapsack Trip," *SCB* 6, no. 5 (June 1908): 291.

68. Browning, *Place Names*, 5, 58, 109, 122–23; Solomons, "Among the Sources of the San Joaquin," 79; "Map of the Yosemite National Park, Prepared for Use of U.S. Troops by N. F. McClure, 1st Lieut., 5th Cavalry, March 1896," attached to "Report of the Acting Superintendent of Yosemite National Park," August 31, 1896; Farquhar, "Place Names" (1924): 63; Francis P. Farquhar, "Place Names of the High Sierra," *SCB* 13, no. 2 (1925): 127.

69. *History of Fresno County, California*, 121, 190, 213, 231–35, 238–39.

70. Map by J. W. A. Wright, 1882, in *History of Fresno County, California*, 231; Lil' Winchell to [Solomons], [April 16, 1896], Bancroft Library, SC Papers, 71-295 c/243: 43; "Notes, Lil' Winchell's accts," 1896, Bancroft Library, Winchell Papers, 243:46.

71. J. N. LeConte to Winchell, February 23, 1903, Bancroft Library, Winchell Papers, 243: 43. Dusy's name still graces a meadow, creek, and an awesome basin. For Dusy's Peak, see Solomons, "Contour Map—Tehipite Valley," January 1897, Bancroft 71-295c/243: 48; for national patterns, see Stewart, *Names on the Land*, 354.

72. Letter from George Davidson to Board of Directors, "The Name 'Mt. Rainier,'" February 20, 1906; "Recent or Modern Methods for Establishing Place Names," *SCB* 6, no. 2 (January 1907): 88–90.

73. Henry Gannett to Club, October 8, 1902, *SCB* 4, no. 3 (February 1903): 239–41.

74. L. A. Nelson, "Mount Meany," *Mountaineer* 13, no. 1 (November 1920): 31.

75. William Colby, "Proposed Summer Outing of the Sierra Club—Report of the Committee," *SCB* 3, no. 3 (February 1901): 250–53.

76. Howard Longley, "Mountain Trips: What to Take, and How to Take It," *SCB* 2, no. 1 (January 1897): 43, 30–31; for food taken, see Goldberg, Bowen & Co. to Senger, June 11, 1897, Bancroft Library, SC Papers, carton 172, file 2.

77. Interview with William Colby conducted by Hal Roth, 1961.

78. Alfred Runte, *National Parks: The American Experience* (Lincoln: University of Nebraska Press, 1987, rev. ed.), 19–32; Anne Farrar Hyde, *An American Vision: Far Western Landscape and National Culture, 1820-1920* (New York: New York University Press, 1990), 7, 11; Starr, *Americans and the California Dream*, 172, 189–90; Michael L. Smith, *Pacific Visions*, 4.

79. For a geographically broad perspective, see William G. Robbins, "Laying Siege to Western History: The Emergence of New Paradigms," in *Trails: Toward a New Western History*, ed. Patricia Nelson Limerick, Clyde A. Milner II, Charles E. Rankin (Lawrence: University Press of Kansas, 1991): 183; Stanford E. Demurs, *The Tourist in Yosemite, 1855-1985* (Salt Lake City: University of Utah Press, 1991): 58–62.

80. Established between 1902 and 1912: New York City's American Alpine Club, the Rocky Mountain Climbers Club, the Alpine Club of Canada, Seattle's Mountaineers, Chicago's Prairie Club, British Columbia's Mountaineering Club, the Dartmouth Outing Club, Vermont's Green Mountain Club, and the Colorado Mountain Club.

81. W. H. Neiswender, "Summer Outing in the Cascades," *Sunset* 7, no. 2–3 (June–July 1901): 71; Theodore S. Solomons, "In the Upper Merced Cañon," *Sunset* 7, no. 2–3 (June–July 1901): 60.

82. Ella M. Sexton, "Where the Red Deer Come Down to Drink," *Sunset* 7, no. 1 (May 1901): 4; Emma M. Greenleaf, "God's First Temples," *Sunset* 9, no. 5 (September 1902): 346.

83. King, *Mountaineering*, 79; Ernest Dawson, "Climbing the Grand Teton," *SCB* 12, no. 4 (1927): 364.

84. On maps and the female body, see Ella Shohat, "Imaging Terra Incognita: The Disciplinary Gaze of Empire," *Public Culture* 3, no. 2 (spring 1991): 46–47; on gender in discourse of discovery, see Louis Montrose, "The Work of Gender in the Discourse of Discovery," *Representations* 33 (winter 1991): 1–41.

85. Map drawn by J. W. A. Wright, 1882, in *History of Fresno County, California*, 231; Robert M. Price, "Exploration of Mount Darwin," *SCB* 11, no. 3 (1922): 285; "Map of the Yosemite National Park," attached to "Report of the Acting Superintendent of Yosemite National Park," 1896.

86. Browning, *Place Names*, 16. Named since 1960: Amelia Earhart Peak, Anna Mills Mount, and Carol Col, sometimes called Puppet Pass.

87. Frank Bond to Walter Huber, December 28, 1925, Bancroft Library, SC Papers, 44:17; Julian H. Steward, "Temple Crag (13,016 feet)," *SCB* 11, no. 3 (1922): 312–13.

88. *History of Fresno County, California*, 231, 244; for invitation to Mills from club, see "Record of Proposal for Membership and Ballots," Bancroft Library, SC Papers, ser. 12, Membership Records, cartons 309–10; Browning, *Place Names*, 72, 135.

89. Henry Gannett to Club, October 8, 1902, *SCB* 4, no. 3 (February 1903): 239–41.

90. Charles E. Fay, "The Annual Address of the President," *Appalachia* 3, no. 1 (June 1882): 7.

91. Harriet Monroe, "The Yosemite Waters," *SCB* 6, no. 5 (June 1908): 307–8. Bridal Veil was also called, "Queen of the Valley" and "Falls of Louise." See Browning, *Place Names*, 26.

92. C. F. Gordon-Cumming, *Granite Crags of California*, 200–201.

93. Joseph LeConte, "A Journal of Ramblings" (1875), reprinted as LeConte, "Ramblings Through the High Sierra," *SCB* 3, no. 1 (January 1900): 45–55, 29; on LeConte's life, see Lester Stephens, *Joseph LeConte, Gentle Prophet of Evolution* (Baton Rouge: Louisiana State University Press, 1982).

94. E. R. Ingraham, "Where Amatil Laughs," *Sunset* 9, no. 1 (May 1902): 65; W. B. May, "Red Letter Day in the Yosemite," *Sunset* 5, no. 2 (May 1900): 29.

95. J. S. Hutchinson, "First Ascent," *SCB* 5, no. 3 (January 1905): 158; Browning, *Place Names*, 64, 140. See also Francis P. Farquhar, "An Introduction to Clarence King's 'The Three Lakes'"; and Clarence King, "The Three Lakes: Marian, Lall, Jan, and How They Were Named," *SCB* 24, no. 3 (June 1939): 109–20.

96. In addition to those mentioned elsewhere, fifty-six lakes were named for women in the Sierra alone; see R. M. Marshall to Colby, July 16, 1935, Bancroft Library, SC Papers, 39:

25; Hitchman, *Place Names of Washington*, 150–55; Marjorie Kennedy, "The Tetons," *Mountaineer* 32, no. 1 (December 15, 1939): 4.

97. David Freeman Hawke, *Those Tremendous Mountains: The Story of the Lewis and Clark Expedition* (New York: Norton, 1980), 131.

98. George Putnam, "Down the Kern-Kaweah," *SCB* 7, no. 1 (January 1909): 35; Sholes, "President's Address for 1896," 281; George H. Harvey Jr., "Our First Sierra Club Outing," *SCB* 12, no. 2 (1925): 161–62; Arthur O. Wheeler, "The Alpine Club of Canada's Expedition to Jasper Park, Yellowhead Pass and Mount Robson Region, 1911," *Canadian Alpine Journal* IV (1912): 63; S. D. Woods, *Lights and Shadows of Life on the Pacific Coast* (New York: Funk & Wagnalls, 1910), 348.

99. Barbara Novak, *Nature and Culture: American Landscape Painting, 1825-1875* (New York: Oxford University Press, 1980), 40–41.

100. See illustrations in Hutchings, *In the Heart of the Sierras*, 1886 ed., [154], 384, 386, 410, 415; Bunnell, *Discovery*, 61, 85; Charles Burckhalter, "An Alpine Lake in the High Sierra," *Sunset* 7 (May–October 1901): 397, 403; John H. Williams, *Yosemite and Its High Sierra* (San Francisco: John H. Williams, 1914), 53, 69, 128.

101. Whitney, *Yosemite*, 69; Nordhoff, *California*, 77; Demurs, *Tourist*, 36; Orland, *Man and Yosemite*, 47–51.

102. C. F. Gordon-Cumming, *Granite Crags of California*, 105; "bosom," Solomons, "In the Upper Merced Cañon," *Sunset* 7 (May–October 1901): 63. See also William Conger Morgan, "A High Sierra Circuit on Headwaters of King's River," *SCB* 12, no. 3 (January 1910): 186.

103. Helen M. Gompertz, "Up and Down Bubb's Creek," *SCB* 2, no. 2 (May 1897): 84.

104. Julie Mortimer, "The 1921 Outing," *SCB* 11, no. 3 (1922): 257.

105. J. N. LeConte, "Among the Sources of the South Fork of King's River," *SCB* 4, no. 4 (June 1903): 259.

106. Mary Austin, *The Land of Little Rain* (1903; reprint, Albuquerque: University of New Mexico Press, 1974), 128. LeConte, "Among the Sources," 259–61.

107. Emily A. Thackvay, "Camps and Tramps for Women," *Outing* 14, no. 5 (August 1889): 340; Jennie Ellsworth Price, "A Woman's Trip Through the Tuolumne Cañon," *SCB* 2, no. 3 (January 1898): 177.

108. John Muir, "Lake Tahoe in Winter," *SCB* 3, no. 2 (May 1900): 122; John Muir, "A Geologist's Winter Walk," *OM* 10, no. 4 (April 1873): 357.

109. Edward T. Parsons, "The Mazamas on Mount Jefferson," *SCB* 3, no. 3 (February 1901): 206; Charles Sproull Thompson, "On Mt. Lefroy, August 3, 1896," *SCB* 2, no. 1 (January 1897): 2; Lena Martha Redington, "The 1913 Outing to the Kings River Cañon," *SCB* 9, no. 3 (January 1914): 161. For the naming of Eleanor's Island, see Bolton Coit Brown, "Another Paradise," *SCB* 3, no. 2 (May 1900): 143.

110. Quote from "Etc." *OM* 11, no. 1 (July 1873): 99. See also Paula Baker, "The Domestication of Politics: Women and American Political Society, 1780–1920," *American Historical Review* 89, no. 3 (June 1984): 620–47.

111. Nathan A. Bowers, quoting the "Creed" of Walter J. Sears, "Capitalizing Scenery: Scenic Appreciation by the Nation and by the Individual," *Mazama* 5, no. 1 (December 1916): 75.

CHAPTER 2. MASCULINE SUBLIMES

1. William O. Douglas, *Of Men and Mountains* (New York: Harper & Brothers, 1950), 314–26.

2. Catharine Savage Brosman, *Reading Behind the Lines: The Interpretation of War* (New Orleans: Graduate School of Tulane University, 1991).

3. Jane Tompkins, *West of Everything: The Inner Life of Westerns* (New York: Oxford University Press, 1992), 6.

4. On romanticism and landscape appreciation, see Matt Cartmill, *A View to a Death in the Morning: Hunting and Nature Through History* (Cambridge: Harvard University Press, 1993), 112–33. Marjorie Hope Nicolson, *Mountain Gloom and Mountain Glory: The Development of the Aesthetic of the Infinite* (New York: Cornell University Press, 1959), 1–33; Simon Schama, *Landscape and Memory* (New York: Knopf, 1995), 11, 447–51; M. L. Pratt, *Imperial Eyes: Travel Writing and Transculturation* (London: Routledge, 1992).

5. Simon Schama, *Landscape and Memory*, 11, 447–51; see also *sublime, elevated, awe,* and *masculinity, Oxford English Dictionary*, 2nd ed., 1989; available at: http://dictionary.oed.com/cgi/display. Accessed December 2, 2003.

6. Samuel Taylor Coleridge, "To Sara Hutchinson," August 6, 1802, in *Collected Letters of Samuel Taylor Coleridge*, ed. Earl Leslie Griggs, 2:1801–6 (Oxford: Clarendon Press, 1956), letter 451, 841–42.

7. For assessments of the sublime as an advanced form of aesthetic appreciation, see Roderick Nash, *Wilderness and the American Mind*, rev. ed. (New Haven: Yale University Press, 1973), 45; Michael P. Cohen, *The Pathless Way: John Muir and American Wilderness* (Madison: University of Wisconsin Press, 1984), 236–40; Michael Smith, *Pacific Visions: California Scientists and the Environment, 1850-1915* (New Haven: Yale University Press, 1987), 73. For primary sources, see Hubert Dyer, "Camping in the Highest Sierras," *Appalachia* 6, no. 4 (January 1892): 283; Charles F. Judson, "An Ascent of the Grand Combin," *Appalachia* 9, no. 2 (March 1900): 127.

8. Emerson's "Nature," in *The Selected Writings of Ralph Waldo Emerson* (New York: Random House, 1950), 11. For this analysis of Coleridge's "On the Principles of Genial Criticism Concerning the Fine Arts," see Cohen, *Pathless Way*, 236–67.

9. Charles E. Fay, "The Mountain as an Influence in Modern Life," *Appalachia* 11, no. 1 (1905): 35.

10. Hazard Stevens, "The Ascent of Takhoma," *Atlantic Monthly* 38 (November 1876): 524–25; George Bagley, "Ascent of Mount Tacoma," *Overland Monthly* [hereafter *OM*] 8 (1886): 266–78; Paul Schullery, *Island in the Sky: Pioneering Accounts of Mount Rainier, 1833-1894* (Seattle: The Mountaineers, 1987): 67, 91–96; Ira A. Williams, "Glaciers of the Three Sisters," *Mazama* 5, no. 1 (December 1916): 14–23.

11. Theodore Solomons, "A Search for A High Mountain Route from the Yosemite to the King's River Cañon," *Sierra Club Bulletin* (hereafter *SCB*) 1, no. 6 (May 1895): 230–31; David Brower, ed., photos by Richard Kaufman, text by John Muir, *Gentle Wilderness: The Sierra Nevada* (San Francisco: Sierra Club, 1967).

12. E. C. Winchell, letter in the San Francisco *Morning Call*, September 11–12, 1872, reprinted as "King's River Cañon in 1868," *SCB* 12, no. 3 (1926): 242, 244.

13. Henry David Thoreau, "Ktaadn," in *The Maine Woods*, ed. Joseph J. Moldenhauer (Princeton: Princeton Universitiy Press, 1972), 70–71; the experience of "Ktaadn," or Katahdin, is interpreted in Nash, *Wilderness*, rev. ed., 81, 91; Max Oelschlaeger, *Idea of Wilderness: From Prehistory to the Age of Ecology* (New Haven: Yale University Press, 1991), 149; Lawrence Buell, *The Environmental Imagination: Thoreau, Nature Writing, and the Formation of American Culture* (Cambridge: Harvard University Press, 1995), 12; for the fullest treatment of the sublime, see Nicolson, *Mountain Gloom and Mountain Glory*, v.

14. Nicolson, *Mountain Gloom and Mountain Glory*, 281–82.

15. John Muir, "The Yosemite National Park," *Atlantic Monthly* 84, no. 502 (August 1899): 145–46.
16. Peter N. Stearns, "Girls, Boys, and Emotions: Redefinitions and Historical Change," *Journal of American History* 80, no. 1 (June 1993): 36–74.
17. Nicolson, *Mountain Gloom and Mountain Glory,* 299–359.
18. Fay, "Mountain as an Influence," 10–11.
19. J. S. Hutchinson Jr., "First Ascent: Mt. Humphreys," *SCB* 5, no. 3 (January 1905): 168.
20. Hilaire Belloc, *The Path to Rome* (New York: G. P. Putnam's Sons, 1902), 140–43.
21. John Muir, *The Mountains of California* (New York: Century Co., 1894), 64–65; Stephen Fox, *John Muir and His Legacy* (Boston: Little, Brown, 1981), 12–13.
22. For similar moments, see Charles E. Fay, "Up to the Crags of Sir Donald," *Appalachia* 7 (1893): 162; Charles F. Saunders, *The Southern Sierras of California* (Boston: Houghton Mifflin, 1923), 16–21; E. Weldon Young, "The Mazamas on Mt. Rainier," *SCB* 3, no. 3 (June 1901): 271; Muir, *Mountains of California,* 251–52.
23. John Muir, "A Geologist's Winter Walk," *OM* 10, no. 4 (April 1873): 355–56.
24. John F. Sears, *Sacred Places: American Tourist Attractions in the Nineteenth Century* (Oxford: Oxford University Press, 1989), 8.
25. William Cronon, "The Trouble with Wilderness," in *Uncommon Ground: Toward Reinventing Wilderness,* ed. William Cronon (New York: Norton, 1995), 74–76.
26. Samuel Taylor Coleridge, "To W. Sotheby," July 13, 1802, *Letters of Samuel Taylor Coleridge,* ed. Ernest Hartley Coleridge (Boston: Houghton Mifflin, 1895), 1:370. For John Muir's love of wild animals and visualization of wilderness as their home, see Lisa Mighetto, "Editor's Preface," in *Muir Among the Animals: The Wildlife Writings of John Muir,* ed. Lisa Mighetto (San Francisco: Sierra Club Books, 1986), xxiii, and C. Hart Merriam, " To the Memory of John Muir," *SCB* 10, no. 2 (January 1917): 146–47.
27. On the historical association of female and nature, see Carolyn Merchant, *The Death of Nature: Women, Ecology and the Scientific Revolution* (San Francisco: Harper and Row, 1989), xv; Annette Kolodny, *The Lay of the Land: Metaphor as Experience and History in American Life and Letters* (Chapel Hill: University of North Carolina Press, 1975); T. J. Jackson Lears, *Fables of Abundance: A Cultural History of Advertising in America* (New York: Basic Books, 1994), 26–39.
28. Allison Blunt and Gillian Rose, "Introduction: Women's Colonial and Postcolonial Geographies," in *Writing Women and Space: Colonial and Postcolonial Geographies,* ed. Allison Blunt and Gillian Rose (New York: Guilford Press, 1994), 10–11.
29. John Muir, "The Hetch Hetchy Valley," *OM* 11, no. 1 (July 1873): 47. Of Wapama, Kolana, and Tueeulála, the latter two survived because of Muir. See also Edwin Way Teale, *The Wilderness World of John Muir* (Boston: Houghton Mifflin, 1954), 311.
30. Muir, "Geologist's Winter Walk," 355, 358.
31. William H. Brewer, *Rocky Mountain Letters, 1869: A Journal of an Early Geological Expedition to the Colorado Rockies* (Denver: Colorado Mountain Club, 1930), 11–12.
32. James M. Hutchings, *In the Heart of the Sierras: The Yo Semite Valley, Both Historical and Descriptive, and Scenes by the Way, Big Tree Groves* (Yosemite: Old Cabin with Pacific Press Publishing House, 1886), 89, 403–6; Josiah D. Whitney, *The Yosemite Guide-Book* (Cambridge, MA: University Press, 1870), 16.
33. Joseph LeConte. "Ramblings Through the High Sierra," *SCB* 3, no. 1 (January 1900): 46; Lester D. Stephens, *Joseph LeConte, Gentle Prophet of Evolution* (Baton Rouge: Louisiana State University Press, 1982), 123, 179, 245–47. Stanford E. Demurs, *The Tourist in Yosemite, 1855-1985* (Salt Lake City: University of Utah Press, 1987), 36.

34. Charles Fay, "The Annual Address of the President," *Appalachia* 3, no. 1 (June 1882): 3.

35. For stresses in the home occasioned by tension between the "values of a deferential, hierarchical, patronage society" represented by the idealized "walled garden" and those of an "increasingly contractual, individualistic society," see Steven Mintz, *A Prison of Expectations: The Family in Victorian Culture* (New York: New York University Press, 1983), 5, 10.

36. Lears, *Fables of Abundance*, 77.

37. For Whitney's theory, see *Yosemite*, 85; for Muir quote, see Muir, *Mountains of California*, xii; for controversy over geological origins of Yosemite, see Lester Stephens, *Joseph LeConte*, 122–23.

38. Muir, "Yosemite National Park," 146.

39. John Muir, "Explorations in the Great Tuolumne Cañon," *OM* 11, no. 139 (August 1873): 147.

40. Quote from John G. Lemmon, "Conifers of the Pacific Slope—How to Distinguish Them," pt. 1, *SCB* 2, no. 2 (May 1897): 61; see also pt. 2, *SCB* 2, no. 3 (January 1898): 156–73; W. W. Price, "Description of a New Grove of Sequoia Gigantea," *SCB* 1, no. 1 (January 1893): 17–22; William Dudley, "Zonal Distribution of Trees and Shrubs in the Southern Sierra," *SCB* 3, no. 4 (June 1901): 298–312; William Dudley, "Trees Along the Tulare Trails," *SCB* 4, no. 2 (June 1902): 153–56; John G. Lemmon, "Conifers of the Pacific Slope—Part III," *SCB* 4, no. 2 (June 1902): 100–131.

41. Mary W. Blanchard, "Boundaries and the Victorian Body: Aesthetic Fashion in Gilded Age America," *American Historical Review* 100, no. 1 (February 1995): 21–51.

42. John R. Glascock, "A California Outing," *SCB* 1, no. 5 (January 1895): 147–67.

43. Gail Bederman, *Manliness and Civilization: A Cultural History of Gender and Race in the United States* (Chicago: University of Chicago Press, 1995), 29, 43–44, 156, 181–86.

44. Nash, *Wilderness*, rev. ed., 146.

45. David G. Pugh, *Sons of Liberty: The Masculine Mind in Nineteenth Century America* (Westport, CT: Greenwood Press, 1983), 6–18.

46. Pugh, *Sons of Liberty*, xv–xvi; see also Kolodny, *Lay of the Land*, xi, 3–12.

47. Peter Gay, *The Cultivation of Hatred: The Bourgeois Experience, Victoria to Freud* (New York: Norton, 1993): 116–23; 425–29.

48. Philip Stanley Abbot, "Three Days on the Zinal Grat," *Appalachia* 7, no. 3 (March 1894): 215; Ernest C. Smith, "A Trip to Mount Rainier," *Appalachia* 7, no. 3 (March 1930): 205.

49. Annette Kolodny, *The Land Before Her: Fantasies and Experience of the Frontier, 1630-1860* (Chapel Hill: University of North Carolina Press, 1984), xi, 3–12.

50. Tompkins, *West of Everything*, 4, 12–13, 5, 48.

51. H. P. Nichols, "Back Range of the Selkirks," *Appalachia* 7, no. 2 (December 1893): 102; Joseph LeConte, "My Trip to the King's River Cañon," *SCB* 4, no. 2 (June 1902): 88; Willoughby Rodman, "Another View of the King's River Outing," *SCB* 4, no. 4 (June 1903): 314–17; J. N. LeConte, "The Ascent of the North Palisades," *SCB* 5, no. 1 (January 1904): 1–2, 19; Edward T. Parsons, "Climbing Mt. Brewer—The Climax of the Sierra Club Outing for 1902," *SCB* 4, no. 4 (June 1903): 282–84; E. T. Parsons, "The Notable Mountaineering of the Sierra Club in 1903," *SCB* 5, no. 1 (January 1904): 49; Fay, "Up to the Crags of Sir Donald," 159; Fay, "Mountain as an Influence," 27; Francis M. Fultz, "The Mt. Ritter Knapsack Trip," *SCB* 6, no. 5 (June 1908): 291; Charles S. Thompson, "The Taking of Mt. Balfour," *SCB* 2, no. 5 (January 1899): 268–69.

52. E. T. Parsons, "Notable Mountaineering," 44; Lincoln Hutchinson Jr., "A Neglected Region of the Sierra," *SCB* 2, no. 5 (January 1899): 278–83; George C. Thompson, "The

Climb of Dunderberg Via Virginia Cañon," *SCB* 10, no. 3 (January 1918): 287–91; Fay, "Mountain as an Influence," 28.

53. Hutchinson, "First Ascent: Mt. Humphreys," 153.

54. Philip Stanley Abbot, "An Ascent of the Weisshorn," *Appalachia* 7, no. 2 (December 1893): 113.

55. Samuel H. Schudder, "A Partial Ascent of Sierra Blanca," *Appalachia* 1, no. 4 (February 1878): 258–66; Charles Sproull Thompson, "On Mt. Lefroy, August 3, 1896," *SCB* 2, no. 1 (January 1897): 5; Lincoln Hutchinson, "Neglected Region of the Sierra," 278.

56. Hutchinson, "First Ascent: Mt. Humphreys," 159.

57. Thomas Weiskel, *The Romantic Sublime: Studies in the Structure and Psychology of Transcendence* (Baltimore: Johns Hopkins University Press, 1976), 12–22.

58. Thompson, "On Mt. Lefroy, August 3, 1896," 5.

59. Fay, "Mountain as an Influence," 40.

60. Thompson, "On Mt. Lefroy, August 3, 1896," 1–9; Charles Sproull Thompson, "On Mt. Lefroy, August 3, 1897," *SCB* 2, no. 3 (January 1898): 149–55.

61. Dean Peabody, "The Canadian Rocky Mountains —1923," *Appalachia* 18 (December 1924): 53.

62. Donna Haraway, *Primate Visions: Gender, Race, and Nature in the World of Modern Science* (New York: Routledge, 1989), 28–29; Blunt and Rose, "Introduction: Women's Colonial and Postcolonial Geographies," 11.

63. J. Federico Fino, "Notes on the Psychology of Mountaineering," *Appalachia*, n.s., 15, no. 12 (December 1949): 425.

64. John Muir, "Ascent of Mount Rainier," *Pacific Monthly* 8, no. 5 (November 1902): 202.

65. Clarence King, *Mountaineering in the Sierra Nevada* (New York: Scribner's, 1907), 348.

66. Abbot, "Three Days on the Zinal Grat," 228.

67. John Knox McLean, "The Choice of a Camp," *SCB* 9, no. 4 (January 1915): 266.

68. Julie Ellison, *Delicate Subjects: Romanticism, Gender, and the Ethics of Understanding* (Ithaca: Cornell University Press, 1990), 151.

69. John C. Van Dyke, *The Grand Canyon of the Colorado* (New York: Charles Scribner's Sons, 1920), v–vi, 1, 4, 9.

70. Walter L. Huber, "The Sierra Club in the Land of the Athabaska," *SCB* 14, no. 1 (February 1929): 1–12; Dyer, "Camping in the Highest Sierras," 283; Hutchinson, "First Ascent: Mt. Humphreys," 153–54.

71. Lincoln Hutchinson, "Red-and-White Peak and the Head-Waters of Fish Creek," *SCB* 4, no. 3 (February, 1903): 198–99.

72. Hubert Dyer, "Camping in the Highest Sierras," 285.

73. "Ushba," *Appalachia* 6, no. 1 (May 1890): 1–2.

74. P. B. Van Trump, "Mount Tahoma," *SCB* 1, no. 4 (May 1894): 121, 124.

75. Charles S. Thompson, "Taking of Mt. Balfour," 266; Joseph LeConte Jr., "An Ascent of Mt. Ritter," *Appalachia* 7, no. 1 (February 1893): 3–6; Dyer, "Camping in the Highest Sierras," 283; Frank Branch Riley, "This Is the Life," *Mazama* 4, no. 3 (December 1914): 28.

76. George C. Thompson, "Climb of Dunderberg Via Virginia Cañon," 288, 291.

77. Lincoln Hutchinson, "The Ascent of 'Matterhorn Peak,'" *SCB* 3, no. 2 (May 1900): 161–62; Fay, "Up to the Crags of Sir Donald," 159.

78. John H. Williams, *Yosemite and Its High Sierra* (Tacoma: John H. Williams, 1914), 40; John H. Williams, *The Mountain that Was God* (Tacoma: John H. Williams, 1910), 33–34.

79. Nash, *Wilderness*, rev. ed., 44–65; James Ramsey Ullman, *The Age of Mountaineering* (Philadelphia: Lippincott, 1964): 15–16.

80. Charles G. Van Brunt, "An Ascent of Sierra Blanca," *Appalachia* 6, no. 2 (December 1890): 164–66; A. E. Douglass, "The Altitudes of Orizaba and Poppocatepetl," *Appalachia* 8, no. 4 (March 1898): 356–61; A. E. Douglass, "An Ascent of Poppocatepetl," *Appalachia* 8, no. 3 (July 1897): 221–24. Charles E. Fay, "In the Sierra Madre Mountains," *Appalachia* 6, no. 3 (July 18910): 208.

81. N. F. McClure, "Explorations Among the Cañons North of the Tuolumne River," *SCB* 1, no. 5 (January 1895): 168–86; "Report of the Acting Superintendent of the Sequoia and General Grant National Parks, August 31, 1896"; "Notes and Correspondence," *SCB* 1, no. 7 (January 1896): 288–89; Francis P. Farquhar, "Nathaniel Fish McClure, 1865–1942," *SCB* 28, no. 3 (June 1943): 96–98.

82. N. F. McClure, "Ascent of 'El Yunque,'" *SCB* 3, no. 2 (May 1900): 127–34.

83. McClure to editors, April 9, 1902, *SCB* 4, no. 2 (June 1902): 172.

84. N. F. McClure, "How Private Burns Climbed Mt. Pinatúbo," *SCB* 5, no. 1 (January 1904): 28.

85. Quotes from Fay, "Mountain as an Influence," 37–38. On Peary's expedition, Lisa Bloom, *Gender on Ice: American Ideologies of Polar Expeditions* (Minneapolis: University of Minnesota Press, 1993).

86. Allston Burr, "Mount Blanc Again," *Appalachia* 15, no. 3 (December 1922): 241.

87. Charles E. Fay, "The First Ascent of Mount Dawson," *Appalachia* 9, nos. 3 and 4 (April 1901): 259; William H. Pickering, "A Climb in the Cordillera of the Andes," *Appalachia* 7, no. 3 (March 1894): 205–12. Scholars have echoed climbers' own assessments. See Roland Barthes, *Mythologies,* trans. Annette Lavers (New York: Hill & Wang, 1972), 74; Schama, *Landscape and Memory,* 502.

88. William Frederic Badè, "An Ascent of the Matterhorn," *SCB* 6, no. 2 (January 1907): 76–83; for a similar climb recollecting Tyndall, see Abbot, "Ascent of the Weisshorn," 122.

89. R. W. Poindexter, "Four Mexican Volcanoes," *SCB* 8, no. 2 (June 1911): 96–109.

90. Willis Linn Jepson, "The Steer's-Head Flower of the Sierra Nevada," *SCB* 8, no. 4 (June 1912): 266–69; Willis Linn Jepson, "Mountain Misery," *SCB* 9, no. 1 (January 1913): 40–42.

91. William Frederic Badè, "The Mountain Bluebird and the Wood Pewee," *SCB* 8, no. 4 (June 1912): 260–65; Reginald Farrer, "Flower Climb," from *Among the Hills* (London: Headley Brothers, 1910), 305–10.

92. Fordyce Grinnell Jr., "A Butterfly of the High Sierra Nevada—Behr's Alpine Sulphur," *SCB* 9, no. 2 (June 1913): 101; Vernon Kellogg, "Butterflies of the Mountain Summits," *SCB* 9, no. 2 (June 1913): 85–94; J. H. Huddleson Jr., "Butterflies of Mount Adams," *Mazama* 4, no. 2 (December 1913): 18–19.

93. On Darwinism and romantic thought, see Cartmill, *View to a Death,* 134–60.

94. Alfred C. Shelton, "Wild Life of the Three Sisters Region," *Mazama* 5, no. 1 (December 1916): 34–37; thrush quotes, Charles Keeler, "Bird Life of Yosemite Park," *SCB* 6, no. 4 (January 1908): 254; see also C. H. Sholes, "The Water-Ouzel, a Poem," *SCB* 6, no. 4 (January 1908): 244. Lester Stephens, *Joseph LeConte,* 256.

95. William Conger Morgan, "A High Sierra Circuit on Headwaters of King's River," *SCB* 7, no. 3 (January 1910): 187.

96. Quote from John Knox McLean, "Choice of a Camp," 267; see also Vernon Kellogg, "Collecting Insects of the High Mountains," *SCB* 9, no. 4 (January 1915): 270; John Muir, "Studies in the Sierra: I. Mountain Sculpture," *SCB* 9, no. 4 (January 1915): 225–39; Lloyd Shaw, *Nature Notes of the Pikes Peak Area* (Colorado Springs: Apex Book, 1916), 27–30.

97. John Muir, "Tehipite Valley," *SCB* 9, no. 3 (January 1914): 125; Muir, "Studies in the Sierra: I. Mountain Sculpture," *SCB* 9, no. 4 (January 1915): 225–39.

98. John Muir, "The Hetch-Hetchy Valley," *SCB* 6, no. 4 (January 1908): 216.

99. For Muir's correspondence with women, see John Muir Papers, University of the Pacific, Stockton, Calif. On his sentimentality, see Keith Kennedy, "Affectionately Yours, John Muir," in Sally M. Miller, *John Muir: Life and Work* (Albuquerque: University of New Mexico Press, 1993), 17–25. On Muir, see also Nash, *Wilderness*, rev. ed., 161–82; Michael Cohen, *The History of the Sierra Club, 1892-1970* (San Francisco: Sierra Club Books, 1988), 22–33; Fox, *John Muir*, 139–47. Nash, Cohen, and Fox do not highlight women's role. Carolyn Merchant does, in "Women of the Progressive Conservation Crusade," *Environmental Review* 8 (spring 1984): 57–86.

100. Frank Branch Riley, "This Is the Life," 31–32.

101. Harriet Monroe, "An Appreciation," *SCB* 10, no. 1 (January 1916): 26–28; Linnie Marsh Wolfe, *Son of the Wilderness: The Life of John Muir* (Madison: University of Wisconsin, 1978); Linnie Marsh Wolfe, ed., *John of the Mountains: The Unpublished Journal of John Muir* (Madison: University of Wisconsin Press, 1979 c. 1938); John Muir, *Travels in Alaska*, ed. Marion Randall Parsons (Boston: Houghton Mifflin, 1924, c. 1915).

102. LeRoy Jeffers, "John Muir: An Appreciation," *Appalachia* 4, no. 4 (June 1916): 390–93.

103. "A Talk By John Muir, June 17, 1911," *SCB* 12, no. 1 (1924): 44; Samuel Merrill, "Personal Recollections of John Muir," *SCB* 13, no. 1 (February 1928): 25–26. Thurman Wilkins, *John Muir: Apostle of Nature* (Norman: University of Oklahoma Press, 1995): 39–60.

104. Charles Keeler, "Recollections of John Muir," *SCB* 10, no. 1 (January 1916): 19; Samuel Merrill, "Personal Recollections of John Muir," 26.

105. On Muir as a climber, see Peter Browning, *Place Names of the Sierra Nevada: From Abbott to Zumwalt* (Berkeley: Wilderness Press, 1986), 184; Steve Roper, *Camp 4: Recollections of a Yosemite Rockclimber* (Seattle: The Mountaineers, 1994): 18.

106. John Muir, "A Rival of the Yosemite: The Cañon of the South Fork of the King's River, California," *Century Illustrated Magazine* 43, no. 1 (November 1891): 93; John Muir, *Mountains of California*, 190; John Muir, *A Thousand Mile Walk to the Gulf* (Boston: Houghton Mifflin, 1916).

107. Benjamin Ide Wheeler, "Inscription on Honorary Doctor of Laws Granted to Muir on May 14, 1913," reproduced in *SCB* 10, no. 1 (January 1916): 24.

108. "A Message and Appreciation from James Bryce," *SCB* 10, no. 1 (January 1916): 1.

109. William S. Ladd, review, *Appalachia*, n.s., 15, no. 7 (June 1949): 388–89; LeRoy Jeffers, "John Muir: An Appreciation," 390–93. On his intimacy with nature, see Robert B. Marshall, "John Muir," *SCB* 10, no. 1 (January 1916): 23; on Muir as "lover of nature," C. Hart Merriam, "To the Memory of John Muir," *SCB* 10, no. 2 (January 1917): 146; Teale, *Wilderness World*, 311.

110. Marion Randall Parsons, "War Service Record," *SCB* 10, no. 3 (January 1918): 325.

111. J. Monroe Thorington, "A War-Time Ascent of Mont," *Mazama* 5, no. 2 (December 1917): 148–54; "War Service Letters," *SCB* 10, no. 4 (January 1919): 450–75.

CHAPTER 3. FEMININE SUBLIMES

1. Quotes from Harriet Monroe, "An Appreciation," *Sierra Club Bulletin* [hereafter *SCB*] 10, no. 1 (January 1916): 27–28; see also Harriet Monroe, "Camping Above the Yosemite—A Summer Outing with the Sierra Club," *Putnam's Magazine* (May 1909): 216–27; Daniel J. Cahill, *Harriet Monroe* (New York: Twayne, 1973); Ellen Williams, *Harriet Monroe and the Poetry Renaissance, The First Ten Years of Poetry: A Magazine of Verse, 1912-22* (Urbana: University of Illinois Press, 1970).

2. Monroe, "Camping Above the Yosemite," *Putnam's*, 223.

3. Barbara Claire Freeman, *The Feminine Sublime: Gender and Excess in Women's Fiction* (Berkeley: University of California Press, 1995), 45. On the shift from feminized,

natural origins of abundance to masculine, commercial, and technological origins, see T. J. Jackson Lears, *Fables of Abundance: A Cultural History of Advertising in America* (New York: Basic Books, 1994), 19, 102–11.

4. Agnes Wright Spring, *A Bloomer Girl on Pike's Peak, 1858: Julia Archibald Holmes, First White Woman to Climb Pike's Peak* (Denver: Denver Public Library, 1949), 5–36.

5. Samuel H. Scudder, "The Alpine Club of Williamstown, Mass.," *Appalachia* 4, no. 1 (December 1884): 45–47; Laura and Guy Waterman, *Forest and Crag: A History of Hiking, Trail Blazing, and Adventure in the Northeast Mountains* (Boston: Appalachian Mountain Club, 1989), 119–24, 183–85.

6. Isabella L. Bird, *A Lady's Life in the Rocky Mountains* (Norman: University of Oklahoma Press, 1966), Bird's note, August 27, 1879, p. 10.

7. Bird, *A Lady's Life in the Rocky Mountains*, 83–101. On this "archetypal Victorian Lady Traveller," see Jane Robinson, *Wayward Women: A Guide to Women Travellers* (Oxford: Oxford University Press, 1990), 82.

8. Miss M. F. Whitman, "A Climb Through Tuckerman's Ravine," *Appalachia* 1, no. 3 (June 1877): 136, 132; Evelyn Marianne Ratcliff, "The Sierra Club's Ascent of Mt. Rainier," *SCB* 6, no. 1 (January 1906): 2; Jennie Ellsworth Price, "A Woman's Trip Through the Tuolumne Cañon," *SCB* 2, no. 3 (January 1898): 174–84.

9. Emily Lindsley Ross, "First White Woman on Mt. St. Helens," *Mazama* 2, no. 3 (July 1903): 130, reproduces text of 1883 climb. For the first white women on Mt. Hood, in 1867, see George H. Himes, "Nomenclature of Northwest Mountains," *Mazama* 4, no. 1 (October 1912): 3. On Helen Brodt, the first up Mt. Lassen (and honored with a lake), see Polly Welts Kaufman, *National Parks and the Woman's Voice: A History* (Albuquerque, University of New Mexico Press, 1996), 15–16.

10. Lafayette Houghton Bunnell, *Discovery of the Yosemite and The Indian War of 1851 Which Led to that Event* (Los Angeles: G. W. Gerlicher, 1911), 314.

11. Lester D. Stephens, *Joseph LeConte, Gentle Prophet of Evolution* (Baton Rouge: Louisiana State University Press, 1982), 121.

12. Kaufman, *National Parks*, 6–7; Michael P. Cohen, *The Pathless Way: John Muir and American Wilderness* (Madison: University of Wisconsin Press, 1984), 322.

13. Anna Mills Johnston, "A Trip to Mt. Whitney in 1878," *Mt. Whitney Club Journal* 1, no. 1 (May 1902): 18–28, in Leonard Daughenbaugh, "On Top of Her World: Anna Mills' Ascent of Mt. Whitney," *California History* 64, no. 1 (winter 1985): 47–51. See also *History of Fresno County, California, with Illustrations Descriptive of Its Scenery, Farms, Residents, Public Buildings* (San Francisco: Wallace W. Elliott, 1882): 243–44; James M. Hutchings, *In the Heart of the Sierras: The Yo Semite Valley, Both Historical and Descriptive, and Scenes by the Way, Big Tree Groves* (Yosemite: Old Cabin with Pacific Press Publishing House, 1886), 473.

14. Cicely Williams, *Women on the Rope: The Feminine Share in Mountain Adventure* (London: Allen and Unwin, 1973); "The Inauguration of New Zealand Alpine Club," *New Zealand Alpine Journal* 1, no. 1 (March 1892): 3–8.

15. From *Appalachia*: "Proceedings of the Club," 1, no. 2 (March 1877): 8; "Members Added Since June 25, 1879," 7, no. 2 (July 1879): 189; "Members of the Corporation," 3, no. 1 (June 1882): 89–97; "Retrospect and Prospect," 5, no. 4 (May 1889): 332; "New Members," 6, no. 2 (December 1890): 106–8. See also Janet Robertson, *The Magnificent Mountain Women: Adventures in the Colorado Rockies* (Lincoln: University of Nebraska Press, 1990): 24.

16. "Excursions of the Season of 1883," *Appalachia* 3, no. 3 (December 1883): 292–96; Emily A. Thackvay, "Camps and Tramps for Women," *Outing* 14, no. 5 (August 1889): 334–35.

17. For analyses of this presumed affinity, see Sherry Ortner, "Is Woman to Nature as Man

is to Culture?," in *Women, Culture, and Society*, ed. Michelle Zimbalist Rosaldo and Louise Lamphere (1974; Stanford, CA: Stanford University Press, 1993), 67–88; Carolyn Merchant, *The Death of Nature: Women, Ecology, and the Scientific Revolution* (San Francisco: Harper and Row, 1983), 1–41;

18. Carroll Smith-Rosenberg, *Disorderly Conduct: Visions of Gender in Victorian America* (Oxford: Oxford University Press, 1986): 176; Barbara Miller Solomon, *In the Company of Educated Women: A History of Women and Higher Education in America* (New Haven: Yale University Press, 1985).

19. Thackvay, "Camps and Tramps for Women," 333–42; "Paintings and Sketches, Exhibited March 14, 1877," *Appalachia* 1, no. 4 (February 1878): 280–81. Women did twenty-five of the forty-seven sketches exhibited.

20. Philip Stanley Abbot, "An Ascent of the Weisshorn," *Appalachia* 7, no. 2 (December 1893): 115.

21. John Muir, address in "Proceedings of the Meeting of the Sierra Club," *SCB* 1, no. 7 (January 1896): 280; Shirley Sargent, *Pioneers in Petticoats: Yosemite's Early Women* (Los Angeles: Trans-Anglo Books, 1966), 50. Sargent quotes women from the *San Francisco Chronicle*, "Down a Glacier a Mile a Minute," for August 25, 1895; Theodore S. Solomons, "An Early Summer Excursion to the Tuolumne Cañon and to Mt. Lyell," *SCB* 2, no. 1 (January 1897): 52; for "college girls" quote, see Theodore S. Solomons, "Explorations in the Sierra Nevada During the Season of 1896," *Appalachia* 8 (July 1897): 243.

22. Charles A. Bailey, "A Yosemite Discovery," *SCB* 2, no. 4 (June 1898): 216–21; Paul Schullery, ed., *Island in the Sky: Pioneering Accounts of Mount Rainier, 1833-1894* (Seattle: The Mountaineers, 1987), 125–40.

23. Fanny Bullock Workman, "Pioneer Ascents in Baltistan (Himalayas)," *Appalachia* 9, nos. 3 and 4 (April 1901): 246–50. On the Workmans, see also David Mazel, ed., *Mountaineering Women: Stories by Early Climbers* (College Station: Texas A & M University Press, 1994), 102.

24. Robinson, *Wayward Women*, 30.

25. Workman, "Pioneer Ascents in Baltistan (Himalayas)," 237–54.

26. Thackvay, "Camps and Tramps for Women," 33–42; Mazel, *Mountaineering Women*, 119, 100, 115.

27. Smith-Rosenberg, *Disorderly Conduct*, 245; Cornelius Beach Bradley, "Exploration of the East Creek Amphitheater," *SCB* 2, no. 5 (January 1899): 270–77.

28. For "seeds," see Thackvay, "Camps and Tramps for Women," 333–42; for "still pretty," see Mrs. L. D. Pychowska, "Walking-Dress for Ladies," *Appalachia* 5, no. 1 (December 1887): 29.

29. John R. Glascock, "A California Outing," *SCB* 1, no. 5 (January 1895): 147–67.

30. Joseph LeConte, "My Trip to King's River Cañon," *SCB* 4, no. 2 (June 1902): 89.

31. Martha Warren Beckwith, "Lassen Buttes: From Prattville to Fall River Mills," *SCB* 3, no. 4 (June 1901): 288–97; Helen M. Gompertz, "Up and Down Bubb's Creek," *SCB* 2, no. 2 (May 1897): 85–86.

32. Marion Randall, "The Second King's River Outing," *SCB* 6, no. 2 (January 1907): 103–4.

33. Quotes from J. E. Church Jr., "A New-Year Outing in the Sierra," *SCB* 4, no. 3 (February 1903): 227; for other mixed-sex groups, see Alice Eastwood, "From Redding to the Snow-Clad Peaks of Trinity County; also, List of Trees and Shrubs Seen en Route," *SCB* 4, no. 2 (June 1902): 39–52; Joseph LeConte, "My Trip to King's River Cañon," 88–99; Edward Parsons, "Climbing Mt. Brewer—The Climax of the Sierra Club Outing for 1902," *SCB* 4, no. 4 (June 1903): 278–84; Helen M. Gompertz, "Up and Down Bubb's Creek," 79–89; Solomons, "Explorations in the Sierra Nevada," 240; Joseph LeConte, "Among

the Sources of the South Fork of King's River—Part I," *SCB* 4, no. 3 (February 1903): 177–84; Joseph LeConte, "Among the Sources of the South Fork of King's River—Part II," *SCB* 4, no. 4 (June 1903): 253–63.

34. Bolton Coit Brown, "Wanderings in the High Sierra, Between Mt. King and Mt. Williamson," *SCB* 2, no. 2 (May 1897): 90–98; Bolton Coit Brown, "Another Paradise," *SCB* 3, 2 (May 1900): 135–49.

35. E. Fay Fuller, "Historians Report for 1894," *Mazama* 1, no. 1 (1896): 17.

36. Katherine Gile, "Mount St. Helens," *Mazama* 2, no. 3 (July 1903): 128; E. Weldon Young, "The Mazamas on Mt. Rainier," *SCB* 3, no. 3 (June 1901): 271.

37. Membership List, *SCB* 1, no. 8 (May 1896): inside cover.

38. William Colby, "Proposed Summer Outing of the Sierra Club—Report of the Committee," *SCB* 33, no. 3 (February 1901): 253.

39. For quotations, see ibid., 252; on participants, see Edward T. Parsons, "The Sierra Club Outing to Tuolumne Meadows (A Man's View of the Outing)," *SCB* 4, no. 1 (January 1902): 20–22.

40. "1906 Mazamas Outing," *Mazama* 3, no. 1 (March 1907): 27. There were twenty-five men and thirty women; twenty-five of the women were single, and one was a medical doctor.

41. "Constitution and By-Laws, Charter Members, New Members," *Mountaineer* (1909): 25–28. In the Mountaineers' first two years, nineteen men and twenty-two women joined.

42. *Canadian Alpine Journal* no. 2 (1908): 182–96. For women's role in establishing the Alpine Club of Canada, see Cyndi Smith, *Off the Beaten Path: Women Adventurers and Mountaineers in Western Canada* (Jasper, Alberta, Canada: Coyote Books, 1989): 69–71.

43. Hugh E. Kingery assisted by Elinor Eppich Kingery, *The Colorado Mountain Club: The First Seventy-five Years of a Highly Individual Corporation 1912-1987* (Evergreen, CO: Cordillera Press, 1988), 24–28.

44. Lee Hall, *Common Threads: A Parade of American Clothing* (Boston: Little, Brown, 1992), 123.

45. "Report of the Councilors. Exploration," *Appalachia* 1, no. 3 (June 1877): 193–94.

46. Mary Edith Griswold, "The Mountain Girl's Dresses," *Sunset* 2, no. 6 (May–October 1903): 222.

47. Edward T. Parsons, "The Sierra Club Outing to Tuolumne Meadows," 21–22; Sexton, "Camp Muir in the Tuolumne Meadows," *SCB*, 12–18.

48. Thackvay, "Camps and Tramps for Women," 335, 341.

49. Sarah A. Gordon, " 'Any Desired Length': Negotiating Gender Through Sports Clothing, 1870–1925," in *Beauty and Business: Commerce, Gender, and Culture in Modern America*, ed. Philip Scranton (New York: Routledge, 2001), 28–29.

50. *San Francisco Chronicle*, June 29, 1902, full page, 10; see also Tulare County *Times* of Fresno, August 7, 1902, front page; Berkeley *Gazette*, July 1, 1902; Oakland *Gazette*, July 1, 1902; Oakland *Enquirer*, August 2, 1902. In Bancroft Library.

51. "Climbing Mount Brewer: The Climax of the Sierra Club's Trip," *San Francisco Chronicle*, August 24, 1902, 7; Edward T. Parsons, "Climbing Mt. Brewer," 278–84.

52. On Climbing in the Rockies, see Pearl Turner Album, August 10 and 22, 1914, University of Colorado, Boulder, Norland Library; on 1911–1912 attire, see Francis P. Farquhar, "Sierra Club Mountaineer and Editor," oral history conducted by Ann and Ray Lage (San Francisco, Sierra Club History Committee, 1974), 4.

53. Harriet Monroe, "Camping Above the Yosemite—A Summer Outing with the Sierra Club," *SCB* 7, no. 2 (June 1909): 86, 91, 95, 97; Harriet Monroe, "Camping Above the Yosemite," *Putnam's*, 223, 226.

54. Helen Gompertz LeConte, "The Sierra Club in the Kings River Canyon," *Sunset* 2, no.

6 (May–October 1903): 250–63; Pearl Turner Album, Rocky Mountains, August 4 and 7, 1914; Ella M. Sexton, "Camp Muir in the Tuolumne Meadows, Where the Sierra Club Went A-Camping (A Woman's View of the Outing)," *SCB* 4, no. 1 (January 1902): 12–18; Miss M. F. Whitman, "Camp Life for Ladies," *Appalachia* 2, no. 1 (June 1879): 44; Mary E. Crawford, "Mountain Climbing for Women," *Canadian Alpine Journal* (1909): 86; Bertha Gorham Pope, "With the Sierra Club in 1914," *SCB* 9, no. 4 (January 1915): 253.

55. Harriet Monroe, *Chosen Poems: A Selection from My Books of Verse* (New York: Macmillan, 1935), 101; Crawford, "Mountain Climbing for Women," 85–91; Helen M. Gompertz, "Up and Down Bubb's Creek," 79–89; Katherine Chandler, "Sierra Wild Flowers," *Sunset* 19, no. 4 (August 1907): 335.

56. Hazel King, "Ski Running: An Impression," *SCB* 9, no. 4 (January 1915): 271–73.

57. Crawford, "Mountain Climbing for Women," 87.

58. Constance Frederica Gordon-Cumming *Granite Crags of California* (Edinburgh: William Blackwood, new ed., 1886), on microfilm; original held by Wisconsin State Historical Society, 256–57; Jennie Ellsworth Price, "A Woman's Trip Through the Tuolumne Cañon," 182–83; Jessie M. Whitehead, "With the Sierra Club in 1927," *SCB* 13, no. 1 (February 1928): 12. For "no terrors," see Elizabeth Marston Badè, "Recollections of William F. Badè and the Early Sierra Club," interview by Eleanor Badè (Sierra Club History Committee, 1976), 3–4.

59. Theodore H. Hittell, "On the Tip-Top of the United States," *Sunset* 9 (1902): 294–303.

60. Walter Huber to Blake, November 22, 1944, Bancroft Library, Sierra Club [hereafter SC] Papers, 4: 26. Huber said women had joined him on many climbs between 1908 and 1932 and that the climbs had been noted in the Sierra Club, "Mountain Records of the Sierra Nevada," Bancroft Library, SC Papers, but that presence of the women had not.

61. Helen M. Gompertz, "Up and Down Bubb's Creek," 83; C. H. Sholes, "The 1908 Perilous Ascent of St. Helens," *Mazama* 6, no. 4 (December 1923): 61–65.

62. Dora Keen, "First Up Mt. Blackburn," *World's Work* 27, no. 1 (November 1913): 80–101; Bill Sherwonit, ed., *Alaska Ascents: World-Class Mountaineers Tell Their Stories* (Anchorage: Alaska Northwest Books, 1996), 46–47. In 1965 the U.S. Board of Geographic Names designated part of Alaska's Chugach Mountains as the Dora Keen Range.

63. "Dora Keene [*sic*] Climbs Blackburn 17,000 feet," *Daily Alaskan* 19 (August 20, 1912), front page; "Reached Highest Point," *Daily Alaskan* 10 (August 9, 1912); "Tourists Besiege Skagway," *Daily Alaskan* 1 (June 21, 1911), front page. Reels 5 and 6, University of Washington Library, Microfilm Collection.

64. Colin F. Kirkus, *Let's Go Climbing!* (London: Thomas Nelson, 1941), 91; quoted in Nea Morin, *A Woman's Reach: Mountaineering Memoirs* (New York: Dodd, Mead, 1968), 198–200.

65. Helen Gompertz LeConte, "High Water in Tehipite," *Sunset* 9, no. 1 (May–October 1902): 326.

66. Mrs. L. D. Pychowska, "Walking-Dress for Ladies," 28.

67. Marion Randall Parsons, "On Mt. St. Helens with the Mazamas," *SCB* 7, no. 3 (January 1910): 176.

68. Harriet Monroe, "The Grand Cañon of the Colorado," *Atlantic Monthly* 84, no. 506 (December 1899): 816–21; for drawing my attention to this quote, I thank Kaufman, *National Park,* 13.

69. Chandler, "Sierra Wild Flowers," 333–35.

70. Elizabeth Van E. Ferguson, "Field Notes of the 1920 Outing," *SCB* 11, no. 2 (January 1921): 150.

71. "Haunts" from Mary T. S. Schaffer, "Botanical Notes," *Canadian Alpine Journal* (1911):

131–35. See also Julia W. Henshaw, "The Mountain Wildflowers of Western Canada," *Canadian Alpine Journal* 2 (1908): 130; Gertrude E. Benham, "The Ascent of Mt. Assiniboine," *Canadian Alpine Journal* (1907): 91; Miss M. F. Whitman, "Climb Through Tuckerman's Ravine," 132–34; Mrs. G. W. Thacher, "Alpine Flowers of Colorado," *Appalachia* 5, no. 3 (December 1888): 284–90.

72. M. M. Pychowska, "Two in the Alpine Pastures," *Appalachia* 5, no. 3 (December 1888): 184–94; Julie Clark, see "Botanical Exhibit," *Appalachia* 6, no. 4 (December 1891): 338; Warren Upham, "Reports of the Councillors for the Autumn of 1892," *Appalachia* 7, no. 1 (February 1893): 81; Mrs. Albion D. Wilde, "Reports of the Councillors for 1921," *Appalachia* 15, no. 3 (December 1922): 373–79.

73. Evelyn Fox Keller, *Reflections on Gender and Science* (New Haven: Yale University Press, 1985), 3–8.

74. Gloria Ricci Lothrop, "Women Pioneers and the California Landscape," *Californians* 4 (May/June 1986): 18–19.

75. Katherine Chandler, "Nature's Drug Store: Timely Tips to Campers About Helpful and Harmful Shrubs and Plants," *Sunset* 19, no. 1 (May 1907): 51–53.

76. "Notes and Correspondence," *SCB* 7, no. 1 (January 1909): 63; Caroline LeConte, "A Californian's Return," *Sunset* 24, no. 2 (February 1910): 212.

77. Emma Homan Thayer, *Wild Flowers of the Pacific Coast: From Original Water Color Sketches Drawn from Nature* (New York: Cassell, 1887), [7].

78. Thackvay, "Camps and Tramps for Women," 333.

79. Chandler, "Sierra Wild Flowers," 333–35; Katherine Chandler, *Habits of California Plants* (San Francisco, 1903).

80. For guidebooks by women, in addition to those otherwise cited, see Julia Wilmotte Henshaw, *Mountain Wild Flowers of America: A Simple and Popular Guide to the Names and Descriptions of the Flowers that Bloom Above the Clouds* (Boston: Ginn, 1906); Mrs. Albion Wilde, *Plants of Mt. Washington, New Hampshire* (Boston: AMC, [1920]); Edith S. Clements, *Flowers of Coast and Sierra* (New York: H. W. Wilson, 1928); Mary Elizabeth Parsons, *The Wild Flower of California: Their Names, Haunts, and Habits* (San Francisco: California School Book Depository, 1897, 1930); Frances Theodora Parsons, *A Selection of Fifty Plates from "How to Know the Wildflowers,"* by Mrs. William Starr Dana and Marion Setterlee (New York: Scribner's Sons, 1894); Alice Eastwood, *A Key to Common Families of Flowering Plants in California* (San Francisco: California Botanical Club, California Academy of Sciences, 1934); Alice Eastwood, *Flora of the Pacific Coast* (Boston: Ginn, 1897).

81. "Wild Flower Show," *SCB* 6, no. 4 (January 1908): 270–74; Jessie Whitehead, "With the Sierra Club in 1927," 12.

82. Eastwood and Muir shared a friendship with Jeanne Carr. Eastwood proposed other women for club membership; see Bancroft Library, SC Records, carton 309, folder 21.

83. Eastwood held the position into the 1940s. Susanna Bryant Dakin, *The Perennial Adventure: A Tribute to Alice Eastwood, 1859-1953* (San Francisco: California Academy of Sciences, 1954), quote from 5; for biographical detail, see preface, and 1–18.

84. Alice Eastwood, *A Flora of the South Fork of the Kings River, from Millwood to the Head Waters of Bubbs Creek* (June 1902), Sierra Club Publication 27.

85. Marcia Myers Bonta, *Women in the Field: America's Pioneering Women Naturalists* (College Station: Texas A & M University Press, 1991), 97; Dakin, *Perennial Adventure,* preface, 1–18. Eastwood's publications included "From Redding to the Snow-Clad Peaks of Trinity County," 39–58, and "Through a Botanical Paradise," *Sunset* 26, no. 3 (March 1911): 350–52.

86. For a similar vision, see M. M. Pychowska, "Two in the Alpine Pastures," 186–87.

87. Alice Eastwood, *A Collection of Popular Articles on the Flora of Mount Tamalpais* (1944; published by the author), 4–13.

88. Michael Cohen, *Pathless Way,* 180.

89. Bancroft Library, SC Records, carton 309, folder 21, proposals for membership.

90. Bonta, *Women in the Field,* 49–60.

91. Barbara R. Stein, *On Her Own Terms: Annie Montague Alexander and the Rise of Science in the American West* (Berkeley: University of California Press, 2001), quote from 50; see also xiii, 3, 122, 152,158, 239, 275.

92. For "lap," see Marion Randall Parsons, "The Twenty-eighth Outing, " *SCB* 15, no. 1 (February 1930): 12–12; for "teems," Elesa M. Gremke, "To Tehipite Through Silver Canyon," *Sunset* 6, no. 5 (March 1901): 136.

93. Nina Eloesser, "Tales of High Trips in the Twenties," oral history by Ann Lage (Sierra Club History Committee, 1985), 20; for interest in animals, see also Dorothy M. Emmet, "A British Student Looks at the Sierra Club Outing," *SCB* 15, no. 1 (February 1930): 24.

94. Quotes from Mary Austin, *The Land of Little Rain* (1903; Albuquerque: University of New Mexico Press, 1974), 152–53, 155, 160; for her sensitivity to western lands and users, see Mary Hunter Austin, *The Flock* (New York: Houghton Mifflin, 1906).

95. Vera Norwood, "Women's Place: Continuity and Change in Response to Western Landscapes," in *Western Women: Their Land, Their Life,* ed. Lillian Schlissel, Vicki L. Ruiz, and Janice Monk (Albuquerque: University of New Mexico Press, 1988), 159; for "desolation" quote, see Austin, *Land of Little Rain,* 120.

96. Quotes from Austin, *Land of Little Rain,* 128–29; see also Mary Austin, *Earth Horizon: Autobiography* (New York: Literary Guild, 1932), 287–88, 290, 294; and Esther F. Lanigan, introduction to *A Mary Austin Reader* (Tucson: University of Arizona Press, 1996), 12–13. Like Austin, Nea Morin recalled, "First I explored the hillsides, scrambling among the masses of alpenrose, to me the most beautiful of all flowers, embodying the very essence of mountains. Then I wandered higher where great *nappes* of late spring snow stretched long arms down to the high pastures, and each day brought the discovery of new flowers." Nea Morin, *Woman's Reach,* 19.

97. Introduction by T. M. Pearce to Mary Austin, *Land of Little Rain,* vii.

98. Lawrence Buell, *The Environmental Imagination: Thoreau, Nature Writing, and the Formation of American Culture* (Cambridge: Harvard University Press, 1995), 79.

99. Austin, *Earth Horizon,* 288–89; Austin, *Land of Little Rain,* 115, 116.

100. Austin, *Land of Little Rain,* preface. For a similar perspective, see Pearl Turner Album, August 21, 1914.

101. Mary Austin, *A Mary Austin Reader,* ed. Ester F. Lanigan (Tucson: University of Arizona Press, 1996), 11–12.

102. On piñon nuts, see Elizabeth Van E. Ferguson, "Field Notes of the 1920 Outing," 150; for other encounters, see Muriel A. Stratford, unpublished manuscript, 1920, 3, Bancroft Library, SC Papers, carton 45, folder 50. Alice Eastwood, "From Redding to the Snow-Clad Peaks of Trinity County," 45-48. For a complimentary description of Quinault, see Marion Randall Parsons, "Through the Olympics with the Mountaineers," *SCB* 9, no. 3 (January 1914): 156; see also Lulie Nettleton, "Climbing the Rockies of Glacier National Park," *Mazama* 4, no. 4 (December 1915): 34–37.

103. Marion Randall Parsons, "The Grand Cañons of the Tuolumne and the Merced," *SCB* 6, no. 4 (January 1908): 236, 240; for "overwhelming," see Lucy Washburn, "The Grand Circuit of the Yosemite National Park," *SCB* 7, no. 3 (January 1910): 152.

104. Thacher, "Alpine Flowers of Colorado," 288–90.
105. Helen M. Gompertz, "A Tramp to Mt. Lyell," *SCB* 1, no. 4 (May 1894): 139–40; Helen M. Gompertz, "Up and Down Bubb's Creek," 79–89.
106. Marion Randall Parsons, "On Mt. St. Helens with the Mazamas," 174.
107. Katherine Oliver, "From an Autumn Camp," *Sunset* 25, no. 4 (October 1910): 457; Evaleen Stein, poem, "The Mountain Torrent," *Sunset* 20, no. 1 (November 1907): 66; Harriet Monroe, "Camping Above the Yosemite," *SCB*, 88, 91.
108. Quote from Helen M. Gompertz, "Tramp to Mount Lyell," 139; similarly, see Eunice T. Gray, "Sleeping in the Open," *Sunset* 27, no. 3 (September 1911): 34; Thackvay, "Camps and Tramps for Women," 337; Edith M. Esterbrook, "Two Women Afoot with Camp Packs," *Appalachia* 15, no. 1 (November 1920): 26; Lena Martha Redington, "The 1913 Outing to the Kings River Cañon," *SCB* 9, no. 3 (January 1914): 160; Olivia R. Johnson, "High Trip Reminiscences, 1904–1945," an oral history conducted by Terry Kirker (Sierra Club History Committee, 1976), 12–13.
109. Harriet Monroe, *Chosen Poems,* 37–39, 97, 40, 42.
110. For emphasis on men and masculinity in early conservation, see Alston Chase, *In a Dark Wood: The Fight over Forests and the Rising Tyranny of Ecology* (Boston: Houghflin Mifflin, 1995); Robert Gottlieb, *Forcing the Spring: The Transformation of the American Environmental Movement* (Washington, DC: Island Press, 1993); Roderick Nash, *Wilderness and the American Mind,* rev. ed. (New Haven: Yale University Press, 1973).
111. The text of the Sierra Club's centennial history does not mention women but their presence is evident in its photographs. See Tom Turner, *A History of the Sierra Club: 100 Years of Protecting Nature* (San Francisco: Sierra Club, 1992), 89, 95, 156, 188, 194; Michael P. Cohen, *The History of the Sierra Club, 1892-1970* (San Francisco: Sierra Club, 1988). See also Francis P. Farquhar, *First Ascents in the United States, 1642-1900* (Berkeley: Grabhorn Press, 1948). Of seventy listed, women made four. The club has published Anne LaBastille, *Women and Wilderness* (San Francisco: Sierra Club, 1980); and Arlene Blum, *Annapurna: A Woman's Place* (San Francisco: Sierra Club, 1980).
112. For complaints of being ignored, see Phyllis Munday, "First Ascent of Mount Robson," *Canadian Alpine Journal* 14 (1924): 68–74, 150, and Blum, *Annapurna,* 1–3. Chris Jones's classic *Climbing in North America* (Berkeley: University of California Press, 1976), 69, 370–71, mentions few women, noting that the Alpine Club of Canada allowed women to join and discussing some modern climbs. For mountaineering as a male, see A. C. Spectorsky, ed., *The Book of the Mountains* (New York: Appleton-Century Crofts, 1955); John Hunt, ed., *My Favorite Mountaineering Stories* (Guilford: Lutterworth Press, 1978), 9.
113. For analyses of this underevaluation, see Vera Norwood, *Made from This Earth: American Women and Nature* (Chapel Hill: University of North Carolina Press, 1993), 53; Lawrence Buell, *Environmental Imagination,* 26.
114. On women in conservation and environmentalism, see Carolyn Merchant, "Women of the Progressive Conservation Crusade," *Environmental Review* 8 (spring 1984): 57–86; Carolyn Merchant, "Earthcare," *Environment* 23 (June 1981): 6–40; Carolyn Merchant, *Earthcare: Women and the Environment* (New York: Routledge, 1995); Suellen Hoy's "Municipal Housekeeping," in *Pollution and Reform in American Cities, 1870-1930,* ed. Martin V. Melosi (Austin: University of Texas Press, 1980), 173–98; Anne Firor Scott, *Natural Allies: Women's Associations in American History* (Urbana: University of Illinois Press, 1991); on women in historic, archaeological, and scenic preservation, see Kaufman, *National Parks;* Hal Rothman, *The Greening of a Nation? Environmentalism in the United States Since 1945* (Fort Worth: Harcourt Brace, 1998), 60; Paula Baker, "The Domestication of Politics, 1780-1920," *American Historical Review*

89 (June 1984): 85-110; Nancy A. Hewitt and Suzanne Lebsock, eds., *Visible Women: New Essays on American Activism* (Urbana: University of Illinois Press, 1993), 1-13, 101-18; Glenda Riley, *Women and Nature: Saving the "Wild" West* (Lincoln: University of Nebraska Press, 1999). On women climbers, see Janet Robertson, *Magnificent Mountain Women;* Shirley Sargent, *Pioneers in Petticoats;* Cyndi Smith, *Off the Beaten Track;* Bill Birkett, *Women Climbing: 200 Years of Achievement* (Seattle: The Mountaineers, 1990); Rachel da Silva, ed., *Leading Out: Women Climbers Reaching for the Top* (Seattle: Seal Press, 1992); David Mazel, *Mountaineering Women: Stories by Early Climbers* (College Station, Texas: Texas A & M University Press, 1994); Anne LaBastille, *Women and Wilderness* (San Francisco: Sierra Club, 1980); Laura and Guy Waterman, *Forest and Crag;* for excellent treatments of climbers and travelers, Kaufman, *National Parks,* 3-26; and Riley, *Women and Nature.*

On European women climbers: Jane Robinson, *Wayward Women;* Jane Robinson, ed., *Unsuitable for Ladies: An Anthology of Women Travellers* (Oxford University Press, 1994), 44-64; Cicely Williams, *Women on the Rope;* Shirley Angell, ed., *Pinnacle Club: A History of Women Climbing* (Glasgow: Pinnacle Club, 1988); David Mazel, *Mountaineering Women.*

115. For discussion of this oversight, see Katherine G. Morrissey, "Engendering the West," in *Under an Open Sky: Rethinking America's Western Past,* ed. William Cronon, George Miles, and Jay Gitlin (New York: Norton, 1992), 132-45. For such general histories, see Joseph M. Petulla, *American Environmental History: Exploitation and Conservation of Natural Resources* (San Francisco: Boyd & Fraser, 1977); for mention of women, see Hans Huth, *Nature and the American: Three Centuries of Changing Attitudes* (Lincoln: University of Nebraska Press, 1990), 26, 61, 79, 83, 115, 126, 197; Max Oelschlaeger discusses ecofeminists in *The Idea of Wilderness: From Prehistory to the Age of Ecology* (New Haven: Yale University Press, 1991), 309-16. On specific women, see Peter J. Schmitt, *Back to Nature: The Arcadian Myth in Urban America* (Baltimore: Johns Hopkins University Press, 1990).

116. Yi-fu Tuan, *Topophilia: A Study of Environmental Perception, Attitudes, and Values* (Englewood Cliffs, NJ: Prentice-Hall, 1974), 111-12, 96-97; Donald W. Meinig, *The Interpretation of Ordinary Landscapes: Geographical Essays* (New York: Oxford University Press, 1979), 2.

117. Lorraine Anderson, ed., *Sisters of the Earth: Women's Prose and Poetry About Nature* (New York: Vintage Books, 1991), xv; China Galland, *Women in the Wilderness* (New York: Harper & Row, 1980); Lisa Bloom, *Gender on Ice: American Ideologies of Polar Expeditions* (Minneapolis: University of Minnesota Press, 1993).

118. Annette Kolodny, *The Land Before Her: Fantasy and Experience of the American Frontier, 1630-1860* (Chapel Hill: University of North Carolina Press, 1984), xi, 3-12; Vera Norwood and Janice Monk, eds., *The Desert Is No Lady: Southwestern Landscapes in Women's Writing and Art* (New Haven: Yale University Press, 1987), 1-9; Norwood, *Made from This Earth.*

119. Smith-Rosenberg, *Disorderly Conduct,* 174.

120. Annette Kobak, "Review of *Unsuitable for Ladies,*" *Times Literary Supplement* no. 4765 (July 29, 1994): 8.

121. Muir to Parsons, September 9, 1913, Bancroft Library, Parsons family papers, box 2.

122. Harriet Monroe, "Shall the Hetch Hetchy Valley be Saved for the Nation? Artists and Nature Lovers Oppose the Selfish Desire of San Francisco to Utilize this Wonder Vale of Yosemite National Park as Source for Its Municipal Water Supply," *Chicago Sunday Tribune,* March 27, 1910.

123. Sierra Club rosters, 1911–1917, Bancroft Library, SC Papers, Membership Records, ser. 12.

124. *Congressional Record* 45, no. 3 (December 20, 1909–March 28, 1910). On the strong role of women in the Hetch Hetchy Valley battle, see Carolyn Merchant, "Women of the Progressive Conservation Crusade," *Environmental Review* 8 (Spring 1984): 57–86; Kaufman, *National Parks,* 30–32.

PART II. OUTDOOR EXPERIENCES AND THE POLITICS OF
CONSERVATION, 1914–1944

1. Bertha M. Rice, "Urgent Need of Protection for the Toyon," *Sierra Club Bulletin* 11, no. 1 (January 1920): 97–98; Bertha M. Rice and Roland Rice, *Popular Studies of California Wild Flowers* (San Francisco: Upton Bros. & Delzelle, 1920).

CHAPTER 4. MOUNTAINS AS HOME AND GARDEN

1. Muir to Mrs. Parsons [May 23, 1914], Bancroft Library, Parsons family papers, Box 2; Marion Randall Parsons, "The Ascent of Mount Olympus," *Mountaineers* 6 (1913): 38, 41; see also Marion Randall Parsons, "Through the Olympics with the Mountaineers," *Sierra Club Bulletin* (hereafter *SCB*) 9, no. 3 (January 1914): 149–58; for "sweet, smiling face," see Oliveria R. Johnson, "High Trip Reminiscences, 1904–1945," oral history conducted by Terry Kirker (Sierra Club History Committee, 1977).

2. Lola Creighton, "The Wallowa Outing, 1918," *Mazama* 5, no. 3 (December 1918): 231–32. By 1919, 185 women and 276 men belonged to the Mazamas; see "Mazamas Membership List, November 1, 1919," *Mazama* 5, no. 4 (December 1919): 374–80; on women in Sierra Club, see Membership Files, 1909–11, Bancroft Library, SC Papers; Julie Mortimer, "The 1921 Outing," *SCB* 11, no. 3 (1922): 255–60; William Colby's notebook for 1917 Outing, Bancroft Library, SC—Colby Papers, carton 39: 14; Mountaineers' 1920 outing included 36 men and 45 women; 15 women and 12 men made four of the ten most demanding ascents. The 1922 trip attracted 108 women and 68 men. *Mountaineer* 13, no. 1 (November 1920); 14, no. 1 (November 1921): 81; 14, no. 2 (January 1922): 2–3; 14, no. 9 (August 1922): 2–3; 15, no. 1 (December 1922): 29; 17, no. 1 (December 1924): 70–71.

3. "In Memoriam: Fanny Bullock Workman," *Appalachia* 18, no. 4 (December 1924): 185–89. Women made three of six ascents over thirteen thousand feet on the Sierra Club's 1925 trip; see Bertha Clark Pope, "The High Trip of 1925," *SCB* 12, no. 3 (1926): 213–23.

4. Horace Kephart, *Camping and Woodcraft* (New York: Outing Publishing, 1919), 163.

5. Advertisements in *SCB* 10, no. 1 (January 1916): inside front cover; *SCB* 11, no. 1 (January 1920): back cover.

6. Pearl Turner Album, August 4, 1947, University of Colorado, Norland Library. The pants of the 1920s were "the sort of thing that the men wore overseas in the First World War. They were khaki pants and they laced at the knees," and they wore heavy wool socks that came up to the knees. See Dorothy "Dot" Leavitt Pepper, "High Trip High Jinks," oral history conducted by Terry Kirker (California State University, Fullerton, 1976), 5.

7. See Spiro's and Leibold & Co.'s advertisements in *SCB* 12, no. 2 (1925): [3, 5]; *SCB* 12, no. 3 (1926): [335]; Sarah E. Gordon, "Any Desired Length: Negotiating Gender Through Sports Clothing, 1870–1925," in *Beauty and Business: Commerce, Gender, and Culture in Modern America,* ed. Philip Scranton (New York: Routledge, 2001), 45–47.

8. Aurelia Harwood, "Southern California Chapter Notes," *SCB* 12, no. 3 (1926): 313; Colby to Harwood, May 1, 1922, June 13, 1923, Mather to Harwood, December 13, 1923, Ban-

croft Library, SC Papers, box 63; Aurelia Reinhardt, "Aurelia Squire Harwood," *SCB* 14, no. 1 (February 1929): 64–67.

9. Reinhardt, "Aurelia Squire Harwood," 67.

10. Not all respondents answered all questions, so that the number of replies to each question varies. Three were born in the 1870s, 21 in the 1880s, 33 in the 1890s, and 17 in or after 1900. Of 77 responses, 32 said they had been born in California, 8 in the eastern United States, 24 in the Midwest, and 7 in the Far West. Seven were foreign born. Only 11 reported that one or more of their parents had been born in California, but a striking 47 said both had been born in the United States, and 9 had one native-born parent. Eleven said both parents had been born abroad.

11. Of reasons for joining, 34 cited hiking and recreation as their only reasons, 11 said hiking and recreation first with social reasons second, and 34 said that hiking, social, and environment were all important, with hiking almost always first. Three were 18 years old or younger when they joined; eight were between 20 and 23; 51 were 24 to 35; eight were between 36 and 43. See replies to questionnaires mailed June 1, 1972, by Marshall Kuhn, Sierra Club History Committee, Bancroft Library.

12. Ethel Rose Taylor Horsfall, "On the Trail with the Sierra Club, 1920s–1960s," oral history conducted by George Baranowski (Sierra Club, underwritten by the National Endowment for the Humanities, 1979), 4.

13. Emily Haag, another native Californian, joined the Sierra Club in 1912 to fight for Hetch Hetchy. Moving to Seattle in 1923, she became active in the Girl Scouts, North Cascades Conservation Council, Olympic Parks Association, Friends of Three Sisters, Save-the-Redwoods League, Washington Roadside Council, Audubon Society, Alpine Lakes Protective Society, Bird Sanctuaries, Nature Conservancy, the fights in the 1950s for French Peter and Glacier Peak in the Cascades, and in the 1970s Washington Environmental Council and Earth Day. See Emily Haag response to June 1, 1972, questionnaire from Marshall Kuhn, Sierra Club History Committee, Bancroft Library.

14. Educational levels included: 2, elementary only; 5, high school plus extension only; 5, business college; 10, some college work; 11, a four-year degree; 4, a two-year normal school degree plus postgraduate work; 3, four years plus postgraduate; 35, held an AB or BS plus a graduate degree. Only 8 listed housewife as their vocation. The teachers had averaged 26.5 years in the classroom by retirement. Removing the 7 teachers who quit to get married, the average was 31 years. Those who were not teachers, businesswomen, or clerical workers included a medical technician, a nurse, a school principal, a professor, a chemist, a journalist, a physical therapist, and two lawyers. The 46 who had married averaged two children, with one-third reporting no children; 36 had remained single. See replies to June 1, 1972, questionnaire from Marshall Kuhn, Sierra Club History Committee, Bancroft Library.

15. Women joined local walks in larger numbers, see "Local Walks of the Sierra Club of San Francisco, Calif.," schedule 27, November 7, 1920, to April 24, 1921, 7; the cost to participants of 1921 Outing into Yosemite National Park, including railroad and stage transportation, was about $100. On this outing, ten men and eleven women climbed Mt. Ritter, scouted by Norman Clyde and led by Mr. Allen. See Julie Mortimer, "The 1921 Outing," *SCB* 11, no. 3 (1922): 255–60.

16. Of 82 responses, 75 reported involvement in women's organizations; 28, in professional groups; 19, in university associations; 18, concerned with cultural activities; and only 14 listed a religious affiliation of any type. See replies to June 1, 1972, questionnaire from Marshall Kuhn, Sierra Club History Committee, quote from Charlotte Mauk's reply, in Bancroft Library.

17. Obituary, "Marion Randall Parsons," *SCB* 38, no. 8 (October 1953): 36.

18. Marion Randall Parsons, "The Grand Cañons of the Tuolumne and the Merced," *SCB* 6, no. 4 (January 1908): 242.

19. Marion Randall Parsons, "Mono Vignette," *SCB* 37, no. 10 (December 1952): 68–74; Marion Randall Parsons, "The Twenty-eighth Outing," *SCB* 15, no. 1 (February 1930): 15–16. Marion Randall Parsons, "Spring in the Tyrol," *SCB* 12, no. 3 (1926): 289–96.

20. Marion Randall Parsons, *Old California Houses: Portraits and Stories* (Berkeley: University of California Press, 1952); Parsons, "Mono Vignette," 68–74.

21. Vera Norwood and Janice Monk, eds., *The Desert Is No Lady: Southwestern Landscapes in Women's Writings and Art* (New Haven: Yale University Press, 1987), 226, 228, 232.

22. Louise Hewlett, "The 1936 Outing," *SCB* 22, no. 1 (February 1937): 63; see also Muriel A. Stratford, unpublished manuscript, 1920, 3, Bancroft Library, SC Papers, carton 45:50. For contrast between "cold, austere beauty" of peaks and "gentle little idyll" of a garden, see Charlotte E. Mauk, "The Nth Itinerary," *SCB* 27, no. 4 (August 1942): 6.

23. Pepper, "High Trip High Jinks," 4.

24. Blanche Stallings, "The End of the Rope," *SCB* 26, no. 1 (February 1941): 25–26.

25. Julie Mortimer, "1921 Outing," 258–59; see also Doris Leonard, "Rock Climbers' Paradise," *SCB* 20, no. 1 (February 1935): 46–49.

26. Marcia Myers Bonta, *Women in the Field: America's Pioneering Women Naturalists* (College Station: Texas A & M University Press, 1991), 114. See also *SCB*, 1933 and 1937 issues.

27. Dorothy M. Emmet, "A British Student Looks at the Sierra Club Outing," *SCB* 15, no. 1 (February 1930): 23; Elizabeth Van E. Ferguson, "Field Notes of the 1920 Outing," *SCB* 11, no. 2 (January 1921): 147–50.

28. Ethel Boulware, "Afoot with the Sierra Club in 1933," *SCB* 19, no. 3 (June 1934): 4; Ethel Boulware, October 29, 1971, reply to June 1, 1972, questionnaire, Bancroft Library.

29. Hewlett, "1936 Outing," 64.

30. Dorothy Miller, "The Artist in Kern River Canyon," *Sunset* 12 (December 1903): 129.

31. Nina Eloesser, "Tales of High Trips in the Twenties," oral history conducted by Ann Lage (Sierra Club History Committee, 1985), 20; see also Bertha Clark Pope, "High Trip of 1925," 220.

32. From Stella Benson, "The Awakening," quoted by Pope, "High Trip of 1925," 213; see also Hewlett, "1936 Outing," 58–68.

33. Blanche Stallings, "A Freshman's Impressions of a High Trip," *SCB* 24, no. 3 (June 1939): 22–24; see also Hewlett, "1936 Outing," 58–68.

34. Lena Martha Redington, "The 1913 Outing to the Kings River Canyon," *SCB* 9, no. 3 (January 1914): 161.

35. For "everyone," see Stallings, "Freshman's Impression," 16; for "look at the sky," see Boulware, "Afoot with the Sierra Club in 1933," 2.

36. Harriet Monroe, "In High Places," *SCB* 11, no. 4 (1923): 420.

37. First quotes from Harriet T. Parsons, "Mountain Medley," *SCB* 24, no. 3 (June 1939): 4; Marion Randall Parsons, "Twenty-eighth Outing," 12–17; "pent-house" from Mildred Thoren, "Impressions," July 7–22, 1933, unpublished poem, in SC Papers, Bancroft Library, 1972 questionnaires file.

38. Pearl Turner Album, Colorado Rockies, July 25, 1924, University of Colorado, Norland Library; Julia W. Henshaw, "The Mountain Wildflowers of Western Canada," *Canadian Alpine Journal* 2 (1908): 130; Helen Emerson Anthony, "A Day on a Mountain," *Appalachia* 16 (1923): 71–75. For an analysis of gardens in women's frontier writings, see Annette Kolodny, *The Land Before Her: Fantasy and Experience of the American Frontier, 1630-1860* (Chapel Hill: University of North Carolina Press, 1984).

39. Harriet Monroe, "Camping Above the Yosemite: A Summer Outing with the Sierra Club," *SCB* 7, no. 2 (June 1909): 90. See also Jennie Price, "A Woman's Trip Through the Tuolumne Cañon," *SCB* 2, no. 3 (January 1898): 181–82; Lena Martha Redington, "1913 Outing," 162; Bertha Pope, "With the Sierra Club in 1914," *SCB* 9, no. 4 (January 1918): 255; Alice Eastwood, "Through a Botanical Paradise," *Sunset* 26, no. 3 (March 1911): 350.

40. Hewlett, "1936 Outing," 66–67.

41. Ethel Boulware, "Afoot with the Sierra Club in 1933," 8–9; for later examples of garden analogy, see Charlotte Mauk, "Nth Itinerary," 5–6; Nancy MacCabe, "Diary of a Base Camp Dilettante," 1949, 39, 44, Bancroft Library, Sierra Club Papers, Mother Lode Chapter Papers, carton 45, folder 61.

42. Quote from Elsie M. Zeile, "Wild Flowers of the Yellowstone Outing," *SCB* 12, no. 4 (1927): 346–48; see also Parsons, "Twenty-eighth Outing," 11; Dorothy Miller, "Artist in Kern River Canyon," 129; Harriet Monroe, "Maternity," in *Chosen Poems: A Selection from My Books of Verse* (New York: Macmillan, 1935), 103.

43. For "pines," see Parsons, "Twenty-eighth Outing," 16–17; Anita Day Hubbard, "The First High Horse Trip," *SCB* 25, no. 1 (February 1940): 22. Other examples of garden analogies: Blanche Stallings, "Freshman's Impression," 24; Marion Randall Parsons, "With the Sierra Club in the Kern Cañon," *SCB* 7, no. 1 (January 1909): 32; Marion Randall Parsons, "On Mt. St. Helens with the Mazamas," *SCB* 7, no. 3 (January 1910): 172; Harriet T. Parsons, "Mountain Medley," 1–15.

44. For evidence of women's sense of comfort with wilderness, see Harriet Monroe, "Camping Above the Yosemite," *SCB*, 94; Monroe, "Camping Above the Yosemite—A Summer Outing with the Sierra Club," *Putnam's Magazine* 5 (May 1909): 225; Lucy Washburn, "The Grand Circuit of the Yosemite National Park," *SCB* 7, no. 3 (1910): 150; Marion Randall Parsons, "Through the Olympics with the Mountaineers," 151; M. M. Pychowska, "Two in the Alpine Pasteurs," *Appalachia* 5, no. 3 (December 1888): 187; Edith M. Esterbook, "Two Women Afoot with Camp Packs," *Appalachia* 15, no. 1 (November 1920): 31; Mary T. S. Schaffer, "The Finding of Lake Naligne," *Canadian Alpine Journal* 4 (1912): 95.

45. Parsons, "The Twenty-eighth Outing," 12, 19; Thoren, "Impressions."

46. Hewlett, "1936 Outing," 66–67, 64. For other women writing of being at home see: Helen M. Gompertz, "A Tramp to Mt. Lyell," *SCB* 1, no. 4 (May 1894): 142; Harriet Monroe, "Camping Above the Yosemite," *SCB*, 94; Lucy Washburn, "The Grand Circuit of the Yosemite National Park," *SCB* 7, no. 3 (January 1910): 150; "a sense of permanent residence," Anita Day Hubbard, "First High Horse Trip," 23; Harriet T. Parsons, "Mountain Medley," 4; Elizabeth Knowlton, "Hill-Lover," *Appalachia* 15, no. 7 (June 1949): 350.

47. For Talbot quote and *home* as code word, see Nancy Woloch, *Women and the American Experience* (New York: Knopf, 1984), 270–71.

48. Skilled women climbers, including Miriam O'Brien and Nea Morin, complained of encountering opposition to their climbing from husbands and other family members, and experienced difficulty in finding women sufficiently free from constraining relatives to climb with them.

49. Ethel Boulware, "Afoot with the Sierra Club in 1933," 8–9, 5.

50. Dorothy Pilley, *Climbing Days* (1935; London: Hogarth, 1989), excerpted in *Mountaineering Women: Stories by Early Climbers*, ed. David Mazel (College Station: Texas A&M University Press, 1994): 135.

51. Pope, "High Trip of 1925," 220. For "awards and tests," see Nea Morin, *A Woman's Reach: Mountaineering Memoirs* (London: Eyre & Spottiswoode, 1968), 155–56. See also Harriet T. Parsons, "Mountain Medley," 4.

52. "Remembering the High Trips," interview with Ruth E. Prager, conducted by Ruth Sumner (Sierra Club History Committee, 1976), 7; Marion Randall Parsons, "On Mt. St. Helens with the Mazamas," *SCB* 7, no. 3 (January 1910): 171; Nancy MacCabe, "Diary of a Base Camp Dilettante," 44; Harriet Monroe, "Camping Above the Yosemite," *SCB*, 90, and *Putnam's*, 221, 225; Mildred Thoren, "Impressions."

53. Pepper, "High Trip High Jinks," 4.

54. Olivia R. Johnson, "High Trip Reminiscences, 1904–1945," 10–12.

55. Pope, "High Trip of 1925," 218–20.

56. Harriette W. Patey, "White Mountain Swimming-Holes," *Appalachia* 17, no. 4 (December 1933): 552–57.

57. Bertha Pope, "With the Sierra Club in 1914," 250. For afternoon teas and swimming, see Lena Martha Redington, "1913 Outing," 160–61.

58. Muriel A. Stratford, unpublished manuscript, 1920, 5, Bancroft Library, SC Papers, carton 45:50.

59. Jessie M. Whitehead, "With the Sierra Club," *SCB* 13, no. 1 (February 1928): 10–12.

60. For "atmosphere," see Blanche Stallings, "Freshman's Impression," 2; Pope, "High Trip of 1925," 218–20.

61. Nora Evans, "Sixty Years with the Sierra Club," interview conducted by Judy Snyder (Sierra Club History Committee, 1976), 4–5; Ethel Boulware, "Afoot with the Sierra Club in 1933," 2–3, 8–9; Anita Day Hubbard, "First High Horse Trip," 23.

62. Whitehead, "With the Sierra Club," 10. She later rock-climbed with Miriam O'Brien Underhill. See Miriam O'Brien Underhill, "Manless Alpine Climbing," *National Geographic* (August 1934): 131–70; see also Dorothy M. Emmet, "British Student," 22–23.

63. Emmet, "British Student," 22–23.

64. Pope, "High Trip of 1925," 213–23; Pearl Turner Album, July 25, 1924; Marion Randall Parsons, "The 1920 Outing: Headwaters of the San Joaquin and the Kings," *SCB* 11, no. 2 (January 1921): 143; Charlotte Mauk, "On the Wilderness Trail," *SCB* 34, no. 6 (June 1949): 4.

65. Charlotte Mauk, "On the Wilderness Trail," 4; Frank Branch Riley, "This is the Life," *Mazama* 4, no. 3 (December 1914): 28–32; Stallings, "Freshman's Impression," 18–19; Pearl Turner Album, July 26 and August 7, 1924. Nora Evans, "Sixty Years with the Sierra Club," 5.

66. For "undemocratic," see Pepper, "High Trip High Jinks," 15; for "in those days," see attachment by Nora Evans to October 29, 1971, questionnaire, Bancroft Library.

67. Some of the uninvited women tramped with Norman Clyde, who was occasionally ignored by the main body of climbers because he was reputed to be taciturn and did not bathe; see Pepper, "High Trip High Jinks," 15–17. Clyde did guide very difficult ascents. Only on the hardest climbs, such as those of Higher Spires and Lower Spires, were women dramatically underrepresented between the late 1910s and mid-1930s. Glen Dawson, "Mountain-Climbing on the 1934 Outing," *SCB* 20, no. 1 (February 1935): 103–4. From 1927 to 1936, 62 men and 15 women received club certificates for having scaled at least five 14,000-foot peaks; see "Fourteen-Thousand-Foot Climbers of the Sierra Club," *SCB* 21, no. 1 (February 1936): 103–4.

68. Elizabeth Knowlton, "These Climbing Americans," *Independent Women* 14, no. 7 (July 1935): 218–19, 228, quoting from Jacques de Lépiney, *Sur Les Cretes du Mont Blanc: Récits déascensions* (Chambéry: M. Dardel, 1929); Jacques and Tom de Lépiney, *Climbs on Mont Blanc*, trans. Sydney Spencer (London: Edward Arnold, 1930).

69. Those using the new technology included Caroline Coleman, Eleanor Bartlett, Mary Alvarez, Marjory Bridge Farquhar, Doris Leonard, and Annie Nilsson. See Harriet Parsons, "A Half-Century of Sierra Club Involvement," oral history conducted by Ann Lage,

funded by the National Endowment for the Humanities and the Sierra Club History Committee (1981), 12.

70. Glen Dawson, "Mountain Climbing on the 1934 Outing," 103–4; on women leading, see Nora Evans, "Sixty Years with the Sierra Club," 6; Ruth E. Prager, "Remembering the High Trips," 7.

71. Miriam E. O'Brien, "Without Men: Some Considerations on the Theory and Practice of Manless Climbing," *Appalachia* 19, no. 2 (December 1932): 187–203; "Climbs," *Appalachia* 19, no. 4 (December 1932): 297–98. See also "Ladies' Mountaineering," *Alpine Journal* (Britain) 44 (1932): 343; Bill Birkett and Bill Peascod, *Women Climbing: 200 Years of Achievement* (Seattle: The Mountaineers, 1990), 31–46.

72. Miriam O'Brien Underhill, *Give Me The Hills* (Riverside, CT: Chatham, 1971; reprint of 1956 edition with an additional chapter), 158.

73. Nea Morin, *Woman's Reach*, 65. On Miriam O'Brien Underhill and Nea Morin, see Birkett and Peascod, *Women Climbing*, 31–46, 58–68.

74. Doris Leonard, "Rock Climbers' Paradise," 44–49; see also Blanche Stallings, "The End of the Rope," 26–27.

75. Pepper, "High Trip High Jinks," 33.

76. Morin, *Woman's Reach*, 155–56, 207, 30, 109, 246.

77. "The Accident," *Mazama* 9, no. 8 (August 1927): 1–2.

78. Ethel Boulware, "Afoot with the Sierra Club in 1933," 14; Edith M. Esterbrook, "Two Women Afoot with Camp Packs," *Appalachia* 15, no. 1 (November 1920): 25–31.

79. Whitehead, "With the Sierra Club," 14–15; see also Julie Mortimer, "1921 Outing," 255.

80. Helen LeConte, "North Palisades," *SCB* 19, no. 3 (June 1934): 24–27.

81. Marion Randall Parsons, review of *Climbing Days* by Dorothy Pilley, *SCB* 21, no. 1 (February 1936): 109–10.

82. Pearl Turner Album, July 25, 1924, Norland Library, University of Colorado, Boulder.

83. Vera Norwood, "Women's Place: Continuity and Change in Response to Western Landscapes," in *Western Women, Their Land, Their Life,* ed. Lillian Schlissel, Vicki L. Ruiz, and Janice Monk (Albuquerque: University of New Mexico Press, 1988), 164. Norwood is drawing here on the work of Patricia Meyer Spacks, *The Female Imagination* (New York: Knopf, 1975), 221–22; see also Joseph Donovan, "The Silence Is Broken," in *Women and Language in Literature and Society,* ed. Sally McConnell-Ginet, Ruth Borker, and Nelly Furman (New York: Praeger, 1980), 205–16.

84. Peter N. Stearns and Timothy Haggerty, "The Role of Fear: Transitions in American Emotional Standards for Children, 1850–1950," *American Historical Review* 96, no. 1 (February 1991): 63; O'Brien quote from Birkett and Peascod, *Women Climbing*, 45.

85. Ruth R. Currier, "Sierran, 1914–1934," *SCB* 20, no. 1 (February 1935): 35–40.

86. Ibid., 35–40; Jennie Price, "Woman's Trip," 181–82.

87. Marjory Bridge [Farquhar], "Mount Humphreys," *SCB* 19, no. 3 (June 1934): 15–19.

88. Glen Dawson, "The Devils Crag," *SCB* 19, no. 3 (June 1934): 19–23. For another example from that same year, of men's language of the climb, see Richard M. Leonard, "Three Teeth of Sawtooth Ridge," *SCB* 19, no. 3 (June 1934): 31–33.

89. Anne Shannon Monroe, "Mazamas in the Mountains," *SCB* 6, no. 2 (December 1921): 18.

90. Bruce Meyer, "Mountaineering on the 1940 High Trip," *SCB* 26, no. 1 (February 1941): 127–29; J. Ed Nelson, "The 1939 Climbing Season," *Mazama* 21, no. 12 (December 1939): 35; Richard Leonard, "Yosemite Climbing Notes," *SCB* 26, no. 1 (February 1941): 135; David R. Brower, "Mountaineering During the 1939 High Trip," *SCB* 25, no. 1 (February 1940): 120–21.

91. "Officers for 1903," *Mazama* 2, no. 3 (July 1903): [1]; "Mazamas Organization for the Year 1916–1917," *Mazama* 4, no. 4 (December 1915): 75. The Appalachian Mountain Club had women members in 1890 but no officers; see "Officers" and "New Members," *Appalachia* 6, no. 2 (December 1890): 106–9.

92. "Report on Mountaineering," *Canadian Alpine Journal* 4 (1912–1914): 148–49.

93. From 1900 to 1950 no woman chaired the Sierra Club's Outing, Mountaineering, Trails, Winter Sports, or Conservation Committees. At various times they chaired the Lodge, Library, Visual Education, and Membership Committees.

94. Mauk to Ada Fish, November 8, 1944, Bancroft Library, Mauk Papers, Outgoing Letters file.

95. Harriet T. Parsons, "Mountain Medley," 14.

96. Mauk, "Nth Itinerary," 1; Mauk, "Homecoming, 1946," *SCB* 32, no. 5 (May 1947): 22–23.

97. Mauk to Fish, November 8, 1944; for a description of Mauk as a "gentle person," see Nathan Clark, "Sierra Club Leader, Outdoorsman, & Engineer," interview by Richard Searle (Sierra Club History Committee, 1977), 70.

98. Elaine Tyler May, *Homeward Bound: American Families in the Cold War Era* (New York: Basic Books, 1988), 37–57.

99. Carroll Smith-Rosenberg, *Disorderly Conduct: Visions of Gender in Victorian America* (Oxford: Oxford University Press, 1985), 245–96.

100. R. Claire Snyder, *Citizen-Soldiers and Manly Warriors: Military Service and Gender in the Civic Republic Tradition* (Lanham, MD: Rowman & Littlefield, 1999), 2.

101. Elizabeth Knowlton, "These Climbing Americans," 228.

102. Stuart Kimball, Miriam Underhill, et al., *Mountain Flowers of New England* (Boston: Appalachian Mountain Club, 1964). O'Brien also edited the Appalachian Mountain Club's bulletin *Appalachia*.

103. Miriam Underhill, *Give Me the Hills,* 169–75.

CHAPTER 5. MOUNTAINS AS THE MEASURE OF MEN

1. Chester H. Rowell, "The Mountain and the Sea," *Sierra Club Bulletin* (hereafter *SCB*) 11, no. 3 (1922): 261–63. Rowell was active in progressive Republican politics, edited the *Fresno Republican* (1898–20), and in 1932 became editor of the *San Francisco Chronicle*.

2. John C. Van Dyke, *The Grand Canyon of the Colorado: Recurrent Studies in Impressions and Appearances* (New York: Charles Scribner's Sons, 1920), v–vi.

3. H. Appleton, "The Himalayas as a Climbing Field," *Mountaineer* 17, no. 1 (December 1924): 9–11.

4. *SCB* 11, no. 2 (January 1921): advertisement, inside back cover; S. L. Foster, "An August Outing in the Upper Merced Cañon," *SCB* 7, no. 1 (January 1909): 39–46.

5. Richard W. Montague, "Why Do We Come Back?" *Mazama* (1920): 23–25.

6. George C. Thompson, review of John C. Van Dyke, *The Mountain: Renewed Studies in Impressions and Appearances* (New York: C. Scribner's Sons, 1916) in *SCB* 10, no. 2 (January 1917): 260–26; Francis P. Farquhar, "First Ascent of the Middle Palisade," *SCB* 11, no. 3 (1922): 264–70; Hilaire Belloc, *The Path to Rome* (New York: G. P. Putnam's Sons, 1902), 248.

7. Philip E. Smith, "Another Ascent of the Black Kaweah (13,752 feet)," *SCB* 11, no. 3 (1922): 311.

8. Letters from Marshall Kuhn, Sierra Club History Committee, to Sierra Club members who had joined before 1930, with questionnaire, June 1–October 29, 1972. Replies in Bancroft Library.

9. Sixty-seven men replied to the questionnaire. Fifteen had joined between 1900 and 1911; and three, during World War I. Forty-six joined between 1920 and 1930. Somewhat

more than one-third had been born in the 1880s, slightly less than one-third in the 1890s, and somewhat over a third between 1900 and 1915. Four were enrolled as life members at birth in the 1920s. The four foreign-born members were from Norway, Holland, Switzerland, and England. Fifty-three gave the birthplace of their parents as America, but fourteen reported that their parents were born abroad. Not every respondent answered all the questions.

10. See 1899 photograph of Farquhar on the top of Saddleback Mountain, Bancroft Library, Pictorial Collection 1971.037 PIC. SC Portrait Miscellany. Quote from Richard Leonard, introduction to Francis Farquhar, "Sierra Club Mountaineer and Editor," oral history conducted by Ann and Ray Lage (Sierra Club History Committee, 1974), iii.

11. Quotes from Francis P. Farquhar, "First Ascent of the Middle Palisade," *SCB* 11 (1921): 264–70; see also Farquhar, "Sierra Club Mountaineer and Editor," 18.

12. Quotes from W. P. Putnam, "The Thumb," *SCB* 11, no. 3 (1922): 272; see also Jacques and Tom de Lépiney, *Climbs on Mont Blanc,* trans. Sydney Spencer (London: Edward Arnold, 1930), 11, 29, 88.

13. Mr. and Mrs. J. W. Hood, "John Hood (1926–1947)," *SCB* 33, no. 3 (March 1948): 119.

14. J. S. Hutchinson, "Goddard and Disappearing Creeks: The Enchanted Gorge," *SCB* 12, no. 1 (1924): 20.

15. Lépiney, *Climbs on Mont Blanc,* 156.

16. First quote from Van Dyke, *Grand Canyon,* v–vi, 1, 4, 9; second quote from J. Monroe Thorington, "Side-Valleys and Peaks of the Yellowstone Trail," *Alpine Journal* 37, no. 230 (May 1925): 47; see also Peter Wild, "Van Dyke's Shoes: Tracking the Aesthetic Behind the Desert Wanderer," *Journal of the Southwest* 29, no. 4 (winter 1987): 412.

17. "George Leigh Mallory," *Appalachia* 18, no. 4 (December 1924): 1; David Pye, *George Leigh Mallory: A Memoir* (London: Oxford University Press, 1927), reviewed in *SCB* 13, no. 1 (February 1928): 97–98.

18. Francis P. Farquhar, review of E. F. Norton's *The Fight for Everest* (New York: Longmans, 1924), in *SCB* 12, no. 3 (1926): 329.

19. Philip E. Smith, "Another Ascent of the Black Kaweah (13,752 Feet)," 311–12. The language of the unknown remained strong as well in European climbing; see Lépiney, *Climbs on Mont Blanc,* 93.

20. Norman Clyde, *El Picacho del Diablo: The Conquest of Lower California's Highest Peak, 1932 and 1937* (Los Angeles: Dawson's Book Shop, 1974), 11–13. For the club's firing of Clyde, see Richard M. Leonard, "Mountaineer, Lawyer, Environmentalist," oral history conducted by Susan Schrepfer (Berkeley: University of California, Bancroft Oral History Office, 1975), 1:15–17.

21. Norman Clyde, "First Ascent of Mount Wilbur," *SCB* 12, no. 1 (1924): 4–6.

22. Norman Clyde, "Up the East Face of Mt. Whitney," *Touring Topics* (December 1931).

23. Norman Clyde, "Climbing the Sierra Nevada from Owens Valley," *SCB* 13, no. 1 (February 1928): 35.

24. J. W. A. Hickson, "Two Lesser First Ascents in the Canadian Rockies, 1925," *Alpine Journal* 38, no. 232 (May 1926): 70; see also Lépiney, *Climbs on Mont Blanc,* 92–93, 13, 128–29, 110.

25. Quote from Clyde, "First Ascent of Mount Wilbur," 4; see also Nathaniel L. Goodrich, "Appalachians in the Sierra," *SCB* 12, no. 4 (1927): 377–81; George H. Harvey Jr., "Our First Sierra Club Outing," *SCB* 12, no. 4 (1925): 161; Robert W. Osborn, "Climb a Mountain Before You Get To It," *Mazama* 2, no. 8 (December 1924): 61–62.

26. C. W. Michael, "First Ascent of the Minarets," *SCB* 12, no. 1 (1924): 33.

27. J. S. Hutchinson, "Goddard and Disappearing Creeks," 13–17.

28. Editorial, "Purposes of the Founders," *SCB* 12, no. 1 (1924): 77–78.

29. Robert M. Price, "Exploration of Mt. Darwin," *SCB* 11, no. 3 (1922): 286.

30. John W. Robinson, introduction to Clyde, *El Picacho del Diablo*, 12.

31. John L. Hart, *Fourteen Thousand Feet: A History of the Naming and Early Ascents of the High Colorado Peaks* (Denver: Colorado Mountain Club, 1925); Hugh E. Kingery, assisted by Elinor Eppich Kingery, *The Colorado Mountain Club: The First Seventy-five Years of a Highly Individual Corporation, 1912-1987* (Evergreen, CO: Cordillera Press, 1988), 53–55; William H. Brewer, *Rocky Mountain Letter, 1869: A Journal of an Early Geological Expedition to the Colorado Rockies* (Denver: Colorado Mountain Club, 1930).

32. Francis P. Farquhar, "Spanish Discovery of the Sierra Nevada," *SCB* 13, no. 1 (February 1928): 54–61; Francis P. Farquhar, *Naming America's Mountains—The Colorado Rockies* (New York: American Alpine Club, 1961); Francis P. Farquhar, ed., *Up and Down California in 1860-1864: The Journal of William H. Brewer*, new ed. (1930; Berkeley: University of California Press, 1949); Earl S. Pomeroy, *In Search of the Golden West: The Tourist in Western America* (New York: Knopf, 1957), 35–45.

33. H. Appleton, "The Himalayas as a Climbing Field," 9–11.

34. John R. White, "Camp-Fires," *SCB* 14, no. 1 (February 1929): 34–38; John R. White, *Bullets and Bolos: Fifteen Years in the Philippine Islands* (New York: Century, 1928). Book review, *SCB* 14, no. 1 (February 1929), 103–4.

35. "The Mount Everest Expedition," *SCB* 12, no. 1 (1924): 78; for similar sentiments, see "Alpina," *Appalachia* 19, no. 4 (December 1933): 592–98; John Noel, *The Story of Everest* (Boston: Little, Brown and Company, 1927); David Pye, *George Leigh Mallory*.

36. "George Leigh Mallory," *Appalachia*, n.s., 18, no. 4 (December 1924): 1–3.

37. George Thompson, review of *The Epic of Mount Everest* by Francis Edward Younghusband (New York: Longmans, Green, 1926), in *SCB* 12, no. 4 (1927): 433–34.

38. J. C. Hutchinson, "Goddard and Disappearing Creeks," 20; "Mountaineering Notes," *SCB* 15, no. 1 (February 1930): 109.

39. Ernest Dawson, "A Sierran's Impression of the Alps," *SCB* 14, no. 1 (February 1929): 85–86.

40. Thompson, review of *Epic of Mount Everest*, 433–34.

41. Joel Hildebrand, "Sierra Club Leader and Ski Mountaineer," oral history conducted by Ann Lage and Ray Lage (Sierra Club History Committee, 1974), 8–16.

42. Putnam, "Thumb," 271–74.

43. H. C. Bradley, "Across the Sierra Nevada on Skis," *SCB* 11, no. 3 (1922): 295–99.

44. Bestor Robinson, "The First Ascent of the Higher Cathedral Spire," *SCB* 19, no. 3 (June 1934): 34.

45. Richard Leonard and David Brower, "A Climber's Guide to the High Sierra, Part IV, Yosemite Valley," *SCB* 25, no. 1 (February 1940): 41–63; Norman Clyde, *American Alpine Journal* 1, no. 2 (1930), and 1, no. 3 (1931).

46. Francis P. Farquhar, "Some Climbs on the North Palisade," *SCB* 17, no. 1 (February 1932): 124–25.

47. Robinson, "First Ascent of Higher Cathedral Spire," 34–37.

48. Ibid., 37; Leonard, "Mountaineer," 1:49.

49. Leonard, "Mountaineer," 1:10.

50. Ibid., 1:11–12.

51. Quotes from David R. Brower, "Far from the Madding Mules: A Knapsacker's Retrospect," *SCB* 20, no. 1 (February 1935): 72–77; on his early climbing, see David R. Brower, "Environmental Activist, Publicist, and Prophet," oral history conducted by Susan R. Schrepfer (Berkeley: Bancroft Oral History Office, 1980), 9–11.

52. Hervey Voge, "Climbs in the Waddington Region—1936," *SCB* 22, no. 1 (February 1937): 31; see also Leonard, "Mountaineer," 1:14–15; Brower, "Environmental Activist," 8, 34, 38.
53. Voge, "Climbs in the Waddington Region—1936," 31, 35–36.
54. Elmo A. Robinson, "Prolegomena to a Philosophy of Mountaineering," quoting Claud Schuster, *Men, Women, and Mountains,* in *SCB* 23, no. 2 (April 1938): 56.
55. Quote from Frank Branch Riley, "This Is the Life," *Mazama* 4, no. 3 (December 1914): 30; see also Richard W. Montague, "Why Do We Come Back?" 23–25.
56. Walter L. Huber, "The Sierra Club in the Land of the Athabaska," *SCB* 14, no. 1 (February 1929): 2–5; "The High Trip of 1923," *SCB* 12, no. 1 (1924): 22, 25.
57. Mary Street Alinder and Andrea Gray Stillman, *Ansel Adams: Letters and Images, 1916-1984* (New York: Little, Brown, 1988): 17.
58. Ansel Adams, "Retrospect: Nineteen Thirty-one," *SCB* 17, no. 1 (February 1932): 1–5.
59. Cedric Wright, *Cedric Wright: Words of the Earth,* ed. Nancy Newhall, foreword by Ansel Adams (San Francisco: Sierra Club, 1960), 13, 33–35.
60. Quotes from Cedric Wright, "Trail Song: Giant Forest and Vicinity: 1927," *SCB* 13, no. 1 (February 1928): 21–22; for photos, see Wright, *Cedric Wright.*
61. Ansel Adams, review of Barbara Morgan, *Summer's Children* (Scarsdale: Morgan and Morgan, 1951), *SCB* 38, no. 8 (October 1953): 77–78.
62. Quote from Ansel Adams, "Retrospect: Nineteen Thirty-one," 1–5; Jonathan Spaulding, *Ansel Adams and the American Landscape* (Berkeley: University of California Press, 1995), 188.
63. Ruth R. Currier, "Sierran, 1914–1934," *SCB* 20, no. 1 (February 1935): 34–41; for similar sentiments, see Jennie Price, "A Woman's Trip Through the Tuolumne Cañon," *SCB* 2, no. 3 (January 1898): 181–82.
64. Cedric Wright, "High Trip Gleanings," *SCB* 20, no. 1 (February 1935): 32–33; on Whitman, see Wright, *Cedric Wright,* 5.
65. Thomas Wolfe, *The Web and the Rock* (New York: Harper & Brothers, 1939), 157, 159.
66. Pearl S. Buck, *Other Gods: An American Legend* (New York: John Day, 1940), 310.
67. Buck, *Other Gods,* 292–93; Wolfe, *The Web and the Rock,* 164.
68. Robert Marshall, "The Problem of Wilderness," *SCB* 32, no. 5 (May 1947): 43–52, first printed in *Scientific American,* February 1930; William James, "The Moral Equivalent of War," *Memories and Studies* (New York: Longmans, Green, 1911), 267–96; John D. Scott, *We Climbed High: A Thumbnail Chronology of the Mazamas, 1894-1964* (Portland: Mazamas, 1969), 37.
69. R. Claire Snyder, *Citizen-Soldiers and Manly Warriors: Military Service and Gender in the Civic Republic Tradition* (Lanham, MD: Rowman & Littlefield, 1999).
70. David R. Brower, "It Couldn't Be Climbed," *Saturday Evening Post,* February 3, 1940, 24–25, 72–75; for attempts by other clubs, see *Trail and Timberline* (December 1937); and *Appalachia* (June 1936).
71. Brower, "It Couldn't Be Climbed," 24–25, 72–75; Bestor Robinson, "The First Ascent of Shiprock," *SCB* 25, no. 1 (February 1940): 1–7; Brower, "A Return to the Peaks," *Sierra* 77, no. 3 (May/June 1992): 93.
72. Snyder, *Citizen-Soldiers and Manly Warriors,* quote from 2; see also 6, 84, 86, 89.
73. Leonard, "Mountaineer," 1:9–10; Richard M. Leonard, *Belaying the Leader* (San Francisco: Sierra Club, 1947).
74. [Harriet T. Parsons], review of H. W. Tilman, *When Men and Mountains Meet* (Cambridge: Cambridge University Press, 1946), in *SCB* 32, no. 5 (May 1947): 142; Leonard, *Belaying the Leader;* Conrad L. Wirth, *Parks, Politics, and the People* (Norman: Univer-

sity of Oklahoma Press, 1980), 232; David Brower, "Pursuit in the Alps," *SCB* 31, no. 7 (December 1946): 32–45; *SCB* 32, no. 5 (May 1947): 141.

75. T. J. Jackson Lears, *Fables of Abundance: A Cultural History of Advertising in America* (New York: Basic Books, 1994), 11, 165, 169, 98, 166.

CHAPTER 6. IN FIRE, BLOSSOMS, AND FLOOD

1. Aldo Leopold, "Conservation Esthetic," *Bird-Lore* 40, no. 2 (March–April 1938): 101.

2. Helen Buckler, Mary F. Fieldler, and Martha F. Allen, editors and compilers, *WO-HE-LO: The Story of the Camp Fire Girls, 1910-1960* (New York: Holt, Rinehart, and Winston, 1961), 20. Juliette Gordon Low established the Girls Scouts of America shortly after the Camp Fire Girls were established.

3. Early advisory meetings for the Camp Fire Girls were held at the Alpine Club in New York City, and the club's Dan Beard remained active in the Camp Fire Girls until his death in 1940. See Buckler, Fieldler, and Allen, *WO-HE-LO*, 27. For the involvement of Sierra Club men and women in scouting, see replies to 1972 questionnaire in Bancroft Library, SC Papers. See also Janet Caldwell, "Mountaineer Activities," *Mountaineers* 46, no. 13 (April 1953): 43.

4. "Here Are the Girl Pioneers of America," *New York Sun,* June 11, 1911, available at http://scoutingarchives.com/gs.html. Accessed February 23, 2004.

5. Luther Gulick, speech, March 22, 1911; text from Buckler, Fieldler, and Allen, *WO-HE-LO,* 21–22.

6. On Luther Gulick and "the efficient life," see T. J. Jackson Lears, *Fables of Abundance: A Cultural History of Advertising in America* (New York: Basic Books, 1994), 167, 179, 222.

7. Robert H. MacDonald, *Sons of the Empire: The Frontier and the Boy Scout Movement, 1890-1918* (Toronto: University of Toronto Press, 1993), 119.

8. Buckler, Fiedler, and Allen, *WO-HE-LO,* 70, 47–48, 21–27.

9. Ibid., 47–48, 70, 25–27.

10. For links between empire, frontier, and scouting, see MacDonald, *Sons of the Empire.*

11. Buckler, Fiedler, and Allen, *WO-HE-LO,* 48, 251; Charles Alexander Eastman, *Indian Scout Talks* (Boston: Little, Brown, 1914), 146–48, 184; Jane L. Stewart, *The Camp Fire Girls on the March,* Camp Fire Girls Series, vol. 5 (Chicago: Saalfield, 1914): frontispiece.

12. Buckler, Fiedler, and Allen, *WO-HE-LO,* 22.

13. Jane L. Stewart, *The Camp Fire Girls in the Mountains,* Camp Fire Girls Series, vol. 4 (Chicago: Saalfield, 1914), 3, 6–7.

14. Buckler, Fiedler, and Allen, *WO-HE-LO,* 257.

15. Nancy Woloch, *Women and the American Experience* (New York: Knopf, 1984), 266.

16. Buckler, Fiedler, and Allen, *WO-HE-LO,* 47–48.

17. Ibid.; Stewart, *The Camp Fire Girls in the Mountains,* 8–13. For membership statistics, I want to thank Jennifer Hillman Helgren, who is completing her dissertation, "A Beautiful and Useful Womanhood: The Camp Fire Girls and Twentieth Century Girls' Culture in America" (Claremont Graduate University).

18. For evidence of activism dating to the 1870s, see John F. Reiger, *American Sportsmen and the Origins of Conservation* (New York: Winchester Press, 1975).

19. W. B. Greeley, "What *Shall We* Do with *Our* Mountains?" *Sunset* 59, no. 6 (December 1927): 14–15, 81–85. The proposal, discussed since 1909, for a San Jacinto aerial tramway became public in 1937. Richard C. Davis, "Wilderness, Politics, and Bureaucracy: Federal and State Policies in the Administration of San Jacinto Mountain, Southern California, 1920–1968" (PhD diss., University of California, Riverside, 1973), 406–28.

20. For Leopold's work on erosion in the 1920s, see Curt Meine, *Aldo Leopold: His Life and Work* (Madison: University of Wisconsin Press, 1988), 209–28. For additional perspectives, see Aldo Leopold, *The Essential Aldo Leopold: Quotations and Commentaries*, ed. Curt Meine and Richard L. Knight (Madison: University of Wisconsin Press, 1999).

21. Aldo Leopold, "The Wilderness and Its Place in Forest Recreational Policy," *Journal of Forestry* 19, no. 7 (1921): 719.

22. Meine, *Aldo Leopold*, 224. Meine quotes "Keep One Wilderness Hunting Ground," from *The Pine Cone*, March 1924, 3.

23. Aldo Leopold, "A Plea for Wilderness Hunting Grounds," *Outdoor Life* (November 1925), reprinted in Aldo Leopold, *Aldo Leopold's Wilderness: Selected Early Writings by the Author of "A Sand County Almanac,"* ed. David E. Brown and Neil B. Carmony (Harrisburg, PA: Stackpole Books, 1990), 155–61.

24. Aldo Leopold, "Conserving the Covered Wagon: Shall We Save Parts of the Far Western Wilderness from Soft 'Improvements'?" *Sunset* 54, no. 3 (March 1925): 21.

25. Aldo Leopold, "Wilderness as a Form of Land Use," *Journal of Land and Public Utilities Economics* 1, no. 3 (July 1925): 398, 400.

26. Leopold, "Wilderness as a Form of Land Use," 401, 403, 404.

27. Aldo Leopold, "Pioneers and Gullies: Why Sweat to Reclaim New Land When We Lack Sense Enough to Hold On to the Old Acres?" *Sunset* 52, no. 5 (May 1924): 15.

28. Leopold, "Conserving the Covered Wagon," 21.

29. "Men of the Blood" from Kipling's "The Song of the Sons," in MacDonald, *Sons of the Empire*, 2; Leopold, "Conserving the Covered Wagon," 21.

30. For a discussion of this problem, see Annette Kolodny, *The Lay of the Land: Metaphor as Experience and History in American Life and Letters* (Chapel Hill: University of North Carolina Press, 1975), 26–70.

31. Leopold, "The Green Lagoons," *American Forests* 51, no. 8 (August 1945): 414; on Leopold and *Babbitt*, see Meine, *Aldo Leopold*, 220–21, 235–36.

32. Leopold, "Conserving the Covered Wagon," 56.

33. Greeley, "What *Shall We* Do With *Our* Mountains?," 81.

34. Leopold "Green Lagoons," 414.

35. The Sierra Club did not, for example, welcome the San Gorgonio Primitive Area and initially supported efforts to make the San Jacinto Primitive Area a state park. See Davis, "Wilderness, Politics, and Bureaucracy," 45–46, 57–58.

36. John Ise, *Our National Park Policy: A Critical History* (Baltimore: Johns Hopkins University Press, 1961): 396–400; on women's role, especially through the General Federation of Women's Clubs, in lobbying for the National Park Service, see Kaufman, *National Parks*, 34–35.

37. William Colby, "The Proposed Enlargement of Sequoia National Park," *Sierra Club Bulletin* (hereafter *SCB*) 12, no. 1 (1924): 76–77; Douglas Strong, *Trees—Or Timber? The Story of Sequoia and Kings Canyon National Parks* (Three Rivers, CA: Sequoia Natural History Association, 1967).

38. Act of July 3, 1926, ch. 744, 44 Stat. 818. With this act, the park included not only the summit but one side of Mt. Whitney, the main canyon of the Kern River, the Big Arroyo, Chagoopah Plateau, the pine forest east of the Kern, the Kaweah Peaks, much of the Great Western Divide, Redwood Meadows, and the granite canyons at the head of the Middle Fork of the Kaweah River.

39. Francis P. Farquhar, "Enlargement of Sequoia National Park," *SCB* 12, no. 4 (1927): 408–9.

40. Peter Philip Mickulas, "Giving, Getting, and Growing: Philanthropy, Science, and the New York Botanical Garden, 1888–1929" (PhD diss., Rutgers University, 2003), 94–97, 391.

41. Emma Lucy Braun published extensively from 1916 into the 1960s. Her earliest work included *The Physiographic Ecology of the Cincinnati Region* (Columbus: Ohio State University, 1916), based on her dissertation, and "The Vegetation of the Mineral Springs Region of Adams County, Ohio," *Ohio State University Bulletin* 32, no. 15 (June 30, 1928): 383–517. Most widely known was her *Deciduous Forests of the Eastern United States* (1950; New York: Hafner, 1964).

42. "In the Beginning," *Wild Flower* 1, no. 1 (January 1, 1924): 1; and *Wild Flower* 1, no. 3 (July 1, 1924): 1.

43. *Wild Flower* 1, no. 4 (October 1, 1924): 33; Philip L. Buttrick, "Various Aspects of Wild Flower Preservation," *Wild Flower* 2, no. 3 (July 1, 1925): 5. On Candice Wheeler's promotion of the aesthetics of flora and fauna, see Mary Blanchard, *Oscar Wilde's America: Counterculture in the Gilded Age, 1876-1893* (New Haven: Yale University Press, 1998).

44. *Wild Flower* 6, no. 2 (April 1, 1929): 14.

45. Buttrick, "Various Aspects of Wild Flower Preservation," 5.

46. Early studies included Thomas Bonser, "Ecological Study of Big Spring Prairie," *Proceedings of the Ohio State Academic Science,* special paper 7 (1903); J. H. Schaffner, O. E. Jennings, and F. J. Tyler, "Ecological Study of Brush Lake," *Proceedings of the Ohio State Academic Science,* special paper 10 (1904); Frederick E. Clements, *Plant Succession and Indicators: A Definitive Edition* (New York: H. W. Wilson, 1928). On the development of ecology, see Donald Worster, *Nature's Economy: A History of Ecological Ideas* (New York: Cambridge University Press, 1994).

47. Robert Clarke, *Ellen Swallow: The Woman Who Founded Ecology* (Chicago: Follett, 1973), 40, 112–20. See also Mary Joy Breton, *Women Pioneers for the Environment* (Boston: Northeastern University Press, 1998), 47–63.

48. Edith S. Clements, *Flowers of Coast and Sierra* (New York: H. W. Wilson, 1928); Frederic E. Clements and Edith S. Clements, *Flower Families and Ancestors* (New York: H. W. Wilson, 1928).

49. E. Lucy Braun, "The Physiographic Ecology of the Cincinnati Region," *Ohio Biological Survey* 11, no. 3 (1916), bulletin 7, published by Ohio State University, Columbus; Frederica Detmers, "An Ecological Study of Buckeye Lake," *Proceedings: Ohio State Academic Science,* special paper 19 (1912).

50. Vera Norwood, *Made from This Earth: American Women and Nature* (Chapel Hill: University of North Carolina Press, 1993).

51. E. Lucy Braun, "Where and Why," *Wild Flower* 1, no. 2 (April 1, 1924): 14.

52. In the 1970s the Sierra Club asked, "Do Trees Have Standing?" and petitioned the U.S. Supreme Court to recognize the rights of nature. Justice William O. Douglas offered a resounding, if dissenting, yes. See Roderick Frazier Nash, *The Rights of Nature: A History of Environmental Ethics* (Madison: University of Wisconsin Press, 1989).

53. Mrs. Francis Edmund Whitley, "A Plea for the Wild Flowers," *Wild Flower* 1, no. 3 (July 1, 1924): 33.

54. *Wild Flower* 5, no. 3 (July 1, 1928): 1; 6, no. 1 (January 1, 1929): 11; 5, no. 3 (July 1, 1928): 33.

55. On women in the Audubon Societies, see Frank Graham Jr., with Carl W. Buchheister, *The Audubon Ark: A History of the National Audubon Society* (New York: Knopf, 1990), 14–17; on women's activism, Nancy A. Hewitt and Suzanne Lebsock, eds., *Visible Women: New Essays on American Activism* (Urbana: University of Illinois Press, 1993).

56. Thomas R. Dunlap, *Saving America's Wildlife* (Princeton: Princeton University Press, 1988), 92–97.

57. Pamphlet, "Steel-Trapping by the Audubon Association," (Emergency Conservation Committee, 1933); pamphlet, "Blood Money for the Audubon Association," (Anti–Steel Trap League, n.d.), Denver Public Library, Rosalie Edge Papers, Box 291.

58. Graham, *Audubon Ark,* 112–17. On predators and sportsmen, see Dunlap, *Saving America's Wildlife;* Meine, *Aldo Leopold;* Susan Flader, *Thinking Like A Mountain: Aldo Leopold and the Evolution of an Ecological Attitude toward Deer, Wolves, and Forests* (Columbia: University of Missouri Press, 1974).

59. Of the sixty-nine donors to the Anti–Steel Trap League in May 1933, fifty-two were women: List of Donors, May 5, 1933, Denver Public Library, Rosalie Edge Papers, Box 291. Western representatives of the Western Federation of Animal Crusaders were women; the British representatives were a couple. The president, vice president, secretary-treasurer, and five of the eight directors of the Vivisection Investigation League were women, as were nine of the sixteen officers of the Anti–Steel Trap League; Wolfe to Edge, January 14 and May 27, 1939, Denver Public Library, Edge Papers, Box 292, FF86.

60. For "domestic irregularities" and suffrage charge, see J. Allen Wiley to Edge, February 23, 1933; for a "rich men's club," see pamphlet, Rosalie Edge, *Sportsmen's Heaven Is Hell for Ducks* (New York: Emergency Conservation Committee, 1938); for "Mr. Featherstone-haugh," see Rosalie Edge, "Killing Wholesale," in *Finishing the Mammals* (New York: ECC publication no. 59, 1936), 7. Denver Public Library, Rosalie Edge Papers, folder 16.

61. [Rosalie Edge], *Fighting the Good Fight* (New York: ECC, 1934), 2; Rosalie Edge, "What Is a Sanctuary?," *The Audubon Steel-Trapping Sanctuary* (New York: ECC, 1934), 1. Denver Public Library, Rosalie Edge Papers, folder 16.

62. For quote, see [Edge], *Fighting the Good Fight,* 2–7, Denver Public Library, Rosalie Edge Papers. Traditionally, little attention was accorded Edge; see Nash, *Rights of Nature;* Roderick Nash, *Wilderness and the American Mind,* 3rd ed. (New Haven: Yale University Press, 1982); Reiger, *American Sportsmen;* James B. Trefethen, *An American Crusade for Wildlife* (New York: Winchester Press, 1975). For Edge's attack on the Audubon Society, see Norwood, *Made from This Earth,* 158, 279–80; Thomas R. Dunlap, *Saving American Wildlife,* 94–96; and Graham, *Audubon Ark,* 107–29. On the Emergency Conservation Committee, see *Encyclopedia of American Forest History,* ed. Richard C. Davis (New York: Macmillan, 1983). For broad discussions of Edge, see Stephen Fox, *John Muir and His Legacy: The American Conservation Movement* (Boston: Little, Brown, 1981); and Polly Kaufman, *National Parks and the Woman's Voice: A History* (Albuquerque: University of New Mexico Press, 1996), 40–43. Clark Bainbridge, at the University of Idaho, is writing a dissertation on Edge.

63. The National Federation of Business and Professional Women's Clubs turned its attention to issues of labor, unemployment, taxation, health, and vocational guidance. "Resolutions Adopted at the Biennial Convention, Chicago, 1933," *Independent Women* 13, no. 8 (August 1934): 233.

64. Susan R. Schrepfer, "Establishing Administrative 'Standing': The Sierra Club and the Forest Service, 1897–1956," *Pacific Historical Review* 58, no. 1 (February 1989): 55–81.

65. S. B. Show, "Primitive Areas in the National Forests of California," *SCB* 18, no. 1 (February 1933): 29, 24–25, 30; Alfred Runte, *National Parks: The American Experience,* 2nd rev. ed (Lincoln: University of Nebraska Press, 1979).

66. Show, "Primitive Areas," 24–25. On primitive areas in the northern Cascades, see Hermann F. Ulrichs, "The Cascade Range in Northern Washington," *SCB* 22, no. 1 (February 1937): 78.

67. Earl Pomeroy, *In Search of the Golden West: The Tourist in Western America* (New York: Knopf, 1957), 157–58.

68. Paul Shriver Sutter, *Driven Wild: How the Fight Against Automobiles Launched the Modern Wilderness Movement* (Seattle: University of Washington Press, 2002).

69. "Minutes of the 1st Meeting of the Organizing Committee to Found the Wilderness Society," Washington, DC, January 20–22, 1935; "Meeting of the New York Members of the Wilderness Society," January 27, 1937; "Minutes of the Organizing Meeting," April 24, 1937, Denver Public Library, Wilderness Society Papers, Minutes.

70. Susan Flader, *Thinking Like a Mountain.*

71. Robert Sterling Yard, Report to Council, no. 2, October 8, 1937, Report to the Council, no. 3, March 1, 1938. Denver Public Library, Wilderness Society Papers, Minutes.

72. "Wilderness Areas and the Forest Service, a Step Forward in November, 1935," Denver Public Library, Wilderness Society Minutes. Entry, "Robert Marshall," in *Encyclopedia of American Forest History,* 702. Marshall attacked management of the primitive areas in *Nature, Scientific Monthly, Living Wilderness,* and the *Journal of Forestry.*

73. Nash, *Wilderness,* 2, 200–208, 220, 224.

74. E. Stanley Jones, "Sierra Club Officer and Los Angeles Chapter Leader, 1931–1975," oral history by Virginia Bennett (Sierra Club History Committee, 1976), 3–4.

75. The female-led Garden Club of America had a National Parks Committee and lobbied for the park. See Mrs. Robert C. Wright to Mrs. Duncan McDuffie, January 16, 1940, Save-the-Redwoods League Office, McDuffie Papers, San Francisco. For legislative history of the park, see Ise, *Our National Park Policy,* 402–3. In the long run, the wilderness status of Kings Canyon was compromised; the road was extended to Copper Creek and the Park Service resisted classifying the backcountry as wilderness under the 1964 Act.

76. In the Rockies, the classified areas included (among others) Cabinet Mountain, Mission Mountain, Pentagon and Sun River, Anaconda Pintler, the Idaho, the Sawtooth, and the Selway Bitterroot in Idaho and Montana. In the eastern Rockies were Spanish Peak, Absaroka, Beartooth, Cloud Peak, North Absaroka, South Absaroka, Teton, Bridger, Popo Agie, Stratified, and Glacier Peak. In Colorado were Mt. Zirkel–Dome Peak, Wilson Mountain, La Garita–Sheep Mountain, Mardon-Snowmass, Gore Range–Eagle Nest, Mt. Shavano, and the high valleys of San Juan and Upper Rio Grande. In the Southwest were the Black Range, White Mountain, Pecos Division, San Pedro Parks, Sycamore Canyon, Pine Mountain, Mazatzal, Superstition, Sierra Ancha, Mt. Baldy, and the upper Gila River watershed. Along the Pacific Coast, classified areas enfolded the peaks of the northern Cascades as well as Oregon's Mts. Jefferson and Hood, Three Sisters, Mountain Lakes, and Eagle Cap. In California, the designation areas spanned Marble Mountain, the Salmon-Trinity Alps, south through Desolation Valley, Emigrant Basin, Mount Dana and the Minarets, down the spine of the Sierra to the High Sierra Wilderness Area itself. In Southern California the areas classified included the mountainous San Raphael, Devils Canyon, Cucamonga, Agua Tibia, San Jacinto, and San Gorgonio (the highest peak in Southern California).

PART III. IN WILDNESS IS THE PRESERVATION OF THE NATION, AND THE WORLD, 1945–1964

1. David Brower, "Wilderness and Survival," Reed College, Portland, Oregon, March 16, 1959, Sierra Club Offices, San Francisco, Minute Books (hereafter SC, MB). See also David Brower, "A Conservationist's Questions About National Forests," U.S. Forest Service, Supervisors Meeting, Portland, Oregon, April 5, 1957, in SC, MB; David Brower, "Wilderness—Conflict and Conscience," *Sierra Club Bulletin* (hereafter *SCB*) 42, no. 6 (June 1957): 9.

2. Quotes from David R. Brower, "Environmental Activist, Publicist, and Prophet," oral history conducted by Susan R. Schrepfer, 1974–1978 (Berkeley: Regional Oral History Office, 1980), "free in the hills," 2, "there in the Sierra," 3, "not a manly thing," 7, and see also 1–14, 39–40; John McPhee, *Encounters with the Archdruid* (New York: Farrar, Strauss & Giroux, 1971), 27–28; Stephen Fox, *John Muir and His Legacy: The American Conservation Movement* (Boston: Little, Brown, 1981), 275.

3. Brower, "Environmental Activist," 1–10.

4. David Brower, "A Return to the Peaks," *Sierra* 77, no. 3 (May/June 1992): 91–95.

5. Brower, review of Richard L. Burdsall and Arthur B. Emmons 3rd, *Men Against the Clouds: The Conquest of Minya Konka* (New York: Harper & Brothers, 1935), in *SCB* 21, no. 1 (February 1936): 108.

6. Brower to Farquhar, October 29, December 10, 1935; Leonard to Brower, December 19, 1935; Voge to Brower, February 10, 1936, Bancroft Library, Brower Papers, carton 3.

7. Leonard to Farquhar, December 15, 1935, Bancroft Library, Brower Papers, carton 3.

8. Brower to Folks, October 20, 1936, June 28, 1937, Brower to R. J. Brower, July 1, 1936, Bancroft Library, Brower Papers, carton 3; Brower, "Environmental Activist," 8–9, 28, 19.

9. Brower, "Environmental Activist," 1–14, 35, 39–40; David Brower, *For Earth's Sake: The Life and Times of David Brower* (Salt Lake City: Peregrine Smith Books, 1990), 1–26; George Perkins Marsh, *Man and Nature: The Earth as Modified by Human Action* (New York: Scribner, Armstrong, 1864).

10. David Brower, "How to Kill a Wilderness," *SCB* 30, no. 4 (August 1945): 2.

11. Brower, "Environmental Activist," 192; Ron Eyerman and Andrew Jamison, *Social Movements: A Cognitive Approach* (University Park: Pennsylvania State University Press, 1991), 4–6.

12. My emphases on professionalism and issues of human survival within the environmental movement are somewhat at variance with the arguments of Samuel P. Hays: that this was a grassroots, consumer movement determined to protect amenities. Samuel P. Hays, *Beauty, Health, and Permanence: Environmental Politics in the United States, 1955-1985* (New York: Cambridge University Press, 1987), 1–40; see also Samuel P. Hays, *A History of Environmental Politics Since 1945* (Pittsburgh: University of Pittsburgh Press, 2000), 1–4.

CHAPTER 7. MOUNTAIN CONQUEST—FAMILY STYLE

1. Virginia Adams and Ansel Adams, *Michael and Ann in the Yosemite Valley* (New York: Studio Publications, 1941), 20–62; Harriet T. Parsons, "Yosemite for Children," *Sierra Club Bulletin* (hereafter *SCB*) 27, no. 4 (August 1942): 143.

2. Helen Dole and Alfred Dole, "A Children's Burro Trip," *SCB* 34, no. 6 (June 1949): 94; Richard M. Leonard, "Ancient Landscapes," *SCB* 34, no. 6 (June 1949): 86; David Brower, ed., photo by Richard Kaufman, text by John Muir, *Gentle Wilderness: The Sierra Nevada* (San Francisco: Sierra Club, 1967).

3. Margaret Thal-Larsen, "Hills of Home," *SCB* 39, no. 6 (June 1954): 57–59.

4. LeGrand Cannon Jr., *Look to the Mountain* (New York: Henry Holt, 1942), 541–42; Norman Bright, "A Soldier's Farewell to the Heights," *SCB* 29, no. 5 (October 1944): 36–39.

5. John D. Mendenhall, "The First Ascent of Mount Confederation," *SCB* 33, no. 3 (March 1948): 114; Leonard, "Ancient Landscapes," 86; for an emphasis on the search for "permanence" and the importance of the postwar period in the transformation of conservation into environmentalism, see Samuel P. Hays, *Beauty, Health, and Permanence: Environmental Politics in the United States, 1955-1985* (New York and Cambridge: Cambridge University Press, 1987).

6. "Mountain 'Conquest' . . . Family Style," *Sunset,* June 1956, 41.
7. John Ise, *Our National Park Policy: A Critical History* (Baltimore: Johns Hopkins University Press, 1961), 451–52; Carl Parcher Russell, *One Hundred Years in Yosemite* (Yosemite National Park, CA: Yosemite Association, 1992; reprint of 1922 and 1959 eds.), 113–14.
8. Adams to Newhall, 1943, in Ansel Adams, *Ansel Adams: Letters and Images, 1916-1984,* ed. Mary Street and Andrea Gray Stillman (New York: Little, Brown, 1988), 143.
9. Quote from Irving M. Clark, "Our Olympic Heritage and Its Defense," *Living Wilderness* 12, no. 21 (June 1947): 2–9; see also J. Ed Nelson, "The 1939 Climbing Season," *Mazama* 21, no. 12 (December 1939): 31.
10. These included the Izaac Walton League, the American Civic Association, the National Parks Association, the National Association of Audubon Societies, the Boone and Crockett Club, and the National Wildlife Federation.
11. Curt Meine, *Aldo Leopold: His Life and Work* (Madison: University of Wisconsin Press, 1988), 480; U.S. Forest Service, "Wilderness and Wild Areas," 1947, Bancroft Library, SC Papers, file 229.
12. McKaye to Council, May 25, 1947; Report, June 20, 1950, Denver Public Library, Western History and Genealogy, Wilderness Society Papers (hereafter DPL, WHG, WS).
13. Benton McKaye, "Restoring the 'Primitive,'" June 3, 1949, address to Wilderness Society Council, in Minutes, 1–3, DPL, WHG, WS; Frank Bernard, "Father of the Appalachian Trail, Benton McKaye," *Journal of Forestry* 45 (April 1947): 236–51.
14. Patricia Limerick, *The Legacy of Conquest: The Unbroken Past of the American West* (New York: Norton, 1987), 323–24.
15. Aldo Leopold, "Wilderness as a Form of Land Use," *Journal of Land and Public Utility Economics* 1, no. 3 (July 1925): 399.
16. Speech by Benton McKaye, Wilderness Society annual meeting, June 20, 1950, DPL, WHG, WS; Charles C. Bradley, "Wilderness and Man," *SCB* 37, no. 10 (December 1952): 59–67.
17. James Ramsey Ullman, *The Age of Mountaineering,* rev. ed. (Philadelphia: J. P. Lippincott, 1964), 320.
18. Aldo Leopold, "The Green Lagoons," *American Forests* 51, no. 8 (August 1945): 414; Aldo Leopold, *A Sand County Almanac and Sketches Here and There* (1949; reprint, London: Oxford University Press, 1968), vii–viii; Meine, *Aldo Leopold,* 484.
19. Leopold, *Sand County Almanac,* 20–22.
20. "Mount Katahdin Beckons You," *Appalachia,* n.s., 15, no. 7 (June 1949): inside cover; Howard Copenhaver, *They Left Their Tracks: Recollections of 60 Years as a Bob Marshall Wilderness Outfitter* (Montana: Stoneydale Press, 1990), 41–46; John D. Mendenhall, "First Ascent of Mount Confederation," 109–14.
21. Edward S. Deevey, "The Hare and the Haruspex: A Cautionary Tale," *SCB* 46, no. 8 (October 1961): 9.
22. Elaine Tyler May, *Homeward Bound: American Families in the Cold War Era* (New York: Basic Books, 1988), ix.
23. David W. Armstrong, "Recreation in a National Emergency," *Recreation* 45, no. 3 (June 1951): 125.
24. Articles from *Recreation:* John J. Collier, "Recreation in Our Changing Times," 52, no. 10 (December 1959): 414–16; "Plans Shape Up for 1959 Congress," 52, no. 6 (June 1959): 226; Warren W. Kershow, "Why Recreation?" 52, no. 2 (February 1959): 40; "Camping Services for Families: An Association," 52, no. 3 (March 1959): 97.

25. Caroline T. Finch, "The Children Loved Them," *SCB* 40, no. 8 (October 1955): 21–23; Lowell S. Nicholson, "A Family Outing," *Appalachia*, n.s., 15, no. 7 (June 1949): 346–50; Robert G. Orr, "Pack up the Kids and Go Camping," *Parents' Magazine* 31 (July 1956): 45, 47, 87–88; "What's Wrong with This Family?," *Better Homes and Gardens* 30 (July 1952): 16–17; "Family Camping," *Consumer Report* 21 (June 1956): 288–91, and 21 (August 1956): 370; Angus Taylor, "A California Family in the Alps," *SCB* 43, no. 9 (November 1958): 53–56; "Camping Services for Families," 97.

26. Helen Dole and Alfred Dole, "A Children's Burro Trip," 94; Finch, "The Children Loved Them," 21–23.

27. Quote from Catherine T. Hammett, "Camping: Its Part in National Defense," *Recreation* 45, no. 3 (June 1951): 158; on the postwar family, see May, *Homeward Bound*.

28. T. J. Jackson Lears, *Fables of Abundance: A Cultural History of Advertising in America* (New York: Basic Books, 1994), 246.

29. Orr, "Pack up the Kids," 45–47, 88.

30. Adams to Newhall, 1943, in Adams, *Ansel Adams*, 145; Joseph Prendergast, "The Past Is Prologue to the Future," *Recreation* 49, no. 1 (January 1956): 4–5.

31. M. J. Voigt, "The Burro and the Family," *SCB* 41, no. 3 (March 1956): 26; David R. Brower, ed., *Going Light—With Backpack or Burro* (1951; reprint, San Francisco: Sierra Club, 1960); "Family Camp at Mazamas Lodge," *Mazama* 47, no. 13 (July 22, 1955): 57–58.

32. Brower, *Going Light*, 102–3. Brower's children became committed to conservation. Roger Hildebrand retraced Whymper up the Matterhorn. Leopold's sons and daughters chose careers in the natural sciences and were active in conservation.

33. Joel Hildebrand, "Sierra Club Leader and Ski Mountaineer," oral history conducted by Ann Lage and Ray Lage (Sierra Club History Committee, 1974), 3–4.

34. Finch, "The Children Loved Them," 21–23; Helen Dole and Alfred Dole, "A Children's Burro Trip," 87–94.

35. Hildebrand, "Sierra Club Leader," 3–4.

36. Charles C. Bradley, "Wilderness and Man," 66.

37. Howard Zahniser, "The Need for Wilderness Areas," *National Parks Magazine* (October–December 1955): 161–66, 187–88; quote taken from 166.

38. "Dear Mom," *McCall's* 82 (July 1955): 16; R. E. Carlson, "Why Send Your Child to Camp?," *Parents' Magazine* 23 (May 1948): 31.

39. *Saturday Evening Post* (hereafter *SEP*) 219, no. 51 (June 21, 1947): cover.

40. Until 1931 the National Recreation Association had been the Playground Association of America. E. C. Mathew, "Camp Opens New Doors," *Hygeia* 25 (July 1947): 510–11; "Camp Fire Girls," *American Photography* 45 (March 1951): 174; "Dear Mom," 16.

41. Carlson, "Why Send Your Child to Camp?," 31, 115–17.

42. Ibid.; Hammett, "Camping: Its Part in National Defense," 158–60.

43. Howard Zahniser, quoting Robert Marshall, in "The Need for Wilderness Areas," 166, 187.

44. Frederick Jackson Turner, "The Significance of the Frontier in American History," in *Frontier and Section* (Englewood Cliffs, NJ: Prentice-Hall, 1961), 36–37. Reprint from American Historical Association, Annual Report for 1893, Washington, DC, 1894, 199–227; Mark Bassin, "Turner, Solov'ev, and the 'Frontier Hypothesis': The Nationalist Signification of Open Spaces," *Journal of Modern History* 65, no. 3 (September 1993): 473–511.

45. Minutes, Wilderness Society, June 3, 1949, 1–2. DPL, WHG, WS; Olaus J. Murie, "Wilderness," *Mazama* 35, no. 13 (December 1953): 38–40.

46. Gail Bederman, *Manliness and Civilization: A Cultural History of Gender and Race in the United States, 1880-1917* (Chicago: University of Chicago Press, 1995), 91-98.
47. Zahniser, "The Need for Wilderness Areas," 166, 187; Brower, *Going Light*, 1-4.
48. Brower, *Going Light*, 5-6.
49. Daniel H. Condit, "Babes in Sierra-Land," *SCB* 33, no. 3 (March 1948): 34-40.
50. Orr, "Pack up the Kids," 45-47, 87-88.
51. David R. Brower, foreword to Ansel Adams and Nancy Newhall, *This Is the American Earth* (1960; reprint, San Francisco: Sierra Club, 1971), xiii.
52. E. Harms, "Nature Study: Aid to Mental Health," *Nature Magazine* 46 (April 1953): 201-4.
53. Zahniser, "The Need for Wilderness Areas," 161, 165.
54. Rudolph W. J. Opperman, "Impressions of Recreation in America," *Recreation* 52, no. 2 (February 1959): 44-45. James Ramsey Ullman's popular novel *The White Tower* (New York: J. B. Lippincott, 1945) centers on the competition between a Nazi and an American for a peak.
55. From *Recreation*: Alexander Reid Martin, "Recreation . . . A Positive Force in Preventive Medicine," 52, no. 7 (September 1959): 265; "Plans Shape Up for 1959 Congress," 52, no. 6 (June 1959): 226; Rudolph W. J. Opperman, "Impressions of Recreation in America," pt. 2, 52, no. 3 (March 1959): 92-93.
56. From *Recreation*: August Heckscher, "The United States at Play in a World at Work," 51, no. 10 (December 1958): 341; Prendergast quoted William Russell of Columbia University: see Joseph Prendergast, "The Past Is Prologue to the Future," 4-5; Sigurd F. Olson, "The Intangible Values in Nature Protection," 48, no. 1 (January 1955): 4-5.
57. Zahniser, "The Need for Wilderness Areas," 163; Charles C. Bradley, "Wilderness and Man," 63-66.
58. Zahniser, "The Need for Wilderness Areas," 163.
59. *Rocky Mountain News* (July 13, 1948): 32, from Hugh Kingery and Elinor Eppich Kingery, *The Colorado Mountain Club* (Evergreen, CO: Cordillera Press, 1988), 50.
60. Pete Martin, "Every Girl for Herself!" *SEP* 223, no. 46 (May 21, 1951): 38-39, 133-36, 139-40.
61. Peter N. Stearns, "Girls, Boys, and Emotions: Redefinitions and Historical Change," *Journal of American History* 80, no. 1 (June 1993): 72-74.
62. In the 1940s and 1950s women published extensively in botany: Viola Brainerd Baird, *Wild Violets of North America* (Berkeley: University of California Press, 1942); Walter L. Huber, review by Roderick Peattie, ed., *The Sierra Nevada: The Range of Light* (New York: Vanguard Press, 1947), in *SCB* 33, no. 3 (March 1948): 131; H. G. Hird, "Two Ladies & a Lake," *Independent Woman* 33 (April 1954): 128-29; Mary Bowerman, *The Flowering Plants and Ferns of Mount Diablo, California; Their Distribution and Association into Plant Communities* (Berkeley: Gillick Press, 1944); Alice Eastwood, *A Collection of Popular Articles on the Flora of Mount Tamalpais* (San Francisco: California Academy of Sciences, 1944).
63. Glenda Riley, *Women and Nature: Saving the "Wild" West* (Lincoln: University of Nebraska Press, 1999), 171.
64. Marjory Farquhar, "Pioneer Woman Rock Climber and Sierra Club Director," oral history conducted by Ann Lage (Sierra Club History Committee, 1977): 35-39. Women serving on the SC board between 1943 and 1968 included: Mauk, 1943-1968; Parsons, 1943-1946; Farquhar, 1951-1955; and Polly Dyer, 1960-1967.
65. For Mauk's early work, see Mauk to Ada Fish, November 8, 1944, Bancroft Library, Mauk Papers, Outgoing Letters file; on her club work, see Nathan C. Clark, "Sierra Club

Leader, Outdoorsman, & Engineer," oral history conducted by Richard Searle (Sierra Club History Committee, 1977), 70.

66. The incident occurred in 1958; the club later retained a series of successful northwest representatives, including Michael McCloskey. See Polly Dyer, "Pacific Northwest Conservationist," oral history conducted by Susan R. Schrepfer, 1983 (Berkeley: Bancroft Oral History Office, 1986), 139–41. The Federation of Western Outdoor Clubs consisted of thirty-three member organizations in 1957.

67. Brower, *Going Light*, 5–7, 88–92.

68. "America's Interesting People: High Life," *American Magazine* 160, no. 5 (November 1955): 47.

69. Elizabeth S. Cowles, "Have You a Mountain Widow in Your Home?," *SCB* 34, no. 6 (June 1949): 17–21, reproduced in Brower, *Going Light*.

70. Monica Jackson and Elizabeth Stark, with foreword by Arlene Blum, *Tents in the Clouds: The First Women's Himalayan Expedition* (1956; Seattle: Seal Press, 2000).

71. Numa F. Vidal, "Who Climbed Mount McKinley?," *SEP* 222, no. 34 (February 18, 1950): 83; Mendenhall, "First Ascent of Mount Confederation," 109–14; on Barbara Washburn and other women climbers in the period, see Polly Kaufman, *National Parks and the Woman's Voice: A History* (Albuquerque: University of New Mexico Press, 1996), 126–28.

72. "High Trip, 1953," *SCB* 39, no. 6 (June 1954): 93–94; "Mountaineering Notes," *SCB* 40, no. 8 (October 1955): 79–81.

73. John D. Scott, *We Climb High: A Thumbnail Chronology of the Mazamas, 1894-1964* (Portland: Mazamas, 1969), 76–77.

74. The 1959 Himalayan expedition aroused public criticism as Claude Kogan and three others were lost; on this and other climbs in the 1950s, see Nea E. Morin, *A Woman's Reach: Mountaineering Memoirs* (New York: Dodd, Mead, 1968), 253–54.

75. Morin, *Woman's Reach*, 198, 253.

76. Morin, *Woman Reach*, 198; for original, see Samivel [Paul Gayet-Tancrède], *L'Amateur d'Abîmes* (Paris: Éditions Stock, Delamain et Boutelleau, 1940), 142. Samivel (1907–1992) was a French writer, artist, and explorer who supported the preservation of mountain wildernesses.

77. Morin, *Woman's Reach*, 205.

78. Allan Macdonald, "Realm of the Overhang," and "Editorial Comments," *SCB* 47, no. 9 (December 1962): 5–22.

79. Anton Nelson, "Climbing the Lost Arrow," *SCB* 32, no. 5 (May 1947): 1, 4–5, 9–10.

80. Samivel, *L'Amateur d'Abîmes*, 140.

81. Dee Molenaar, "St. Elias: The First American Ascent," *SCB* 32, no. 5 (May 1947): 63–70; Alfred W. Baxter Jr., "First Ascent to St. Elias Range," *SCB* 37, no. 10 (December 1952): 28. Baxter's team named 13,400-foot Mt. Jordan for Stanford's early president.

82. Alfred Baxter Jr., Fritz Lippman, Allen P. Steck, and Lawrence Swan, "The Himalayas Since the War," *SCB* 37, no. 10 (December 1952): 16.

83. Richard C. Houston and William Long, "The California Himalayan Expedition to Makalu," *SCB* 40, no. 8 (October 1955): 1–17.

84. Allen Steck, "Terror on Makalu," *SEP* 227, no. 46 (May 14, 1955): 32–33, 65–66, 70, 74, 76; Allen Steck, "Why Climb Mountains?," *SEP* 227, no. 46 (May 14, 1949); Houston and Long, "California Himalayan Expedition," 1–17; Vidal, "Who Climbed Mount McKinley?," 83; Richard K. Irvin, "American Andean Ascents, 1954," *SCB* 40, no. 8 (October 1955): 34–39.

85. Maurice Herzog, *Annapurna: First Conquest of an 8000-Meter Peak (26,493 Feet)* (New York: E. P. Dutton, 1953).

86. Sir John Hunt, *The Conquest of Everest with a Chapter on the Final Assault by Sir Edmund Hillary* (New York: E. P. Dutton, 1954), 1, 8, 3–6, 9; Ullman, *Age of Mountaineering*, 320.

87. Nepal Hunt, *Conquest of Everest*, 205–6; Hunt, "Why Climb Mountains?" *Rotarian* 85, no. 3 (September 1954): 28–30; Ullman, *Age of Mountaineering*, 293–94.

88. Minutes, Wilderness Society Council, June 3, 1949, and May 25, 1947; McKaye to Council, DPL, WHG, WS.

89. Benton McKaye, "Restoring the Primitive." McKaye cited Robert Marshall, "Problem of Wilderness," *Scientific Monthly* (February 1930).

90. Harold E. Perry, "Native Daughter," *SCB* 37, no. 10 (December 1952): 17–20; see also review by Ella Clark, "Indian Legends of the Pacific Northwest," *SCB* 39, no. 6 (June 1954): 103; Clifford V. Heimbucher, "Exploring Navajo Canyon," *SCB* 39, no. 6 (June 1954): 61–70.

91. John S. Duryea, "The Spiritual Values of the Wilderness," *SCB* 39, no. 6 (June 1954): 45–47; see also Erna Gunther, "The Indians of the Northwest," *Mountaineer* 46, no. 13 (December 15, 1953): 17–19.

92. Barbara Morgan, *Summer's Children* (Scarsdale, NY: Morgan & Morgan, 1951). In reviewing Morgan's book, Adams praised her for drawing a connection between wilderness and child development, see *SCB* (October 1953), 77–78.

93. Minutes, Wilderness Society Council 1947; McKaye to Council, May 25, 1947, DPL, WSP.

94. Margaret Murie, *Two in the Far North* (New York: Knopf, 1962).

95. On Sierra, see Lowell Sumner and Richard M. Leonard, "Protecting Mountain Meadows," *SCB* 32, no. 5 (May 1947): 53–62; on damage elsewhere, see Alfred Baxter Jr., Fritz Lippman, Allen P. Steck, and Lawrence Swan, "The Himalayas Since the War," 11; Alfred Baxter Jr., "First Ascent to St. Elias Range," 21.

CHAPTER 8. MOUNTAINS MADE WILDERNESS

1. Richard E. McArdle, "The Concept of Multiple Use of Forest and Associated Lands—Its Values and Limitations," Fifth World Forestry Congress, Seattle, August 29–September 10, 1960 (Seattle: University of Washington Press, 1962), 143–45; copy at University of California, Berkeley, Bancroft Library, Brower Papers, carton 13.

2. Sierra Club, *Outdoor Newsletter* 1, no. 6 (August 22, 1960), [6]. Durham, North Carolina, Forest History Society, Society of American Foresters Papers.

3. Adams to N. Clark, June 27, 1959, Bancroft Library, Sierra Club (hereafter SC) Papers, Charlotte Mauk files; Brower to SC, Board of Directors, October 12, 1960, McArdle to N. Clark, October 28, 1960, Brower to N. Clark, November 28, 1960, Bancroft Library, Sierra Club Papers, Brower Papers, carton 19; David Brower, "How Bold Shall We Be?," December 5, 1959, transcript, Sierra Club Office, San Francisco, Minute Books (hereafter SC, MB).

4. Adam Rome, "'Give Earth a Chance': The Environmental Movement and the Sixties," *Journal of American History* 90, no. 2 (September 2003): 3.

5. Wallace Stegner letter, reprinted in Stewart L. Udall, "Conservation and the 1960s," first published in David Brower, ed., *Wilderness: America's Living Heritage* (San Francisco: Sierra Club, 1961), reprinted in William Schwartz, ed., *Voices for the Wilderness* (New York: Ballantine Books, 1969), 283.

6. Stephen Fox described the club under Brower as swooping "in from the west" to become the "focal point of modern American conservation"; see Stephen R. Fox, *John Muir and His Legacy: The American Conservation Movement* (Boston: Little, Brown, 1981), 272, 281. William Devall writes: "Brower's commitment to environmentalism drew

him ahead of his fellow leaders." William Devall, "David Brower," *Environmental Review* 9, no. 3 (1985): 239. For Brower as a "troublemaker," see Michael P. Cohen, *The History of the Sierra Club, 1892-1970* (San Francisco: Sierra Club Books, 1988), 250. On 1950s activism, see Mark W. T. Harvey, *A Symbol of Wilderness: Echo Park and the American Conservation Movement* (Albuquerque: University of New Mexico Press, 1994), 287–301; David De Leon, *Everything is Changing: Contemporary U.S. Movements in Historical Perspective* (New York: Praeger, 1988), 143.

7. Arthur Brittan, *Masculinity and Power* (Oxford: Basil Blackwell, 1989), 1–2.

8. David R. Simons, "These Are the Shining Mountains," *Sierra Club Bulletin* (hereafter *SCB*) 44, no. 7 (October 1959): 1–13.

9. Brower, "The Sierra Club: National, Regional, or State," address to directors, Minutes, May 3, 1952, Bancroft Library, SC Papers; "New Chapter," *SCB* 39, no. 10 (December 1954): 12.

10. Harold E. Crowe, "Announcement from the President," *SCB* 38, no. 1 (January 1953): 3–4.

11. David Brower, "Tour of Duty," *SCB* 38 no. 4 (April 1953): 4; Leonard Grant to Brower, July 28, 1953, Bancroft Library, SC Papers—Brower files, box 204.

12. Roderick Nash, *Wilderness and the American Mind*, rev. ed. (New Haven: Yale University Press, 1973), 209–17; Cohen, *History of the Sierra Club*, 160.

13. On the meeting at the Leonard house, see Cicely M. Christy, "Contributions to the Sierra Club and the San Francisco Bay Chapter, 1938–1970s," oral history conducted by Ann Lage and Ray Lage (Sierra Club History Committee, 1982), 19–20; see also Kathleen Goddard Jones, "Defender of California's Nipomo Dunes," oral history conducted by Anne Van Tyne (Sierra Club History Committee, 1984), 8.

14. Brower, "Preserving the National Monument Without Impairment," Statement on Upper Colorado River Storage Project, Committee on Interior and Insular Affairs, House of Representatives, Washington, DC, January 18, 1954, and following days, Bancroft Library, SC Papers, box 175; David R. Brower, "Preserving Dinosaur Unimpaired," *SCB* 39, no. 6 (June 1954): 7; Zahniser to Leonard, January 29, 1954, Bancroft Library, Wayburn Papers, box 1; Harvey, *Symbol*, 191–96.

15. Quote from David R. Brower, "Environmental Activist, Publicist, and Prophet," oral history conducted by Susan R. Schrepfer (Berkeley: Regional Oral History Office, Bancroft Library, 1980), 133, see also 118–23; "Dinosaur Bill Out of Committee," *SCB* 39, no. 5 (May 1954): 3–4; Bernard DeVoto, "And Fractions Drive Me Mad," *Harpers* 209 (September 1954): 10–11; David R. Brower, "Dinosaur: Hour of Decision," *SCB* 40, no. 5 (May 1955): 3; David R. Brower, "Dinosaurs, Parks, and Dams," *Pacific Spectator* 8 (spring 1954): 158; Harvey, *Symbol*, 287–301.

16. Brower to the *Denver Post*, February 16, 1954; Sierra Club Press Release, January 27, 1954, Bancroft Library, SC Papers, box 175; Brower, "Preserving the National Monument," 1–10; Brower to McKay, January 26, May 20, and July 7, 1955, SC, MB; Sierra Club, "Upper Colorado Controversy: Sound Development and Unimpaired Parks—A Way to Have Both," 7 June 20, 1955, Bancroft Library, Brower Papers, carton 6; Harvey, *Symbol*, 271.

17. Minutes, SC, Executive Committee, June 25, 1955. Bancroft Library, SC Papers; Richard M. Leonard, "Mountaineer, Lawyer, Environmentalist," oral history conducted by Susan R. Schrepfer (Berkeley: Regional Oral History Office, Bancroft Library, 1975), 49; Harvey, *Symbol*, 153–58; Fox, *John Muir*, 286.

18. Susan R. Schrepfer, "Establishing Administrative 'Standing': The Sierra Club and the Forest Service, 1897–1956," *Pacific Historical Review* (1988): 66–67; on Three Sisters, SC, Board of Directors, Minutes, May 3, 1952, February 27, 1954.

19. George Van Dusen, "Politics of Partnership: The Eisenhower Administration and Conservation, 1952–1960" (PhD diss., Loyola University, 1974), 24–32, 228–30, 253, 286–91; Donald Cate, "Recreation and the U.S. Forest Service: A Study of Organizational Response to Changing Demands" (PhD diss., Stanford University, 1963), 32.

20. James P. Gilligan, "The Contradiction of Wilderness Preservation in a Democracy," Society of American Foresters, October 26, 1954, in *Congressional Record*, 84th Cong., 2d sess., July 11, 1956; James P. Gilligan, "The Development of Policy and Administration of Forest Service Primitive and Wilderness Areas in the Western United States" (PhD diss., University of Michigan, 1954); Brower, "Environmental Activist," 87; Sierra Club, Fact Sheet, April 17, 1957, SC, MB.

21. McArdle to Brower, November 8, 1955, SC, MB; "Gross Acreage in the National Wilderness Preservation System by Areas and Categories," July 1957, Bancroft Library, SC Papers, box 219.

22. SC, Board of Directors, February 4, 1950; Brower, "The Meaning of Wilderness to Recreation," 41st National Recreation Congress, October 1, 1959, Chicago, Bancroft Library, Brower Papers, carton 1.

23. Brower, "Statement on Timber Access Roads and the Timber Resources Review," to Joint Congressional Committee on Federal Timber, Redding, CA, November 14, 1955, Bancroft Library, SC Papers—Art Blake files, box 112.

24. Hubert Humphrey to A. Hildebrand, March 29, 1956, Bancroft Library, SC Papers—Wilderness Bills; *Congressional Record*, Sen., 84th Cong., 2d sess., June 7 and July 11, 1956.

25. U.S. Forest Service, Pacific Northwest Region, "Glacier Peak Land Management Study," February 7, 1957.

26. Brower to Wesley D'Ewart, July 24, 1956, Bancroft Library, SC—Arthur Blake, box 112; SC, Board of Directors, Minutes, October 15, 1955; SC, Conservation Committee, Minutes, September 13, 1956; Wayburn-Stone correspondence, February 24 and March 15, 1956, Bancroft Library, SC Papers; Brower, "Will We Discover the Northern Cascades in Time?," *SCB* 42, no. 6 (June 1957): 13–15; SC, Board of Directors, Minutes, July 4–5, 1957; Brower, "Your Wilderness!," *SCB* 43, no. 6 (June 1958): 3–4; Brower, "Wilderness in the Conservation Movement," Theodore Roosevelt Conservation Conference, October 2, 1958, Denver, Bancroft Library, Brower Papers, carton 1.

27. For "perpetual snow," see SC, Fact Sheet, April 17, 1957, SC, MB; for "Rorschach blot," see Simons, "These Are the Shining Mountains," 11–12, SC, MB; for "symphony," see Brower, "Wilderness and Survival," March 16, 1959; David Brower, "Crisis in the North Cascades: The Missing Millions," *SCB* 44, no. 2 (February 1959): 15; see also *Friends of Three Sisters Wilderness Bulletin* 15 (March 7, 1961), University of Washington, Brock Evans Papers, carton 17; Brower, "Environmental Activist," 94–96; Brower to Executive Committee, SC, December 14, 1960, SC, MB.

28. "For ourselves," from Brower, "Glacier Peak Wilderness Proposal of Mountaineers is Commended: Region 6 Proposal for the Area is Considered Inadequate," testimony, October 16, 1959, Bancroft Library, SC—Litton Papers, box 137; "medicine men," from Brower, "How Bold Should We Be?"

29. Brower to Farquhar, July 23, 1958, Bancroft Library, Brower Papers, carton 17; Brower, "Wilderness and Survival," March 16, 1959; on specialization, see Paul A. Carter, *Another Part of the Fifties* (New York: Columbia University Press, 1983), 92–94.

30. Brower to Farquhar, July 23, 1958, SC, MB; David Brower, "A Conservationist's Questions About National Forests," U.S. Forest Service, Supervisors Meeting, Portland, Oregon, April 5, 1957, SC, MB; David Brower, "Scenic Resources and the American Conscience," introductory remarks at Fifth Biennial Wilderness Conference, in San

Francisco, March 15, 1957, Bancroft Library, SC Papers, box 199; David Brower, "Wilderness—Conflict and Conscience," *SCB* 42, no. 6 (June 1957): 9; Brower, "Sierra Roads and the Sierra Wilderness," Statement Before Meeting of Fresno and Madera County Supervisors, Fresno, April 20, 1956, Bancroft Library, SC—Bradley Papers, box 116.

31. Minutes, Executive Committee, Sierra Club, November 14, 1953, May 22, 1954, November 20, 1955; September 18–19, 1956, January 1957, Bancroft Library, SC Papers, Board of Directors files; Brower, "Conservationist's Questions"; Brower, "The Resolution of Conflicts," Fifth Biennial Wilderness Conference, San Francisco, March 15, 1957, Bancroft Library, SC Papers, box 199; Brower, "Wilderness in the Conservation Movement."

32. For example, in 1953 he addressed the National Geographic Society; see Grant to Brower, July 28, 1953; in 1955, the Associated Sportsmen of California, see Difani to Brower, August 2, 1955; and in 1957, the Council of Churches and a Water Resources Conference in Missoula, see Warrant to Brower, March 26, 1958. In 1958 Brower also spoke to the City Club of Portland, Theodore Roosevelt Conservation Conference in Denver, Associated Society of Agricultural Engineers, Montana Conservation Council in Butte, and Forestry Club at Oregon State College School of Forestry. See W. Berry to Brower, March 11, 1958; Cooney to Brower, April 30, 1958; Hornick to Brower, May 13, 1958; Peters to Brower, October 21, 1958. In 1959 he addressed, among others, the Wildlife Management Institute in New York and Reed College. Bancroft Library, Brower Papers, box 204.

33. Cyril Northcote Parkinson, *The Evolution of Political Thought* (Boston: Houghton Mifflin, 1958); Cyril Northcote Parkinson, *Parkinson's Law and Other Studies in Administration* (Boston: Houghton Mifflin, 1957); Brower, "How Bold Shall We Be?"; Herbert Kaufman, *The Forest Ranger: A Study in Administrative Behavior* (1960; reprint, Baltimore: Johns Hopkins University Press, 1986), 4–5, 207–9, 231–32.

34. Brower, "Wilderness and Survival," March 16, 1959; Vance Packard, *The Hidden Persuaders* (New York: Pocket Books, 1957). See illustrations in Alex Calhoun, "Must Logging Destroy Streams," *SCB* 47, no. 9 (December 1962): 60–64.

35. Proceedings of the 8th Wilderness Conference, printed in François Leydet, ed., *Tomorrow's Wilderness* (San Francisco: Sierra Club, 1963), [36–48].

36. Brower, "Wilderness in the Conservation Movement."

37. David Brower, "How Bold Shall We Be?"; David Brower, "The Citizen Acts—As Lobbyist," 66th National Conference on Government, Phoenix, November 15, 1960, Bancroft Library, Brower Papers, carton 1; see also SC, Board of Directors, December 5–6, 1959; Leonard, "Mountaineer," 342–43; Brower, "Environmental Activist," 90.

38. Brower, "How Bold Shall We Be?" Brower quoted Russell Lynes, "Time on Our Hands," *Harpers* 217, no. 1298 (July 1958): 34–39; for references to Riesman and Galbraith, see Brower, "Wilderness and Survival," Harvard Travellers Club, Boston, May 20, 1958, Brower to Farquhar, July 23, 1958, SC, MB; John Kenneth Galbraith, *The Affluent Society* (New York: New American Library, 1958); Brower, "Preserving the Dinosaur National Monument without Impairment," January 18, 1954.

39. Brower, "Wilderness—Conflict and Conscience," *SCB* 42, no. 6 (June, 1957): 6, 12, 23; Brower, "Resolution of Conflicts."

40. Brower, "Reply: Wilderness Needs an Automatic Stay of Invasion," *SCB* 44, no. 1 (January 1959): 12; "Sierra Club Policy and Standards for National Park and Other Scenic Roads," *SCB* 45, no. 9 (December 1960): 59; Brower, "Wilderness in the Conservation Movement."

41. Brower to N. Clark, August 14, 1959, Bancroft Library, SC Papers—Bradley files, box 116; Donald C. Swain, *Wilderness Defender: Horace M. Albright and Conservation* (Chicago: University of Chicago Press, 1970), 42–43, 56–58, 123.

42. Quote from Conrad Wirth, *Parks, Politics, and the People* (Norman: University of Oklahoma Press, 1980), 359; David Perlman, "Mission 66: Parks' 10-Year Plan," *SCB* 42, no. 1 (January 1957): 12; David Brower with Howard Zahniser, "Wilderness Is Where You *Keep* It," *SCB* 42, no. 1 (January 1957): 4.

43. Adams to N. Clark, June 27, 1959, Bancroft Library, SC Papers—Mauk files, Box 144; Ansel Adams, "Tenaya Tragedy," *SCB* 43, no. 9 (November 1958): 1–4. See also Alfred Runte, *National Parks: The American Experience* (Lincoln: University of Nebraska Press, 1979), 173. For photographs of construction, see Yosemite Park Service, Museum Archives, Tioga Road files.

44. Brower to SC, Board of Directors, January 14, 1959, SC, MB; Leonard, "Mountaineer," 342; Brower, "Environmental Activist," 54–55, 58; Brower to N. Clark, August 14, 1959, Bancroft Library, SC Papers—Bradley files, box 114; "Sierra Club Policy and Standards for National Parks and other Scenic Roads," *SCB* 45, no. 9 (December 1960): 57.

45. On early controversies, see Schrepfer, "Establishing Administrative 'Standing,'" 55–81; on logging in the Sierra, see Timothy P. Duane, *Shaping the Sierra: Nature, Culture, and Conflict in the Changing West* (Berkeley: University of California Press, 1999).

46. U.S. Forest Service, "Resource Management Plan, Kern Plateau," 1956; David Brower, ed., photographs by Richard Kaufman, text by John Muir, *Gentle Wilderness: The Sierra Nevada* (San Francisco: Sierra Club, 1967); Martin Litton, "Sierra Club Director and Uncompromising Preservationist, 1950s–1970s," oral history conducted by Ann Lage (Berkeley: Regional Oral History Office, Bancroft Library, 1983), 11.

47. Wayburn to Connaughton, June 19, 1956, SC, MB; Brower, "Conservationist's Questions"; SC, Board of Directors, May 3, 1958.

48. U.S. Forest Service, "Recreation Plan for the Kern Plateau," 1959; Richard McArdle to Clair Engle, July 31, 1959, Eldon E. Ball to Newell Charde, August 7, 1959, Bancroft Library, SC Papers—Kern files.

49. Brower, diary, June 11–12, 1960, Bancroft Library Brower Papers, carton 3; Brower, "Los Angeles Kern Plateau Trip Sets Records," *Southern Sierran* (June 14, 1960): 1–2; Sierra Club, *Outdoor Newsletter* 1, no. 6 (August 22, 1960); Brower to Executive Committee, SC, December 14, 1960, Bancroft Library, SC Papers—Bob Golden files, box 136; Brower, "Wilderness and Survival," March 16, 1959; Brower, "Conservationist's Questions."

50. Brower, "Meaning of Wilderness to Recreation"; Brower, "Wilderness in the Conservation Movement"; Brower, "Wilderness—Conflict and Conscience," *SCB* (1957), 1; Brower, "Primitive and Wild Areas in Relation to Public Works," June 23, 1958, American Society for Agricultural Engineers, Santa Barbara, SC, MB; Brower, "Wilderness and Survival," March 16, 1959, and May 20, 1958; David Brower, "How Dense Should People Be?," *SCB* 44, no. 4 (April 1959): 12–13.

51. Brower, "Wilderness and Survival," March 16, 1959; Brower, "The Citizen Acts—As Lobbyist"; Brower, "How Dense," 12–13.

52. "Malthusian," from Brower, "Wilderness and Survival," May 20, 1958; "rivalry," from Brower, "Meaning of Wilderness to Recreation"; Brower, "Wilderness and Survival," March 16, 1959; "blind," from Brower, "How Dense," 13.

53. *San Francisco Chronicle*, "How to Survive the Onslaught of Peace?," September 25, 1959; for liberal response to the visit, see Richard H. Pells, *The Liberal Mind in a Conservative Age: American Intellectuals in the 1940s and 1950s* (Middletown, CT: Wesleyan University Press, 1989), 349.

54. Bertrand Russell, *In Praise of Idleness and Other Essays* (New York: Norton, 1935); Brower, "Meaning of Wilderness to Recreation"; Brower, "How Dense," 12–13.

55. "Sierra Club Population Policy," SCB 50, no. 4 (April 1965): 11; "Further Comments on the Question of Expanding Population," *SCB* 44, no. 6 (September 1959): 4–6; Brower, "How Dense," 12–13; Thomas R. Vale, ed., *Progress Against Growth: Daniel B. Luten on the American Landscape* (New York: Guilford Press, 1986), 7; Huxley to Brower, May 20, 1959, Mumford to Brower, May 19, 1959, Lowell Sumner to Brower, May 18, 1959, SC, MB; Brower, "Meaning of Wilderness to Recreation"; Brower, "Wilderness and Survival," May 20, 1958.

56. Phoebe Anne Sumner, "The Last Citadel," *SCB* 35, no. 6 (June 1950): 77.

57. Lowell Sumner and Richard M. Leonard, "Protecting Mountain Meadows," *SCB* 32, no. 5 (May 1947): 53–62.

58. Brower, "Wilderness and Survival," March 16, 1959; Brower, "Reply," 12; Brower, "The Citizen Acts—As Lobbyist"; Brower, "Wilderness and Survival," May 20, 1958.

59. Robert Marshall, "The Problem of the Wilderness," *SCB* 32, no. 5 (May 1947): 42–46. Reprinted from *Scientific American*, February 1930.

60. Brower, "The Real Cost of the Oversold Mammoth Roads," in Brower to Chester Warlow, June 16, 1958, Bancroft Library, SC—Brower files, carton 17.

61. Brower, "Wilderness and Survival," March 16, 1959; Brower, "Primitive and Wild Areas"; Brower, "Meaning of Wilderness to Recreation"; Brower, "The Citizen Acts—As Lobbyist"; Brower, "Reply," 12.

62. Paul Sears, "On Coming to Terms with Our Environment," *SCB* 44, no. 7 (October 1959): 43, 37–42.

63. Ansel Adams and Nancy Newhall, *This Is the American Earth* (San Francisco: Sierra Club, 1960), 32, 35, 44, 36–40, 62, iii.

64. Ibid.; Brower to Executive Committee, December 14, 1960; Brower, "Angeles Kern Plateau Trip Sets Record," 1–2.

65. On the use of academic work in the conservation movement, see Ben W. Twight, *Organizational Values and Political Power: The Forest Service versus the Olympic National Park* (University Park: Pennsylvania State University Press, 1983), 108–9.

66. "Sierra Club—Confidential Draft Only," [February 16, 1955]; Brower, "Wilderness and Survival," March 16, 1959; William H. Whyte Jr., *The Organization Man* (New York: Simon and Schuster, 1956).

67. Brower, "Environmental Activist," 81; Brower to Murray, April 29, 1960, Bancroft Library, SC Papers—Flannery files, box 124; Brower, Diary, May 21–22, 1960, Bancroft Library, Brower Papers, carton 6; for evidence Brower cited Kaufman, *Forest Ranger*, 4–5, 91, 126, 165–66, 182, 207, 209, 231–32.

68. Brower to W. F. McCullock, May 17, 1956, to McArdle, May 17, 1956, to A. L. Strand, May 17, 1956, SC, MB; Brower to Clair Engle, March 7, 1957, Bancroft Library, SC Papers, box 229; N. Clark to Henry Vaux, December 29, 1960, Bancroft Library, SC Papers—Brower files, box 19; Brower, "Confidential memo to 28 individuals including Horace Albright, Colby, Drury, Gabrielson, Gutermuth, Krutch, Luna Leopold, and Olaus Murie," June 3, 1960, Bancroft Library, SC—Brower files, box 13.

69. Brower to Murray, April 29, 1960; Sierra Club, *Outdoor Newsletter*, 1, no. 6 (August 22, 1960); Sierra Club, Press Release, "Sierra Club Urges Field Hearings for 'Multiple Use' Forest Bill," May 13, 1960, Bancroft Library, SC Papers—Brower files, box 13; Grant McConnell, "The Multiple Use Concept in Forest Service Policy," *SCB* 44, no. 7 (October 1959): 24 (also reprinted by SC, no. 3, 1960, Bancroft Library, SC Papers, Bradley files, box 4); Gilligan, "The Development of Policy," 282.

70. Brower quoted Stegner, cited John Ise, *The United States Forest Policy* (New Haven: Yale

University Press, 1920), and cited L. F. Cronemiller, "State Forestry in Oregon" (MA thesis, Oregon State College, 1936). See Brower to Murray, April 29, 1960; Brower, "Wilderness and Survival," March 16, 1959; McConnell, "Multiple Use Concept," 14–28.

71. Brower to Murray, April 29, 1960; Brower's annotations on McArdle to Clark, October 28, 1960, in Bancroft Library, Brower Papers, carton 1; Brower, "Environmental Activist," 66, 81; Brower, "Wilderness and Survival," March 16, 1959; Brower, "Conservationist's Questions." Brower used a quotation from Kenneth G. Crawford, *The Pressure Boys: The Inside Story of Lobbying in America* (New York: J. Messner, 1939), 199; Brower, "Beware of Multiple-Usemanship!," *SCB* 43, no. 4 (April 1958): 5–6.

72. Grant McConnell, "Multiple Use Concept," 28.

73. Brower to Murray, April 29, 1960; SC, Press Release, May 13, 1960; SC, Board of Directors Minutes, September 17 and October 15, 1960; Clark to Murray, May 11, 1960.

74. Brower, "Needed—A Credo for Leadership," speech in Diary 1961. Bancroft Library, Brower Papers, carton 1; Brower, "Suggested Points for Consideration, Meeting with Dr. Selke," June 6, 1961, Bancroft Library, Brower Papers, carton 19; "Sierra Club Exhibits," *SCB* 44, no. 2 (February 1959), 6; Brower, "Confidential Memo to 28 Individuals."

75. Quote from marginal notes by David Brower and Polly Dyer on McArdle, "Concept of Multiple Use." See also Brower, "Confidential memo to 28 individuals," June 3, 1960; Brower, "Wilderness and Survival," May 16, 1959.

76. Sierra Club, *Outdoor Newsletter* 1, no. 6 (August 22, 1960); Clepper to Clark, November 18, 1960, Durham, N.C., Forest History Society, Society of American Foresters, box 160; Brower to SC Board of Directors, October 12, 1960; Brower to Clark, November 25, 1960, Brower to Clepper, November 28, 1960, Bancroft Library, SC Papers—Brower files, carton 19.

77. Clark to Clepper, November 21, 1960, Durham, NC, Forest History Society, Society of American Foresters, box 160.

78. Samuel P. Hays, *Beauty, Health, and Permanence: Environmental Politics in the United States, 1955-1985* (New York: Cambridge University Press, 1987), 1–40; see also Samuel P. Hays, *A History of Environmental Politics Since 1945* (Pittsburgh: University of Pittsburgh Press, 2000).

79. Between 1947 and 1952 the Sierra Club's membership increased at an average annual rate of 4.3 percent; by the late 1950s the annual rate of increase was 10 percent. There were 10,000 members in 1956, and 13,500 by 1959.

80. Ron Eyerman and Andrew Jamison, *Social Movements: A Cognitive Approach* (University Park: Pennsylvania State University Press, 1991), 4–6; Brower to Executive Board, SC, October 12, 1960, SC, MB.

81. SC, Executive Committee, May 6, 1951, June 27, 1946, Bancroft Library, SC Papers.

82. Editorial, *Christian Science Monitor*, December 3, 1960. Petition was defeated, 6,724 to 1,108. Minutes, SC, Board of Directors, October 10, 1960; Ballot of November 15, 1960, University of Washington, Library, Pauline Dyer Papers, box 3. For a copy of the "Proposed Loyalty Oath for Sierra Club Membership, 1960," with related correspondence, see appendices to Thomas Amneus, "New Directions for the Sierra Club Los Angeles Chapter," oral history conducted by Eric Redd (Sierra Club History Committee, 1977), 34–35.

83. Brower, "Needed—A Credo for Leadership." On public opinion, see "As We Go To Press," *Recreation* (September 1963): 303.

84. Quote from John Kenneth Galbraith, *Affluent Society* (1971 ed.), 4–5; on the 1950s, see Pells, *Liberal Mind*, 346, 165–74, 187, 142; William O'Neill, *American High: The Years of*

Confidence, 1945-1960 (New York: Free Press, 1986), 24-27; Brower, "Wilderness and Survival," March 16, 1959, Reed College, Portland, SC, MB.

85. John McCormick, *Reclaiming Paradise, The Global Environmental Movement* (Bloomington: Indiana University Press, 1989), 46, 48, 55; Rome, "Give Earth a Chance," 1-33.

86. Brower, "Conservationist's Questions"; Brower, "Wilderness—Conflict and Conscience," *SCB* (1957), 9; Brower, "Wilderness and Survival," March 16, 1959. On postwar liberals in general, see Pells, *Liberal Mind*, 237.

87. "Issues" quote from Brower, "A Balanced Program for Conservation and Natural Resources," Remarks before Democratic National Committee, Denver, May 27, 1960, Bancroft Library, SC Papers—Brower speeches; "Kids" quote from Brower, "The Citizen Acts—As Lobbyist." For invitation to speak, see Paul Butler, Democratic National Committee, to Brower, May 17, 1960, Bancroft Library, Brower Papers, carton 204.

88. That November, Brower talked with Udall in Phoenix, see Brower diary, November 5, 1960, Bancroft Library, Brower Papers, box 6, vol. 20; Brower to Udall, January 13, 1961, University of Arizona, Tucson, Udall Papers, Boxes 190-94. At the cabinet meeting on January 1, Udall expressed interest in new national seashores and the wilderness bill. See Udall to the President, May 19, 1961, John F. Kennedy Library, box 641.

89. Brower to Frank Masland, February 26, 1961, Bancroft Library, SC Papers—Brower files, box 19; "Sierra Club Policy and Standards for National Parks and Other Roads," *SCB* 45, no. 9 (December 1960): 59.

90. Brower, "Meaning of Wilderness to Recreation"; Brower, "The Citizen Acts—As Lobbyist"; Brower to Clark, August 14, 1959.

91. Rome, "Give Earth a Chance," 12-16.

92. Polly Dyer, "Pacific Northwest Conservationist," oral history conducted by Susan R. Schrepfer, 1983 (Berkeley: Regional Oral History Office, Bancroft Library, 1986), 9, 139-40; on women separating into organizations run by women, see Polly Welts Kaufman, *National Parks and the Woman's Voice* (Albuquerque: University of New Mexico Press, 1996), 36-40; see also Mary Joy Breton, *Women Pioneers for the Environment* (Boston: Northeastern University Press, 1998), 173-78. For Club's inclusion of women, see Royal Robbins, "Wyoming's Range of Light," *SCB* 49, no. 9 (December 1964): 80.

93. Quote from Cicely M. Christy, "Contributions to the Sierra Club," 33-36; see also Marjory Bridge Farquhar, "Pioneer Woman Rock Climber and Sierra Club Director," oral history conducted by Ann Lage and Ray Lage (Sierra Club History Committee, 1977), 50-54; Ethel Rose Taylor Horsfall, "On the Trail with the Sierra Club, 1920s-1960s," oral history conducted by George Baranowski (Sierra Club History Committee, 1982), 14; Harriet T. Parsons, "A Half-Century of Sierra Club Involvement," oral history conducted by Ann Lage (Sierra Club History Committee, 1981).

94. Rome, "Give Earth a Chance," 14.

95. "The Silent Spring of Rachel Carson" and Clarence Cottam, "The Gentle Scholar," *SCB* 49, no. 4 (May 1964): 6-7.

96. Also in 1964 Congress established the Land and Water Conservation Fund and debated measures that later became law to protect wild rivers, to establish a Youth Corps, to create the Bureau of Outdoor Recreation, to undertake a nationwide Outdoor Recreation Resources Review, and to establish, among other parks, a Cascades and a Redwood National Park.

97. "Establish a National Wilderness Preservation System," Conference Report No. 1829, 88th Congress, 2d sess., August 19, 1964. Act signed into law on September 3, 1964, PL 88-577, 78 Stat. 890.

98. Dyer, "Pacific Northwest Conservationist," 89.

99. Ashley Montagu, "Wilderness and Humanity," in *Wilderness in a Changing World*, ed. Bruce M. Kilgore (San Francisco: Sierra Club, 1966), 226.

100. William Schwartz, *Voices*, 116.

101. Sigurd F. Olson, "The Spiritual Need," in *Wilderness in a Changing World*, ed. Bruce M. Kilgore (San Francisco: Sierra Club, 1966), 218–19.

102. Brower, "Wilderness—Conflict and Conscience," from *Wildlands in Our Civilization* (San Francisco: Sierra Club, 1964), 52.

103. Quotes from Paul Brooks, "Wilderness in Western Culture," in François Leydet, *Tomorrow's Wilderness*, 84, 87; for other references to romantic literature, see Schwartz, *Voices*, 38, 41, 51, 127–28, 130, 162; Ashley Montagu, "Wilderness and Humanity," 224–27.

104. Schwartz, *Voices*, 86.

105. Quote from A. Starker Leopold, in "A Vignette of Primitive America," *SCB* 48, no. 3 (March 1963): 11.

106. Schwartz, *Voices*, 140.

107. Ibid., 91.

108. Ibid., 141.

109. Quote from Steven Marts, "Rock!" *SCB* 55, no. 7 (July 1970): 7; on club trips, see Genny Schumacher, "Sierra Club Outings, 1957–1967," *SCB* 52, no. 10 (November 1967): 13.

110. Gerald Piel, "Wilderness and the American Dream," in *Wilderness: America's Living Heritage*, ed. David Brower (San Francisco, Sierra Club, 1961), reprinted in Schwartz, *Voices*, 47.

111. George Marshall, "Howard Zahniser and the Preservation of Wilderness," *SCB* 49, no. 9 (December 1964): 71.

112. Few women spoke at the Sierra Club's first six Biennial Wilderness Conferences, 1949–1964. David R. Brower, ed., *Wildlands in Our Civilization* (San Francisco: Sierra Club, 1964), contents, 130–75; Leydet, *Tomorrow's Wilderness*, 29–30.

113. Margaret W. Owings, "Facets of Wilderness," in Wilderness in a Changing World, ed. Bruce Kilgore (San Francisco: Sierra Club, 1966), 233.

114. Ibid., 234.

EPILOGUE

1. Patricia Limerick, "Disorientation and Reorientation: The American Landscape Discovered from the West," in *Discovering America: Essays on the Search for an Identity*, ed. David Thelen and Frederick E. Hoxie (Urbana: University of Illinois Press, 1994), 190, 187–215.

2. Mary Yates, "To Be a Woman," Redbook Magazine (November 1976), 108–10. Yates narrated her 1973 ascent of Mt. Rainier.

3. Nancy Faber, "Adventure: Team of Women to Climb Annapurna," People 10 (July 31, 1978): 70–71; Marty Olmsted, "Talking with Mountain Climber Margi Rushmore, Who is Climbing the Himalayas This Month," Glamour 76 (spring 1978): 11–18; Theresa J. Mocabee, "Go for It," Seventeen 35 (May 1976): 132, 194; "The 25 Most Intriguing People of 1978," *People* 10, no. 26 (December 25–January 1, 1979): 78.

4. David Breashears, *High Exposure: An Enduring Passion for Everest and Unforgiving Places* (New York: Simon and Schuster, 1999), 292.

5. Yi-fu Tuan, *Topophilia: A Study of Environmental Perception, Attitudes, and Values* (Englewood Cliffs, NJ: Prentice-Hall, 1974), 111–12, 96–97.

6. Gene Marine, *America the Raped: The Engineering Mentality and the Devastation of a Continent* (New York: Simon and Schuster, 1969); Sam D. Gill, *Mother Earth: An American Story* (Chicago: University of Chicago Press, 1987).

7. William Cronon, "The Trouble with Wilderness; or Getting Back to the Wrong Nature," in William Cronon, ed., *Uncommon Ground: Toward Reinventing Nature* (New York: Norton, 1995), 74–75.

8. Steve Roper, Camp 4: *Recollections of a Yosemite Rock Climber* (Seattle: The Mountaineers, 1994), 158; Harvey Manning, ed., *Mountaineering, The Freedom of the Hills* (Seattle: The Mountaineers, 1960), vi, 57, 80.

9. Richard G. Mitchell, Mountain Experience: *The Psychology and Sociology of Adventure* (Chicago: University of Chicago Press, 1983), viii, 185.

10. Todd Skinner, "Storming the Tower," *National Geographic* 189, no. 4 (April 1996): 32–51.

11. Breashears, *High Exposure*, 289, 294.

12. For an outstanding example, see Linda Hogan, Deena Metzger, and Brenda Peterson, eds., *Intimate Nature: The Bond Between Women and Animals* (New York: Fawcett Books, 1998). On the implications and origins of the continued associations between the feminine and nature, see Catherine M. Roach, *Mother/Nature: Popular Culture and Environmental Ethics* (Bloomington: Indiana University Press, 2003).

13. On ecofeminism, see Glenda Riley, *Women and Nature: Saving the "Wild West"* (Lincoln: University of Nebraska Press, 1997), 171–73; on women's environmental activism since the 1960s, see Temma Kaplan, *Crazy for Democracy: Women in Grassroots Movements* (New York: Routledge, 1997), 1–14.

14. Carolyn Merchant, *Earthcare: Women and the Environment* (New York: Routledge, 1995).

15. Vandana Shiva, *Staying Alive: Women, Ecology and Development* (London: Zed Books, 1988), 1–13; Nalini Visvanathan, Lynn Duggan, Laurie Nisonoff, and Nan Wiegersma, eds., *The Women, Gender and Development Reader* (London: Zed Books, 1997), 6–67.

16. Sue Ellen Campbell, *Bringing the Mountain Home* (Tucson: University of Arizona Press, 1996); Anne LaBastille, *Women and Wilderness* (San Francisco: Sierra Club, 1980); Irene Diamond and Gloria Feman Orenstein, eds., *Reweaving the World: The Emergence of Ecofeminism* (San Francisco: Sierra Club, 1990); Lorraine Anderson, *Sisters of the Earth* (New York: Vintage, 1991); Susan Griffin, *Women and Nature: The Roaring Inside Her* (New York: Harper and Row, 1978).

17. Ruth Anne Kocour, *Facing the Extreme: One Woman's Story of True Courage, Death Defying Survival, and Her Quest for the Summit* (New York: St. Martin's Paperback, 1998), 2–6.

18. William Cronon, "The Trouble with Wilderness," 74–75; Rebecca Solnit in James Gorman, "Yosemite and the Invention of Wilderness," *New York Times*, September 2, 2003, F1.

19. "This wilderness is a need. The idea of wilderness as an area without man's influence is man's own concept." See Howard Zahniser, "The Need for Wilderness Areas," *National Parks Magazine* (October–December 1955): 163.

INDEX

Coe Glacier, 119
Cohen, Michael, 88
Colby, William, 29, 75, 76, 138p, 268n2
Colby Pass, 113
Coleman, Caroline, 272n69
Coleridge, Samuel Taylor, 41, 44, 48, 84, 225,
    227, 233
    on Nature, 42, 57
    rituals and, 54
Colorado Mountain Club, 76, 119, 133, 194
    clothing and, 103
    establishment of, 252n80
Colorado Water Project, 210–11
Columbus, Christopher, 13
Commercial interests, 45, 183
Congressional Record, 211
Conservation, xii, 3, 106, 161, 177, 221, 236
    environmentalism and, 283n5
    masculinity and, 266n110
    mountaineering and, 130, 209
    support for, 5–6, 93, 158
    wilderness, 216, 223, 232
    women and, 107, 124, 235, 266n114
Conservation Associates, 223
Conservationists, 40, 97, 164, 207, 240
    Brower and, 179–80
    Muir and, 65
    psychological theories and, 186
    survival and, 191
Conservation movement, 4, 68, 195, 234,
    293n65
Consumerism, 93, 188, 223
Coolidge, Calvin, 163
Cooper, James Fenimore, 227
Cooper, Susan Fenimore, 13, 20
Cooper Creek, 174
Cordée féminine, 198, 236
Corpron, Doug, 39–40
Cotter, Richard, 10p
Cowles, Elizabeth, 197
Cowles, Henry C., 166
Crack in the Picture Window, The (Keats), 222
Crater Lake National Park, 163, 171, 210,
    248n37
Crawford, Mary, 80
Crockett, Davy, 191
Cronon, William, 47, 238
Cultural heritage, 219, 228, 231, 238, 241
Culture, 93
    nature and, 58

Victorian, 85, 154
    Wilderness Act and, 227
Curran, Mary Catherine, 86
Currier, Ruth, 120, 121, 122, 144
Curtis, Asahel: photo by, 35

Daily Alaskan, on Keen, 82
Dartmouth Outing Club, 252n80
Darwin, Charles, 26, 62
Daughters of the American Revolution, 174
Daughters of the Golden West, 174
Davis, Milton F., 28p
Dawson, Glen, 120, 121, 135
Death Valley, 90
De Fremery, Virginia, 115
Delancy, Paul, 201p
De Lépiney, Tom, 116
Democratic National Committee, 222–23
Democratic Party, environment and, 225
Department of Agriculture, 162, 224
Department of Research and Develop-
    ment, 202
Department of the Interior, 63, 172, 183
    national parks and, 162
Depression, 123, 124, 178
Detmers, Federica, 166
Devall, William, 288n6
Devils Crags, 121
Diamond Peak, 210, 211
Dinosaur National Monument, 210–11
Division of Forestry, 27
Division of Ornithology, 81
Division of Recreation Lands, 173
Dixon, Joseph: photo by, 205
Dole, Alfred: photo by, 189
Dole, Helen, 189
Domesticity, 156, 157, 167, 240, 281n60
    ideology of, 6, 68, 74
    women and, 86, 112, 120
Dora Keen Range, 263n62
Douglas, William O., 41, 44, 177, 233
    conservation and, 40
    Kloochman and, 39–40, 55
    on mountains, 226
    Sierra Club and, 280n52
    Wilderness Act and, 7
Drus, 198
Dryads, 35p
Dudley, William, 27
Dusy, Frank, xii, 29, 30p, 251n71